GW00645444

Stevenage Ltd

International Library of Sociology

Founded by Karl Mannheim

Editor: John Rex, University of Aston in Birmingham

Arbor Scientiae
Arbor Vitae

A catalogue of the books available in the **International Library of Sociology** and other series of Social Science books published by Routledge & Kegan Paul will be found at the end of this volume.

Stevenage Ltd

Aspects of the planning and politics of Stevenage New Town 1945-78

Bob Mullan

School of Economic and Social Studies
University of East Anglia

Routledge & Kegan Paul

London, Boston and Henley

First published in 1980
by Routledge & Kegan Paul Ltd
39 Store Street,
London WC1E 7DD,
9 Park Street,
Boston, Mass. 02108, USA and
Broadway House,
Newtown Road,
Henley-on-Thames,
Oxon RG9 1EN
Printed in Great Britain by
Redwood Burn Limited
Trowbridge & Esher
© Bob Mullan 1980
No part of this book may be reproduced in
any form without permission from the
publisher, except for the quotation of brief
passages in criticism

British Library Cataloguing in Publication Data
Mullan, Bob
  Stevenage Ltd – (International library
  of sociology).
  1. City planning – England – History
  2. Stevenage, Eng. – City planning
  – History
  I. Title   II. Series
  711.4'0942582   HT169.G7S6   80–49941

ISBN 0 7100 0538 5

To Mary and Jessica

Contents

Illustrations

Maps

Appendices

Preface

This book is concerned with aspects of the politics and planning of Stevenage New Town from its inception in 1945 up to, and including, the events of 1978. It could well be said that the book, more accurately, is about the politics *of* planning, in that the structure and action of the urban managers, including planners, is the focus of the work. What is intended in the book is an examination of the constraints which have operated on both the structure and action of the Stevenage urban managers over the past thirty years or so. These constraints include three sets of actors: 'politicians', industrialists, and pressure groups/protest movements.

While the analysis of particular aspects of the development of the town goes beyond the actors' perspectives and action, attention is nevertheless paid to such perspectives and action. For example, in the analysis of the protest movements, I share with John Rex the view that 'one has actually to study movements run by real pimpled people, and systematic analysis has to make sense of their observed action' (Rex, 1978, p. 568).

Perhaps it is important to account here for an impression that may be formed, viz. that the planners simply 'cannot win', in that they are criticised for not being flexible enough in their action and yet are also criticised for being too flexible! The point I am trying to make, however, is that planners ought both to be far more reflexive, and systematically to locate their 'technical' activity within the crucial wider economic and political context. I am not in any sense arguing against the legitimacy of the planning activity: simply commenting on its weaknesses as presently (sometimes) practised.

Acknowledgments

There are several people I would like to thank for the help that they have given me. The following were kind enough to grant me interviews, often at extremely short notice: Jack Balchin, Charles Burr, Baroness Denington, Philip Ireton, and Ernest Lenderyou (all of the Stevenage Development Corporation), Simon Bowes-Lyon of the Hertfordshire Society, Steve Halls of the Department of Employment (local office), John Hubble of the Stevenage Valley Association, Geoffrey Hughes of the Stevenage Industrial Employers Group, Ian Johnson, agent for the Hertford and Stevenage Constituency Conservative Party, Tom McCombie of the Campaign Against Stevenage Expansion, Shirley Williams, and Cynthia Wood of the Aston Parish Council. I also received an enormous amount of information and advice from the following people: Alan Cudmore, Steve Dunn, Jack Greenwood, Geoff Marsh, and Bob Sulzbach (all of the Stevenage Development Corporation), Jim Caldwell of the Stevenage Labour Party, Michael Downing of the Stevenage Trades Council, John Rodger of the University of Edinburgh, John Silkin MP, and Leslie Sklair (LSE), who has provided continuous and constructive advice. Finally, I would like to thank Mary Mullan for the help she has given me throughout.

Janet Garland transcribed the interviews, Barbara Dewing, Richard Johnson, and David Mews produced the maps, illustrations, and figures, and Sally Baits diligently typed the numerous tables.

Introduction

The explorer of power structures confronts many difficulties. Voltaire described the hero of one of his
stories as a person whose principal talent lay in dis-
covering the truth, which all men seek to obscure.
People in power have more reason for obscuring the
truth than others, although not always for the same
reasons. Politicians and businessmen are alike concerned, at times, to exaggerate their own influence
and achievements; at other times, they obstruct
efforts to penetrate the details. The structure of
wealth is notoriously difficult to examine. Official
records can be misleading. Journalistic accounts range
from the totally dishonest to the merely ignorant.
                                        S.Encel (1978), p.47

This case study of Stevenage New Town is used to illustrate both the strengths and weaknesses of the thesis of
'urban managerialism'. Ray Pahl, quite correctly, states
that:

Since the urban managers are the central mediators
between urban populations and the capitalist economy
and since they also serve to generate and maintain the
ideology of Welfare-Statism, their role remains crucial
in the urban problematic. (1)

It is, indeed, the urban managers' specific role that is
under examination here. Their role - in this particular
case, the role of the Stevenage Development Corporation -
will be examined by virtue of the specification and
evaluation of the constraints (specifically, central
government, local authorities, local industrialists, and
local protest groups) placed upon them: both on their
structure and on their action.

The case study traces certain aspects of the development
of Stevenage New Town from its beginnings in 1946 through

to 1978. There is within the study a focus both on the
years 1970-8, and thoughout on the activities of planners,
politicians, industrialists, and Stevenage protest groups.
 The study is based on a variety of sources, using
official statistics and documents, formal and informal
interviews, analysis of documentation, and (especially in
the years 1975-7) participant observation.
 As Hindess points out, official statistics are indeed
useful, provided they are used within the context of a
systematic argument, (2) and that is what I attempt here.
The interviews which were carried out are enumerated in
appendix 1. In the analysis of documentation, and particularly that of the Stevenage Development Corporation,
I received an enormous amount of assistance from members
and officers of the Corporation (as has been ac-
knowledged); however, eighteen months after the com-
mencement of the study it became evident that in order to
'test some hypotheses' and to 'get beyond the surface of
things' I needed data of a much less easily available and
public nature. Thus, following consultations with several
'informed' persons, I decided that it was the minutes (3)
of the Corporation Board that were required, and so both
formally and informally I approached the General Manager
and Chairman of the Corporation, requesting permission to
see and use the minutes. I was informed, with no specific
reason given, that I could not see them, so I wrote to the
Chairman, Baroness Evelyn Denington, asking for a reason
for the refusal. I received no reply, so I then wrote to
the Department of the Environment's New Towns Directorate,
seeking Ministry instructions on the matter. On 16 September 1977 the Department replied, stating that:
      corporations are bodies corporate, and management and
      administration matters have been devolved to them.
      The Stevenage Board's decision about disclosure of
      their minutes is properly one for them to take, and
      this is not something in which Central Government can
      intervene. (4)
I then decided to attempt to obtain a view of the minutes
without permission, and accordingly, through a number of
sources, I was in fact able to obtain copies of the Corporation's full set of minutes. (5) In the meantime I
received a letter from the Corporation's General Manager -
on instruction from the Chairman - stating that:
      after the time and assistance which has been afforded
      to you by hard pressed Members and Officers, your
      action, without any hint to us, in asking the
      Department of the Environment to over-rule the
      Chairman's instruction that minutes should not be
      made available - as they contain much confidential

matter which it would be improper to disclose - to you
was not received kindly. On the contrary, it was seen
as a rather poor way of saying thank you. (6)

It is my opinion that the nature of the information
contained in the minutes is of such value, particularly in
relation to the central factor of the housing allocation
process, that the use of it outweighs any other considerations.

Of course it is important to ascertain whether or not the
minutes were an accurate reflection of what was 'going on'
in the Corporation, for as Dennis points out:

above a certain level of abstraction, the fabricators
of illusions and the falsifiers of the record come more
and more into their own. The student of power should
therefore keep his researches close to the details
which the generalised reports will eventually purport
to describe and from which they will be claimed to have
been derived. (7)

In this study there is supporting evidence - and on
occasion, plausible reasoning - to substantiate points
made in the minutes, and, moreover, the minutes are used
in conjunction with a set of hypotheses, systematically
examined throughout the text. A further reason to believe
that the minutes were representative of Corporation action
and ideology is the rather plausible argument that the
Corporation Board would not have felt that it had anything
to hide anyway (and even if it had, the 'private minute
book' could have been used).

Chapter 1 describes some facets of the planning profession: it is not in any sense intended as an exhaustive
survey, but merely to be of some assistance to the reader.
Some of the points made, for example the manner in which
planners tend to rely rather excessively on 'predictions'
of one kind and another, recur in the case study.
Chapter 2 describes some historical and structural facts
about the British, and particularly the London, New Towns.
Again, it is not meant as an exhaustive summary of the
literature, but merely as a guide through particular parts
of the case study. Chapters 3-10 describe the case study,
while chapters 11-14 discuss the relation between the
empirical evidence of the study and certain theoretical
issues. Chapter 11 discusses the industrial base of
Stevenage, pointing to the constraining nature that it
had on the Corporation, particularly in relation to
housing policy. In chapter 12 there is a discussion of
'urban managerialism', both theoretically and in relation
to the Stevenage data, particularly that pertaining to the
Corporation. Both the structure and the efficacy of the
protest organisations are under scrutiny in chapter 13,

the analysis being related to literature on public participation and particularly that on 'urban social
movements'. Chapter 14 concentrates on the relation
between local authorities and new town development corporations. The empirical input to the chapter both gives
consideration to the 'future' of the town and summarises
the text, particularly in relation to the constraints
placed on 'urban managers'.

Finally, the widespread use of quotation and annotation
is considered to be necessary because of the contentious
and ambiguous statements made both by various individual
actors and contained in numerous documents, most notably
the Corporation Board minutes.

NOTE

There exists no stylistically elegant method of avoiding
the appearance of sexism when the third person singular
is used repeatedly. The reader is asked to excuse the
fact that, in the pages that follow, the masculine is
used at times.

Abbreviations

AR	Annual Report
BAC	British Aircraft Corporation
CASE	Campaign Against Stevenage Expansion
CAUSE	Campaign Against Unnecessary Stevenage Expansion
CDP	Community Development Project
CE	Chief Engineer
CEO	Chief Estates Officer
CES	Centre for Environmental Studies
CIS	Counter Information Service
CODOT	Classification of Occupations and Directory of Occupational Titles
CPRE	Council for the Preservation of Rural England
DE	Department of Employment
DEG	Department of Employment Gazette
DOE	Department of the Environment
EA	Employment Area
EEA	Employment Exchange Area
ERV/ERV1	Department of Employment returns. ERVs refer to the number of unemployed persons, and ERV1s to the number of unfilled vacancies (for my particular use of them see ch.3, n.73).
GHS	General Household Survey
GLC	Greater London Council
HSD	Hawker Siddeley Dynamics
IDC	Industrial Development Certificate
JHL	Joint Housing List
LCC	London County Council
MAFF	Ministry of Agriculture, Food and Fisheries
MLH	Minimum List Heading
NETS	New and Expanding Towns Register
NFU	National Farmers' Union
OPCS	Office of Population Censuses and Surveys
RIM	Research, Information and Monitoring
SBC	Stevenage Borough Council

SDC	Stevenage Development Corporation
SDO	Social Development Office (of the SDC)
SEEPC	South East Economic Planning Council
SHA	Special Housing Allocation
SIC	Standard Industrial Classification
SIEG	Stevenage Industrial Employers' Group
SOS	Save Our Stevenage Campaign
SPSE	Strategic Plan for the South East
SUDC	Stevenage Urban District Council
SVA	Stevenage Valley Association
TCPA	Town and Country Planning Association

Part one

1 Some themes in urban planning

> It is difficult for ordinary councillors to handle the
> problems created by an official virtuoso who can throw
> in references to the growth of American car ownership
> during the depression as being centrally relevant to
> the fate of two little houses in Newcastle's West End.
> Jon Gower Davies (1977), p.439

1 GENERAL CONSIDERATIONS

Within sociology there are essentially two quite different
conceptualisations advanced in relation to the role and
actions of urban planners in contemporary Western societies. There is first the work of Norman Dennis and Jon
Gower Davies - both concerned with the nature of representative democracy - who amply demonstrate the potency
of the 'dictatorship of the official' thesis within the
planning context. (1) On the other hand there is the
Marxist perspective, most notably in the work of Manuel
Castells, which suggests that planners are in fact far
less autonomous and more constrained in their practices.
Castells puts the argument in the following manner:

> If it is true that the State expresses, *in the last
> instance and through the necessary mediations,* the
> overall interests of the dominant classes, then urban
> planning cannot be an instrument of social change, but
> only one of domination, integration and *regulation of
> contradictions*. (2)

Mellor, writing more historically, makes the important
point that planning has not yet resolved the tension in
aims, evident from its earliest days as both an activity
of government and as a social movement: 'As the former
it was concerned with land use, property interests and
environmental planning, as the latter with community

betterment.' (3) This is an important point to make,
particularly as the sociological critiques have tended to
result in an impression that planning is a priori a regressive or reactionary activity. Planning and the
planning profession have to be evaluated in the same
manner as other professions and occupational strata: the
state of the society at a particular moment in time has to
be considered, the function and structure of the profession at that moment, variations in ideology and
practice within the profession, the differing constraints
which refer to particular planning functions and duties,
and so on. For example, there is the very question of the
status of planning as a profession, and indeed the
question 'what is a profession?' itself. Mellor again
makes an important observation concerning the lack of
authority accredited to the planning profession, and
suggests that in part this is derived from its pragmatic
tendencies:

> If planning becomes the practice of planning, then the
> planners cannot justify what they do except by what
> they do, i.e., their methodology. It is not possible
> to demonstrate that a proposal is the best or the
> truest one, only that at this moment in time it is the
> most useful for attaining certain objectives. So the
> way is open for the layman to draw his own, and differ-
> ent, conclusions from the analysis of the situation.
> (4)

Perhaps more important, particularly in terms of its
status and relations to other occupational strata, and in
order to avoid either its deification or indeed its de-
nunciation, is the nature of professions in contemporary
societies. Esland points to the complexity of the problem
when he rightly observes that one of the paradoxes of the
social position of the new professional workers is that
'they have become both agents of capitalist control and
also the professionally trained servants of capitalism'.
(5) Esland hypothesises that through the logic of
capitalism some professions are becoming 'proletarianised'
and are thus simply service agents for the owners of
capital, the higher administrators in government departments, and so on. It is important, however, to remember that:

> professional workers nevertheless constitute a powerful
> group - particularly those who are recruited or pro-
> moted to higher managerial positions. (6)

Esland describes the emergence of the professions as a
very clear example of the process of bureaucratic rationalisation which has become so dominant a feature of advanced industrial societies. He continues to suggest that

not only have the professional occupations themselves
undergone substantial rationalisation in organisation,
curricula and the validation of expertise and qualification, but they have been instrumental in the progressive
rationalisation of the economic organisation of society
itself. (7)   Indeed, what can be considered as the opposite tendency to the 'proletarianisation' process is the
existence and development of the 'professional mandate'.
Everett Hughes describes the professional mandate in the
following manner:

> Professions, perhaps more than other kinds of
> occupation ... claim a broad legal, moral and intel-
> lectual mandate. Not only do the practitioners, by
> virtue of gaining admission to the charmed circle of
> the profession, individually exercise a licence to do
> things others do not do, but collectively they presume
> to tell society what is good and right for it in a
> broad and crucial aspect of life. Indeed, they set
> the very terms of thinking about it. When such a
> presumption is granted as legitimate, a profession in
> the full sense has come into being. (8)

Hughes is here describing one of the mainsprings of a
profession's authority. Indeed a major threat to a claim
for monopoly is the existence of other occupational groups
claiming similar benefits for society and offering different but apparently equivalent skills. This realisation on
the part of a profession leads to a major characteristic
of the professional mandate, namely that it is dependent
for its justification on a rather negative view of the lay
public. As Esland remarks:

> The concept of the 'lay public' is an important one in
> that it legitimates a profession's raison d'être - that
> is, that it has a right to do things for and to people.
> (9)

Perhaps it is now appropriate to move on to more specific
elements of the practice of planning: however, what must
be understood is that the descriptions are concerned with
the dominant tendencies within planning, and not with
planning per se.

2   PLANNING

Karl Mannheim asserts that 'planning' is foresight deliberately applied to human affairs in order that the
social progress of societies is no longer merely the
product of conflict and competition. (10)   The question
is, however, whether this definition of 'planning' can
be equated with the practices, both in terms of ideas

and interventions, of urban planners? Norman Dennis, like
Mannheim, defining planning as a process which is intended
to increase the predictability of life and the scope for
orderly control, states that because the planners ignore
the fact of uncertainty and the realities of power they in
fact decrease both predictability and control. (11)

What is certain, however, is that urban planning is a
political activity. This can be assumed either through
definitional fiat, for example, by defining the planner
as the master allocator of scarce resources, or through
an acceptance of technical rationality as political, or
through the effects of planning. For example, the consequences of urban renewal are first the displacement of
neighbourhoods, and second, a consequence following from
this, a regressive income redistribution, with lower-
income groups who consume at the lower end of the housing
stock suffering the most. (12)

There have of course long been criticisms of planners'
practices but these have tended to be merely anarchistic,
such as the work of Jane Jacobs and Richard Sennett who
plead, respectively, for Darwin and disorder. (13)

3 PLANNING IDEOLOGY

As stated earlier, what is intended here is a description
of the dominant tendencies within planning. Similarly,
the view held here is that ideological processes are
invariably contradictory and partially heterogeneous:
they are never completely clear-cut and neat. Current
terms (and, potentially, practices) in vogue at present
within planning are those like 'flexibility', 'monitoring', 'open-ended', and so on, all terms indicating
that planners are indeed becoming increasingly aware of
the limitations of strict determinism. However, whether
this awareness will lead to a radical change in practice
is a very different question, and, further, if an acceptance of the reality of uncertainty were to become
widespread this could endanger the actual existence of
the planning activity. Therefore perhaps a concentration
on traditional ideology is in order.

Jon Davies suggests that the planner looks at things 'as
a whole' and indeed 'comprehensively', and that there is
a distinct connection between 'comprehensiveness' and
another 'technological and ideological flourish of
planning', namely the need to bring the future into being
today. (14) This can be termed 'futurism' and, as Irene
Taviss suggests, the futurologist by producing images of
the future is indeed influential in producing that future.

Of course, another aspect of this futurism is that 'facts' become even more tenuous, or, as Dennis puts it, 'anchorless data'. (15)   What is characteristic of the average futurologist is 'optimism', and this Taviss suggests is because of the:

> self-selection process whereby those who choose to study the future are recruited from among the people who maintain a strong faith in the scientific method and in man's ability to control his destiny.   This world view tends to be inherently optimistic. (16)

Futurism is itself linked to another keystone of the planner's ideology, namely the belief in 'progress'. Sklair indicates that statements about progress, be it in the educational, scientific or housing field, often conceal rather more than they reveal, and this is particularly true 'when we discover that a particular piece of progress' takes place 'at the expense of one social group and benefits another group'.   He thus suggests that there are three fundamental questions to be asked of progress: who benefits from progress?;   who defines progress in particular societies, and are there different definitions of progress for different concrete groups?; where progress for some is at the expense of others, who decides what level of expense is tolerable for what degree of progress? (17)   Both futurism and progress are once again linked with another of the planner's ideological characteristics, namely the belief in the ability to 'predict', whether this be related to populations, future car drivers or whatever.   This issue will be returned to later in the text, and just one example of the consequences that can occur with the 'prediction business' will be cited here.   Malcolm MacEwen notes that the:

> difficulty of prophesying is shown by [Peter Hall's] sad experience, for within a week of the publication of his book 'London 2000' he had to admit that he had been overtaken by events, and that the census figures showed that the growth of population and employment in the South East would be 80 per cent bigger by 2000 than he had estimated, that the demand for houses would be correspondingly greater, and that the number of new towns required, which he had estimated at 17, would have to be doubled. (18)

Another, less widely discussed, imperative of planners is what can be termed the 'naturalistic fallacy' or, put another way, 'can implies ought'.   Ozbekham states that increasingly within the planner's world, 'can', a conditional and neutral expression of feasibility, begins to be read as if it were written 'ought', which is an ethical statement connoting an imperative.   He adds that feasi-

bility, which is a strategic concept, is elevated to the
status of a normative concept, with the result that
whatever technological reality indicates we can do, it is
taken as implying that it must be done. (19)
  The final three elements of the ideology are more common
and thus require less explanation. First there is what
can only be termed the tendency to 'think big', which is,
of course, intimately related to notions of 'growth', and,
as Wildavsky asserts, planners do tend to be spenders with
the emphasis on the large and the loud over the small and
the quiet. He continues to state that the stock in trade
of the planner is the big model, which sometimes appears
more important the bigger and more complex it becomes,
even though it may actually be nothing more than a long
list of variables. He concludes by pointing out that the
planner's:

> fame and fortune depend on identification with visible
> objects and these are not to be found in the feeder
> road. (20)

Second there is 'architectural determinism', that is to
say, a belief in the one-way process in which the physical
environment is the independent variable with human
behaviour the dependent variable. (21) Finally, there is
the firm belief in the 'technocratic solution', a belief,
as Eversley puts it, that there are 'no problems which
cannot be solved by intelligent men of goodwill by the
application of Benthamite principles allied to modern
technology'. (22)

4   PUBLIC PARTICIPATION IN PLANNING

The issue of public participation in planning has not only
been the predominant area of concern for sociologists
interested in planning over the past few years, it has
also been the thorn in the flesh - or at least a chief
preoccupation - for the majority of planners, and has been
so for the past decade since the Town and Country Planning
Act (1968) and the Skeffington Report: People and Planning
(1969) formalised participation in planning.
  C.Wright Mills sets the context:

> democracy implies that those vitally affected by any
> decision men make have an effective voice in that
> decision. This, in turn, means that all power to make
> such decisions be publicly legitimated and that the
> makers of such decisions be held publicly accountable.
> (23)

Damer and Hague in a review of the area suggest that the
growth of public participation in planning - as an idea -

in the United Kingdom can be explained with reference to
five interrelated factors: the example of the American
planning experience; the social ethic of planning; the
general interest in participatory rather than representative democracy; the history of bottlenecks and hold-ups
in the administrative process of plans; the growth of
public interest in the urban environment. (24) However,
to the extent that planning has not been the only area of
'social policy' (25) where demands have been made for participation, the following observation of Gyford's is particularly pertinent, and it rearranges Damer and Hague's
five factors into a reverse order of importance:

> The fact that the demands for more participation were
> especially strident in the field of local planning may
> thus reflect the fact that planning produced the most
> readily visible - and once completed often the least
> reversible - forms of social change, removing or
> rehousing familiar faces, and destroying familiar
> places. (26)

The Skeffington Report has been thoroughly discussed and
evaluated elsewhere, (27) so suffice it to say here that
essentially the Committee saw the only credible source of
conflict between the planners and the public as lying in
the public's ignorance of planning matters, and furthermore it was their hope that such ignorance could be
eradicated by the education of the public through participation, together with a sympathetic mass media. As
Levin and Donnison observe, the Committee 'assume too
readily that the conventions of a Quaker meeting can be
adapted in the commercial, political, professional and
racial rough-house in which planning decisions are actually made'. (28)

The likelihood of the public actually participating in
planning matters to the degree of exercising influence
(let alone power) has been demonstrated by Norman Dennis
to be negligible, and indeed Dennis suggests that 'only a
mentally ill person would expend his energies for any
length of time on an activity in which the prospects of a
pay-off were negligible or nil'. (29) The question may
quite rightly be asked: why is this so?

The general view on the matter is that participation can
only be properly understood if it is seen in terms of
social control: for example Arnstein, in her discussion
of participation, talks in terms of a 'ladder of participation' with each rung related to either degrees of
tokenism or degrees of power. (30) The next question is,
of course, how do planners exercise social control over
potential participants, and indeed actual participants?
The first method of control can be termed 'information

control', the importance of which Dennis, Alford, Cohen and Lukes demonstrate. (31)   Berger, in his discussion of 'cognitive participation', puts the matter rather well:

> Once a situation has been defined in certain terms, a number of practical options are ipso facto foreclosed. It is a very limited notion of participation to let an elite define a situation in complete disregard of the ways in which this situation is *already defined* by those who live in it - and then to allow the latter a voice in the decisions made on the basis of the pre-ordained definition. A more meaningful notion of participation will include a voice in the definitions of the situation that underlie this or that decision-making option. (32)

Of course it must be remembered that a 'definition of the situation' need not take place (always) at the level of 'you need your roof mending, I should know as I am the expert' (within the planning context): it may also take the form of who is defined as being a legitimate actor in (say) a participation programme. For example, Dennis states that in the 'Planning Progress Report', the relationship between the Sunderland Corporation and the Residents' Association was characterised as 'reasonableness', while Jordan et al., discussing the Chester Conservation Area Advisory Committee, state that the Committee has 'certainly been a very *responsible* body'. (33)

Another method of control is that of 'co-optation'. Selznick describes co-optation as the process whereby new elements are absorbed into the leadership or policy-determining structure of an organisation as a means of averting threats to its stability or existence. (34) Dunleavy gives such an example in his study of Newham, and in particular in terms of the activities of a housing pressure group. He describes a situation where at public meetings many residents reacted to the council's immovable stance with feelings of despair, and as the 'rehousing date receded further into the future so the protest movement began to decay'. Dunleavy goes on to state that two of the protest leaders were then 'offered and accepted houses and then the committee fell apart, split by bitter personal animosities'. (35)

Rose and Hanmer, together with Dennis, talk of a process similar to that of co-optation, namely the 'encapsulation of individuals', while Dennis further describes the processes of 'complication' and of 'authorities saying they are using the power on behalf of someone else'. (36) Finally Davies describes the process whereby the planner, in anticipation of opposition to ideas or actions, is provided with a device enabling him to deny the rationality

of the criticism, namely that what is 'inevitable is also
irrelevant'. (37)
   So far it has been implied that participation is desirable in that it is more likely to further social justice.
However, there are of course contrary arguments, for
example Sapolsky suggests that the experience with fluoridation confirms the inappropriateness of direct citizen
involvement in policy making, as the technical intricacies
of the problem are too great for the average voter to
resolve. (38)   Moreover, of course, there are arguments
that too much involvement and participation is harmful and
not beneficial to the democratic process. (39)   Finally
there is the important observation of Barrington Moore,
namely that sharing in the decision-making process does
not automatically diminish suffering or raise the level of
human dignity:

   Beyond a certain point it can have quite the opposite
   results. Homo Committicus, to coin an appropriate
   barbarism, is not the only species of homo sapiens and
   not necessarily the most admirable one. A very
   precious part of human freedom is that *not* to make
   decisions. What would life be like if it were necessary to attend a meeting every day to decide at which
   hour the street lights should go on? (40)

   Before moving on to the next chapter it is important to
stress that this has been a selective review of a body of
literature, and so both the general and more specific
statements made here about planning, planning ideology and
public participation must be considered as ideal typical.
It is for the case study to bring to light the strengths
and weaknesses of the various arguments.

2 The London new towns
An overview

new towns cannot be appreciated by just reading books
and pamphlets. To those who are interested in human
affairs and in the physical fabric that is the
background to living; to those who take pride in this
nation's achievements in the field of social advance;
to those who are concerned to improve the conditions
in which many millions of their fellow-countrymen still
live; to those who want to judge for themselves
whether in the new towns can be seen an encouraging
glimpse of the future; to all these, the best advice
that can be given is: 'Go and see'. The miracle of
today may be the commonplace of tomorrow.

Frank Schaffer (1970), p.256

I do not intend here to provide a history of the new town
movement, as that has been the subject of many texts, (1)
but rather to give an outline of some of the fundamental
aspects of new towns, both historical and structural, in
order to place the case study in context.

It is important, before beginning, to place the new town
movement in perspective, for as Goodey quite rightly
states, 'new towns have assumed an importance out of
proportion to their housing contribution'. (2) For
example, new communities under the new and expanding towns
legislation have only provided 4.5 per cent of the
dwellings built in Britain since 1945, the new towns
claiming twice as many as the expanding. (3) The question
thus has to be asked, why have the new towns assumed such
importance? Goodey makes the following observations.
First, he suggests that to begin with they represent an
important experiment in environmental policy and in development administration which is directly endorsed and
maintained by national government. Second, Goodey
suggests that 'they permit design innovation through a
master plan process, they attract dynamic staff and a

MAP 1   NEW TOWNS
Under the New Towns Act 1965 and
the New Towns (Scotland) Act 1968

Source: 'The New Towns', DOE (1978, p.3)
Reproduced by permission of the Controller of Her
Majesty's Stationery Office

perpetual train of academic and professional commentators and observers'. Finally he suggests that resulting from the above two reasons, 'they have been sold to the world as a bold British product'. He makes the important point that:

> for a few, vocal and politically significant people, new towns are an emotional issue. The literature of the Town and Country Planning Association, its journal, variously called 'The Garden City', 'Garden Cities and Town Planning' and 'Town and Country Planning', and successive accounts in the TCPA mould together with annual field trips for visitors and conferences which often focus on the new towns, have all reflected and helped to create a 'new town mystique'. (4)

Goodey concludes, quite accurately, that unquestioning loyalty to the new town ideal - evident in much TCPA-inspired comment - has permeated official images of the new towns at least in so far as they are reflected in government publicity and public relations.

1   IDEOLOGICAL ORIGINS

It is anti-urbanism that lies at the root of the new town movement, as it did with the garden city movement. This anti-urbanism is to be found in the writings of, for example, Robert Owen, William Morris, and most importantly Ebenezer Howard, who, according to Jane Jacobs, set

> spinning powerful and city-destroying ideas.... He focused on the provision of wholesome housing as the central problem, to which everything else was subsidiary; furthermore he defined wholesome housing in terms only of suburban physical qualities and small-town social qualities. (5)

Carter, furthermore, suggests that Howard paid no attention at all to the problem which has now become of central concern, namely the regeneration of the centres of the old cities, but instead 'fled, emotionally and practically, to the creation of entirely new towns'. (6)

Indeed new towns were the epitome of 'architectural determinism', (7) which of course is a source from which arose many of the problems that were to face new towns much later. Hirsch and Sorenblum similarly talk of the 'agrarian myth' as being an extremely important factor in the creation of later urban strains in the USA. (8)   Ruth Glass states the case against the architectural determinism of the new town movement with clarity:

> It is not clear ... why the resuscitation of village life within urban communities should be regarded as

being so delightful and so progressive nor how it is to
be accomplished.... The mere shortening of the
physical distance between different social groups can
hardly bring them together unless, at the same time,
the social distance between them is also reduced. (9)
Indeed Lionel March discusses a CES pilot study where
three master plans - Stevenage, Hook, and Milton Keynes -
were compared over a whole range of indices of spatial
performance. It was found that when the planned towns
were tested against a 'natural' town - in this particular
case, Reading - most indices were poorer in the planned
situations. Furthermore the 'natural' plan showed greater
resilience to changes in preference structure: for example, whether people preferred ease of interaction or
more spaciousness made little difference to the measured
effectiveness of Reading. (10)

2   THE RAISON D'ÊTRE OF THE NEW TOWNS

The discussion here will be confined to the early new
towns and in particular the London New Towns. (11)
On 19 October 1945 Lewis Silkin, Minister of Town and
Country Planning, appointed a New Towns Committee whose
terms of reference were:
    To consider the general questions of the establishment,
    development, organization and administration that will
    arise in the promotion of New Towns in furtherance of
    a policy of planned decentralization from congested
    urban areas; and in accordance therewith to suggest
    guiding principles on which such towns should be
    established and developed as self-contained and
    balanced communities for work and living. (12)
Thus both historically and officially the purpose of the
new towns was related to the decentralisation of congested
urban areas. Now there are two quite distinct perspectives on this policy, the first one being represented
particularly by Manuel Castells, who asserts that the new
towns were above all a response to the urban crisis of the
London region, resulting from excessive industrial concentration produced by the technological and economic
evolution of British capitalism, 'according to the well
known movement of the formation of the metropolitan
regions'. Castells goes on to say that this concentration
was particularly acute in Britain as a result of the
'transformations' produced within the old industrial base,
centred on raw materials and on the conglomerates of
traditional textiles. In answer to the question 'why was
intervention, in the form of the 1946 Act following the

1944 Abercrombie Plan, carried out with such vigour?',
Castells asserts that the destruction caused by the Nazis
considerably aggravated the housing crisis, but:

> the decisive element, without any doubt, was the
> political conjuncture, with the upsurge of working-
> class political awareness and the electoral triumph
> of the Labour Party, which reinforced the pressure for
> change and required satisfaction on the level of
> demand, in order not to radicalize the class struggle
> (given the reformist outlook of the Labour Party). (13)

So the new towns, according to Castells, were a resumption of the ideology of social reform through the
modification of the environment. Using the language more
of Baran and Sweezy, Hudson, in his study of the North
East New Towns, produces an argument similar to that of
Castells. He states that the new towns represent attempts
by the state to reduce the costs of production to private
industry by a policy of infrastructure provision, and the
gathering of labour through the nominated housing system
into locations suited to the needs of new industry 'as
capital is withdrawn from traditional sectors, continuing
the underdevelopment of the region and exploitation (in
the strict sense of extraction of surplus value) of its
working class'. (14)

In order to examine, albeit briefly, the argument of
Castells it is necessary to consider what the state of the
Labour Party and the working class was following the
Second World War. The New Towns Act of 1946 was not, of
course, the only piece of legislation passed in the Second
World War period. Other pieces of legislation with a
social policy aim included the Education Act (1944), the
National Health Service Act (1946), the National Insurance
Act (1946), the Town and Country Planning Act (1947), and
the National Assistance Act (1948). Thus it is quite
apparent that a perspective on the 'welfare state' and
its origins is more or less equivalent to a perspective
on the meaning of the new town legislation in itself.

Ralph Miliband considers that the welfare state, for all
its importance in humanising the existing social order,
did not constitute any particular threat to power and
privilege. (15) In another text he suggests that the
war-time radicalism of Britain was not a formed socialist
ideology, although in its

> mixture of bitter memories and positive hopes, in its
> antagonisms to a mean past, in its recoil from Con-
> servative rule, in its impatience of a traditional
> class structure, in its hostility to the claims of
> property and privilege, in its determination not to
> be robbed again of the fruits of victory, in its ex-

pectations of social justice, it was a radicalism eager
for major, even fundamental, changes in British Society
after the war. (16)
He adds that the Labour leaders also thought and spoke of
the 'new society' that must follow the ordeals of war, but
of course the impact of war upon them, Miliband observes,
was very different from the impact it had on their supporters, and indeed there was much common ground between
Labour Ministers and their Conservative colleagues on the
shape of the post-war settlement. (17)
Runciman suggests that the Labour victory was not nearly
'so climactic' as the large parliamentary majority and the
surprise with which it was greeted might suggest. He
states that it might in one sense seem plausible to
describe it as a working-class victory but, he continues,
just as a Conservative government cannot come to power
without the support of a sizable minority of manual
workers and their families, so a Labour dovernment depends
on the support of a sizable minority of the middle class,
and indeed in 1945 millions of middle-class voters supported Labour whilst millions of working-class voters
still did not. (18)
So there is a measure of agreement that there was indeed
a radicalism at the time, though, if as Castells argues
measures had to be taken - albeit merely reformist ones -
to prevent the 'radicalisation of the class struggle',
those taken in the area of land use and housing were meek
indeed. For example, Marwick, discussing the Town and
Country Planning Act and the New Towns Act, states that
the Uthwatt Committee advising the Attlee Government
suggested that the 'old socialist nostrum' of land
nationalisation in practice offered too many compli-
cations, and accordingly the Government took the step
of nationalising not the land itself but the development
rights rights in it. (19)
The second perspective is less cynical than the first in
terms of the reasons behind the immediate implementation
of the Act. Hilary Rose focuses on the destruction caused
by the Second World War, noting that London itself
possessed one-third of all the nation's war-damaged
houses, while Bailey talks of the relief of overcrowding
and also of the bad housing of the working class. Bourne
talks of the reaction to the urgent problem of housing
overspill populations, and finally Blair talks of the
post-war innovation. (20) There is here no suggestion
of a more deep-seated reason for the policy in contrast
to Castells who sees the intervention in terms of the development of capitalism with its integral contradictions.
Deakin and Ungerson bring the perspectives a little

closer in a sense when they discuss new town policy, and
in fact assert that the policy is characterised by tension
between at least three types of 'goal', mediated by institutions of three kinds - private capital, local authorities, and national bureaucracies - whose aims are the
reduction of urban densities, regional equity, and
provision for people in housing 'need'. (21)   It is
perhaps closer to the truth to suggest that it is in fact
tension between the three institutions rather than the
goals that brings about the configuration of new town
policy.

Of course there are more extreme and 'idealist' views on
the new towns, such as those of Peter Self - a member of
the important new town lobby, the TCPA - who asserts that
the new town concept is a natural instrument for the 'new
humanism' which questions traditional 'laws' of economic
and technological progress, and which seeks to revitalise
human, community and civic values through a better
ordering of spatial relationships; (22)   and those of
Creese who (while discussing Henry Moore's 'Family Group'
sculpture in Harlow) describes the change from the Second
World War to the post-war mentality which produced the new
towns as follows:

> The essential change is from weary numbness into the
> realm of feeling, from artificial darkness up into
> natural light, from individual loneliness into ex-
> pansive association, and from twentieth-century de-
> structivity into procreation again. (23)

3   STRUCTURE OF THE NEW TOWNS

i   Development corporation boards

The Reith Committee proposed - proposals which were to be
institutionalised in the form of the 1946 Act - that the
new towns be run on a day-to-day basis, with direct
Treasury funding, by development corporations responsible
to Parliament, but free of interference in daily management.   As Peter Hall comments, 'the formula, in other
words, was rather like that of Reith's own beloved BBC'.
(24)   Cullingworth interestingly asserts that it was
obvious that the local government machinery was not suited
to undertake building on the scale contemplated, even if
local housing situations made it politically viable that
local authorities could contemplate a major building
programme for non-local people: 'the basic solution,
therefore, was the building of new towns by new and ad
hoc agencies'. (25)

Development corporations are similar to local authorities
in management structure, except that the officers, instead
of (theoretically) being responsible to the councillors,
are responsible to an appointed board. The Reith
Committee made numerous recommendations regarding the
boards: the following are the most important ones:
   Members should include persons who, among them, have
   experience of land development, of economic and social
   conditions and labour relations, of business and local
   government, and appreciation of cultural requirements...
   Some members should be chosen after consultation with
   the local authorities concerned, it being necessary to
   secure local contacts and good-will, but it is essential that no member of the governing body should
   regard himself or act as a delegate of any other
   authority or organization...
   The Chairman should be of recognised public standing,
   and able to devote adequate time to the work...
   It is desirable that some of the members should live
   in the town...
   The Chairman and other members should be adequately
   paid...
   The board should appoint the chief executive who
   should not be a member of the board... (26)
In practice, and through the various New Town Acts,
boards have tended to have nine members, including the
Chairman and Deputy Chairman, all appointed on a part-time
basis, with the ordinary members merely attending board
and sub-committee meetings say once or twice a month,
while the Chairman could spend two or even three days a
week on board business.
The principal problems in relation to the boards have
been perceived as their 'appointed' nature, together with
the possibility of 'political' appointments, and the
position of the board member who is also a member of the
local council.
Schaffer states that the Act (as amended by the 1965 and
1975 Acts) requires that, of the members, one must be
'local'. However, as he further points out, the Minister
need not succeed as the Act actually states that he must
'have regard' to the 'desirability of securing the
services of one or more persons resident in or having
special knowledge of the locality in which the new town
will be situated'. (27) Schaffer also makes the point
that successive ministers have appointed members of a
variety of skills and professions, and further that they
have invariably included at least one woman member. Dame
Evelyn Sharp, former Permanent Secretary at the Ministry

of Housing and Local Government, states that selecting
members and even chairmen is apt to be a pretty haphazard
business, and that, more importantly, the temptation to
government is to make political appointments:

> People prominent in political life will often be first-
> class for the job; but they should not be chosen
> because they are politicians. What ought to be done,
> but is not always done, is first to analyse the quali-
> ties and experience needed on the particular board of
> management ... and then to set out to find them, re-
> gardless of politics. Sometimes it seems that boards
> are chosen ... on the basis of the interests they
> represent instead of the skill and experience they can
> bring to the job.... The composition of the board
> really can make a very great difference to the quality
> of the town; and no trouble is too great to get it
> right. (28)

Richard Crossman, the minister she 'worked with' for a
short and stormy time, was certainly in favour of political appointments, while Eric Moonman MP, writing in 1972,
noted that recent Labour Party regional conferences at
Crewe and Newcastle-upon-Tyne had passed resolutions
calling for local authorities to be given at least 40 per
cent of the seats on development corporation boards. He
suggested for his part that this would have the advantage
of ensuring that the boards reflected to some extent the
composition of local opinion, regardless of who was in
office at central government level. Yet, he continued, it
must not be forgotten that these boards were making decisions about housing, work and amenities which were financed by central government and should therefore reflect
the political attitudes of the party in power - thus the
Labour Party when in government should ensure that the
majority of seats on these boards were held by people
sympathetic to the party and its aims, in the context of
the new towns. (29) The basic argument against this is,
for example, that offered by Frank Schaffer who asserts
that the fact that members do not have to stand for
election relieves them of the need to canvass people for
popularity, and enables them perhaps to take a more detached approach to problems than can the average local
councillor. (30)

The Minister of course has considerable power regarding
the selection of members, particularly as the 1965 Act
(schedule 2, section 5) gives him broad powers such as
the following:

> If the Minister is satisfied that a member of the
> corporation ... is *unsuitable* to continue as a member,
> the Minister may remove him from his office as a member
> of the corporation. (31, emphasis added)

So the 'unsuitability' is left totally undefined, and thus the Minister, for any reason he likes, may merely remove at a stroke and replace a member with someone else of whom he approves.

In terms of payment to the members, Dame Evelyn Sharp suggests that the pay is 'modest', while Schaffer talks of a 'small salary', and the DOE talk of a 'small amount' - 'in fact you could call the post honorarium'. (32)   The salaries are in fact quite considerable, particularly that of the Chairmen: furthermore, it must be remembered that members receive full salary even though they may be unable to attend a particular board meeting.

However, that is not all, in that under the New Towns Act (1975), there is a clause (chapter 42, section 2(1), paragraph 7a) titled 'pension benefits for chairmen', which states that any person who is, or has been, a chairman of a corporation, may be paid - by the Secretary of State - a pension, allowance or gratuity 'as may be so determined'.   They are the only part-time public servants to obtain for themselves such an arrangement.

Annual Remuneration of Members
of New Town Corporation Boards

	Chairman	Deputy Chairman	Members
1946	£1,500	£ 750	£400
1963 (1 Jan)	2,000	1,000	500
1970 (1 Jan)	2,750	1,375	700
1971 (1 Jan)	3,500	1,500	700
1973 (1 April)	3,700	1,600	700
1973 (7 Nov)	4,200	1,850	700
1974 (1 Jan)	4,340	1,920	700

(From 1974 the pay for chairmen and deputy chairmen has been increased by threshold supplements authorised under the (then) pay code at December 1974, and had risen by £7.66 per week for chairmen and £3.83 per week for deputy chairmen, and has remained at that figure ever since.) (33)

ii   Finance

In theory, corporations plan and develop the town according to their own ideas: however, for every major item

of expenditure and indeed every development proposal they
have to obtain the Ministry's approval, and the Ministry
in turn must obtain Treasury consent, and as Schaffer
points out, this close financial control has long been a
bone of contention. (34)

All the capital needed by a corporation is borrowed from
central government, and has to be repaid - with interest -
over a period of (normally) sixty years. The money for
the repayments comes predominantly from the rents of the
housing stock, shops and industrial space and factories.
The risk is the government's of course, in that if there
were an overall loss on any town it would fall on the
taxpayer; however, if on the other hand a town were to
make a surplus, the Treasury could claim it. The government, in addition to capital loans, also pays a small
subsidy towards housing built for letting, which comes out
of general taxation and is not repayable. Finally, to
assist a new corporation on to its feet, the government
has in the past made a small contribution towards the
first three years' deficiency.

Of course the cost of building a new town comes from a
variety of sources other than central government: the
local authority services have to be met by the responsible
authority and are paid out of local rates. Some of these
services, for example schools and roads, are of course
themselves subsidised by central government (as in any
type of town). The Corporations can also themselves
contribute to the cost falling on the local authorities -
but any capital monies provided by the corporation in relation to such services must be borrowed from central
government and again have to be repaid over sixty years.
Similarly, statutory undertakers such as the gas or water
boards have to fulfill their responsibilities, but the
Corporation may have to pay for any special arrangements.

Some of the new town building is financed by private
capital, but there is no fixed rule concerning this, and
thus it varies with both the economic climate and the
organisations concerned. Many of the industrial and
commercial firms have built their own factories and
offices, and the same goes for the large retailers.
Furthermore, the financing of churches and places of
commercial entertainment has to come from those wishing
to build. Schaffer points out that a good deal of building in the town centres has been financed by estate development companies and insurance companies, who build
offices and shops as a commercial investment, or through
pension funds which provide the capital and lease the
buildings back to the development corporation for
management. (35)

In 1946 the first estimates put the cost of a new town
for 50,000 people at £19 million, of which it was thought
that £15 million would be borne by the corporations and
the remainder by the local authorities, but this was
quickly discovered to be an underestimate, and by 1948
£25 million worth of public money was considered to be the
required sum. Since that time building costs have increased enormously - as land is more expensive and as
overheads are higher - and by 1972 the figure was approaching £250 million for a town of 50,000 people.

The amount of public money spent by corporations is
subject to control through Parliament, but the money is
not all voted for at once, as the cost of building a town
is spread over some twenty years or more and Parliament
only provides enough money for a few years ahead. Interest rates are fixed by the Treasury, mediated by the
Minister, and have varied over the years between 3 per
cent and 14 per cent, with an average of approximately
6 per cent.

It is essential, asserts Schaffer, to take a long view of
new town finances, particularly as a town is bound to show
a deficit in its early years before it becomes fully
revenue producing. (36) It is also important to take a
comprehensive view, in that the towns purport to have
social as well as economic objectives: thus even if a
town shows a loss in the accounts it may be the cheapest
way of doing an essential job. For example, the £7
million Middle Lee Regional Drainage Scheme, which, although financed largely by the Harlow and Stevenage Development Corporations, serves a large area of Hertfordshire, is still carried on the accounts of these two
towns.

Finally, Schaffer suggests that it is necessary to
consider the new towns as a single national investment.
Some of the London new towns began producing a surplus
after only ten years, whilst others have not yet reached
that stage, and indeed the latest designated towns could
very well show a deficit for even longer. Taking the
British new towns as a whole, there is deficit on general
revenue account of £12 million a year on capital advances
of about £1,000 million, but substantial capital profits
are being made from the sale of land and houses, and thus
the revenue balance for a single year is but one of many
factors to be considered in judging the financial situation as a whole.

    What is certain is that with forty to fifty years of
    the loan repayments still to run, the expenditure bids
    fair to become one of the best investments ever made of
    the taxpayer's money... (37)

suggests Schaffer, who concludes that capital appreciation
must also not be overlooked.

iii   Industry

Cresswell and Thomas quite rightly point out that the new
towns have attracted mostly light modern industries, and
typically they have a high proportion of employment in
manufacturing and a low proportion in primary and most
service industries (although in parallel with national
trends this is rapidly changing); and within manufacturing there is usually a high proportion of employment in
light engineering. Cresswell and Thomas then point to the
exceptions: Corby with a dependence on steel; Welwyn
Garden City on chemicals; Stevenage on vehicle production
(in the form of aerospace); Basildon, Cwmbran, and East
Kilbride all on vehicle production. (38) Trimble asserts
that new town firms are not representative, but rather are
growth industries, with electrical engineering and particularly computers and electronics as the largest components. (39)
 Luttrell suggests that there are a number of reasons why
the new towns in their build-up phase should have been
based on an inflow of manufacturing plants, the first
being that quite a number of factories are fairly mobile,
especially the type of manufacture that is growing
rapidly, namely light engineering. The second reason is
however a negative one, being that the 'local service'
jobs are created by the existence of a resident population. (40) A more up-to-date survey is the one undertaken by Deakin and Ungerson, who suggest that the new
town industries highlight the changing structure of
industry in general:
    the continuing contraction of the extractive indus-
    tries, slower expansion of the manufacturing indus-
    tries and rapid expansion of service industries...,
and they continue to point out that manufacturing is
becoming more capital-intensive with the following consequence:
    Capital-intensive plants create fewer jobs; and the
    employment structure is increasingly weighted in favour
    of the skilled and those with professional qualifi-
    cations. (41)
 This of course is a frequent comment, and indeed
Cresswell and Thomas make a similar point, stating that
the largest form of imbalance which arises in the
structure of employment is related to the nature of the
dominant industries, which being mostly modern in character tend to employ a low proportion of unskilled workers.
(42)

Ray Thomas in his study of the London new towns describes
the process of industrial attraction in an extremely
interesting manner. He states that the process of getting
new industry usually started with discussions between the
firm and the corporation, the backing of the corporation
strengthening the case of the firm in obtaining an IDC
from the (then) Board of Trade. Many of the new towns,
he asserts, soon became extremely discriminating in the
type of employer they were willing to encourage, as they
tried to avoid a situation of domination by a single large
employer or single large industry. However, Thomas continues, a particularly large firm, confident that it could
get an IDC, might not bother to spend much time negoti-
ating with the corporation but instead go direct to the
Board of Trade, and having got approval there, the corporation concerned had little choice but to accept them -
and following acceptance by the corporation a firm could
expect to get housing for all of its employees within the
town. (43)

Concentrating solely on the London new towns, it can be
observed that there are four methods by which Londoners
can move to new (and expanding) towns. (44) To begin with
they can go on to the New and Expanding Towns Register
(NETS), which was formerly the Industrial Selection
Scheme. Second, a firm moving to a new town can offer
present employees a move; third, particular 'linking'
arrangements have been made between specific London
Boroughs and specific new towns; and finally an individual may move - though this is highly unlikely - to a particular town entirely on his own initiative.

The most important method is the NETS register, and it is
that which will be described here (note that it is the
most important in that once a firm has moved into a new
town, its labour force can do what it pleases, let alone
retire or die, and thus the firm has to once again turn to
London). (45) The scheme, assert Deakin and Ungerson,
attempts to reconcile two primary objectives, namely re-
lieving housing need in London (as defined by the GLC) and
meeting new town labour demands. (46) Those who register
with NETS (and the GLC) must satisfy two main requirements: first, they must be resident in the Greater London
area or be tenants of the GLC outside of that area, and
second, they must be willing to take up employment in the
new town. Provision is also made, however, for servicemen
recently discharged, workers who move with their firms out
of London, and pensioners with relatives in a new or
expanding town. Deakin and Ungerson go on to state that:

It is therefore clear that the prime determinant of the
sorts of people who move to new or expanding towns is

the type of *jobs* that are available in those towns;
also that it is the employers who, within broad limits,
control migration to those towns. (47)

They continue furthermore to suggest that those who
operate the scheme, and particularly the manner in which
they choose to define priorities in terms of housing need,
are almost equally important. For example, they state
that tenants of the GLC, London Borough Councils, and
Housing Associations are given priority, although assumed
to be in satisfactory housing, on the basis of the assumption that their movement to new or expanding towns
creates vacancies in London for those in 'housing need'.
(48) Mann counters this reasoning:

Nor can we assume that those left behind in the inner
areas will then move into the dwellings vacated by the
skilled emigrants for among overspill groups 'household
splitting' has been a frequent occurrence. This means
that the emigrants did not exist as a separate
household before they moved, and thus 'split away' from
the rest of the household on moving, leaving the
conurbation dwellings still occupied. This occurs particularly with the young married couples who form such
a large part of overspill groups: prior to the move
they were forced to live with parents. (49)

iv Balanced and self-contained communities?

Two concepts and goals to which the new towns aspire are
those of 'balance' and 'self-containment'. Cresswell and
Thomas state that there are three criteria relating to the
concept of balance:
(a) the level of the population should be supported by a
    roughly equivalent level of employment;
(b) the structure of employment should not be dominated by
    a single firm or type of industry; and
(c) the towns are not to be one-class communities. (50)

Taking (b) first, it has already been pointed out that in
certain new towns there is domination either by a single
firm or type of industry, for example Stevenage with aerospace, and Corby with steel. Regarding point (a) there is
increasing evidence that both in- and out-commuting are on
the increase, and particularly so when the town has
produced its second generation of residents (of school-
leaving age) and is thus faced with a possible excess of
labour. (51) Point (c) has received far more coverage
although it could well be argued that it is the least
important point. Lewis Silkin, the first New Towns
Minister, stated in 1948 that he was

very concerned indeed, not merely to get different

classes of the community, people of different occupations, living together in a community, but to get
them actually mixing together.... We have therefore
to consider what is the right arrangement, the right
layout of the estate, to ensure that the intermingling
of people of different classes of society is facili-
tated. (52)

Wendy Sarkissian, in a historical review of the idea of
'social mix', suggests that there are in fact nine different goals of social mix, which of course may or may not be
used in combination: to raise the standards of the lower
classes by nurturing the spirit of emulation; to
encourage aesthetic diversity and thus raise aesthetic
standards; to encourage cultural cross-fertilisation;
to increase equality of opportunity; to promote social
conflict in order to foster individual/social maturity;
to promote social harmony by reducing social and racial
tensions; (53) to improve the physical functioning of the
city and its inhabitants; to help to maintain stable
residential areas; and to reflect the diversity of the
urbanised modern world. (54) She continues to point out
that there was a particularly strong revival of the idea
following the Second World War, which in fact can be seen
in the attempt at 'classlessness' in planning models and
concepts like, for example, the 'socially-balanced
neighbourhood'. She concludes with reference to new town
planners:

Without ever being precise about the way they would
like to see people live, many planners have relied on
physical solutions to solve social problems. (55)

Cresswell, Ogilvy, and Cherry all make the same point,
whilst Bolwell et al. point out that there has been a particular increase in the population of the middle-class
sector of Crawley. (56) Heraud in a more general study
suggests that while class heterogeneity on a town basis
has more or less been achieved, on a local or neighbourhood basis a certain social homogeneity has developed, in
which different neighbourhoods have taken on distinctive
class characteristics, (57) a conclusion borne out to some
degree by the Stevenage Development Corporation's Social
Development Officer:

I think housing management policy has to some degree
steered people into certain areas of the town, certainly not so much into large areas like Bedwell or
Broadhall ... but particular parts of areas they've
allowed to recome recognised as (say) problem family
areas... (58)

The self-containment goal refers to the desire that the
town should provide all the necessary facilities for its

TABLE 1 Social structure of the new towns: Socio-economic groups of economically active males (age 15 and over) (Comparison with national and regional averages)

Area	Total	Employers and managers %	Professional workers %	Intermediate non-manual %	Junior non-manual %	Foremen and supervisory manual %	Skilled manual %	Semi-skilled manual %	Unskilled manual %	Personal service and own account %	Farmers, forces, and indefinite %
Averages:											
England and Wales	14,490,540	10.1	4.6	4.5	12.7	3.6	31.3	14.9	8.1	4.6	5.6
Greater London	2,468,300	12.0	5.6	5.4	18.1	3.3	27.6	12.7	8.0	5.9	1.4
South East Region	5,157,197	12.3	5.9	5.4	15.7	3.3	27.8	12.5	7.2	5.5	4.4
New towns:											
Basildon	19,950	6.0	3.4	4.8	12.4	5.3	33.8	22.3	7.1	4.2	0.7
Bracknell	7,450	9.0	8.7	5.6	13.7	4.3	32.9	15.4	5.2	2.1	3.1
Crawley	19,120	10.0	7.7	6.2	15.4	3.8	33.6	13.4	4.9	4.2	0.8
Harlow	19,740	10.3	6.8	6.2	12.3	4.9	34.9	14.9	4.2	4.8	0.7
Hatfield	7,330	7.6	6.7	4.6	14.7	5.0	37.2	13.8	6.4	3.3	0.7
Hemel Hempstead	19,610	10.1	6.7	5.5	11.6	4.6	34.1	17.1	5.6	4.2	0.5
Stevenage	17,030	8.4	7.5	7.8	14.4	4.0	33.5	16.3	4.6	2.8	0.7
Welwyn Garden City	11,970	11.4	10.9	9.0	14.5	4.2	27.9	12.2	4.3	2.7	0.7
Total, London new towns	122,200	9.1	7.0	6.2	13.5	4.5	33.5	16.3	5.3	3.8	0.8

Source: Census 1966.
Note: Classification is by area of residence, not place of work. Retired people are excluded.

inhabitants.   To begin with there is obviously an overlap
here with the other goal, and in so far as there is an
increase of out-commuting because of employment needs, the
goal is obviously not being realised.   With more specific
facets like educational facilities, general amenities and
so on, each town obviously has its own particular
strengths and weaknesses. (59)   Thomas and Cresswell put
it well when they suggest that the conclusion that the new
towns have achieved a certain level of self-containment
relative to other places around London is tempered by
several considerations.   First, they point to the fact
that as the new towns become more established, more of the
initial immigrants will change either their place of
residence or work.   Second, they note that the recent
policy of encouraging the sale of development corporation
dwellings to tenants in new towns, in order to raise the
level of owner-occupation nearer to the national average,
is likely to decrease self-containment, and finally they
add that:

> It is also likely that, in time, the new towns as areas
> of balanced population and employment or employment
> centres will become more attractive as places to work
> in for people living in surrounding areas. (60)

v   Social structure

Table 1 gives a relatively clear and consistent picture of
the social structure of the new towns, with the usual
pattern of bias towards 'skill' of various kinds.   Thomas
and Cresswell state that a comparison of the industrial
structure of the new towns with the socio-economic group
distributions that industries generate for the whole of
Great Britain, suggests that the industrial structure is
a major factor in determining the class structure, and
that the majority of the new towns have a bias towards
firms in the engineering industry which in fact employ
an above-average proportion of professionally qualified
personnel.   Interestingly they add that:

> Professional workers, those in socio-economic group 3
> and 4, are over-represented in the workforces of the
> London new towns but not to the same extent among
> residents since a large proportion of this group,
> larger than for any other group, chooses to live
> outside. (61)

Barr notes that there is an exceedingly small number of
black people resident in new towns, and indeed calculates
this as 0.003 per cent of the total population of the
towns, as compared with a national average of 1.7 per
cent. (62)

The more frequent criticism of the London new towns is that they attract the young and the skilled, indeed cream off the best from London, and in so doing leave London more deeply entrenched in its own problems. Berry, Heraud, Roderick, and Willmott all make this point, and Boer and Greendale make a similar observation in relation to the new towns of the USA, stating that such towns are only for the affluent, the young and the skilled. (63) Deakin and Ungerson assert that as long as the emphasis on the new towns (and similarly with the expanded towns) programme is ultimately determined by the objective of securing economic vitality and social equilibrium of the receiving areas, there will be limits placed on the contribution that these programmes can make to the solution of the economic and social problems of the conurbations, and indeed they go on to state that the parts of London with the least housing stress benefit disproportionately from the new towns policy. Deakin and Ungerson conclude by asserting that

the notions of employers in new and expanding towns concerning the reliability and contributions to profit-ability of potential employees, and of housing managers concerning cleanliness and financial stability of potential tenants combine to ensure that screening of applicants through the [NETS] ... especially favours the 'respectable working class' - that is, skilled manual workers. (64)

Deakin and Ungerson in fact add that the people who actually do move to the new towns are themselves simply 'seeking a rather easier, less stressful way of life'. (65)

4   FUTURE OWNERSHIP

The Reith Committee analysed the problem of the future ownership of the new towns when it sat in 1945, but it went no further than analysis, stating instead that it would be unlikely that the matter would need to be decided upon for some twenty years!

It is of course extremely difficult, as Schaffer points out, to stop a new town once it has started, in that its very success generates fresh demands as industry expands and children grow up, marry and have their own families. Indeed with nearly half the inhabitants under the age of 20 years, with over three-quarters over 45 and less than four per cent over 60, new births will exceed deaths and removals by a substantial margin, and hence it will be many years before the age grouping becomes normal. (66)

Furthermore, Schaffer continues, in order to leave room
for this 'natural expansion', the period of rapid growth
has to stop a good deal short of the ultimate population
for which the town is planned, and indeed the precise
point will vary according to the age structure in the
particular town, although in general it has been found
necessary to leave about a 25 per cent margin. (67)

The 1946 Act in fact granted power to the Minister to
'wind up' corporations, but this provision was repealed
by the New Towns Act (1959) which established the New
Towns Commission, a national body with members appointed
by the Minister in a similar manner as are members of a
development corporation. As Thomas and Creswell observe:

> The reason given for this amendment was that it was
> undesirable on social grounds for a local authority to
> own almost all the properties in their area and was
> outside the function of elected authorities. J.R.
> Bevins, Parliamentary Secretary to the Minister of
> Housing at that time, stated that 'Estate management
> should be stable and it is unwise to mix it with
> politics'. (68)

The Commission, which was set up by the Conservative
Government, was to take over and manage the property of
the towns as and when each was completed. The Labour
opposition was highly suspicious at the time the Bill was
going through Parliament, particularly of Conservative
'ulterior motives', and particularly as at the same time
Labour was advocating the transfer of all privately rented
houses to the local authority. (69) The Conservative move
was perceived as a threat, and furthermore it was considered that the Conservative proposals would lead to the
setting up of a Commission that would merely act as a
'disposal board' for selling off to private owners the
valuable publicly-owned assets. In the event the Commission was set up in 1961, and in 1979 owned assets in
four of the new towns.

In 1968 a resolution was made at the Labour Party Conference advocating the transfer to local authorities of
houses and neighbourhood shops, but for the industrial and
commercial properties, including town-centre shops, the
suggestion was for a transfer to a new central government
agency - a 'New Towns Industrial Corporation' was one of
the specific suggestions. In 1975 the Labour Government
in fact produced a bill which received the Royal Assent,
and became operational on 15 November 1976. The New Towns
(Amendment) Act (1976) contains the statutory provisions
for the transfer by development corporations to district
(and borough) councils, of their housing and allied
properties. Specifically the Act provides for the

transfer of all corporation-built housing in tenancy, all
community centres, public houses, amenity areas and play
spaces, together with neighbourhood shopping centres and
estate offices and depots.

The Commission still exists and, until a change in policy
is contemplated with more vigour, it will take over and
manage the industrial and commercial assets of new towns
following the handing over of their other assets.

Thus, in conclusion, the argument for the handing over of
assets to local authorities is that such a measure would
result in more local autonomy and control, whilst the
objection to the hand-over rests on the argument that, as
William Robson puts it,

> there would be a serious risk of corruption if property
> worth many millions of pounds were transferred to quite
> small district councils, whose members and electors may
> have a personal interest in some part of it. (70)

5   INHERENT PROBLEMS

Obviously under this heading come the real and potential
problems of employment bases which may be either vulnerable in the sense of having restricted markets, thus being
unable to diversify products if need be, or vulnerable in
that if second-generation residents of the towns do not
possess the skills needed by industries - which is indeed
highly likely - then if industry is prevented from im-
porting labour (through the promise of a house), following
the local authority take-over, it could be in serious
trouble unless an industry has invested in training
facilities - which again is highly unlikely.

Perhaps however the first observation to be made is of
the radical significance of new town policy changes.   To
begin with it must be appreciated that the overall context
within which the eight London new towns were intended to
fit changed almost as soon as the 1946 Act was passed.   In
the early 1940s it was assumed that the birth-rate would
continue to decline and that therefore one of the long-
term difficulties facing the post-war planners would be
population stagnation.   In the event, the population of
the South East began to increase at an unexpectedly rapid
rate as the birth-rate turned upwards following the war,
and thus the major role initially envisaged for the new
towns as the centrepiece in a planned dispersal policy
failed to materialise, and instead these broader goals
were blurred by the initial teething problems encountered
by the corporations as they struggled to launch the new
towns amidst acute shortages and competition for scarce

resources, and then they were submerged by the unplanned growth of population.

Furthermore, more specific goals - notably of a more social nature - have been abandoned through changes in policy. Aldridge, in her review of the reports of the Government's Expenditure Committee on the administration, planning and financing of new towns, describes the situation:

> What emerges is an impression not of efficiency, but of an understaffed division of the Department of the Environment administering legislation which, if it once had any social and economic objectives, has been profoundly modified by unsystematic and incremental policy changes, particularly in the late 1960s and early 1970s. These included the tacit abandonment of self-containment, coupled with a major shift to owner-occupied rather than publicly rented housing and a growing emphasis on short-run financial viability as the justification for policies regarding land acquisition, commercial and industrial composition and the attraction of retail and leisure facilities. Not only has new towns policy contrived to maintain an almost apolitical tradition for thirty years, but other departments make few concessions to it. (71)

Michael Mann, after stating that new town schemes depend critically on their ability to attract industry and commerce from the conurbations together with a substantial proportion of their employees, points to another problem. He suggests that after twenty years of relative success, a crisis has now been reached in that 'many signs indicate that industry is reluctant to move and some planners consider the reluctance to be justified'. He considers that the crux of the problem is that there simply is not enough mobile industry to carry out all governmental policies. (72)

Goodey, in his study of 'images of new towns', suggests that negative image themes seem to arise from one of two sources - sources which indicate problem areas. The first source is aesthetic, and is the 'undifferentiated modernity of the new town structure as glimpsed in the TV shot, the press photograph, or the view from the road'. The other source, Goodey suggests, is the more complex one of the human problems inherent in the 'rapid development of new place'. (73)

The final problem to be observed is that of the difficulties of co-existence between the locally-accountable local authority and the more autocratic and appointed development corporation, within the same town. Orlans, in his excellent study of the first five years of the new town

of Stevenage, considers the problem to be of crucial
importance:

> the most fundamental problem posed by the Stevenage
> experience [is] ... the extent to which efficient
> executive action is compatible with the democratic
> process.... It is strange how socialist and monopoly
> capitalist doctrines coincide in the New Town. For
> surely it is more a difference in name than substance
> that separates the social principles of, let us say,
> the Metropolitan Life Insurance Company's Parkchester
> development in New York City and the Ministry of Town
> and Country Planning's Stevenage New Town. In both
> there is to be found the same monopolistic ownership
> of land by one agency, the same leasehold restrictions
> on the freedom of the individual, the same lack of
> democracy in the appointment of the governing body,
> the same bureaucratic rule by remote officials. (74)

With the passing of the New Towns (Amendment) Act (1976),
housing assets have been transferred to the local authorities and thus the end of the two-organisation towns is in
sight, although past history will not be easily erased.
Richard Crossman's various accounts of the new towns are
illustrative of the problems which have been encountered.
He talks of the 'curious distance which seemed to exist in
every new town between the elected representatives on the
local council and the members of the corporation appointed
by the Ministry', and that 'the fact that they can get on
with their job without consulting public opinion is the
great thing, according to Dame Evelyn Sharp', and that the
'Ministry, which is autocratic anyway and very remote, has
displayed far too obvious a prejudice in favour of its
privileged children and against the local authorities'.
Crossman adds:

> This has made the UDCs intensely jealous and difficult
> to handle; I am pretty sure changes will have to take
> place *as soon as the Dame disappears*. (75, emphasis
> added)

The way in which Crossman 'hints' continuously at the
power of the Ministry's officials is interesting, (76) and
yet the impression is still formed of his own ultimate
control.

A final illustration comes from Crossman again and
suggests the context in which different authorities in
different new towns worked out their relationships. He
talks firstly of a visit to Runcorn where the UDC 'felt
the usual hate and suspicion of the corporation with their
brand new offices, their big salaries and their air of
being the feudal masters', and then of a trip to Corby
where, following talks with the councillors, he was

'hauled away by the corporation and went round the town
to see *their* housing and to be shown how much better it
was than the UDC housing':

> Corby makes it pretty clear what psychological and
> political problems are created by planting a develop-
> ment corporation next door to a disgruntled, competi-
> tive UDC. I tried to make the corporation see that
> it was *their* duty to make the running in friendly co-
> operation. (77)

General Duff, one time General Manager of Stevenage Development Corporation, interestingly suggests in his book
on the British new towns that corporations strive to be
strictly non-political. However, he adds that when a
Conservative government is in office, the policies which
the corporations have to carry out are bound to have a
Conservative flavour and this obviously does not make for
harmony when dealing with predominantly Labour councils.
Duff concludes that the

> best that is likely to be achieved is a veneer of
> politeness covering a great deal of back-stage
> squabbling. (78)

The corporations themselves have quite a lot to say on
the matter, with, for example, Wyndham Thomas, General
Manager of Peterborough Development Corporation for twelve
years, and member of the Commission for the New Towns and
the Hemel Hempstead Development Corporation, stating that
relations now are generally much better than they were in
the 1950s, the reason being, he suggests, 'the new breed
of general managers'. (79) In relation to draft planning
proposals he suggests that public participation is largely
a fruitless exercise, it being much better to be simply
'accessible and approachable', and to be this with
'sympathetic efficiency' which will, he asserts, convince
the public that corporations are generally as sensitive
and as responsive to public opinion as the very best local
authorities. (80) It is the naive beliefs of the aforementioned general manager, and the blasé ones, like the
following assertion by Stevenage Development Corporation's
General Manager (1969-76), that has irritated local
councillors over the years, and it is with this comment of
Jack Balchin's that attention is turned to the case study:

> there are no Clay Cross Corporations. The law's the
> law, and the Minister's policies are the Corporation's
> policies. (81)

Part two

3 Stevenage 1945-60
Beginnings

> Bevan never ceased to rail against what he called 'the
> whistle-blowing' planning of the Treasury experts in
> manipulation of capital investment programmes. They
> thought when they moved figures on charts, men moved
> too; 'they thought a building worker in Liverpool
> became a cowman in Kent'.
>
> Michael Foot (1975), p.95

In January 1945 the Stevenage Urban District Council's
Town Planning and Development Committee agreed that the
proposal to site a satellite town at Stevenage be approved
in principle, subject to reservations with regard to financial provisions and any necessary boundary revisions.
(1) This agreement was, in no small measure, related to
pressure from the Committee's Chairman, Councillor Philip
Ireton, a Council member of the new towns lobby of the
Town and Country Planning Association (TCPA): indeed as
Councillor Ireton himself put it:

> I *got* my committee to welcome and support a new town of
> Stevenage... (2)

In the same year both the Tottenham Borough Council and
the Thames Valley and District First Housing Association
offered to develop a garden city at Stevenage: both
offers were investigated and considered before being
subsequently declined. (3)

Lewis Silkin, the Minister of Town and Country Planning
in the Attlee Government, had decided to designate
Stevenage as the first new town, (4) and in early 1946
began to make the necessary prologue. This beginning
turned out to be one of the most important and interesting
events of post-war town planning. In April the Minister
decided to visit Stevenage and address a public meeting
both to spread the news of the impending social revolution
and to allay any fears. Already, however, the Council was
developing a posture of resentment; indeed on hearing of

the meeting the Council resolved to put on record its very
serious view of the lack of information supplied by the
Ministry on the matter of the proposed satellite town,
together with the general lack of co-operation in this
matter. (5)   As Schaffer points out, Silkin had tried to
make a start at Stevenage using the very limited and
inadequate powers of the Town and Country Planning Act of
1932. (6)   This was met with considerable protest, with,
for example, the railway station boards being changed to
'Silkingrad', and with Silkin himself being called a
'Dictator' and a 'Gestapo'. (7)   The Council by this time,
July 1946, at a meeting of the New Town Inquiry Committee
(without Councillor Ireton in attendance), recorded that

It is expected that the New Town Bill will receive the
Royal Assent on the 2nd August, that the advertisement
of the Draft Order proposing to designate Stevenage as
the site of a New Town will appear in the local press
in the week following. The Bill provides that not less
than 28 days shall be given for the submission of
objections, it is probable therefore that the Inquiry
will take place not earlier than the second week in
September.

Objection to Draft Order. It was resolved to recommend
that this Council object to the proposed Order for the
following reasons: (i) It is not practicable to super-
impose a new and larger town on an old one. The necessity of demolishing property is one of the most
important indications of the impracticability of the
proposal. (ii) A site 30 miles from London is not
desirable, with improved transport facilities the town
will tend to become a dormitory town. A New Town of
the size proposed, between Welwyn Garden City and
Letchworth will create a conurbation in North Herts.
(iii) The site is on good agricultural land; the
number of agricultural holdings being particularly
large. (iv) The siting of a New Town at Stevenage
will destroy the character and traditions of the
present town. (8)

The legal adviser was instructed to prepare the objections
in detail on these grounds for submission to the Minister
after the advertisement of the Draft Order. Following a
heated local inquiry, (9) the Designation Order - from
which flow all the statutory powers: the right to buy
land compulsorily, the freezing of land values, the use of
Exchequer money - was finally made. (10) However, the
Order was immediately challenged in the courts on the
grounds that by announcing at the public meeting before-
hand that he intended to have a new town at Stevenage, the
Minister was biased and could not have fairly considered

the objections. Mr Justice Henn Collins in the King's
Bench Division held that the Minister was clearly biased,
while the Court of Appeal took the opposite view and supported the Minister. The objectors then took the case to
the House of Lords where they again were defeated.
Schaffer states that the Law Lords went thoroughly into
the whole nature of the Minister's actions and obligations
and decided that the Minister was not acting in a judicial
or quasi-judicial capacity. He was taking a purely administrative decision and had properly complied with all
the legal requirements. (11) Orlans notes that the public
inquiry was compared by a prominent Stevenage Conservative
of the time with the 'Courts of the Star Chamber of Tudor
and Stuart times'; more importantly he goes on to say
that, in effect, the House of Lords ruling amounted to the
fact that the balance of evidence submitted at a public
inquiry need not determine the Minister's decision, which
might be based in the final analysis simply upon government policy. (12) Lucas puts the matter in the following
manner:

> [Silkin] was flouting this most fundamental principle
> of justice. The right to be heard carries with it some
> right to be heeded. (13)

S.A.de Smith describes the case - Franklin v. Minister of
Town and Country Planning - in more detail. He states
that objectors challenged the validity of the order in the
courts, claiming that the Minister had failed to act
judicially. He had 'manifested bias or a real likelihood
of bias' in favour of his proposal from the outset; and
'the fact that he had made the final order while important
technical problems (water supply and sewage disposal)
remained unsolved showed that his bias had continued to
the end'. The House of Lords, de Smith continues, held
that the standard of impartiality imposed on an independent tribunal was inapplicable to this type of situation: 'the Minister's role made it inevitable that he
would incline in favour of his own scheme'. The only
'duties cast upon him were to cause a properly conducted
inquiry to be held and to consider the objections and the
report fairly, with a mind not closed to argument'. He
adds that the Minister's functions were 'purely administrative'. In conclusion, de Smith suggests that:

> The decision in this case was sensible, though the term
> 'purely administrative' may have been unfortunate. A
> duty to act fairly may imply a duty to behave like an
> adjudicator *for certain purposes* - for example, in
> ensuring that everyone directly concerned is adequately
> informed of his rights, knows the case he has to meet
> and has a proper chance to put his case, and that

reasons are given for decisions. In other words it was held that no duty to observe natural justice was cast on the Minister. (14)

Thus on 17 November 1946 Stevenage, a North Hertfordshire town of 6,237 inhabitants, was designated as the site of the first new town, which was planned to reach an ultimate population of 60,000, drawing inhabitants from overcrowded areas of London. As E.M.Forster, a one-time dweller of Stevenage, put it:

Stevenage fell out of a blue sky like a meteorite upon the ancient and delicate scenery of Hertfordshire. (15)

The Minister's own defence of his action was given at a meeting held in November, when speaking on the proposals to build a satellite town at Hemel Hempstead:

It has been criticized that I should constitute myself as judge and jury and that no man ought to be judge in his own court. That is an entire misconception of the functions of the inquiries. Before ever the inquiry was held, I had to be satisfied, after consultation with any of the local authorities that it is expedient in the national interest that the area should be developed as a new town. That is a responsibility which I think ought to be placed upon a Minister, but having satisfied myself, it would be quite wrong to submit the whole thing to the judgement of an outside person who has no responsibility at all and who may not have the knowledge or background or information to enable him to make a decision. If I find objections are sound, I am bound to take them into consideration and either drop the scheme or modify it. (16)

However, as has already been argued, the Minister has only to consider any objections to be unsound to reject them.

As has been indicated, resistance to the designation was readily manifest. Orlans, in his study of Stevenage, divides the opponents to the designation into seven classes: agricultural interests, the rural cult (conservationists), property interests, ratepayer interests, 'class antagonism' (in other words, particular middle-class residents apprehensive of a repeat of the class incongruity which occurred when working-class evacuees and workers were billeted in Stevenage during the Second World War), the Residents' Protection Association (an organization of some 1,200 members), and finally those who were opposed to 'planning' in that it was deemed to be the opposite of 'freedom'. (17) Orlans quite rightly points to the ambivalent posture of the town's traders, in that although being predominantly Conservative, ratepaying, and property owning, they were also aware of what rewards future business could bring. (18)

This resistance to the designation of Stevenage was not
of course an isolated event, as much later, in 1961, according to Hilary Rose, a new town planned for Hook in
Hampshire was stifled by local interest groups:

> Local feelings were appeased, but overcrowded people
> living in London lost out and remained sharing with
> their in-laws - people on waiting lists inadequately
> housed with no chance of change. To planners calcu-
> lating the overspill from any redevelopment scheme,
> to London's housing managers confronted with lists
> of 180,000 waiting for council houses, or to the actual
> people wanting to move to a New Town, the interests of
> a few were seen to prevail over the needs of many. (19)

The local supporters of the new town project at Stevenage
were, essentially, the Trades Council who welcomed the
possibility of more and varied employment (as did numerous
individual workers); those who were attracted to the
'city lights' notion of Stevenage as a citadel of entertainment; and the Labour Party supporters (although
Orlans suggests that the real political division between
supporters and opponents was not so much between Labour
and Conservative, as between progressives and conservatives, some of whom were inside the ranks of both
parties). (20) There were of course the 'disinterested'.
As Orlans notes, the 'Brave New World' planning and politics interested only a varying proportion of the inhabitants, the rest being preoccupied with dogs, beer,
gardening, poetry, their digestion or their neighbour's
wife. (21) More importantly he makes the fundamental
point that the crucial fight on the new town was fought
not in local assemblies, the streets or ballot boxes,
but in judicial and Ministerial Chambers where 'law' and
'learned argument' reigned supreme. (22)

The first Stevenage Development Corporation Board was
assembled by Silkin in late 1946 - following the 'Advisory Committee' he had set up earlier while his bill
was proceeding through Parliament - and consisted of
the nine members of the Committee. The Chairman, who
relinquished the position some eight months later, was
the prominent architect Clough (later Sir Clough)
Williams-Ellis, a TCPA Council member with Labour Party
leanings (he was brother-in-law to John Strachey). The
Deputy Chairman was Monica Felton, a member of the Reith
Committee, an academic with leanings towards the left
of the Labour Party. The other members included a
journalist, a manager, two London councillors, another
TCPA Council member and writer, Stevenage's Councillor
Ireton (receiving his reward for his part in the designation), and retired Chief of the Post Office, Sir Thomas

Gardiner.* In all, seven of the nine members had socialist leanings.

It was formally announced that the new town was to be
planned to accommodate a 'balanced' community of 60,000
persons with industry and commerce of varied types, sufficient to provide employment for the inhabitants. (23)
It is of some interest to note at this juncture the fact
that previous to designation, Stevenage possessed a considerable concentration of sizeable manufacturing industry
compared with other London New Towns designated shortly
afterwards. For example, Stevenage had 4 occupiers
employing 2,600 employees, Hemel Hempstead had 36 occupiers employing 6,200 employees, and Welwyn Garden City
had 69 occupiers employing 8,000 employees (24) (NB ratio
equivalence of employers to number of employees).

The final House of Lords judgement was not in fact given
until the end of July 1947, by which time it had become
apparent that a period of austerity was at hand, what with
the fuel crisis, the Dalton resignation over the Budget
leak, and a total of 1,916,000 unemployed. (25)   The
Chairman reported that at the last meeting of the Standing
Ministerial Conference the Minister had stated that no
commitments involving capital expenditure should be made
and no further senior staff should be appointed. (26)
These restrictions, particularly in relation to land
acquisition, caused concern to the Corporation, who
suggested that these measures

> may prove to have been unfortunate.... It is feared
> that, as a result of the delay in authorising the
> acquisition of the land, entry may have to be effected
> at shorter notice than is desirable in the interests of
> food production, of the farmer personally and conse-
> quently of local public relations. (27)

Whilst the first General Manager of the Corporation -
General Duff, (28) a professional soldier with a reputation for being excessively formal (e.g., other Corporation officers were invited to confer with him by the
single word 'speak' written at the bottom of the subject
concerned) - was being appointed, relations with both the
Council and the public were deteriorating. The Council
was again concerned about the lack of information it was
receiving from the Corporation and hence requested an
early meeting to formally discuss future developments,
(29) while the public, both bemused and puzzled at the
'plans' together with the dearth of action, was again

---

* Full profiles of all the Corporation members for the
  period 1946-76, together with length of service and
  attendance record, are given in appendix 2.

restless. At the same time within the Corporation a
quorum could not be mustered to interview candidates for
the post of Chief Architect, (30) and in December 1947 the
Board, due no doubt in considerable measure to the growing
attacks on the organisation, agreed that the minutes of
its meetings should be marked 'confidential' and circulated to members of the Corporation and Chief Officers
only, and that they should not be made available to staff.
Any matters of interest to staff would be notified to
those affected either personally or through the staff
representatives, as might be appropriate. (31) This
process in fact went even further when in July 1948 it
was agreed by the Board that any decisions made at private
meetings which were not suitable for general discussion
and circulation, should be recorded in a separate minute
book to be kept in the sole possession of the General
Manager. (32)

The year 1948 started reasonably optimistically for the
Corporation with fifty applications from firms requesting
sites, but as it dragged on progress was nil and no major
work of construction had been accomplished. (33) During
the year there had been a change in Chairman when Sir
Thomas Gardiner, who had held the position from October
1947, resigned just one year later, to be replaced by
Alderman the Rev.Charles Jenkinson, Leader of the Leeds
City Council, who in turn died the following August. This
turn of events could of course have strengthened the hand
of the General Manager who was involved in the Corporation
on a day-to-day basis.

At about the same time the political style of the Corporation was emerging. For example, in May 1948 a member of
the Board of Trade had been asked by the Stevenage
Chamber of Commerce to give a talk on industry in the new
town. Mr Burkitt, the representative of the Board of
Trade, subsequently wrote to the General Manager of the
Corporation requesting co-operation in order that the
policy he was to outline in his talk should not conflict
with the views of the Corporation, and this was subsequently arranged. (34) Another example was in relation to
objections regarding proposed water charges. The Legal
Officer of the Corporation thought that it should be
possible by negotiation to settle most of the objections,
but thought that 'unfortunately' a public inquiry to hear
the objections of the Stevenage Residents Protection
Association and a Mr Berry appeared to be inevitable. (35)
Both incidents demonstrate, of course, the rather cynical
workings of the prevailing 'democratic' system.

The Corporation now had a staff of 96 whose remuneration,
together with administration costs, totalled £41,820 per

annum and furthermore the Corporation had received
advances from the Minister to the total of £147,000. In
June it was reported that only two people in the town were
unemployed.

The year 1949 brought a new Chairman, Monica Felton, who
had been an original Board member but had left for a brief
spell as Chairman of Peterlee Development Corporation.
Overall, it can be positively asserted that 1949 was a
dismal year for the Corporation. Orlans sums up the
situation rather well:

> [the Corporation] unable to build one permanent house
> in over three years' activity, struck the observer's
> eye and contributed to the impression (certainly shared
> by many of the Corporation's staff) of inefficiency and
> waste. The Corporation's officers and staff were, for
> the most part, extremely competent professionally, and
> their work was undoubtedly of a high standard. How-
> ever, in the period under review, it consisted exclu-
> sively of plans and surveys - forebodings, not accom-
> plishments.... The poor showing of New Town Corpora-
> tions was due primarily not to mismanagement, but to
> the chronic shortage of capital (especially in
> dollars), labour, and materials from which the entire
> nation suffered at the time, and the lack of adequate
> Government priority.... Finally, there were causes
> peculiar to Stevenage: the court action, the change in
> the Chief Architect and the frequent change of
> Chairmen, the special problem of sewerage, and the fact
> that - unlike the situation in some other New Towns -
> there was almost no land which was available locally
> with main services already installed upon which houses
> could be erected even before the Master Plan was ap-
> proved. (36)

Once again indications of political style were emerging
in 1949. The Board asked Councillor Ireton (a Board
member) to raise the matter of the Stevenage Residents
Protection Association's protest concerning the water
charges, at the next Council meeting, in the hope that
further efforts would be made to persuade the Association
to withdraw their objections. Councillor Ireton did in
fact raise the matter with the Council, which in turn
replied that it was not prepared to ask favours of the
Association. (37) This of course had put Councillor
Ireton in an extremely difficult position, and it high-
lighted the differences at that time between the Corporation and the Council. The differences of course were
related to structure and function, with the Council
functioning in terms of 'community interest', and having
some regard to democratic rights (as well as, of course,
being a little envious of the Corporation). The Corpo-

ration, on the other hand, was in the early and crucial
stage of development and could not achieve its goals
without a clear and determined - and not too prolonged -
sense of purpose. Next on the agenda was the forthcoming
public inquiry into the Master Plan. Mr Dobbie of the
Ministry of Town and Country Planning informed the Corporation that

> the Ministry would not take any active part in the
> Inquiry and their only *representative* would be the
> Inspector. (38, emphasis added)

This of course suggested that somehow the Inspector would
not be taking an 'active part' in the Inquiry, a somewhat
misleading suggestion. Mr Dobbie went on to say that although the local authorities could not be debarred from
making representations at the Inquiry, they would be
invited instead to attend a private meeting at the
Ministry, when any objections they might have could be
discussed. (39) The General Manager thought that the
County Council would probably accept this proposal -
indeed they did - but doubted whether the Urban District
Council would be prepared to do so. In the event the
Urban District Council stated that they

> wished to make their representations at the Public
> Inquiry. They would be willing, however, to meet the
> Ministry's officials for discussion *after* the Inquiry.
> (40, emphasis added)

This is again an indication of the quite different perspective on public participation held by the Council, a
difference related to the different 'politics' of the two
bodies, as noted earlier. Following the Inquiry, the
General Manager reported that he had visited the Ministry
to find out what it intended to do in regard to the discussions with the other government departments and with
the County Council, and how soon a decision would be given
on the Master Plan. The Ministry had indicated to him
that it intended to handle the discussions with the County
Council and government departments alone, and doubted
whether it would be necessary to refer any matters to the
Corporation. (41) This of course was hardly a surprising
Ministry initiative, in that the Corporation was both
rather inexperienced and indeed a small organisation.
 By 1949 the Corporation had an accumulated deficit on
General Revenue Account of £3,000, whilst two events of
a more ideological nature took place towards the end of
the year. First, the Corporation issued a handbook to
both tenants and prospective tenants, stating that within
fifteen to twenty years the Corporation would be wound up,
and second, the Social Development Office was at that
moment wound up. The Corporation itself put it in this
way:

>the Corporation has decided to disband the Social
>Development Department ... social development is not
>a thing apart and must be the direct concern of every
>one of the Corporation's officers. (42)

This seemingly laudable action was in fact motivated more
by the disagreements which occurred between the Social Development Office - headed by a sociologist - and other
Corporation Departments, rather than a universal concern
for 'social development'.

The new year began with a further instance of the inability to form a quorum, this time for the Board meeting
of 10 January. (43)   The Master Plan finally received
approval on 22 February, and substantial changes took
place on the Board, among which were the appointments of
S.Gestetner, head of the Gestetner empire, and, most
importantly, of Evelyn Denington of the LCC and the TCPA
(and who was later to become the longest-serving Chairman
of the Corporation).

In March the subject of industry was discussed intensively by the Board, and ideas were formulated which were to
be of historic importance.   To begin with the Board discussed the quantity of industry which would be necessary
to fill the accommodation as programmed: indeed the Board
asserted that the planning of industrial development must
depend upon the revised programme for building residential
accommodation. (44)   This notion of industrial development
following residential development was soon to be brought
to an end.   A discussion also took place concerning a
report giving full details of a discussion which had taken
place with Messrs Geo.W.King Ltd (a pre-new-town industry), on the possibility of their Hitchin factory being
moved to Stevenage.   Councillor Ireton pointed out that
the Corporation was responsible for the decentralisation
of industry from London, and asked whether it would be
right for a local factory to be allowed to expand, even
though it would bring labour from London.   However, eleven
days later the Board

>agreed that Messrs Geo.W.King Limited should be allowed
>to extend their factory premises in Stevenage to the
>extent which they proposed... (45)

This was an early example of the disjunction between the
'aims and ideals' of new town policy, and the decisions
taken by, or forced upon, the Corporation.   Once again
relations with the Council were strained.   For instance,
the Chairman read a letter which she had received from
the Chairman of the Urban District Council, concerning
the visit to the Corporation headquarters on 7 June by
Lewis Silkin.   The Chairman of the Council thanked the
Corporation for inviting his Council to meet the Minister,

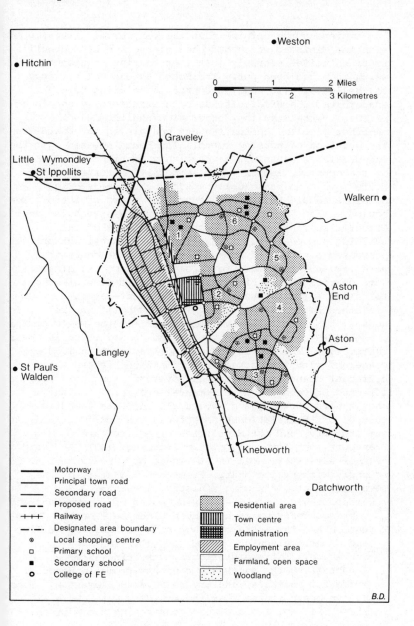

Weston

Hitchin

0   1   2 Miles
0   1   2   3 Kilometres

Graveley

Little Wymondley
St Ippollits

Walkern

6

1

5

Aston
End

2

4

Aston

Langley

St Paul's
Walden

3

Knebworth

Datchworth

	Motorway
	Principal town road
	Secondary road
	Proposed road
	Railway
	Designated area boundary
⊚	Local shopping centre
□	Primary school
■	Secondary school
○	College of FE

	Residential area
	Town centre
	Administration
	Employment area
	Farmland, open space
	Woodland

B.D.

MAP 2   Stevenage master plan 1949

but expressed the opinion that the very brief interview
with the Minister which had been granted to his Council's
representatives scarcely justified the inconvenience to
which they had been put. The Board agreed not to reply
to the letter, (46) and of course in so doing merely
exacerbated the difficulties, both structurally and inter-
personally, between the Corporation and the Council.

 Another problem confronting and concerning the Board was
the question of housing rents. The Board noticed that the
Corporation's rents would invariably be higher than those
of the Council, and thus was seriously perturbed at the
difference, and was equally anxious that everything
possible should be done to reduce the rents of Corporation
houses. (47) The problem of course was a structural one:
Corporation rents reflected the 'true' cost of unit
building and overheads. That is to say, local authorities
possessed a number of pre-war houses let at rents that
were low, but were able to raise these rents to offset
some portion of the high rents they would otherwise have
to charge for new houses built at present-day costs. On
the other hand the Corporation, having built no pre-war
houses, had no alternative but to reflect the whole of the
present-day costs of development and construction in their
rents. (48) The final problem made manifest in 1950 was
concerned with the lack of co-ordination between the
different branches of national government and how this
affected Stevenage's developmental progress. Chisholm
and Manners, Orlans, and Rodwin all indicate the difficulties of the relationships between the Board of Trade,
the Treasury, and the Ministries of Agriculture,
Transport, and Town and Country Planning. (49) An example
of this was experienced in Stevenage at a Board meeting in
October, with Evelyn Sharp, Permanent Secretary of the
Town and Country Planning Ministry, present:

   A report was circulated giving notes of discussions and
   correspondence which had taken place between the Corporation and the Board of Trade and the Ministry of Town
   and Country Planning on the moving of industry to
   Stevenage. Extreme difficulty was being experienced
   in obtaining the necessary consents from the Board of
   Trade for suitable industry to move to Stevenage. Dame
   Evelyn Sharp stated that the Ministry were aware of
   these difficulties and were considering the advisabili-
   ty of approaching the Board of Trade. (50)

 The year 1951 brought the deficit on the General Revenue
Account to £15,000, but also saw the beginnings of large-
scale development, with the process of purchasing one
third of the 6,000 acres of property within the designated
area. It also saw the sacking of the Chairman, Monica

Felton, for visiting Korea without prior permission and
whilst there publicising the belief of the North Korean
Government that the Americans were engaged in germ
warfare. (51) Her replacement was a prominent architect,
and Chairman of Crawley Development Corporation, Sir
Thomas Bennett. Although there was an acceleration in the
building programme, there was at the same time a labour
shortage. In February the Board agreed that the Chief
Estate Officer should ascertain from the London Boroughs
to which Stevenage was linked, the number, with particu-
lars, of building operatives on their housing lists. It
was further agreed that should the number of bricklayers
from the Greater London area be insufficient for the
Corporation's needs, they should be recruited from any
part of the country if necessary, and made an offer of
living accommodation. (52)

The Corporation, in its Annual Report to Parliament, once
again raised the problem of high rents and stated that to
justify them

> Corporations must not only attract industry to their
> towns: they must provide for that industry the best
> possible working conditions.... They must likewise
> provide an exceptional standard of housing and ameni-
> ties. Only thus will the public come to realise that
> the payment of these rents is worthwhile. If Corpo-
> rations can in fact achieve this high standard, they
> will be performing a valuable service by relieving the
> rate burden and establishing housing, subject to the
> statutory subsidies, upon an economic basis. (53)

De Havilland, the aircraft manufacturers, were let a site
of fourteen acres, proceeded to build their factory themselves, and then informed the Corporation that they
desired to pay an annual rent of £215 per acre, who in
reply stated that the required sum was in fact £250 per
acre. However the Board decided in September that it
would accept De Havilland's lower figure as it needed
them (this bargaining was particularly marked in the early
years). (54) As the General Manager, General Duff, later
stated in relation to industrial rents generally:

> It is better to be satisfied with a reasonable return
> and a contented customer. (55)

At the same time as the Conservative Party regained power
nationally, the Board agreed the principle of a scheme for
advancing money to persons wishing to build their own
houses in the designated area, and thus approved a token
provision in the Budget for 1953 of £20,000 for this
purpose. (56)

There were four new appointments to the Board in 1952,
consisting of a surveyor and a one-time member of the

Reith Committee, an accountant, and two retired Army
officers, one of whom, Major A.G.Howard, was just com-
pleting his term as Chairman of the SUDC and was put on
the Board presumably to strengthen local membership. The
other was Lt General Sir Charles King, ex-Engineer in
Chief at the War Office, who was put on the Board as
Deputy Chairman.

De Havilland again figured prominently in the early
months of 1952. The Corporation's Chief Legal Officer
mentioned that exception had been taken by the Company to
the clause which prohibited them from increasing the floor
space of the factory to more than 200,000 sq ft without
the consent of the Corporation, in the giving or with-
holding of which the Corporation might have in regard to
the 'balance of industry' in Stevenage. The Board agreed
that while the clause should require the consent of the
Corporation to the increase over 200,000 sq ft in the
floor area of the building, the words relating to the
balance of industry could be deleted if this would help
towards agreement. (57) Once again a further indication
of the disjunction between the Reithian idea of 'balanced'
communities and the actions of the Development Corporation, albeit a Corporation constrained in its actions by
the 'routine' workings of the industrial location process.

The other company who were to figure even more prominently in Stevenage's development, English Electric Limited,
also made their move in 1952. In July the Chairman of the
Corporation received a letter from Sir Frank Lee, Permanent Secretary at the Board of Trade, refusing GEC Limited
permission to erect a factory at Stevenage and directing
them instead to Portsmouth. The Chairman noted this
decision with concern, but the General Manager reported
that he had written to the English Electric Company
informing them that the Corporation could now offer a
wider choice of site, and that the company, if they so
wished, could inherit a considerable amount of design work
which had already been carried out. (58) A month later
English Electric stated that they would be prepared to
move provided that the whole of their establishment from
Luton could be moved to Stevenage. The Corporation
agreed, and furthermore agreed to English Electric's
request for an immediate allocation of twenty-five houses
for their employees. (59)

Rents again posed problems, so much so that in a letter
to the Minister of Housing and Local Government the Corporation reported that

   Rents in New Towns have now reached a level which gives
   rise for serious concern ... the tenants themselves
   show increasing signs of reluctance in accepting a

tenancy of a Corporation house ... some have already
refused to do so ... unless some measures are taken the
Stevenage Corporation desires to place on record that
it regards the future with the gravest apprehension.
If something is not done, and done quickly, it appears
to the Corporation that the whole project of the development of New Towns is heading rapidly towards
financial disaster... (60)

At the end of 1952 the Corporation estimated that it had
a surplus of 109 houses, and decided to attempt to fill 70
or more of them by offering tenancies to industrial
workers who were willing to move from London to a house in
Stevenage and work in Hitchin or Letchworth. Other
problems included tenants with rent arrears: for example,
just before Christmas 1952, the Board agreed that unless
a particular tenant who was £90 in arrears paid his rent
regularly and paid off his arrears weekly, notice to quit
would be served. (61) The year ended with a £65,000 deficit on General Revenue Account being reported.

The population in 1953 had reached 13,000, whilst industrial development was rapid, with the Corporation
owning nearly three-quarters of the land which was to be
developed. Construction workers engaged in development
numbered 1,900. Half-way through the year Sir Thomas
Bennett, the Chairman, relinquished his position because
of pressure of business. The Corporation, in tribute,
stated that

Sir Thomas Bennett's period of Chairmanship was marked
by substantial progress at Stevenage, which was due in
no small part to Sir Thomas's influence and direction.
(62)

He was replaced by a man who, unlike his predecessors,
stayed for a considerable period of time, in fact just
under nine years. The new Chairman was Sir Roydon Dash,
a surveyor and ex-Chief Valuer at the Board of Inland
Revenue, and, like Bennett, a Conservative. Councillor
Ireton, a fellow Board member, suggested that Dash was
put in 'to make or break Stevenage', as the administration
at the time had acquired a bad reputation. Furthermore he
considered that Dash was completely in the officers'
hands. (63) This assertion of course seems perfectly
reasonable in that the General Manager, General Duff, had
been with the Corporation for a continuous period of six
years, in which time there had been five Chairmen.
Councillor Ireton went on to say that:

Dash wasn't all that interested in Stevenage. He was
interested in Tennis ... in Golf ... in Bridge, and
Whisky and Cigars, but his interest didn't extend much
beyond those. He was a retired man and you know it was
a job that carried a little bit of money. (64)

Of course, even if the assessment of Sir Roydon Dash is
somewhat exaggerated, the process of selection at the time
was such that it tended to recruit persons who had completed their 'careers' rather than persons in the middle
of careers, who would invariably be more likely to be
highly motivated.

Relations with the public were again a little strained,
and, further, a glimpse of the Corporation's evolving political style can be elicited from a consideration of two
isolated events. First, the Stevenage Residents' Association had been pressing for a breakdown of rent figures,
and without much consideration the Board agreed that the
information the Corporation had produced should be given
orally to the Association at a meeting with their representatives, but that on no account should a written
statement be submitted. (65) The Corporation here were
blandly utilising the rather negative and protective
mechanisms of bureaucratic management. The Corporation
also anticipated potential difficulties with a marked
degree of sluggishness and insensibility. For instance,
the Chief Estate Officer circulated copies of correspondence with the Ministry, in which the Minister expressed concern at the small number of middle-class houses
being built in new towns, and accordingly asked what steps
the Corporation was taking to overcome this difficulty.
The Board's response to this - with the exception of
Councillor Ireton who dissented from the decision - was
to inform the Urban District Council that the land the
Corporation had previously offered to it for housebuilding
was now needed by the Corporation for its own purposes.
(66) Once again this did nothing to improve the poor relations between the Corporation and the Council.

The designated area of the new town was disproportionately divided between the Urban District Council, Hitchin
Rural District Council and Hertford Rural District
Council. However, on April Fool's Day an Order became
effective which adjusted the boundaries and placed practically the whole of the designated area within the
Stevenage Urban District.

The continued resentment of landowners to the new town
was made apparent in late 1953 in relation to Section 6(4)
Orders of the New Towns Act (1946), which enabled any
owner of an interest in land within the designated area of
a new town, which had not been acquired by the development
corporation at the expiry of seven years from the establishment of the town, to require the development corporation to acquire that interest. Section 6(4) became
operative at Stevenage in the November, and the Corporation in its Annual Report noted that

Since that date eleven notices only under the section
have been served upon the Corporation: *more had been
expected*. (67, emphasis added)

The year 1953 saw, at their maximum levels, national unemployment of just below half a million, and a total of
1,370,000 workers involved in industrial disputes. By
December the Stevenage unemployment total had reached 72.
The Corporation was steadily becoming 'big business', and
in 1954 its cumulative capital expenditure amounted to
£10,134,904, while at the same time it was the employer
of some 315 people. The housing allocation system - as
well as the general housing situation - together with the
employment structure and opportunities in the town, were
at this time in the process of clarification. In terms of
general housing progress, Stevenage was lagging behind
certain other London new towns: for example in the period
ending 31 December 1954 Stevenage had built a total of
3,003 houses, as compared with Hemel Hempstead's 4,008 and
Harlow's 5,343 - two new towns designated a year later
than Stevenage. (68) Regarding housing allocation procedures the Corporation both clarified and confused the
system, when in replying to a query from the Trades
Council the Corporation agreed that its responsibility

did not extend beyond providing accommodation for
anyone coming from London who could find employment in
Stevenage. Once a house had been occupied, the tenant
would not be moved provided he was satisfactory as a
tenant. Where he chose to work was not the concern of
the Corporation, although they would prefer that he
worked in Stevenage. (69, emphasis added)

However, a few months later the Corporation was asked by
the Stevenage Industrial Employers' Group (SIEG) if
industry could recruit certain tradesmen, such as radial
drillers, millers, lathe setters, and so on, from outside
Greater London - SIEG did not clearly indicate that they
could not find these skills locally - and the Corporation
gave them an immediate 'yes'. (70) The Board also instructed housing management that in future, parents of
tenants should be offered accommodation whether retired
or not, and furthermore the Board considered that the time
was ripe for making some arrangement with the Urban
District Council to assist it in housing the people on
its housing list. (71) All of this, of course, was indicative of the fact that there were extremely difficult
structural problems to be overcome before there would be
reason to talk of new town successes. Further indications
of these structural imbalances were that already - according to the Chief Estates Officer - over 15 per cent
of the population were employed outside of the town, (72)

and, most importantly, there was the beginning of an
employment imbalance, the course and pattern of which
would unfold over the years: in 1954, in Stevenage, there
were 409 unfilled vacancies and 18 persons unemployed,
(73) an indication that there was obviously a need for
different industries (and skills) to be brought into
Stevenage at that time, before an irreversible pattern
was set.

The revision of the Master Plan was completed and presented in 1955, the revision taking the form of 'tighten-
ing up the somewhat scattered nature of the land uses'.
(74) The Corporation was now developing into a comparatively large organisation, a large property owner, and
parallel with this were outbreaks of rebellion, such as
rent marches and rent strikes.

In its Annual Report for 1956 the Corporation stated
that housing development was now considerably behind industrial expansion, and that subsequently there was a
waiting period of several weeks before the needs of
housing applicants could be satisfied and thus allocations
to industry had to be temporarily reduced. (75) Meanwhile
the Board, whilst concurring with the above statement,
went on to assert that unless further industry could be
attracted to Stevenage, and the construction of premises
by or for them begun by the end of 1955, difficulties
might be experienced in finding suitable tenants for
Corporation houses towards the end of 1956. (76) This was
simply illogical: housing development lagged behind industrial expansion, yet the Corporation desired further
industrial expansion.

Relevant national events in 1955 included a balance-of-
payments crisis, the appointment of 'housing supremo'
Harold Macmillan as the Minister of Housing and Local
Government (the Ministry that replaced the Town and
Country Planning Ministry), while locally the population
had reached 21,000 with almost 14,000 persons in Corpo-
ration property, housing rents continuing to give concern.
Finally, the Corporation noted that

   the sturdiness and well-being of the children is proof
   of the advantages they derive from living in a New
   Town. (77)

In 1956 a national newspaper described Stevenage as
Britain's craziest centre of bumbling bureaucracy, indeed
a 'Goon Town'. (78) However, the year began with Councillor Ireton asking a question of his fellow Board members,
a question to be reiterated over the years, namely at what
stage was it proposed to stop development to allow for the
natural growth of the town? No answer was offered, (79)
of course, because - unlike Councillor Ireton - the other

members of the Board were beginning to see the Corporation
as an end in itself, rather than simply the means to development.

Housing was again the main issue of the year. First, the
Corporation was informed by the Ministry that it desired
corporations to provide better-class housing in new towns,
even if such development incurred a loss in the formative
years. The Corporation agreed to encourage private house
development in the town and subsequently sold land to
private developers. (80) Rents had to be raised by two
pence per week, the Corporation decided, and in so doing
admitted that there undoubtedly existed some hardship due
to the high level of rents, and once again stated that the
whole financing of 'this great social and economic experiment of the New Towns' needed re-examining. (81) The
evolving political style could again be observed in relation to the housing situation. To begin with, in relation to the rent rise, the Chairman reported that he
had been

> appointed to attend the quarterly meeting of the
> Stevenage Residents Federation to be held on the 27th
> July. Housing rents would be the main topic of dis-
> cussion at this meeting, and it had been felt that,
> as Dame Evelyn Sharp was to open the Broadhall
> Community Centre on the 28th July, it might be
> advisable to postpone the date of the meeting to avoid
> the possibility of demonstrations at the opening cere-
> mony. Arrangements had therefore been made for the
> meeting to be held on the 30th July. (82)

Furthermore, at the same time the Corporation introduced
a rent rebate scheme (related of course to the Macmillan
Housing Subsidies Act (1956), plus the Housing Subsidies
Order 1956 which effectively abolished general needs
subsidies). A few months following its introduction the
Corporation introduced a minor change in the scheme which
would be advantageous to the recipient, and subsequently
decided that no public announcement of this minor change
should be made, and that this marginal rebate should be
given only when claimed by the tenant. (83) This patently
unjust decision was merely 'routine' behaviour of the
Corporation. Simultaneously, the Corporation agreed that
the Ministry be

> informed that the Industrial Employers' Group is a
> *highly responsible* body... (84, emphasis added)

Thus, while ordinary residents were being kept somewhat
uninformed regarding the nuances of the rent rebate
scheme, the Corporation was at the same time arguing that
the Industrial Employers' Group should be included in the
arena of decision-making.

The year ended with the continuation of a campaign by the
Residents' Federation for a public inquiry into the
affairs of the Corporation, while the General Manager of
the Corporation reported to the Board that a deputation
from the Urban District Council would be received by the
Permanent Secretary early in January, with two resolutions
from the Council on the agenda. One was the resolution
asking for an inquiry into the Corporation's affairs,
whilst the other concerned the sewerage contribution and
the effect on the local rates. The Permanent Secretary,
Dame Evelyn Sharp, indicated to the Corporation that the
Minister wanted to be fully briefed, (85) an understandable but rather cynical move.

Macmillan was replaced as Minister by Duncan Sandys, who
began his term of office by making Board changes. He
replaced John Watson, a surveyor, with Mr Peter Pryor, a
local farmer-cum-Director of Trumans the brewers.
Councillor Ireton described the nature of the change in
the following manner: 'he was turfed off by Duncan
Sandys, the Minister, to put on a particular associate
of his ... both Eton you know'. (86) Sandys also appointed a local industrialist and member of SIEG, Geoffrey
Hughes, an appointment of some (later) importance. Also
in 1957 General Duff retired after ten years as General
Manager, to be replaced by Richard McDougall, the former
County Treasurer, who was perceived as a public relations
and prestige-projects type, and who, like Duff, eventually
served a term of ten years.

The influence of the Conservative administration was
beginning to show itself: for instance, the Corporation
was informed by the Ministry that it could sell land to
speculative builders at market value, as certified by the
District Valuer, whether it enabled the Corporation to
cover its costs or not, and furthermore the Corporation
was encouraged to sell to sitting tenants. Indeed, the
Corporation announced in its Annual Report for 1958 that
it had reached the conclusion that

> the best way for the present of securing private owner-
> ship in the town is to encourage the private estate de-
> veloper. (87)

However, even though most of the people had 'never had
it so good', private sales were difficult to achieve in
1957: New Ideal Homesteads Limited attempted to sell its
houses in the town but could manage just over 50 per cent
sales.

The pattern of both the housing allocation system and the
industrial structure was again becoming clearer. The
Board recognised, correctly, that the most pressing future
housing problem would arise from the age structure of the

population, and particularly the great numbers of children and adolescents - *'exceptional* measures will be needed'. (88)   The Housing Management's quarterly minutes for June indicated that compared with the 3,872 Londoners (this refers to heads of households), 1,067 non-Londoners had been housed, an indication indeed of the exceptional measures which would be needed in future years if the children of the indigenous population were to be housed. (89)   The pattern is somewhat complicated, however, when from the same minutes it can be observed that the in-dustrialists - who were drawing in the non-Londoners to meet their occupational needs - had not taken up 58 of the houses allocated to them.   To further complicate the situation it was announced that Vauxhall of Luton were employing 300 Stevenage people as compared with only 72 less than two years earlier. (90)

These problems were a product of the town's industrial structure together with its occupational structure, which consisted, in the main, of the production of nuclear weapons and computers, industries which required special-ised skills.   The Board of course was aware of this mismatch, and in fact stated in its Annual Report:

> The success of the initial industrial development and
> the rapid expansion of the first new factories has
> hitherto restricted the introduction of fresh firms to
> the area, but new and possibly smaller businesses can
> now be encouraged to come to Stevenage. (91)

This affirmation of both the need and the desire to di-versify the industrial base of the town, has - as will be demonstrated - been mainly just that: an affirmation, a promise followed by little action.   The uncertainty as to the 'life of the Corporation' was making it difficult for the Corporation to obtain qualified staff in adequate numbers, in certain particular areas, at the end of 1957. (92)

By 1958 the Corporation had received advances from Central Government of nearly £3.25 million, with a capital expenditure figure of £24.5 million, whilst it had a defi-cit on General Revenue Account of £251,000.   Employees of the Corporation now totalled 322, of whom 224 were engaged in professional and administrative duties. (93)

An announcement of rent increases was to be made to all tenants in early February, but the Board received a tele-gram from the Chairman of SIEG in January, urging the Corporation to postpone the announcement.   This incident was an initial indication of the usefulness, for SIEG, of having a member, Geoffrey Hughes, on the Corporation's Board. (94)   The Board, however, refused SIEG's request and announced the rent increases.   The Chief Estates

Officer reported that all of the rent increase notices had
been served and that there had been no unfavourable reactions. However, at the very same time, a deputation
from the Residents' Federation was in London, lobbying
Members of Parliament. (95)

In June the English Electric Company, now the town's
dominating industry, enquired whether the Corporation
would be prepared to build a Technical College for them,
whilst also in June the Housing Management returns showed
that, cumulatively, 5,287 Londoners had been housed as
compared with 1,733 non-Londoners. (96)

The 1959 Annual Report announced that the Corporation had
been asked to revise the Master Plan in such a way as to
look to an ultimate population of 80,000, and again the
point was made by the Corporation that it was aware of the
need to introduce new industries which would bring varied
employment opportunities, and also employ the large
numbers of school-leavers who would be wanting jobs during
the coming years. (97) At Board level, however, the
picture was somewhat different, in that the Board agreed
that as the stage had

> now been reached where it was necessary to decide
> *whether industry in Stevenage should be focused on
> electronics or whether it should be diversified,* the
> matter should be raised at the next meeting of the
> Corporation in conjunction with a report on youth
> employment during the next few years. (98, emphasis
> added)

This further indication that the Corporation was somewhat
constrained by the electronics (not to mention aerospace)
industry, was reinforced by an incident which related to
industrial pressure in general. Geoffrey Hughes, of both
SIEG and the Corporation Board, reported to the Board that
SIEG had met and stated that unless some more labour was
drawn from outside London, production could not be
maintained, and furthermore that the suggestion of a 5 per
cent cut in housing allocations to allow for hardship
cases was rejected by the industrialists.* The views of
SIEG were duly noted. (100) However, barely five months
later the Board

> expressed great concern about the lack of nominations
> from industrialists and consequent high number of

---

* Industrial housing allocation takes the following
  pattern. The industrialists inform the Corporation that
  in year x they will need y number of houses. The Corporation then allocate the industrialists fewer houses as
  it considers that the industrialists exaggerate their
  projections. (99)

vacant dwellings and it was *agreed* that if the industrialists fail to take up their housing allocations,
the houses be allocated to other people in need of
them. (101)

This theme of the industrialists not taking up their full
quota of houses, the subsequent allocation of the residue
to 'people in need of them', and the Corporation's relative compliance with the whole system, can be seen to
recur over the next seventeen or so years.

The Master Plan revision was continuing towards the end
of the year, with the hope that the work would be completed the following year. The Board also decided to
amend the Corporation's 'Standing Regulations', and of
particular importance was the insertion of two particular
regulations. Regulation 15a concerned the General
Manager's 'authority', and stated that the

General Manager of the Corporation is authorised to
take appropriate action on all matters not expressly
referable to the Committees; provided that no action
shall be taken on any matter requiring a resolution of
the Corporation to carry it into effect until the
resolution has been passed,

while regulation 16 concerning 'special powers' stated
that

In exceptional cases of urgency where it is not possible to await the next meeting of the Corporation or a
Committee, the Chairman of the Corporation or the
Committee or in his absence another member may author-
ise any necessary action... (102)

In other words unlimited powers were introduced into the
administration, for whoever desired, or was able, to use
them.

It was announced in 1959 that all the 'Big Five' banks
were to have premises in the town centre, that the basic
work on the revised Master Plan had been completed, and
that there was increased private housing development.
(103) However, the Corporation still accepted that it
faced problems. For example there was the need to diversify the industrial base, there was the problem of the
increase in the value of the agricultural land that the
Corporation would have to acquire (the increase due to the
effect on land values of the Town and Country Planning Act
of 1959), and there was the problem of a declining construction work-force. In its 1960 Annual Report the
Corporation stated that the number of construction workers
was down to 809, and that unless some improvement could be
obtained the house-building programme would suffer. (104)
Concern was further expressed over the increasing number
of non-Londoners being housed: the Housing Management

figures showed a cumulative total of 2,622, as compared
with 6,640 Londoners, at the end of 1959, and thus the
Board agreed that

> the whole problem should be reviewed with the Stevenage
> and District Employers' Group at the next meeting of
> the Housing Allocations sub-committee, and that the
> question of a five per cent cut in housing allocations
> for hardship cases should be discussed again with the
> Employers' Group. (105)

General housing progress was quite reasonable, the Corpo-
ration having now completed 8,696 dwellings, although this
compared unfavourably with Harlow, designated a year after
Stevenage, which had completed a total of 12,062. (106)
A new Board member was appointed during the year: A.F.
Tuke, a local banker who was eventually to stay on the
Corporation Board for five years, and later still was to
become Chairman of Barclays Bank.

Finally, questions of a more philosophical nature were
posed in 1959. First, the 'Direct Action Committee
Against Nuclear War' organisation campaigned in Stevenage
for ten days and obtained 1,000 signatories to a petition,
to which the Corporation responded:

> the question whether war-like materials should be
> manufactured is a political issue on which the Corpo-
> ration has no comment to make. (107)

And 'Purpose', the Corporation's quarterly booklet to
tenants, brought the year to its close in the following
manner:

> How seriously ... does Stevenage really take itself?
> Judging by its voting record in local government
> elections and by-elections of recent years one would
> say not very seriously. Polls rarely reach 30 per
> cent... (108)

4   Stevenage 1960-9
Consolidation and contradictions

The British believe in mobilizing extremely small
numbers of people to deal with very large problems.
> A CPRS (Central Policy Review Staff) official,
> quoted in Heclo and Wildavsky (1974), p.304

The 1960s marked the real beginnings of the financial
strength of the Corporation, and from a peak deficit on
General Revenue Account in 1956 of £277,000, there was in
1960 a surplus of £75,000.

The Corporation, anxious to remedy the problem of housing
vacancies, asked housing management for an analysis of the
structure of vacancies. Thus in February the Board was
told that of 445 vacancies, 32.6 per cent of the previous
tenants were buying their own houses, 28.1 per cent were
changing their employment, and 10.2 per cent just could
not settle - the residual category being of a miscellaneous nature. (1)

In the Annual Report the Corporation once again touched
on the need for more industrial diversification and an
employment base which would provide for a greater capacity
to employ young people immediately on leaving school, and
indeed the Corporation appeared a little confident and
optimistic when it suggested that 'all could be well'
as soon as the

> commercial world awakes to the realisation that
> offices can be obtained in New Towns at a fraction of
> their cost in London and can be staffed more efficient-
> ly with employees who do not have to suffer the ex-
> haustion of long journeys by public transport to and
> from work. (2)

The Corporation announced also that it was to build a
group of fifteen unit factories, each of about 1,800
sq ft, to be let mainly to small firms vacating premises
in London, or firms engaged in sub-contract work for the
bigger concerns in Stevenage. (3) So here again is a

policy whose long-term consequence could be to strengthen
the existing employment base rather than to diversify it.
 The defence expenditure of the Government then in office
was a healthy £1,596 million, a matter of intimate concern
to Stevenage. At the same time in Stevenage there were
44 unemployed persons together with a total of 432 unfilled vacancies. Rent increases were announced with
very little hostility from tenants. The Corporation also
recognised the growing problem of the 'second generation':

> At this stage in the town's development there are many
> children of tenants who have grown up in Stevenage and
> are marrying. It is impossible to accept applications
> from all of these for housing in view of the *constant
> pressures* from new and expanding industry and from the
> town's trade and services on the limited supply of new
> houses. But provided the man works in Stevenage,
> applications are accepted. So far 101 such couples
> have been housed, 30 in the past year. (4, emphasis
> added)

As has been evident earlier in terms of non-take-up by
the industrialists, it was not so much 'constant pressure'
but rather a statement of the Corporation's policy and
priorities.
 A New Towns Circular of 1957 (28.6.57/NT) allowed development corporations to sell houses to sitting tenants,
and as the Corporation perceived that there was in fact
such a demand it decided to encourage leasehold sales. (5)
This action of course was taking place within a 'property-
owning political and ideological environment', and indeed
the Ministry had informed the Corporation that it wanted
to see more middle-class houses built, ostensibly to
prevent commuting. (6) Again, the Corporation considered
that the demand for privately-built houses was quite in
evidence and thus decided to reserve more sites for this
type of development, and, moreover, it felt it more appropriate for owner-occupied houses to be grouped together
rather than scattered throughout the town, and therefore
decided to dispose only of detached and semi-detached
houses in certain areas. (7) Hardly a Reithian gesture.
 The total of construction workers engaged in building the
town had now reached a low of 543, a decline which the
Corporation was attempting to offset by 'administrative
and organizational means', (8) whatever that might have
meant.
 The Rector of Stevenage, the Rev.E.W.B.Cordingly, was
appointed to the Board and his presence was felt in the
Corporation's Annual Report:

> The outstanding feature of the year has been the
> growing social cohesion of the town ... Stevenage was

> attaining a consciousness of and a pride in itself....
> The physical, mental and moral quality of adolescents
> in Stevenage is very high.... In what other parish of
> 40,000 people does the Bishop of the Diocese hold three
> or four confirmation services every year? (9)

Meanwhile another member of the Board, Sir Arthur Rucker
(the Deputy Chairman), who had been private secretary to
successive Ministers of Health in the years 1928-36,
informed the Board that he would be going to Nigeria in
October for two months on business (10) (an action which
demonstrated the difficulties involved in appointing to
public life persons who could give maximum time and
commitment).

The year 1961 saw the surplus on General Revenue Account
rise to £372,000, and the building of the 10,000th Corporation house. (11) The same year saw Britain applying to
join the European Economic Community, and the introduction
of the Housing Act (1961), legislation which restored
general needs subsidies but in a form designed to pressure
local authorities into charging 'economic' rents (with
rebates).

The usefulness of two members of the Board was demonstrated early in the year. SIEG, after discussing the
question of diversification, approached the Corporation
with the suggestion that any new industry which showed an
interest in coming to the town ought to be referred to it
in confidence. The Board pointed out, however, that it
was usual for such firms not to want their names mentioned
until negotiations were advanced to the point where they
could advise their employees on the proposed move; at
this stage it was usual for the Corporation to refer the
firm to the Employers' Group to discuss the availability
of labour, and so on. The Board finally resolved that as
Mr Hughes was a member of both the Corporation and the
Employers' Group, he should draw the attention of the
Corporation to any case where he thought it advisable for
the Group to be consulted. (12)

The second case concerned Councillor Ireton. English
Electric Limited wanted to construct a factory of some
4,000 sq ft to process beryllium, a procedure which
carried with it considerable health risks. The Board
agreed that no decision on the company's proposal be taken
until a letter from the appropriate government department
had been received, giving full details of the risks involved and the safeguards to be applied in the processing.
It was further agreed that Councillor Ireton should
request the Stevenage Urban District Council to postpone
further consideration of the proposal until such information had been received and made available to them. (13)

Of course, however useful Councillor Ireton was to the
Board in situations like this particular one, it made his
position uncomfortable, and did not particularly enhance
Corporation/Council relations.

It is an understatement to say that 1962 proved to be an
'interesting' year. The Corporation with a surplus on
General Revenue Account of £648,000, with cumulative
capital expenditure totalling £36 million, and a staff of
393, was now indeed big business.

To begin with there were Board changes. The Chairman,
Sir Roydon Dash resigned and was subsequently eulogised
by the Corporation in the following manner:

> His long experience of property management and the
> knowledge he acquired as Chief Valuer to the Board of
> Inland Revenue were invaluable to him at Stevenage, but
> one would particularly stress his qualities as a leader
> who evoked a firm loyalty from members, officers and
> staff of the Corporation and also commanded enormous
> respect in the town. (14)

Dash was replaced as Chairman by the Deputy Chairman,
Sir Arthur Rucker. Two other Board appointments were
made: an ex-Naval Officer, Commander P.B.Martineau, who
was a local solicitor, was installed as new Deputy
Chairman, and Sam Clarke, director of a Government water
research establishment based in Stevenage joined the
Board.

Construction workers were at this time most concerned
about the future availability of employment, particularly
as the Government had the previous August called for
'restraint'. The Stevenage building workers decided in
February 1962 to demonstrate and march to the Town Square
in order to coincide with a meeting of the Corporation and
Union officials. On hearing of this, the Corporation
decided to cancel the meeting, for as the Board put it

> the Corporation, already faced with serious delays in
> housing completions, cannot afford to lose the services
> of the building workers for such a march... (15)

The Corporation also reported that its 95 per cent
mortgage scheme which had commenced in January 1961 was,
as expected, increasing the number of houses sold to
tenants. The Corporation further resolved to provide more
land for private development so as to ensure, as far as
possible and without interference with its own housing
programme, a continuous supply of houses for sale. (16)

In April Mrs Denington, who by this time had acquired
considerable influence on the Board (due first to her
having been a member for almost twelve years; second
because of her considerable involvement in London County
Council politics; and finally as Chairman of the New and

Expanding Towns Committee and a member of the Central
Housing Advice Committee), reported that she had been
approached in confidence by a member of the Sutton Trust
(of which she was to become a member in 1976). The Trust
was considering setting up a housing association and
wanted to know whether the Corporation might have land
available on which it could build some thirty houses.
The Board agreed to investigate and decide on the matter.
(17)

July, 1962, can be seen as the prelude to a series of
events, at best confusing and at worst bizarre, which
concerned the possibilities of expanding the size of the
town. In 1979 this protracted affair was far from dead.
A letter was received by the Corporation on 10 July from
the Permanent Secretary at the Ministry, Dame Evelyn
Sharp, concerning the 'growth' problems of the South East.
She expounded, as she put it, her 'provisional views'
before the actual regional study of the South East was
completed. Her letter is reproduced here in detail in
order to illustrate the beginnings of the affair:

> I am less certain about Stevenage ... because if you
> plan for a town much if at all larger than 80,000 it
> will be necessary to duplicate the trunk sewer to Rye
> Meads. This will be an expensive job. *It seems to
> follow* that the expansion of Stevenage would only be
> economic if it were large, perhaps to an ultimate popu-
> lation of as much as 150,000. I am not so sure that so
> large a growth is feasible without distorting the town
> or getting too close to other towns. We would, how-
> ever, wish you to make a technical assessment of the
> maximum size to which you think the town could grow,
> taking into account the points I have mentioned, disre-
> garding the designated area, but having regard to water
> supply and sewerage. We would want *approximate* esti-
> mates of the cost likely to be involved in the ex-
> pansion of services.
>
> I appreciate that your position is complicated because
> you have just about finished the preparation of a
> revised Master Plan for an ultimate population of
> 80,000, and that the decision on the land which your
> Corporation want to acquire urgently for housing in
> the northern part of the town is linked with the
> revised Master Plan. I began by thinking that your
> best course would be to go ahead with submission of
> your revised Master Plan and with any proposals linked
> with it. For I had understood that the plan would be
> ready for submission now; and since it is impossible
> to tell how long it will take to reach conclusions
> about an enlarged target (and the upshot may well be

to decide against it anyway) it seemed a pity not to
push on. We shall be making it public that we are
asking you to work out the possibilities of enlarging
the target so you would be able to explain when producing your 80,000 plan (and using it to defend any
proposed acquisition) much of what was going on.

It would be one stage in evolution; and as I have
said it might in the event prove to be the last one.
However, I am now told that you are not as far forward
with production of the 80,000 plan as we supposed. In
the circumstances you may prefer to hold it up until
you have worked out the possibilities of enlarging the
target. If your *hunch* is that enlargement will prove
sensible, despite my doubts, you may want to get your
people working on revision of the plan on this assumption. *Whatever is to be the ultimate target we
obviously want a final plan just as soon as we can
get it.*

I ought perhaps to emphasise that what we are asking
you to make at this point in time is a technical study
of the problem. A decision whether Stevenage's target
should be changed must depend upon the results of your
study and the consultations which will have to follow
it; *and entails consideration of policy which we are
not looking at until we have the technical appreciation.* (18, emphasis added)

The rather problematic aspects of the planning 'logic'
are quite evident in Dame Evelyn Sharp's letter: 'it
seems to follow' that only 'large' expansion would be
economic; that only 'approximate' estimates of the cost
were required; and that 'whatever' was to be the ultimate
target a 'final plan' was needed as soon as possible. The
problem arises of course by virtue of the fact that
'planning' which, by definition, is an attempt at control
and prediction, is intrinsically - and often in a contradictory manner - related to the ever-changing and unpre-
dictable wider economic and political structure.

With a staff of highly qualified technicians, ranging
from engineers to planners, the possibility of an extension of its 'life', let alone the prestige attached
to 'growth', meant that the Corporation was in no doubt
as to what action to take. The Corporation resolved that
work on the technical study be undertaken with 'all
speed', and that, pending its completion, submission to
the Minister of the revised Master Plan for an 80,000
population be deferred. The General Manager further
reported that the Ministry was to notify the County
Council and the Urban District Council the following
day of its request to the Corporation to consider the

possibilities of enlarging the town, and would also be issuing a statement to the press. (19) Work began in a mildly clandestine manner just two days later, when the General Manager assembled the staff and informed them that as the Corporation was looking into the possible size of the town there would be considerable speculation as to what was going to happen. Staff should be silent about where, if at all, development might take place as values in land changed dramatically in circumstances such 'as these', and that it was very important for the good name of the Corporation and its officers that there could be no suggestion that there had been 'leaks'. (20)

The Urban District Council's response was predictable, albeit rather mild. It resolved, on 31 July, that the Minister be informed that although the Council would be prepared to co-operate with the Development Corporation in the preparation of a technical study to assess the maximum population which Stevenage could accommodate, it was strongly opposed in principle to the expansion of the town to a population in excess of 80,000. The Council wished to remind the Minister that it had welcomed the establishment of the new town of Stevenage, but now felt that to expand the town substantially beyond the size first envisaged was undesirable in view of the socio-logical and planning problems which were bound to arise. (21) Dramatically the discussions were interrupted when on 10 August redundancy notices were served at English Electric factories in Stevenage and Luton, following the sudden cancellation of a defence contract for the Blue Water Guided Missile, on which £25 million had already been spent. (22)

Dorothy Wedderburn, in her study of the redundancies, tells the story well. (23) The English Electric factories were engaged almost exclusively on government work, and when the contract was cancelled the missile was approach-ing the end of its engineering development stage, but was not in full-scale production. It was clear, suggests Wedderburn, in informed circles at the time that yet another review of government defence policy was under way. The workers dismissed, who were in fact given three months' notice, were predominantly technicians and quali-fied manpower. The British Aircraft Corporation, of which English Electric was a part, finally decided to make 1,000 workers redundant and rely on 'natural wastage' to remove another 500, and it was further decided to close down the Luton factory and thus concentrate future activity in Stevenage. In Stevenage the redundancy was confined to about 800 direct and indirect engineering staff, although English Electric simultaneously announced that it was bringing more bench work into its Stevenage factory, and suggested to the Corporation that it might need a further 200 houses to accommodate new staff. (24)

Wedderburn points out that until 1962 redundancy and unemployment seemed a long way off, and not many people of the new town were much troubled by the nature of the product - guided weapons - upon which the economy of the town rested. Both Luton and Stevenage had enjoyed very high levels of employment, but during 1962 the picture appeared to change with dismissals at Electrolux in Luton and Kodak at Stevenage. Wedderburn did estimate, however, that some 89 per cent of the redundant men started work again within six weeks of leaving.

To conclude Wedderburn's account, it is interesting to note how she illustrates, in relation to the Stevenage case, the particular rationality of certain aspects of capitalist enterprise:

> during the early weeks after the announcement, press publicity was given to the fact that the Company continued work on some aspects of the contract, the implication being that this was extremely wasteful. Had this not been done, however, the Company would either have had to dismiss temporarily some employees until the alternative work which they subsequently obtained had been introduced into the Division, or men would have been standing idle with the consequent danger of disrupting morale, and of losing skilled men who would be urgently needed later. (25)

The Corporation was pressing the Ministry at this time to open a National Assistance Board in Stevenage, and was also making the point to tenants that it was anxious to play its role as landlord, recognising that one of the difficulties would be the problem of rent payments for tenants who because of a change in work, or unemployment, might find their incomes substantially reduced. The Corporation stated that it would 'consider on their merits individual cases of difficulty that may arise, but will naturally expect full advantage to be taken of facilities available through other agencies'. (26)

In the 1963 Annual Report the Corporation talked of the unexpected threat of unemployment on a serious scale, and asserted that even though the crisis had been less severe than it could have been it served to re-emphasise the importance of industrial diversification. (27) Once again this was merely the Corporation *talking* about the importance of industrial diversification, while not particularly acting on its insight, although it must be noted that the Corporation was constrained to a certain extent by the machinations of a relatively 'free' industrial

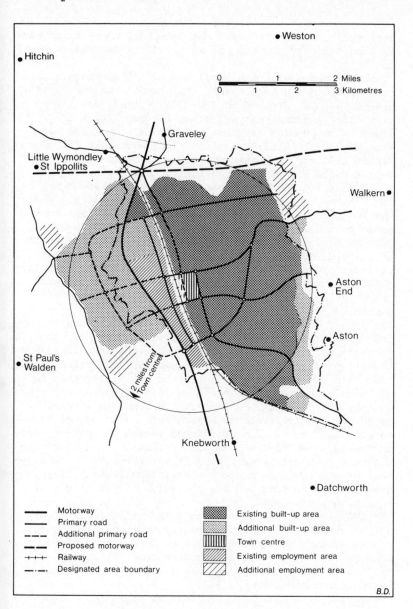

MAP 3 Stevenage expansion proposals 1963

structure: that is to say, the Corporation was in no way in a position to dictate the nature of industrial location.

The year ended with the local slogan - 'Stevenage a gloom town, no longer a boom town'. The surplus on the General Revenue Account dropped to £567,000 in 1963, not surprisingly, and the year was generally quiet with the emphasis on housing progress and allocations, together with the question of expansion. In January the Corporation informed the Minister, who was now Dr C.Hill (the Second World War's 'radio doctor'), that expansion to 130,000 or 140,000 was technically feasible, would not be too late to be successful, and would be economical. (28) The following month the Corporation announced that there would be a semi-public meeting at the local College of Further Education, when its report would be explained to an invited audience of people *representative of the various interests* in the town'. (29, emphasis added) This was, of course, an example of how the Corporation went about the shaping (and manipulation) of public participation.

In June the Stevenage Residents' Protection Association sent a memorandum to the Minister, setting out its objections to expansion, and just over two months later the Council produced a document outlining its objections. The Council's two principal objections were, first, that on sociological grounds the building up of a corporate life quickly in a town raised immense problems and expansion would simply exacerbate such problems; and second, that on planning grounds the purpose of fixing an optimum population in a new town was to enable sensible and purposeful planning to be achieved: if half way through the development of the town the maximum population substantially increased, the Council argued, the value of planning would have been lost. (30)

In 1963 housing completions amounted to 50 per cent of normal output, due of course partly to the extraordinarily severe weather together with labour disputes, although the Corporation was pleased to announce that its policy of selling 'better standard' houses as they became vacant had gathered momentum. (31)

The employment situation was further clarified during the year. Despite their regular protestations to the Corporation that there were not enough houses available to meet their needs, the industrialists' actual position became abundantly clear. For example, the following are a few points raised at the Industrial Housing Allocation meeting of 1963 attended by members of the Corporation and of SIEG. The General Manager reported that:

During the past quarter there had been, on average, 100
houses standing empty ... as a result of allocations
not being taken up in the last quarter...,
and he went on to state that
there had been a dramatic change in the employment
situation in Stevenage. If the Corporation build 1,000
houses a year for the next three or four years and
there are 700/800 school leavers each year, something
like 5,000/6,000 extra jobs will have to be available
during this period.
To which SIEG observed:
it was unlikely that existing industry could offer this
number of jobs and if the Corporation indicated that
they were keen to introduce new industry, *they would
not oppose them*. (32, emphasis added)
Yet in its Annual Report the Corporation blandly stated
that
in the past year there has been an increase in the
number of vacancies for industrial workers which cannot
be filled quickly enough because housing has not been
readily available. (33)
In the same Annual Report another example of what Robert
Thouless would term 'crooked thinking' (34) was considerably in evidence. It was stated that compared nationally,
the age structure of Stevenage was very much out of
balance, with the greatest contrasts being in the 0-14 and
25-39 age-groups which were in excess, and the 45-74 age-
group which was underrepresented. A few pages later it
was noted that it was not proposed to provide maternity
accommodation in the first stage of construction of the
new General Hospital - in an area of very high birth rate.
(35)
To complete a year of idiosyncrasy the Corporation
agreed, following a discussion on the 'uncertainty as to
the possible size of Stevenage', that the Chief Architect
and Planner would prepare a scheme for a larger town
centre, and if necessary in order to carry out the plans
would engage additional staff. It is important to note
here that the Chief Architect and Planner, L.Vincent, had
earlier in the year set up in private practice, and
arrangements had been made with his firm (and partner)
for them to work as consultants to the Corporation. Thus
Mr Vincent in his capacity as the Corporation's Chief
Architect and Planner could call upon himself (and
partner) to act as consultants if he considered it appropriate, which of course was a particularly unsatis-
factory monopolistic arrangement. (36)
The year 1964 saw the surplus on the General Revenue
Account reach £913,000, and the establishment of a 'pro-

fessional' staff at the Corporation of 257, together with
37 unfilled vacancies. In January the General Manager
considered the delay regarding the question of expansion
'embarrassing', particularly as the Corporation's housing
programme was based on the assumption that gradually over
the next few years the rate of production of houses would
be diminishing, and if a decision were made to expand the
town, the public, and any Minister, would expect the
Corporation's housing programme to be stepped up within
a year or two of such a decision. The General Manager,
together with the Board, agreed that the Ministry should
be informed of the difficulties in which the Corporation
was now placed. (37) Of course the reality of the situation was not about difficulties but rather about motivation - the hope of the Corporation that a 'yes' to
expansion would be given. At the time the housing situation was as follows. The industrialists, at the end of
1964, had not taken up 42 houses allocated to them (and
indeed earlier in the year Taylor Instruments Limited had
informed the Corporation that its requirements for 1964-5
could be reduced from 350 to 200); a cumulative total of
4,666 non-Londoners had been housed (31 per cent of the
total housed); and the waiting lists for children and
parents of tenants were 455 and 912 respectively. (38)
Finally, according to the ERV1 and ERV returns, there
were at the time 509 unfilled vacancies together with
97 unemployed persons.

On 7 August the Ministry published the Draft Stevenage
New Town (Designation) Amendment Order 19, which the
accompanying statement described as enlarging the designated area by 1,550 acres, through the addition of some
1,450 acres to the west of the town and some 100 acres to
the north-east of it. The Board obviously was informed of
this well before the public, for on 21 July it was discussing the expansion programme. (39) Following objections to the Draft Order, a public inquiry was announced and programmed for December. Nationally in the
meantime the Housing Act (1964) was introduced, legislation which established the 'Housing Corporation', and
furthermore attempted to encourage the development and
growth of Housing Associations. Most importantly, a
Labour Government was narrowly elected in the October
election, and Shirley Williams won the Hitchin constituency, of which Stevenage was a part - it being only the
second time since 1885 that the seat had been taken by
Labour.

The new Minister of Housing and Local Government was
Richard Crossman, whose version of the events leading up
to the December Public Inquiry is most illuminating:

Shirley Williams asked to see me urgently and said she
wanted to give evidence at the public inquiry on
Stevenage.   This related to a proposal to enlarge three
of our New Towns, Basildon, Harlow and Stevenage, as
part of the method of dealing with London overspill.
The idea had been accepted without too much opposition
by Basildon and Harlow.   But Stevenage has reacted
furiously against the proposal that their town should
be doubled in size by the device of adding a kind of
twin town on the far side of the motorway and the
railway track.   And of course Stevenage is right.
What sane planner would place a motorway and a main
railway line plumb between two halves of a city?   All
my sympathies are with Stevenage....   Now they are
apparently going to be ordered by the Ministry to
accept an enlargement which in their view will destroy
their whole unity as a town.   When I heard about this
from Shirley, I ordered a seminar where Mr Beddoes and
the Chief Architect put the case to me.   I then tested
it out by asking all the Ministry officials sitting
there what they thought.   James, our Chief Planner,
said he was schizophrenic and two others were highly
doubtful.   Really, the only supporter of Dame Evelyn
was her ambitious Deputy, Mr Jones, and the Engineer.
(40)

Again, on 2 December, merely five days before the Inquiry
was due to begin, Crossman recalls finding a 'less urgent'
paper on his desk with a note attached stating that 'you
might like to see what will be said on your behalf by the
Architect at the Stevenage Inquiry':

I glanced at it ... and saw to my astonishment that our
Ministry Architect was going to Stevenage ... to make
the most powerful case for doubling the size of the
town.   I had already had a seminar on this and made it
quite clear I was personally not in any sense committed
to the Ministry proposal ... and was going to leave
myself open to make up my mind after the Inquiry.
After I had made my position clear I had been asked by
the Ministry whether I would cancel the Inquiry ...
'No, I don't mind holding it; it would be extremely
useful because then we would be able to look at the
whole case again and I could announce my decision inde-
pendently at that point.'   I remember the Dame said,
'But you know there will have to be a statement by the
Chief Architect.   We must just make sure it's neutral.'
Remembering this conversation, I was absolutely infuri-
ated by the discovery that this little document had
been put in my less urgent papers as a mere formality
... [next day] I insisted that there should be in-

serted at the top of the draft statement by the Chief
Architect: 'The paper which follows shows the Ministry
policy as it was before the change of Government. It
is not to be understood to prejudice the present
Minister's view on the matter.' (41)

The Inquiry got under way on the 7th, the Inspector being
Mr S.Lloyd-Jones, Ll M. He announced that there were 84
objectors, 44 of whom belonged to the Hertfordshire
Society, and that there had been 99 letters of objection.
Furthermore, he stated that the following organisations
had lodged objections: Hertfordshire County Council,
Stevenage Urban District Council, six District Councils,
the National Farmers' Union, the County Landowners'
Association, and the Stevenage Residents' Protection
Association.

Within the Inquiry the Inspector arranged for the proceedings to be held on one evening so as to provide a more
convenient opportunity for any person not represented to
be able to contribute. Mr Lloyd-Jones took his seat on
the rostrum promptly at 7.30 pm one particular evening
with merely thirty members of the public in attendance,
and in fact the whole evening's proceedings were completed
in eighty minutes. The Inspector could only conclude -
rather naively - that 'the people of Stevenage do not feel
strongly in favour of or against the proposed expansion'.
(42)

Supporters of the expansion proposals were: the rather
'growth obsessed' SIEG; the Trades Council; the Amalgam-
ated Union of Building Workers; the Association of Super-
visory Staffs, Executives and Technicians; and the North
Herts Liberal Association. (43) Following the Inquiry the
Inspector's recommendation was that the Draft Order should
not be confirmed in respect of the 1,450 acres to the
west, but that it should be for the 100 acres in the
north-east. (44)

In January 1965 the Corporation Board calculated that its
contribution to the costs of the ten-day Inquiry would be
approximately £4,000. (45) However, surplus on General
Revenue Account for 1965 reached the million mark -
£1,172,000 to be precise. In March the Labour Government
established the 'Prices and Incomes Board' followed, a few
months later, by the publication of the first National
Economic Plan, while closer to home Mr Crossman appointed
two Urban District Councillors to the Corporation Board.

The Minister made his decision on expansion, and it was
announced on 6 April:

The Minister has ... decided that he should not enlarge
the designated area to the west of the motorway. He
will include the 100 acres to the north-east and pro-

poses to make a designation amendment order accordingly. In reaching this conclusion the Minister notes the
Inspector's view that the town thus enlarged could
provide for a population of 91,000. *But this he thinks
needs further study.* (46, emphasis added)
Thus, as the letter from the Ministry indicates, the
issue of the ultimate size of Stevenage was far from
settled.
Following the decision, the Corporation immediately
decided that the preparation of a new Master Plan be put
in hand by the Consultant Architect and Planner. (47)
However in June the situation reached an even further
level of complexity when the Ministry informed the Corporation that, in relation to the revision of the Master
Plan, it did not want to give the Corporation a population
target at that juncture:
> We think it would be wiser for you to consider the land
> available for development and to put forward proposals
> to us for the population which you can accommodate, on
> the assumptions that the Minister will want you to
> provide for as large a population, including as many
> Londoners as possible, consistent with no fall in the
> standard of provision and broadly no change in the
> density policy which has governed your development.
> (48)
'Completion of a revised Master Plan is a matter of
urgency' was the Board's response. (49)
In the March General Election of 1966 Shirley Williams
increased her majority, the Labour Government remained in
office, an event which precipitated a Sterling crisis and,
consequently, the Prices and Incomes Act (1966). Unemployment was now at more than half a million, and again
defence expenditure was slowly rising, the total annual
budget being £2,145 million.
The Corporation's surplus on General Revenue Account had
now reached £1,527,000, cumulative capital expenditure
£48 million, and the Corporation was at the time employing
some 429 people, of whom 288 worked in professional or
administrative capacities. The population of the town
had now reached 56,700, with a male work force of 18,400
and a female work force of 8,900. 12,851 dwellings had
been let, while only 456 had been sold, and finally
3,514,388 sq ft of industrial and commercial development
had been achieved, all indications of the ever-growing
strength of the Corporation.
An important Board change took place early in the year
when Evelyn Denington replaced Sir Arthur Rucker, who had
resigned, as Chairman and was given a tribute from the
Board who commented on his 'personal qualities and wise

leadership'. (50)   Meanwhile Mrs Denington was increasing
her own influence in other places as well, in that she had
become Chairman of the GLC's Housing Committee.

Richard Crossman visited Stevenage early in April, his
purpose being to

> indicate that in future the Corporation will have to
> play a much more political role, in direct relationship
> with the politicians. The UDC was quite pleased
> because I had put two of their members on the Corpo-
> ration. As for the Corporation, it was sitting under
> its new Chairman, Mrs Denington, whom I had appointed
> from the GLC. She raged at me over a new way of di-
> viding up the Ministry's subsidy of New Towns, of which
> she had been informed but of which I was completely
> ignorant. Apparently my officials and the Treasury
> have been deciding things behind my back again. (51)

The Consultant Planner of the Corporation was at the time
pointing out to the Board that the number of commuters had
remained steady at 2:1 for the past ten years, that is to
say, that 4,000 workers were coming into Stevenage while
2,000 were going outside to work. The Board agreed with
Mr Vincent when he further stated that 'it was quite
impossible to consider Stevenage as a single unit': (52)
yet another example of the disjunction of the Reithian
aims and ideals of the new town policy and practical
actions. The example is important in that it serves to
reinforce the point made earlier that certain crucial
planning goals could only be achieved if there was control
of wider economic and political forces, more than simply
control over the purely 'technical' aspects of the
planning process.

In May the Ministry instructed the new town corporations
to institute a 15 per cent Special Housing Allocation
(SHA) list, which in effect requested the corporations to
provide for unskilled and semi-skilled Londoners 15 per
cent of the total dwellings which became available in any
single year, for in-migrants with employment in the towns
(in other words, 15 per cent of 'key worker' allocations
were to be used for housing this category of applicant).
(53)

The ERV1 and ERV returns at the end of the year demonstrated that during the year 253 vacancies had remained
unfilled while 210 persons remained unemployed - a slight,
though hardly surprising, occupational mismatch. The
Housing Management quarterly figures indicated that the
industrialists had not taken up 232 houses which had been
allocated to them, that 241 rent rebates had been granted
in the year, and that the 'children and parents of
tenants' waiting lists had risen to 555 and 858 respectively. (54)

Revision of the Master Plan was in progress, and the
Board agreed in April 1966 on the following strategy for
preliminary land use: to begin with an ultimate population of 105,000 was to be aimed for, which was to be
accommodated within the designated area, and which would
result in an average density of about 47 persons to the
acre for the new development, with a gross density of
about 38. It was further agreed that planned migration
should generally cease in about 1975 when the estimated
population would be of the order of approximately 80,000,
or indeed earlier if housebuilding could be speeded up.
(55)

The Master Plan, fully revised, was submitted to the
Minister on 30 September and was eventually subject to a
public inquiry which was programmed for early 1967. Two
points are worth noting at this juncture regarding the
1966 revised Master Plan. To begin with, it became quite
apparent just a few years later - as will be demonstrated
- that the planners had grossly miscalculated the future
household size, although it must be remembered that the
revision took place immediately following a Ministerial
decision which effectively suggested that the Corporation
was overestimating possibilities, and thus it is not surprising that the Corporation attempted to maintain a low
planning profile. Further, paragraph 14.10 on page 105
of the Plan stated quite categorically that

> the present induced large-scale immigration from London
> should continue until about 1975 when the town's popu-
> lation would be about 80,000. *Thereafter development*
> *would continue more slowly and the new houses would be*
> *built mainly for children of the present population.*
> (56, emphasis added)

This important statement of intent, together with the
proposed planning strategy, will be examined later in the
text in respect to the decade to follow.

The Public Inquiry took place in Stevenage from 17 to 20
January 1967, and the proceedings lasted a total of
thirty-five hours. The Inspector was Mr J.G.Jefferson,
formerly Planning Officer for West Sussex. There were 106
objections including those from the County Council, the
Urban District Council, most of the surrounding Rural
District and Parish Councils, the Stevenage Labour Party,
the Trades Council, the NFU, London Transport, and SIEG,
who objected because of 'the proposed control of further
development of the existing industrial area west of the
railway'. (57)

In June the Minister announced his decision, which was
that he had decided that the Corporation should continue
to build for planned immigration until a population of
some 80,000 was reached, by about 1975. (58)

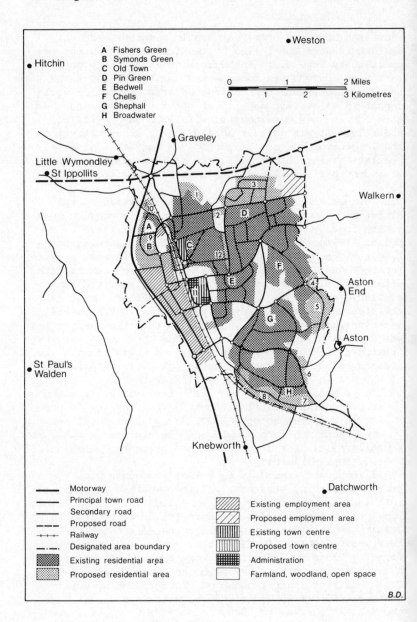

MAP 4   Stevenage master plan 1966

The year 1967 saw the appointment of a new General
Manager, K.Gale, to replace Richard McDougall who had
recently retired. The new General Manager had worked
his way up through the Corporation's Finance Department,
and in fact had been Chief Finance Officer since 1961.
A contemporary of Mr Gale's suggested that 'he fancied
himself greatly as a man of action, and scarcely gave
himself, or anyone else, time to think about anything'.
(59) Another even more important change was the appointment of a new Deputy Chairman to replace Commander
Martineau who had 'relinquished his post', although he
remained on the Board as an ordinary member. (60) The
new Deputy Chairman was Harold Campbell, a prominent
member of various branches of the Co-operative movement,
and someone who later was to become involved in the
Housing Corporation and numerous housing associations.
Councillor Ireton suggested that Martineau had given up
his post 'so that some reshuffle could take place', (61)
and whether or not that was so, certainly the combination
of Denington and Campbell (not to mention two years later
the addition of a powerful General Manager, Jack Balchin)
proved to be quite a driving force, urging the Corporation
on to 'bigger and better' projects.
  The housing 'costs yardstick' was introduced in 1967
through the Housing Subsidies Act, and the yardstick as
applied to Stevenage meant that, according to the Corporation,

> they had to build houses of smaller space standards
> than they have been building in recent years. There
> is an urgent need for the yardstick to be revised in
> line with costs at Stevenage; unless this can be done
> very shortly the housing programme, already delayed
> because of the difficulty in meeting the cost yard-
> stick, will be seriously affected. (62)

In May the Corporation received a circular from the
Ministry concerning owner-occupation in new towns, which
set a target for *new* new towns of 50 per cent owner-
occupation, by the time the target population was reached.
A different strategy would have to be used, the Ministry
recognised, regarding the 'older overspill' new towns:

> it would be unrealistic to suppose that anything like
> 50 per cent of planned intake in overspill New Towns
> will be people able and willing to buy a house on *first
> coming there*. Consequently the demand for houses for
> owner-occupation in the early years of the growth of
> the New Town may well be relatively low. But it is
> important that some houses for sale should be available
> from the beginning to test the market. (63)

The circular concluded by stressing the need for increased

participation by private enterprise in the provision of
houses for sale in the towns. The Ministry produced
another interesting document just a few months later
titled 'Return of Lettings and Departing Tenants - London
New Towns', which calculated that the total vacancies
caused by departing tenants within the period 1 July 1965
to 30 June 1967 was: Crawley 578, Bracknell 678, Hemel
Hempstead 729, Basildon 1,177, Stevenage 1,262, and Harlow
1,768. (64) Now of course one cannot deduce too much from
such statistics at face value, but it is of interest to
note that Stevenage (let alone Harlow) had twice as many
vacancies as both Crawley and Hemel Hempstead, towns of a
similar size.

The Chief Estates Officer pointed out in the year, in
reply to a question about the 15 per cent SHA, that there
were no vacancies in Stevenage at that moment which
required unskilled or semi-skilled labour. (65) This of
course was a quite disturbing statement in view of the
mismatch problem. Employment was the main topic on the
agenda of a joint meeting of representatives of the County
and Urban District Councils, together with the Corporation. The General Manager's Report was read out at the
meeting and was quite a revealing document, and accordingly is reproduced here in detail:

instead of the expected increase in employment in
manufacturing industry during 1966/67 of 1,000 jobs
there was an actual decline of 228.... In accordance
with the approved Master Plan, 6,500 new jobs should be
provided in manufacturing industry and about 4,000 new
jobs in service industry by 1975 and that current proposals for new manufacturing industry provided only
some 600 new jobs and for service industry a total of
1,100 jobs. Making allowance for the total provisions
shown above a further 5,900 jobs in manufacturing
industry and 2,900 in services would be required by
1975. (66)

The Board's response to this quite devastating report was
to naively ask industry 'to expand', and failing that, to
encourage new industry to settle in Stevenage. (67) It is
important to note here that the Board did not specify what
kind of industry ought to be encouraged to set up in the
town. Finally, SIEG announced during the year that the
results of its 'traffic survey' reinforced the views of
the Corporation, namely that it was indeed necessary to
look at the employment facilities of North Herts as 'one
entity', and that the theoretical balance of industry and
population within the town was impracticable and possibly
even an 'undesirable objective'. (68) So now SIEG was
seeking to redefine the 'objectives' of the new town

policy, and had considered that the Reithian ideal of
'balance' was 'undesirable'.
In 1968 the surplus on General Revenue Account reached
£2 million. The Chairman, in the same year, pointed out
that the Ministry was pressing Stevenage to absorb more
Londoners and that in order to do so it was essential - in
her view - to introduce industry which would provide a
large amount of unskilled employment! (69) An examination
of the Housing Management return for the final quarter of
the year does indeed indicate the problem. To begin with
the industrialists took up 265 houses less than their
allocation of 829, while out of an allocation of 166
dwellings to the 15 per cent SHA category only 8 were
actually used, and the cumulative total of the housing of
non-Londoners was 6,806 (33 per cent of the total housing
stock). Finally, the waiting lists for parents and
children of tenants were 1,029 and 566 respectively, with
the waiting time for the latter group being in the order
of approximately eighteen months. (70)
However, 1968 could well be called the year of 'Road 9',
a contentious issue which concerned the proposal to build
a 'principal road' through an open space of recreation
land. The principal opponent to the building of the road
was a group called the 'Stevenage Valley Association'
(SVA), an organisation which figured prominently in the
later years 1972-6 when expansion was recalled to the
agenda. The Corporation, in its Annual Report, stated
that:
    Whilst the Corporation appreciates the feeling aroused
    by the proposals to build Road 9, it is convinced that
    the Road is necessary and in design has done all it can
    to mitigate the effect of the Road on the valley. (71)
The SVA, a small middle-class organisation, was formed to
protest against the building of Road 9 as it was shown on
the 1966 Master Plan: it obtained its credibility in
1968-9 with publicity in the 'Times' and 'London Evening
Standard', a petition of 12,000 signatures, and with its
strategy of posting handbills all over Stevenage. (72)
Its case against Road 9 was, essentially, that it would
account for one tenth of the Valley's open land, and that
it would be unsightly, noisy, and would be dangerous and
a divider. However a much closer examination of the
Road 9 issue serves as a useful prologue to what was
to follow in the later years.
The SVA produced a report, 'The Amenity Aspect of
Fairlands Valley as a Park', which was seventy pages long
together with maps, diagrams, and so on, and was produced
in order to clearly state its case. The SVA described
Fairlands Valley as a 'green strip running between resi-

dential housing areas in the town', and continued to
assert that for 'whatever reason it was left so, it has
come to be accepted by Stevenage people as "the Valley",
a protected open space'. The SVA then proceeded to
contest the arguments and 'evidence' of the traffic consultants whose report on future traffic needs resulted in
the Road 9 proposal. 'The whole report was based on the
assumption that the town of the future would be oriented
around the private car for the majority of the travel
movements', the SVA argued, and further that this
'laissez-faire policy to transport in Stevenage is in
direct contradiction with the basis of the thinking concerning provision for every other major social activity
of the population':

> The implied assumption that almost all the active adult
> citizens will be able to drive is not valid. (73)

The SVA went on to assert that the

> Corporation (following the report) assume (i) car usage
> by 1974 will reach a level above that predicted by the
> Minister of Transport for the year 2000; (ii) a rate
> of decline in public transport which, if continued,
> would eliminate it altogether by 1985; and (iii) take
> no account of the 24-hour goods traffic build-up which
> Road 9 would encourage to pass through the town.

The SVA then proceeded to point out that after approving
the plans for Road 9, the Corporation commissioned a study
into the possibility of a public-transport-oriented system
in the town. (74) The Corporation's traffic consultants,
the SVA argued, 'now say that this study (yet to be published) could totally invalidate the 1966 Master Plan
traffic report on which all current road plans for
Stevenage are based; but the Corporation and the traffic
consultants have chosen to assume that this will not
happen'. The SVA continued to suggest that:

> There is no justification for this assumption and
> further roadworks cannot be justified until this study
> is available ... *there is authoritative, documented
> evidence* that Road 9 is intended to serve external
> traffic and to link with the proposed East-West trunk
> route. This would bring traffic of motorway pro-
> portions from Broadhall Way (A602 connecting with
> Al(M)) through the Valley and Verity Way. (75, emphasis
> added)

What in fact the 'authoritative and documented evidence'
consisted of, and indeed where it was to be obtained, is
difficult to ascertain, but the important feature to
recognise here is the terms of discourse the planners and
opponents engaged in: 'tendentious', 'hypothetical', and
'futurological'.

The year 1969 introduced new elements into the Road 9
issue. The Council, who like the SVA opposed the proposed
construction of Road 9, received a letter from the Ministry of Housing and Local Government, dated 13 July and
titled 'New Towns Act 1965 Section 6(1)* Proposal No 118:
Road 9: Fairlands Valley'. The Ministry pointed out that
the Corporation's intention was to construct a new primary
road (Road 9), to single carriageway width, and further to
reserve sufficient land for the construction of a second
carriageway. The Minister considered that because of
problems of congestion, there was at that moment 'a prima
facie case for constructing Road 9 as soon as possible'.
The letter continued adding an extra - and rather contentious - justification for a quick start to the construction of the project, which was to cost well over
£500,000:

> There is a further important argument for not delaying
> construction of the road. During the period 1971 to
> 1975 the Corporation will be engaged on a heavy
> programme of improvements to the primary road network
> including the dualling of roads 4 and 5 to the east of
> the town centre. In ... [the Minister's] opinion the
> existence of Road 9 will make a valuable contribution
> to the avoidance of serious traffic congestion during
> that period. (76)

The letter ends with the announcement that the Minister
had accordingly decided to approve the Corporation's proposal to construct Road 9 to single carriageway width, but
not to approve the Corporation's further proposal to
reserve land for the construction of a second carriageway.
(77) To conclude, for the moment, the Road 9 issue, below
is an extract from the SVA's press release of 4 August
following the Minister's decision:

> The Minister appears to have made our concession in
> that he will only approve single carriageway width and
> not permit the Corporation to reserve land for a
> further carriageway if the need arises. However since
> *Road 9 is to be a principal road to take external*
> *traffic* the Ministry of Transport have powers at any
> time to requisition land on either side for road im-
> provements so the Corporation have no need to reserve
> the land. (78)

The SVA finished its statement by stating that its
campaign, although 'wonderfully organized' and supported
from start to finish, had not even 'dented the Corporation's mammoth indifference and complacency.' (79)

---

* Section 6(1) proposals are concerned with the granting
  (or otherwise) of development.

Indeed the years to follow were to provide confirmation of that indifference.

A new General Manager was appointed in 1969 who, together with the Chairman and Deputy Chairman, was to prove a considerable force in relation to the town's development and image. Jack Balchin had risen through the administrative and housing apparatus of the LCC, later the GLC, to become Senior Assistant Director of Housing at a time when Mrs Denington, the Corporation's Chairman, was Chairman of the GLC's Housing Committee. Mr Balchin resigned his post with the GLC soon after the Conservatives took control, and came to Stevenage with a reputation of 'complete ruthlessness' and the 'complete organization man'. (80)

The year began with the Corporation discussing the New Towns Circular (No.86) of December 1968, 'Private Enterprise Housing in New Towns', which informed corporations that they were expected to arrange for at least two-thirds of new houses for sale in their town (in effect one-third of the future new town building programme) to be provided by private enterprise. (81)

In June the Corporation's officers were asked to make a draft scheme for offering for sale to sitting tenants all houses built by the Corporation and occupied on short tenancies. Three months later the Board reported that three Building Societies - the Halifax, Co-operative, and Abbey National - were showing interest, and indeed the Board anticipated that the Halifax would be willing to find up to £1 million in instalments over a whole year to assist sitting tenants to buy their own houses, with the Abbey National offering up to £250,000. (82) An official announcement from the Corporation was made in November, which stated that it was offering all of its houses (except those built for special purposes, e.g., those built for disabled persons) for sale to sitting tenants. Arrangements had been made with three of the 'largest building societies' to make mortgage funds available and a comprehensive booklet was printed and issued to some 12,500 tenants. The Corporation announced a little later in the year that some 130 tenants had so far expressed interest in purchase, and of these 16 had made a firm offer to purchase. (83)

In October the Ministry approved the Corporation's proposals for a rent increase to take effect from 1 April 1970, which was to average 4 shillings per dwelling per week, but on the understanding that the Corporation would make further increases the following year as might be necessary in order to prevent its housing revenue account from running into cumulative deficit at the end of 1971-2.

(84)   Still on the subject of housing, Mr Hughes (of both
the Corporation and SIEG) informed the Board that the
Employers' Group was concerned that there were not sufficient houses available to meet industrial needs.   Yet
the Housing Management quarterly report of the following
month demonstrated the recurring pattern, namely that the
industrialists had not taken up 123 of the 847 houses
allocated to them. (85)   The report also indicated that
out of an allocation of 194 to the 15 per cent SHA category only 9 were able to be used.   Furthermore the parents
and children of tenants waiting lists accounted for 1039
and 738 respectively, with the waiting period for the
parents being of the order of sixteen months.

The year came to a close with the Corporation discussing
the Skeffington Report with the County and Urban District
Councils, and

the best arrangements that can be made to enable the
residents of Stevenage to participate as fully as
possible in the planning of their town. (86)

An ironic gesture it turned out to be.

5 Stevenage 1970-1
Rumours of things to come

If men were angels, government would not be necessary.
                                    C.B.Macpherson (1972), p.39

In early 1970 the Corporation received New Town Circular No.144 from the Ministry, which referred to the 'Financing of Sales of Corporation Houses'. (1) The Circular noted that:

> The policy of encouraging the growth of owner-occu-
> pation in New Towns obviously requires that sales of
> Corporation houses should not be inhibited by lack of
> finance. At the same time it is necessary to secure to
> Corporations early and substantial cash flows from
> sales, thereby reducing the need for further Exchequer
> borrowing. These considerations point to the joint
> financing of sales by building societies and Corpo-
> rations in co-operation. (2)

The Ministry then continued to state that they were thus authorising and encouraging development corporations to grant second mortgages to purchasers after a building society had given a 70 per cent mortgage (note that the Building Society Association readily accepted and en- couraged the arrangement that had been made between them- selves and the Ministry). (3) The following month the Corporation stated that, in response to enquiry, the Ministry had made it abundantly clear that this arrange- ment was intended to mean 100 per cent mortgages when they were asked for, (4) and therefore it had revised its scheme accordingly and hoped for a renewed interest by tenants. (5)

The population had now reached 65,000, the total work- force being of the order of 30,500, the number of dwellings built by the Corporation 16,070, and a surplus on the General Revenue Account of just over £2,250,000. Furthermore the Corporation was now an employer of some 563 persons (together with 34 unfilled posts), who were

accounting for £616,976 per annum, whilst the nine Board
Members were costing £6,965 per annum, and indeed annual
administration costs were running close to the million
mark - £908,566 to be precise.
 Board changes took place again with the appointment of
two new members, one of whom was a Conservative County
Councillor, K.C.McKechnie, presumably appointed to create
a little more 'political balance'; whilst the other
appointee, J.D.Crane, an accountant and Commercial
Director of Hawker Siddeley Dynamics Limited, Stevenage's
second largest employer, was put on presumably to add a
little more 'professionalism' to a Board now determined
to forge ahead.
 The Corporation, in the Annual Report, stated that the
offer to sell houses to sitting tenants at market value
had received a relatively poor response, despite the
special financial arrangements which had been made. (6)
It also reasserted that Road 9 should be built as soon as
it was possible to do so. The report also mentioned that
for the first time since 1962-3, 1,000 houses had been
completed during the year, but went on to say that there
was concern that a serious hiatus would occur between the
completion of the St Nicholas housing area and the development of the next major housing area at Symonds Green.
Moreover, if this did occur, the present 'surge' would be
dissipated with 'grave repercussions' on the building
labour force and on the town's 'employment potential'.
The Corporation pointed out that while the Area Plan for
Symonds Green and Fishers Green (Sectors 9 and 10) had
received Ministerial assent in September 1969, the subsequent Section 6(1) proposals had given rise to objections
by the County and Urban District Councils, partly
    because of the Corporation's proposals to complete
    houses on land intended under the 1966 Master Plan for
    natural expansion *owing to lower occupancy rates than
    anticipated*. (7, emphasis added)
 Most importantly, the Corporation suggested that although
development within the framework of the 1966 Master Plan
had made good progress, already the need had become apparent for updating the plan in the light of 'changing
circumstances'! (8) To this effect the Corporation sent
a report that it had completed to Peter Walker the new
Minister (following Labour's defeat in the June election),
in November 1970. The report was titled 'Population,
Employment and Housing in Stevenage', and consisted of
two volumes, one technical and the other more general,
which will be briefly outlined. The report began by
saying that during 1969 the Corporation's Consultant
Planner and the research staff of the Social Relations

Department examined afresh the subjects of population,
employment and housing in Stevenage, with their implications for planning. Parallel with these studies SIEG,
it was stated, was studying the housing requirements of
industrial expansion in Stevenage. Furthermore,

> it has become apparent that the assumed average
> household size will prove to be *significantly* too
> high.... *This means that more dwellings will be
> required for the 80,000 population (target) and more
> land will be needed in which to erect them.* (9,
> emphasis added)

On the foregoing facts the Corporation felt that 'there
was no justification for delaying their careful scrutiny
until the formal review of the Master Plan due in 1971'.
(10) The report continued to state that in the Corporation's view a new dwelling target for 1975 should be put
to the SUDC, County Council and the Minister of Housing
and Local Government:

> we realise the apprehension that may be felt about the
> Corporation using up land in the area now designated,
> but earmarked to meet later generation's needs. The
> answer, however, *is to seek land for the additional
> dwellings needed in the 1990s either now or at least
> in the 1980s by which time the demographic trends will
> have become clearer.* Even if no enlargement of the
> designated area is sought now, some kind of under-
> standing should be reached with the authorities con-
> cerned that, at the appropriate time, new land allo-
> cations shall be considered so as not to prejudice the
> housing of later families. *Stevenage has to grow* - in
> our submission - *and to continue to grow fast. Our
> proposals are made to this end.* (11, emphasis added)

A little later in the year the Corporation was asked by
the Department of the Environment (which had been established in 1970 and had replaced the existing Ministry)
(12) for its comments on 'The South East Joint Planning
Study', to which the Corporation replied that it had
'prepared a number of strategic planning studies to
examine the possibilities for further growth beyond
present targets'. Furthermore the Corporation stated
that it was confident that there were 'no technical difficulties in increasing the ultimate planned population to
about 150,000 by the year 2000 or even more if this were
in the national interest':

> Such a growth ... could make a positive contribution to
> the problems of the region. Moreover it would have the
> merit of offering early implementation as the organ-
> ization exists within the Development Corporation for
> planning and construction. *That organization will*

> *otherwise begin to be wound up within the next five*
> *years or so and there would be a distinct advantage if*
> *the timing of any proposed future enlargement could*
> *obviate the dissipation of organization, professional*
> *staff and a substantial building labour force. It*
> *would be helpful therefore if some early indication*
> *could be given of possibilities in this respect.* (13,
> emphasis added)

It was now clearly evident that the Board was indeed attempting to 'drive on', and indicative of this was the use
of the 'organisation' argument together with the ideological term of the 'national interest'. An examination
of the housing situation of the year illustrates the
political pattern which had been emerging, and which was
to reproduce itself manyfold over the coming years.

The housing management figures indicated that (in relation to the quarter ending 31.12.70) of the 954 allocations to industry, 180 were not taken up, that the
cumulative total of non-Londoners housed was 7,972 (34 per
cent of the total), that only 47 of the allocation of 179
to the 15 per cent SHA category had been able to be used,
and that the waiting lists for children and parents of
tenants were 726 and 991 respectively, with a waiting time
of fourteen months. The aforementioned pattern can best
be illustrated with an extract of some of the points
raised at a 'special meeting of the Board', the purpose of
which was to discuss the Corporation's 'Population,
Employment and Housing in Stevenage' document:

> We should make it clear that the *rare* occasions on
> which a slackening of demand for housing by industrial-
> ists were not the primary cause of the increased allo-
> cation to children of tenants and parents of
> tenants.... If the Corporation's supply of housing had
> met the *greater industrial demand* this might have en-
> couraged industrial growth beyond that recorded. *Their*
> *slower rate of growth should not be used as an argument*
> *for using a smaller assumed rate of future growth and*
> *of future housing demand. If greater response could*
> *be given to the industrialists' calls for houses a*
> *faster build-up of industry might ensue.* (14, emphasis
> added)

Thus the pattern could in fact be described as (i) the
Corporation's refusal to acknowledge the long-term, consistent and structural inability of the industrialists as
a whole* to take up their housing allocation, (ii) the

---

* This categorisation of the industrialists 'as a whole'
  and its corollary, individual industrialists, will be
  explained in chapter 11.

implication that in part the industrialists were controlling the Corporation, (iii) a Corporation eager to perpetuate its own 'life', together with its inbuilt 'growth
obsession' - related to its optimistic and futurological
posture, and (iv) the low priority accorded to both the
children and parents of tenants.

On the employment front the ERV1 and ERV returns of the
year showed that there were 464 unfilled vacancies and
340 unemployed persons. (15)

The County Council began 1971, much to the Corporation's
consternation, by deferring the contribution to the
building of Road 9 until further traffic studies had been
undertaken. The Corporation, in a press release, stated
that the situation was even more serious than it appeared
when it was realised that Road 9 would take two years to
build anyway. (16) The SVA, enthusing over the County's
decision but angry at the Corporation's attempt to involve
the Ministry, affirmed that if the Minister now provided
the finance for the road he would in effect be trampling
on the rights of the elected representatives (and themselves), and that he could only do that because Stevenage
was a new town without the rights which other towns took
for granted:

> The real question is, does Stevenage have a Democracy
> or a Dictatorship? (17)

The Annual Report stated that tenants had responded to
the Corporation's new scheme of offering (with prior
Ministerial permission) for sale all its rented stock
with concessions of up to 20 per cent off market value:
462 sales had been completed since the scheme was introduced, and about the same number were in the final stages
with solicitors. The Corporation continued to mention
that these promising results were due, in great measure,
to the ready co-operation of many building societies and
insurance companies by making mortgage funds available.*
The Corporation also stated that the gross proceeds from
the sale of houses totalled over £2,500,000, an amount
which considerably affected cash flow, the extent of
necessary borrowing and, therefore, the General Revenue
Account. (18)

The Ministry (DOE) further pressurised development corporations into an owner-occupation posture by virtue of its
Circular No.206 of 18 May titled 'House Building For
Sale'. It stated that the building of houses for sale in
new towns had made little progress, and particularly so
building by private enterprise. In 1970, 'the total
number of private houses built in all English new towns

---

* See appendix 4 for the Building Societies concerned.

did not reach 1,000', which represented only about 10 per
cent of all the house building in these particular new
towns. It continued to state that the Secretary of State
- Peter Walker, not particularly noted for his aversion to
speculative building - wished to see over the next few
years a much more rapid development in the building of
houses for sale, and 'he considers moreover that in the
new towns as elsewhere it is private builders who should
provide for this market'. (19) Importantly, the Secretary
of State desired a lifting of the restrictions relating to
land disposal, that is, the restrictions the majority of
development corporations place upon private builders
imposing conditions about the categories of people to
whom houses may be sold:

> For instance, it may be required that all or a speci-
> fied proportion may be sold only to people living or
> working in the town, or who come from an exporting
> area. The Secretary of State considers such conditions
> incompatible with the free market conditions which are
> needed to secury a greater spread of owner-occupation
> in new towns and they should therefore not be imposed
> on any future disposals of land to private builders.
> (20)

Finally the circular asserted that 'the need for Development Corporations themselves to build for sale will largely disappear, and Corporations should not in future therefore take it as a matter of course that they should build
for sale'. (21) Continuing with housing, it can be noted
that the Corporation announced the detailed proposals for
Sector 9 (South), and indeed the site development work was
proceeding following the Ministry's approval, but that
yardstick difficulties were holding up housing construction in the sector with the result that building
labour was being lost to the town. Furthermore, it was
announced, as subsequent output by the Corporation depended on the progress of Sector 9 (Symonds Green) where the
first contract for site development had begun, but where
the building contract had encountered yardstick difficulties, the 'prospect for 1973-4 was no brighter'. (22)
Housing management quarterly figures for the period
ending 31 December again demonstrated that out of an
allocation of 706 the industrialists had only used 527.
There was a slight cumulative increase in the housing of
non-Londoners with the total now being 8,683 (39 per cent
of the total), and on the Joint Housing List (JHL)* 357 of

---

* The Joint Housing List (Corporation/Council) was set up
  in 1969 to combine waiting lists, together with other
  related matters.

the 388 allocations were utilised. Waiting lists for
parents and children of tenants were 947 and 727 respectively, with waiting periods of merely five months,
an indication of the industrialists' over-estimation of
their needs together with the Corporation's compliance.
 The Corporation in its Annual Report stated that the year
had predominantly been occupied with updating the Master
Plan, and furthermore it announced that at

> the same time, though, they go beyond updating, in that
> full account is being taken of the implications of the
> Strategic Plan for the South East and the proposals
> contained in Hertfordshire County Council's consulta-
> tive document 'Hertfordshire 1981'. If arising out of
> these or other Government decisions Stevenage were to
> be further expanded, *updating would not be enough; a
> revised Master Plan would be required.* (23, emphasis
> added)

The Corporation's 'growth mania' was again in evidence.
Finally, the Annual Report also revealed that administration costs now topped the one million mark - £1,043,648 to
be exact.
 SIEG brought out a report in the year which was based on
an employment survey carried out in August 1970, titled
'Second Report on Labour Availability in Stevenage', and
marked for 'private circulation only'. A few extracts
will indicate the nature of, and the thinking behind, the
document:

> Companies did not expand *as expected* during 1969-70 and
> the forward position indicates a slower rate of growth
> than *anticipated* in 1969.... However this situation is
> a direct effect of the national economic climate and
> ... *[we]* consider that the position will change during
> 1971 and 1972 which *may* result in an increased demand
> for housing in the 1972-73 housing year...
> In the 1969 survey ... *all companies confirmed that
> they were unable to get the houses they needed to meet
> their recruitment plans...* (24, emphasis added)

This somewhat misleading and inaccurate report brought
forth an interesting response from the Social Development
Office, a department within the Corporation which tended
to identify less with the employers' interests let alone
the Board, than the other departments. In a memorandum
to the General Manager, the Office stated that in its
opinion

> the Corporation would be justified in asking for a
> public retraction of the statement repeatedly made in
> recent months by representatives of local employers
> that only failure of the Corporation to provide enough
> houses was holding back industrial expansion in

Stevenage - but perhaps the special respect accorded
the Industrial Employers' Group prohibits that. (25)
In July the ERV1 and ERV returns gave an unusual picture
of there being more persons unemployed than unfilled
vacancies, the figures being 383 persons unemployed and
288 unfilled vacancies. This was due to 325 sackings at
the Stevenage branch of International Computers Limited,
who stated that the reason for the action was deferment
of orders in the private sector. Amusingly, the ICL
representative stated that 'this does not represent a
major cut-back'. (26) Employment problems of course were
not confined to Stevenage, for 1971 was the year when
unemployment was approaching one million, when two one-day
strikes against the Industrial Relations Bill brought out
over 750,000 workers, and when 20,000 marchers protesting
against the Government's 'employment policy' clashed with
police at the House of Commons.

Locally, in July, a report was published for the Council
in reply to the previous year's Corporation report 'Population, Employment and Housing in Stevenage'. The
Council's contribution to the debate was in the form of a
document prepared by a team of management consultants -
Llewellyn-Davies, Weeks, Forestier-Walker, and Bor - and
was titled 'Stevenage: Advisory Report to Stevenage Urban
District Council'. (27) The report began by stating that
in their opinion the Corporation's 1970 report was
'competent' but was, however, based 'on a number of assumptions which are questionable', and on 'detailed examination it seemed very unlikely that all those assumptions
would in fact prove accurate, partly because economic
forces could change them and partly because alternative
policies could change them'. The statement seems hardly
worth repeating. However, the report continued in less
general a manner to point out, correctly, that the industrial structure of the town relied excessively 'on a
few large firms; and nearly 40 per cent of the employment
in manufacturing is in vulnerable sectors'. (28) Furthermore the report reiterated the point that has already been
made, namely that the employment structure was biased
towards skilled workers. Of the conclusions two are particularly noteworthy. First, it was suggested that there
was 'no urgency for a decision on a policy of growth in
the town after 1976' and accordingly it was recommended
that a major review of the availability of housing land
be deferred for about five years. Second:
Although the expected employment growth rate over the
next five years is reasonable, the employment structure
of the town is rather vulnerable to adverse trading
conditions and the future supply of labour in the town

is likely to diverge from the future demand by
employers. It is recommended that the Development
Corporation be asked to give more weight to the
following principles when selecting new firms:
(a) the extent to which the firm will diversify the
existing industrial structure;
(b) the firm's potential for employing people other
than skilled manual workers;
(c) the firm's history of training and the advancement
of its employees. (29)

6 Stevenage 1972-3
'Expansion '73' — the case is presented

> Max Weber ... never wavered in his insistence that *both* reason and illogic were essential to the comprehension of the human world.
>
> H.Stuart Hughes (1974), p.431

The year 1972 began with the Chairman of the Corporation reacting angrily to the public circulation of a survey which had been carried out by the Social Development Office, and which was found to be freely available for consultation in the public library. The General Manager consoled the Chairman by stating that a new 'drill' was being specified for determining what documents should be made public and when, if at all. However, the Chairman insisted that pending that stage *all* documents were to be endorsed 'not for publication' or 'confidential'. (1)

The document in question was 'Social Indices in Stevenage', which was the publication of the results of a social survey carried out in 1971. (2) The report was merely an embarrassment to a Board which was forever patting itself on the back, informing the public at regular intervals that (say) three town planners from Honolulu had been to see the 'miracle', that last year they 'had more official visitors than ever before', and that there was a society in Stevenage to cater for every need, like the 'Starline Majorettes', the 'Stevenage Sword Dancers', and the 'Lancaster Bomber International Research Group' (the Secretary of which was Councillor McKechnie, a Board member). The 'Social Indices' report merely pointed out that Stevenage was not unlike any other town, with, for example - within a period of one year - 575 truancies, 743 free school meals provided, 279 child guidance referrals, 88 known attempted suicides, 98 referrals to mental health departments, and so on. Perhaps the most embarrassing feature concerned the concentration of families with problems within specific areas, but more

importantly that there was 'no indication that the
problems have become more concentrated in (these) areas,
and indeed there are signs that new areas of the town are
sharing in the problems, particularly those of a financial
nature'. (3)

In March the Board met to discuss 'unemployment and other
related issues', and at the meeting the Chairman pointed
out that over 23 per cent of the total work-force in the
industrial area lived outside Stevenage. However,

> as the New Town was now being regarded as a regional
> centre it should provide employment for people in that
> region. (4, emphasis added)

Of course what must be added here is that the town was
being regarded as a regional centre by virtue of the
Corporation's selfsame definition: it was not an official
policy change, but merely reinforces the earlier point
made that 'town planning' as it is practised, cannot
dictate or determine wider economic processes such as
those associated with industrial location.

At the same meeting the Chairman reiterated the point
that more industry was wanted in Stevenage, for which more
land would, in turn, be needed. (5)

In April a public meeting was held to discuss the
'Updating of the 1966 Master Plan', a meeting which was to
indicate the manner in which the future battles of 1972-6
were to be fought, both by the Corporation and its opponents.

The Corporation at the beginning of the meeting stated
that it was to make a tape recording of the meeting in
order that every point made should be fully recorded, so
that 'we can then play back the comments that are made,
and make sure that we have thoroughly understood' them,
because 'we are really after public participation in what
we are about to do'. (6) The General Manager pointed out
that 'it is very difficult indeed to predict and forecast
what the population trends will be', and then continued to
give precise quantified predictions. (7) Trouble started
when the Chairman, Mrs Denington, proceeded to talk about
the need for more land because of the extra needs thrown
up by the lower household sizes, and of course to provide
a 'bit more space' for people's gardens, the children's
play space, and so on. But, most importantly, she continued:

> we must bring in more industry and diversified industry
> and again I come back to it, this will mean a greater
> demand on land outside our present designated area...
> (8, emphasis added)

This contained a flawed logic, as the Secretary of the
Trades Council pointed out, when he argued that it 'would

be futile in my opinion, and in the opinion of many trade
unionists, to even talk of expansion when we cannot even
talk about jobs'. (9)

Road 9 was raised, with the SVA again denying the need
for its future construction. The Chief Engineer of the
Corporation informed the SVA that

> obviously when you say that the road is not necessary
> and we say that the road is necessary, there is some
> difference of approach to what 'necessary' means. I
> have spent a lifetime in this game and have some
> knowledge of transportation, and traffic, traffic
> generation and road capacity, and I would welcome to
> be told, if I'm wrong, what is the right way of
> creating the statistics and forecasting that produces
> the right answer.

He went on to say that 'you claim to have it sir. I would
welcome you please to let me have it and I would gladly
personally discuss with you about it. I can do no more'.
(10) A representative of the SVA, Ken Poole, a local
librarian, bitterly complained at the patronising treatment his organisation was receiving:

> I have to say, Madam Chairman, that this is the answer
> that we have often had in the past from the officers of
> the Corporation. There seems to be some belief on
> their part that the fact that they are experts means
> that people who are not experts but who are acquainted
> with the problem, somehow are necessarily talking
> through their hats - I think there have been too many
> examples in the recent past, to show that indeed
> planners are not always right ... it does seem to me
> that when you look at things, the Development Corpo-
> ration does seem to have a dinky toy complex when it
> comes to road building. Indeed when you look at that
> plan and see the interlacing of roads that are on it,
> you sometimes wonder whether in fact the roads weren't
> laid down first of all and the houses simply shoved in
> between... [cheers] (11)

These kinds of interchanges were to be repeated time and
time again over the following four years.

There were two new Board appointments in the year: Peter
Metcalfe, a Stevenage Councillor, ex-Labour Party Agent,
and 'Shirley Williams's best friend', (12) and Group
Captain Douglas Bader who was, it was suggested by fellow
Board member Councillor Ireton, merely 'keeping the seat
warm for someone else', and was 'a bit of a joke'. (13)

The first volume of the updating exercise was published
in April, 'Stevenage 72: Updating of the Master Plan:
Goals and Objectives', with the next volume 'Stevenage 72:
Updating of the Master Plan: Consultation Document',
following quite soon afterwards.

The goals and objectives were indecisive to say the least. For example, page 4, paragraph 4 of the first volume talked of the goal of 'Prosperity, efficiency and economic use of resources', which is to say 'the fullest use of natural resources and of economic and social investment'. Meaning what precisely? Again, page 5, paragraph 5 stressed the objective of 'Flexibility for change', which was to 'provide increased opportunity for improved living standards, prosperity and social mobility'.

The second volume was a little more precise. It stressed the need for more land as the household size had declined, and furthermore because 60,000 jobs *may* be required:

> This is about 6,000 more than the 1966 Master Plan envisaged for a town population of 105,000 plus workers from outside. Extra land is therefore required for this larger working population. Furthermore, increasing mechanisation in industry and the demand for extensive warehouse distribution depots, has meant lower employment densities. More work space will therefore be required for the working population previously *estimated*. (14, emphasis added)

The principal function of the volume was to discuss comments on the general planning of Stevenage arising from the updating exhibition, and public meetings of October and November 1971. According to the Corporation the principal concern of the public was related to uncertainty about any future expansion of the town. In reply the Corporation stated that updating related to the present designated area and terms of reference, viz., a population of about 80,000 including as many Londoners as possible by about 1976, expanding to about 105,000 by the end of the century. The Corporation furthermore stated that the DOE had not yet taken any decision on any land allocation for possible further population growth in the Hatfield/Hitchin corridor (which included Stevenage), as suggested in the 'Strategic Plan for the South East' (SPSE). (15) Again in April the Chairman reported to the Board that she had made an appointment with the Minister in order to discuss the possible enlargement of Stevenage and its population targets, together with miscellaneous matters. (16) One month later she reported her meeting with the Minister to the Board:

> regarding the advancement of the enlargement to meet the Strategic Plan's population targets but with an earlier start than 1981. *The Minister had given her encouragement to think that a proposal on these lines would not be unwelcome to the Department.* (17, emphasis added)

On 15 June the General Manager reported to the Board that
the Secretary of State had met County planning authorities
from the South East Region, to discuss the provision of
further land for private housing development. The General
Manager expected that the Minister would be writing shortly to the Corporation inviting it to commission a feasibility study for expansion and at the same time would be
informing the Urban District Council of such a request.
As a first step the Consultant Planner would produce to
the July Corporation meeting a strategic planning study.
The General Manager continued to suggest that it 'was left
to the Chairman with the Deputy Chairman to choose the
opportune time to talk to the District Council about
the proposed expansion'. (18)
On 27 June the letter arrived from the Secretary of
State, Peter Walker:

It is the Government's desire that further provision be
made for private housing development in certain New
Towns including Stevenage. Some provision can be found
within the existing designated area of such towns: but
in the case of Stevenage it seems right to consider in
addition a substantial extension of the Designated Area
in which further large-scale private development may
take place.

Accordingly the Secretary of State invites the Development Corporation to consider, and after consultation with the Hertfordshire County Council and the
Stevenage Urban District Council, make proposals for
the appropriate size and location of this extended
area. It should be sufficient to bring into use during
the 1970s a minimum of 1,000 acres for private housing
development. Provision would also need to be made for
complementary housing production by the public sector
and by housing societies as well as for housing needs
arising out of natural growth. To allow for this the
Secretary of State accepts that the total extension
area might have to be in the order of 3,000-4,000 acres
if the needs of *comprehensive* town development are to
be met in the year 2000.

The Corporation will no doubt wish to commission
studies leading to recommendations for a revised
Designated Area for Stevenage. He hopes that the
Corporation will proceed *quickly* with these so that the
necessary measures may be taken to bring more residential land into development for private housing. The
Secretary of State invites the Corporation also to consider *whether more land within the existing Designated
Area can be brought into use for private development
while the extension of the Area is being pursued. He*

recognises that much of this residential land has been phased for development after 1980: but this provision for later years could be amply made good in any enlarged area which was eventually designated. By rephasing such areas for development over the next few years, substantial land provision could be made available for private housing and thus enable Stevenage to make an earlier contribution towards the provision of more housing for owner occupation.

The Secretary of State understands that the proportion of owner-occupied dwellings in Stevenage is little more than 10 per cent. Although the Corporation is making good progress in the sale of rented houses to sitting tenants and has also increased the sites allocated for private housing, there is still far to go before the 50:50 ratio of owner-occupied/rented housing that is commonly accepted as desirable is achieved. This present suggestion would go far in this direction. (19, emphasis added)

Thus the Secretary of State desired a 'comprehensive' and 'quick' achievement of an expansion in order to encourage a more even balance of owner-occupation and rented housing. Bearing in mind the procedures which would have to be undertaken before the proposals could materialise - e.g., objections, public inquiry, and so on -, the Secretary of State seemed in no doubt that he would have his way, namely the idea of bringing forward planned development, which of course makes nonsense of the notion of 'planning'.

The desire to encourage owner-occupation in housing is, of course, certainly not uncommon to Conservatism, indeed it is seen by the more cynical as the means by which to end any signs of socialist zeal. (20) This particular situation, though, was much more specific in origin, namely rising house prices. For example in 1969 average house prices (at mortgage completion stage) in Greater London were £6,195 and in the South East (excluding Greater London) £5,772; in 1972 they had risen to £11,113 and £9,914 respectively, and by 1973 to £14,447 and £13,164. (21) Another important factor here was the growth of the Department of the Environment, which was now an employer (at 1 April 1971) of 38,806 civil servants, and was therefore an increasingly powerful Ministry, and moreover the new towns were its 'pet poodle'. (22)

The Corporation was of course able to respond immediately as 'Stevenage 72', the updating report, had taken full account of the SPSE and 'Hertfordshire 1981', (23) as the Corporation pointed out in its Annual Report. However, when the 'written statement' - the most specific volume -

of 'Stevenage 72' was published in October 1972, it was
stated on page 7, paragraph 1.3(e):

> This report *has not,* however, taken into account ...
> the effect of proposals made in the 'Strategic Plan
> for the South East'... (24, emphasis added)

It is of course difficult to ascertain - by virtue of the
nature of planning logic - whether or not the Corporation
had 'taken into account' the implications of the SPSE, and
moreover it is in fact difficult to see whether the two
opposing statements are simply the result of an error, a
misrepresentation, or whatever. The most likely explanation is that it is simply another indication of the
nature of planning logic: namely, that in an ever-
changing situation the best strategy is vagueness.

Before continuing with the reactions to Mr Walker's proposals, the Corporation's plans and so on, a brief examination of the 'written statement' is in order, in that
although not published until October it was formulated
and written *before* Mr Walker's letter, and moreover it is
indicative of the Corporation's *future* planning reports.

Page 1 stated that the Corporation had adopted
'Stevenage 72' as the updating of the Master Plan 1966,
that its value lay in 'its current application to a
changing situation which demands up-to-date framework
references', and that it was intended to serve as a
working document until such time as a revised or full
review Master Plan was produced. (25) 'Factors of change'
occupy pages 7 to 9, and these include 'the decline in the
birth rate and the reduction in the size of the average
household since 1965, and the effect on housing and land
requirements' and 'the changing structure of industry and
employment'. (26)

How exactly was this change conceived? The Corporation,
on page 12, suggested that the 'factors examined in the
report indicate that an *open-ended plan* is required as the
basis for implementation', and furthermore that it was
'*not desirable* to visualise a finite community or to determine an ultimate population'. (27, emphasis added)
However, barely a page later was the assertion that
because of the decline in household size more land would
be required to house 'the *ultimate* population'. (28,
emphasis added)

In July the Consultant Planner produced for the Board
five possible strategies for expansion, and amongst other
points raised the traffic and communications problem,
namely the line of the proposed east-west link between the
M1 and M11. There were at least four possible lines, he
continued, which the DOE's consultants Messrs Atkins and
Partners were investigating, and most of them could

directly impinge on Stevenage, a point the consultants
were aware of. The minutes continue:

> (Atkins) have until 1974 to complete their studies and
> submit their report to the Department. If their con-
> clusions were long delayed this could hamper a decision
> on Stevenage expansion. The Corporation had agreed, in
> principle, to appoint Messrs Atkins and Partners as its
> own Transportation Consultants for Stevenage Expansion
> and this would secure that parallel advice on both
> fronts would be forthcoming from the consultants who
> would integrate their thinking on these two matters
> and perhaps advance the time when a firm view as to
> the line of this particular highway could be reached.
> (29)

This was indeed a most useful strategy. The same Board
meeting reported on a meeting the Corporation Officers and
Board members had just had with representatives from the
Urban District Council. It can be noted that two of the
points that had been raised by the Council were first that
the Secretary of State was encouraging land speculation
and that the Corporation was supporting him, and second
that 'Londoners were being prejudiced against by the
"free-for-all" that would follow in the private developer's wake'. (30) Comments like these were to be
repeated time and time again as the plans were prepared
the following year.

From July 1972 onwards there was a steady build-up of
letter-writing to the newspapers, and occasional press
statements, all opposing expansion and expressing distrust
of both the DOE and the Corporation. For example in July
the prospective Liberal Party candidate for Stevenage, Tom
Willis, stated that he and his party were against what
seemed to be an excessive emphasis on house purchase:
'it looks distressingly like an effort to add a block of
Conservative-voting-middle-class-home-owners to the New
Town, to bolster up the sagging performance of Conservative candidates', while Shirley Williams stated that she
was against expansion if it was to be built by private
developers, and an Urban District Councillor, Brian
Underwood, angry about delaying tactics of the DOE in
avoiding meeting a deputation of councillors, stated that
'we live in this town and should be told what is going
on'. (31) More militaristic-type protestations were also
made, for instance the one made by an Old Town resident,
Mr Hutchinson, when he claimed that 'the Old Town must
now realise that they have been subject to a "pincer
movement", completely encircled'. (32)

Meanwhile at the Corporation more paradoxical statements
were being made. The Corporation never ceased to inform

the public that it was merely a 'servant of the Minister',
yet certainly seemed quite pleased with Mr Walker's proposals, and indeed stated - in relation to a discussion
on the updating volumes 'Stevenage 72' - that it would
have to watch 'very carefully the percentage of houses in
Stevenage which are becoming owner-occupied':

> The General Manager anticipated that by the mid-1980s
> there would be a 50 per cent owner-occupation of all
> housing in Stevenage. (33)

And of course this was not taking into account
Mr Walker's proposals! Again:

> Assuming that most sales in the pipeline are completed,
> owner-occupation which has risen in two years from 10
> per cent to more than 20 per cent will have reached
> 35 per cent during 1974. (34)

In the same document as the previous assertion, namely
the Annual Report, the Corporation lamented the downturn
in public sector building during the year, due to the
building strike and yardstick constraints, and stated that
'the pressures for public sector housing are still very
great and we view with much concern our inability to respond'. (35)

November saw the official announcement by the Stevenage
Councillors - with the exception of the three Conservative
Councillors - that they were opposed to the proposed expansion. As Councillor Corner put it: 'There are 250,000
homeless people in London, but not one of those people
could come to Stevenage to get a house under the terms
which this Government would want expansion', whilst the
Conservative leader - Councillor Boyd - suggested that
they 'should wait until the Development Corporation
prepare their plans'. (36) The Conservative response was
understandable in that as the Conservatives would be unlikely to ever obtain control in Stevenage (as is usual
with the majority of new towns), they would obviously
prefer the Corporation to a potentially powerful Labour
council.

The Corporation Board, in response, merely noted the sign
of disenchantment, although Councillor Cotter, who was
both a member of the Council and the Board, thought that
their pronouncement might be 'the outcome of extreme
concern on the part of the Council who, while not knowing
in what direction such expansion might take place, preferred to make an early overall objection rather than
allow plans to progress irretractably'. (37) Once again
the difficulties of relations between the Corporation and
the Council were evident, and, of importance in this
instance, resulted in an unconstructive partisan attitude.

The Stevenage Valley Association also entered the breach

in November with a press release, stating that the
expansion proposals were not intended to help the homeless
of Stevenage or the poor of London, but 'only to get a
politician out of a difficulty (i.e., to show that Peter
Walker was doing something - anything - to curb soaring
land prices...)', and they went on to demand that the proposals should be scrapped and that the Corporation Board
be reconstituted in order to properly represent the
interests of the 'people' of Hertfordshire. (38)   In
December a report was published by SIEG titled 'Labour
Availability in Stevenage 1972: a survey by a Committee
of Personnel Managers representing SIEG'. One of the
conclusions the report arrived at, rather irresistibly,
was that:

> Whilst the anticipated rates of expansion do not
> compare well with those foreseen in 1969 and 1970,
> taking into account the economic trough experienced in
> 1971, it would not be unreasonable to anticipate seeing
> increases in the foreseen growth rate in the 1972
> survey...,

but, more importantly:

> The reduction in availability of SDC housing to new
> employees is a cause of ... concern. The development
> of private dwellings is considered not to provide an
> adequate supply to the required population of new
> employees. The consequences of this are such that the
> SDC are recommended to consider re-examining their
> policy on house sales and private development and enter
> into any necessary discussion with Government
> Departments to maintain the overall philosophy of new
> town development. (39)

SIEG thus again indicated its 'growth obsession'; once
more complained about the lack of public housing; and
finally, and related to the second point, desired the
Corporation to keep in step with the 'overall philosophy
of new town development', whatever that might have meant
to the group: it certainly had not prevented SIEG in the
past from demanding that it should be allowed to recruit
workers from outside London, and so on. As for SIEG's
complaint about lack of housing, the Housing Management
quarterly figures for the period ending 31.12.72 stated
that out of an allocation to the industrialists of 548
houses, only 406 had been taken up.
  Regarding this point the Corporation itself in its Annual
Report stated that 'greater industrial demand for housing
has come at a time when it cannot be met', and hence
'industrial quotas will be more than halved, and second
generation applicants coming on to the housing list may
have to wait a long time before being offered accommo-

dation'; for example, 'whilst in the summer of 1972 industrial nominees could be offered housing within twelve
weeks, the period is now more than nine months', and 'for
children of tenants, the previous normal fifteen months'
waiting period has to be stretched out to three or four
years'. (40) As can be seen it just does not add up:
327 allocated to the JHL, 375 housed!

At the end of 1972 the population of the town was 70,000,
with a work-force of some 34,000; there were 18,106
Corporation dwellings (over 2,200 of these sold), and
1,701 (including second generation) applicants on waiting
lists. The employment returns at the end of the year
showed totals of 155 unfilled vacancies and 753 unemployed
persons. Finally, 1972 was the year of the Housing
Finance Act, an Act which introduced into council housing
(and new town housing) the concept of 'fair rents'.

By early 1973 the Consultant Planner had produced five
alternative feasibility studies in terms of expansion and
presented them to the Board:

> Mr Vincent explained that *any part of any feasibility
> study could theoretically be adapted to parts of other
> studies and total expansion was capable of contraction
> or enlargement on the 150,000 population target* which
> each study area achieved. (41, emphasis added)

It must be noted here that what is of concern is
'planning', meaning the attempt to 'order and control the
environment'!

At the same Board meeting the function of consultation
and participation was made clear, viz. to 'get better
measure of all the considerations that the Corporation had
to weigh before reaching the decision on what area should
be recommended to the Secretary of State'. (42) However,
merely two weeks later the General Manager stated at a
public meeting that expansion was not 'an issue ... participation will only work if people accept the expansion
as necessary'! (43)

The Corporation decided to approach the consultation and
participation aspect of the operation in the following
manner. It was to 'receive and publish without commitment
or comment the report of the planning team'; to publish a
summary of the report and 'to circulate it to every
household within Stevenage and about two miles beyond its
boundary inviting comments on the alternative feasibility
studies and on various issues to which they give rise';
to hold 'public meetings in Stevenage and in villages
within or adjacent to the area of search to answer
questions and to listen to comment'; and finally to
'consult with local authorities, statutory bodies, and
non-statutory bodies within the same area about the

studies'. (44)   The consultation and participation period
was to last for a period of eight weeks, from 25 January
until 22 March, following the distribution of the summary
and comment form. (45)

 Five alternative expansion strategies were produced:
Strategy M - with the main expansion west of the Designated Area,
Strategy N - with the main expansion extending mainly to
   the north and east,
Strategy P - with the main expansion extending mainly to
   the north,
Strategy R - with the main expansion area extending mainly
   south,
Strategy Q - a peripheral extension in all areas except
   south-east and south-west.

 The reaction to the published proposals was quite vehe-
ment, as a few of the news headlines demonstrated - 'Super
plans, a plot', 'Horror Super City', 'Commuter Peril to
New Town', 'Super City another Birmingham', and so on.
(46)   On the same day as the participation scheme officially commenced, 25 January, the Corporation issued a
press release stating that 'to remedy the housing shortage
it would help if they got an early decision *in favour* of
expanding Stevenage' (47, emphasis added).   This was only
a few days after the Corporation had stated that it would
publish the planning report 'without commitment or
comment', indeed that its whole approach to expansion was
that the

   Corporation recognised its function as the Government's
   agent in this matter and *irrespective of any views it*
   might have had as to the desirability of extending the
   designated area of Stevenage it put the work in hand at
   once. (48, emphasis added)

The press release did nothing for good relations with the
public. Meetings were quickly organised to discuss the
proposals, and letters poured into the local papers.   The
Trades Council, following a heated discussion, came out in
favour of expanding the town, but only if the emphasis
would be on rented housing instead of owner-occupation
which was an attempt in its view - indeed a plot - to
'introduce Tory elements'. Aston Village Society urged
people to write 'no expansion' across the comment forms,
and as a local newspaper put it:

   A clash between a charity organization in the tiny
   village of Aston and Stevenage Development Corporation
   is in the offing over Whitehall's 'jumboville' plans
   for the expansion of the New Town. (49)

 Ian Cuthill of the SVA, in a letter to the 'Stevenage
Gazette', suggested that if Stevenage was to have a symbol

'it would be a road drill', that 'once again the new proposals are initiated by a Minister who lives and works 30
miles away, and to whom the New Towns are a convenient
dump for his poor homeless', and finally suggested that
'the next few weeks may be some of the most critical since
the days of Silkingrad'. (50) Much of the early protest
was highly emotive and a little beside the point: for
example Mr Cuthill's remark about Stevenage being a
'convenient dump for [the] homeless' when in fact the
proposals were about increased owner-occupation.

The relations between the Corporation and the Council
rapidly deteriorated when the Corporation accused the
Council of causing the housing shortage by opposing development in Fishers Green and Symonds Green and thus
holding up the process, whilst Councillor Hall asserted
that 'every time the Corporation nears the end of its
planned life they come up with another plan', and that
'a new Klondyke is being created in Stevenage, every land
and property speculator will beat a rapid path to
Stevenage because there is money to be made'. (51)

There were four public meetings organised by the Corporation in Stevenage, and many more in the surrounding
villages. The Corporation's analysis of the Stevenage
public meetings was as follows: (52)

| Date | Attendance | Attitude Towards Expansion | | |
		For	Against	Don't Know
24.1.73	425	–	–	–
1.2.73	149	–	–	–
7.2.73	144	16	58	70
8.2.73	123	7	75	41

The Corporation quite rightly stated that attendance was
small in relation to the adult population of over 40,000,
and furthermore the Chairman, Mrs Denington, stated that
she had attended some of the public meetings and had been
very pleased with the response and the 'good humour which
has characterised the meetings'. (53) However, other
observers saw things rather differently (which may account
for the Corporation's inability or reluctance to give
voting figures for the first two meetings). The Gazette
described 'stormy meetings', particularly the first one,
where the consensus was 'no' to expansion and typical
remarks were like the following one:

> The Corporation should clear up the abortion they have
> made on this side of the railway line before they make
> a bigger mess on the other side [cheers/applause]. (54)

The Corporation's own Social Development Office again
suggested that the Corporation was surprised that the
> people were not so apathetic as they thought they might
> be. Some of the public meetings really took the form
> of demonstrations; there was one public meeting where
> Mrs Denington found it almost impossible to continue
> the meeting, and she said at one point, 'Do you want
> me to go on?', and everyone roared 'No!', and the
> Deputy Chairman, who was chairing the meeting, had to
> really appeal to their chivalry - 'Let the lady
> continue', and 'You wouldn't stop a lady in her tracks
> would you?' - and that was the only way in which she
> was able to continue the meeting. (55)

The village meetings were naturally very well attended
and equally hostile, for, as the Corporation itself put
it, 'this was no doubt due to their anxious concern about
a town expansion that might envelop their village'. (56)
There was an enormous amount of criticism levelled at the
Corporation's comment form:* basically the argument was
that it was biased in that there was no question as to
whether or not *expansion itself* was considered desirable,
and there were objections to the wording of particular
questions. The Corporation replied - quite correctly,
formally speaking - to the allegations of bias, stating,
for example, that the Corporation was not conducting a
town poll to obtain residents' views on the desirability
of expansion, it was 'seeking rather to get public comment
that might help it in discharging the only task which the
Secretary of State had clearly given it, viz. to make
recommendations on the size and location of expansion
which the Government had expressed the wish to see', and
furthermore 'the form *had* been designed to provide anybody
with scope for general comment and there was ample space
in which total opposition to expansion could be recorded
if respondents held that view'. (57) The Corporation's
response was simply not acceptable to all critics including the Council who, according to the Corporation,
'impugned the Corporation's integrity with allegations of
"self-interest" and "bias"'. (58) Furthermore the Council
then decided to conduct its own poll, as did local
villages, the Corporation suggesting that as these polls
were accompanied by extensive advertising and official
comment opposing expansion (the village polls indeed being
conducted by defenders of 'the villages' physical integrity'), they
> may with greater justice be exposed to the criticism of
> 'self-interest' and 'bias' initially levelled at the
> Corporation's attempt at consultation. (59)

---

* The 1973 SDC comment form is reproduced in appendix 5.

The Corporation's analysis of its comment forms showed a response rate of 17 per cent for Stevenage and 29 per cent for the villages. 44 per cent of the Stevenage respondents (who, according to the Corporation, 'comprise about 7 per cent of all households') (60) opposed *any* expansion. Only 6 per cent expressed a favourable response to expansion. In the villages, two out of three respondents stated their opposition, whilst the number in favour was negligible. Interestingly, the Corporation further stated that:

> Some of the villages were on the periphery of or even outside the area of search. The smaller response expected from such areas did not always happen. *Much depended on the way opposition in the area was organized...* (61, emphasis added),

a point to be returned to later. The response rate of 17 per cent from Stevenage produced a remark from Mrs Denington, the Corporation's Chairman, which was to greatly exacerbate antagonisms:

> The Corporation is somewhat disappointed that only 17 per cent of Stevenage households returned forms. It is not an unreasonable inference to draw that those who remained silent were not disturbed by the idea of expansion. (62)

The Chairman's lack of understanding of the contextualisation of forms of public participation and the problems which arise, was echoed by the General Manager who stated that 'the public were so preoccupied to debate the "whether" question, that they really didn't get down, as much as they might have done, to the "where"...'. (63) Indeed his general attitude towards participation may be illustrated by a statement he made (retrospectively), concerning the 1973 proposals:

> Anyone will sign any petition on any subject whatsoever - you know, if it's something like 'I ought to be shot', now will you sign? - half of them would sign it without understanding what was being said. (64)

Furthermore, the Corporation was also at the time able to utilise the rather idiosyncratic nature of the local press to promote its own case. For example, an early headline stated that the Corporation was 'set for REFERENDUM', (65) a nonsense of course in that this suggested that the Corporation was giving people some kind of deciding vote, but the Corporation would then go to press with statements like 'half way through the participation programme, the response to the Corporation's questionnaire has been poor, but has been split 50-50 in terms of attitude towards expansion', (66) again untrue. Indeed, the Corporation's own Social Development Office, in an internal memorandum, made an attempt to communicate the Press Officer's untruths to the Board: 'There has never at any time been more than an extremely small minority of forms recording support for expansion'. (67)

In March the same department produced an internal report titled 'Stevenage Expansion 1973: the comment form and the desirability of expansion', which stated that at the outset the majority of people pointed out that the question of whether it was desirable that Stevenage should be further expanded was one which should logically take priority over the decision on the expansion area to be recommended to the Secretary of State, which was put forward as the objective at the head of the comment form. (68) The report went on to assert that it was 'not obvious what bearing some of the questions, e.g., question 4, had upon the choice between the various feasibility studies', (69), a point also made by the Urban District Council who stated that some of the questions had been phrased to give the impression that some form of expansion was imminent or inevitable:

> Through a series of obvious statements about the
> present shortcomings of Stevenage (see questions 4 and
> 5), it implied that reduction of commuting; increased
> employment; more housing; more shops and social
> facilities, were all dependant upon further expansion.
> (70)

The report by the Social Development Office concluded by stating that it was clear

> from an examination of completed comment forms, as it
> had been from other parts of the 'participation'
> exercise, that the question of the desirability or
> otherwise of the proposed expansion was the central
> issue of concern to most people who express a view of
> any kind...
> That being the case it can only be a matter for regret
> that the comment form made no specific provision for
> the expression of views upon this issue, and that a
> substantial minority of those who went to the trouble
> of completing a form have been, in effect, disen-
> franchised upon this major issue. (71)

As previously mentioned, the Council, because of its dissatisfaction with the Corporation's comment form, had decided to carry out its own poll of the town's residents. The Council stated that its poll was an 'independent' survey of public opinion, and in contrast to the Corporation's survey basis of 35,000 heads of households, its survey, 'for reasons of efficiency as well as economy is based on a 12.5 per cent sample of the electorate'! Furthermore the Council asserted that its question-

naire* concentrated attention on the central issues of the
proposal, namely:
    (i) should expansion take place and by what increase
    beyond the current population target (102,000 by 2001);
    (ii) should there be an equal or unequal division
    between housing provided for renting and that built for
    owner-occupation;   (iii) *what sort of agency should be
    trusted with the control of new development, in view of
    the existing sizeable population of Stevenage.* (72,
    emphasis added)
Thus the Council's questionnaire did appear to focus on
the 'central issues of the proposal', although point (iii)
hardly lends credence to the Council's claim that its poll
was 'independent'. In any event the Council reported a
response rate of 87.8 per cent, together with the 'facts'
that 64.3 per cent of the sample preferred to see no
expansion whatsoever, and moreover that 75.7 per cent
voted in favour of an elected council taking control of
future development! (73)
Meanwhile the consultation process was producing responses from various local authorities and official
bodies. Hertfordshire County Council opposed the proposed
expansion because it raised 'strategic issues which are
contrary to concepts already approved by the Secretary of
State', namely that Stevenage had been rejected as a
location for 'medium growth' in the SPSE, and furthermore
there was in the County's opinion sufficient land available in Hertfordshire to meet the housing demands of the
region and the locality up until 1981. Most importantly,
the County objected because of its own interests. For
example, it stated that the 'programme for preparing the
Hertfordshire Structure Plan will enable the needs of the
region and the County after 1981 to be satisfied in the
most appropriate way, without affecting the capacity of
the building industry to acquire adequate land for these
purposes'. (74) The County Council added that:
    the process of planning in Hertfordshire is sufficient-
    ly expeditious and of sufficiently high repute as to
    ensure an adequate supply of land for the estimated
    population growth during the late 70s without further
    expansion of Stevenage. (75)
The Urban District Council objected to the proposals
because of rather different reasons. First, the Council
stated that as the Government policy was biased in favour
of the speculatively-developed dwelling, this would mean
that in Stevenage such dwellings would be sold for a
minimum of £15,000, a price beyond the reach of most

---

* The Council's questionnaire is reproduced in appendix 6.

people. Second, and following on from such a policy,
children of tenants would not be able to find an adequate
supply of rented housing within their home town. (76)
Finally the Council suggested that the amenities of the
town were inadequate at the present time for the existing
population, and that the situation would be made that
much worse by expansion. (77)

The Letchworth Urban District Council opposed the proposals because of 'fear of coalescence', as did the
Letchworth Garden City Corporation; Hitchin Urban
District Council was opposed as it considered that expansion would bring Stevenage closer and 'so threaten the
independence of Hitchin'; Datchworth Parish Council
simply did not agree 'to any extension whatever of the
designated area of Stevenage', (78) and these views were
repeated by all the surrounding District, Rural, and
Parish Councils.

The NFU objected, as expected, 'to any proposals which
jeopardize the livelihood of its members', holding that
good agricultural land just could not be sacrificed, and
moreover that the past twenty-five years had seen 'much
hardship caused in this area by farmers being displaced
and losing their livelihoods':

> To add to this burden, on two previous occasions the
> neighbourhood has been thrown into alarm at the possi-
> bility of an extension of the Designated Area. We
> consider the time has now come when the people of this
> neighbourhood, especially the farmers, should be
> allowed to live in peace, making the best of the diffi-
> culties which have inevitably arisen from having a
> large town placed in their midst. (79)

The NFU concluded that it felt so 'strongly that the
concept of expanding Stevenage is wrong in principle that
it would be irrelevant to consider or comment on the
feasibility studies'. (80)

The SIEG stated that it was certainly not opposed to expansion, but added that it desired more rented dwellings
to be included in the plans, while the Stevenage Chamber
of Trade - as in 1946 - stated that it had 'no convictions
that the expansion proposal was beneficial or indeed
necessary to Hertfordshire: but recognised that growth of
the town would benefit town centre traders'. (81)

The Board, in late March, were discussing the draft of
Volume 2 of 'Stevenage Expansion 1973', which was the
volume which described in detail the Corporation's actual
proposals. Mrs Denington, the Chairman, asked members if
this was the kind of report they wished to see published.
Councillor Ireton stated that he had been under the impression that certain aspects were going to be discussed,

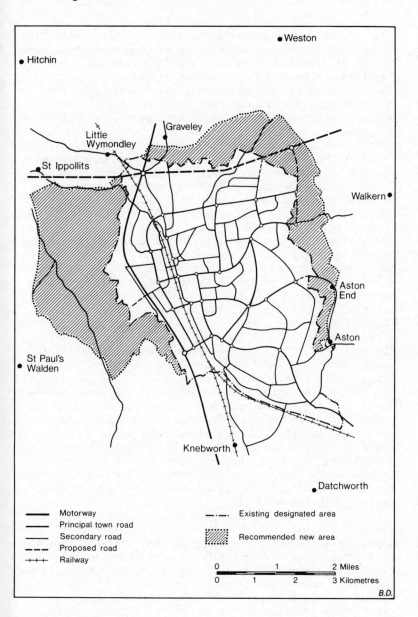

MAP 5 Stevenage expansion proposals 1973

such as traffic consultants' reports, the town centre, and
so on, and moreover that until these were studied it could
not be said that there was a case for expansion. Councillor Ireton also asked what effect expansion would have on
the police, fire, and educational services. (82) The
Chairman then pointed out that by 17 April the Corporation
would have to make up its mind as to what it was going to
recommend to the Minister. The minutes continue:

> A discussion followed on whether the Corporation could
> say to the Minister that it did not recommend ex-ansio
> pansion. Mr McKechnie said that as far as the Minister
> is concerned we were not asked for a negative answer.
> The Corporation should have said this much earlier if
> it was so minded. He felt that we should say that we
> are 'for'. (83)

Councillor Ireton stated that he could not support expansion on the basis of the information he had so far, and
the Chairman stated that 'until a more detailed report was
received covering particularly the points that have been
raised, it seemed that the Corporation would not be in a
position to make any decision'. (84)

March saw another spate of 'protest' letter writing. The
local branch of the 'Action Group for the Improvement of
the Environment' stated that expansion was a 'threat to
animal and plant life', the senior Social Development
Officer of the Corporation, writing in a personal capacity, stated that 'five out of the nine Board members were
local' and that three out of the five were active in the
Labour Party, and thus he felt that 'the Corporation
should act in the interests of Stevenage people and not
those of the Minister', and finally Ian Cuthill of the SVA
stated that the Valley Association would employ both a
'public and a professional strategy': it would 'organize
public protest' and that there would be some back-room
delving into records. (85)

Late in March saw the publication of Volume 2, titled
'Stevenage Expansion 1973: Volume 2, Proposals for
Expansion'. In the preface Mrs Denington stated that the
objections to expansion which had been made had 'been
carefully considered' by the Corporation but they were not
felt to be so weighty or insuperable as to justify
abandoning the proposal for further growth'. (86) The
report also stated that the Secretary of State 'talked of
a land take of 3-4,000 acres':

> the Corporation adheres to the gross land take of the
> order of 3,500 acres, and accepts the feasibility
> studies as properly representing the extent of land
> needed in the recommended expansion area. The exact
> area would of course be affected by the precise bounda-

ries shown and the need to avoid severance of farm
holdings. *The recommended area may be somewhat greater
or less than the 3,500 acres.* (87, emphasis added)
Only the previous month the General Manager had outlined
'new planning techniques for more scientific evaluation
and weighting of subjective value-judgments affecting
decisions such as town expansion', and in fact had asked
the Board 'to play the "evaluation game" with Chief
Officers'! (88)

The Corporation announced that the final decision had
been taken to recommend only a minor expansion to the east
and north, but with a major expansion westwards. It was
asserted that such a strategy would have the following
advantages: (i) it would take an area of relatively low
landscape value overall, (ii) it would involve less en-
croachment on villages than any other strategy, (89)
(iii) fewer historical buildings would be affected,
(iv) the area would be more accessible to the town centre
and contribute to a more geographically 'balanced' town,
(v) the strategy 'recognised the alternative most favoured
by the public', and (vi) in infrastructure terms it would
offer good opportunities for a public transport system and
balanced traffic movement. (90) In acreage terms the proposals amounted to 2,200 acres to the west, 800 to the
north, and 600 to the east. The Corporation's planning
logic is well illustrated by its statement that it:

felt that such a western expansion should be a major
one. This would help to meet the apprehensions expressed by many people that a smaller western expansion
might create a sense of isolation. (91)!

The Corporation was at pains to point out that the 'plan
presented is in no way merely a paper exercise. We have
walked over the area and made our decisions on the
ground'! (92) Tucked away in appendix 4 was a letter from
the General Manager to the Secretary at the DOE, dated 17
March, which included the following:

[These] consultations ... produced expressions of
rigorous opposition to any expansion of Stevenage
whatsoever. The strength of feeling diverted some
authorities and individuals from a readiness to comment
on the feasibility studies themselves. In this respect
the consultations have not quite fulfilled what the
Corporation had hoped. (93)

As always the Corporation was disappointed that the
public had not participated in the manner in which it had
wanted.

Geoffrey Rippon replaced Peter Walker as Secretary of
State in a Government reshuffle, and was instrumental in
introducing the White Paper 'Widening the Choice: the next

steps in housing', which in April announced that the
Government's intention was both to reinforce the momentum
towards home ownership and to look at new towns to build
for rent in areas where this was needed! (94) Mr Rippon
also commented on the mounting opposition to Stevenage
expansion: 'I'm afraid in many cases the attitude is:
"We don't have heaven crammed, let all the rest be
damned!".' (95)

In May the General Manager informed the Board that it
seemed unlikely that a Designation Order would be confirmed before June 1974, so ways and means might 'thus be
explored to recover lost time'. The General Manager made
certain suggestions for an early start on the preparation
of a Master Plan, and simultaneous submission with the
Master Plan of Area Plans for the first areas to be developed. Hearing this Mr Campbell, the Deputy Chairman,
together with Councillor Ireton, doubted

> whether the Corporation could properly go ahead with
> the planning and preparing of a Master Plan *in antici-*
> *pation of the Minister's approval of the Designation*
> *Order*. (96, emphasis added)

However, the meeting decided that 'much depended on the
Department of the Environment's attitude, and the General
Manager undertook to report further on this' at the next
Board meeting. (97) Also in May it was reported that
Geoffrey Rippon had informed Shirley Williams - the MP for
Stevenage - that if there 'was one objection (if he made a
draft order) he will call a public inquiry'. Furthermore,
and also in May, it was suggested in an article in the
'Guardian' that the 'Government's strategy for growth in
the South-East region may have to be changed', as pro-
jections 'based on latest population forecasts indicate
that 750,000 fewer people could need housing outside
London than was expected two and a half years ago'. (98)

An interesting little note appeared in the 'Luton Evening
Post' on 29 May, titled 'Farmers refuse to answer city
probe', which referred to the fact that a survey carried
out by the Corporation's Agricultural Consultant M.A.B.
Boddington, had been abandoned because of NFU opposition.
Mr Boddington, it was reported, had however rejected
suggestions that the survey was an attempt to gauge
compensation.

Although Volume 3 of 'Stevenage Expansion 1973' did not
appear until December - and in the period May to December
considerable protest activity took place - it is pertinent
to consider the report here as this volume was the actual
planning report, that is, the logic the protestors had to
try to defeat. Page 26 stated that the scale of house
provision considered necessary was 'for 26,000 more

dwellings', about 20,000 of these on land outside the designated area (i.e., within the expansion area), and about 6,000 on land within the existing designated area. Furthermore, according to paras 5.3 and 5.5:

> The expectation is that a 50:50 ratio of private/public housing will be achieved both in new house building and in ultimate tenure distribution. 13,000 houses would be provided by private agencies and a like figure by public bodies.

> With the continued sale of Corporation houses to sitting tenants it is expected that the owner-occupier ratio in Stevenage will reach 50 per cent *in or after 1986* and continue to increase gradually in line with national trends. (emphasis added)

How long after 1986, it could well be asked. At the heart of the Corporation's calculations were population projections (the fallibility of the procedure being amply demonstrated elsewhere) (99) as follows. Projection 1 was the base population projection - and as with the other projections was to the nearest thousand - and was in effect a recalculation of 'Projection D' which was used in the 1972 up-dating of the Master Plan, incorporating the more recent birth-rate trends together with the results of the 1971 Census and the (then) current building programme.

Projection 1   Stevenage Population 1971-2006 (100)

1971	1976	1981	1986	1991	1996	2001	2006
67,000	80,000	85,000	90,000	94,000	98,000	102,000	105,000

Projection 2 was arrived at by using the above base level and a rate of private house building on 1,000 acres (additional) in the expanded area, and of 500 additional acres for public housing. Furthermore a building rate of 1,800 dwellings a year was assumed by the Corporation, over a peak period. Moreover, it had 'now been assumed that four fifths of all new houses would be occupied by immigrants, a higher figure than before', and 'has been further assumed that the occupation of new houses by existing Stevenage residents would result in the re-occupation of empty houses by immigrant households', and thus 'on this basis the second projection is as follows':

Projection 2   Stevenage Population 1971-2006 (101)

1971	1976	1981	1986	1991	1996	2001	2006
67,000	80,000	105,000	133,000	141,000	148,000	154,000	161,000

Finally a third projection was produced which assumed that 'instead of 500 acres for public housing, 750 acres are added to provide an increased allocation', and that a 'slower rate of housing production per annum over the build-up period is more likely to be achieved: viz. 750 houses in each sector over the period 1976-1991', and therefore 'the overall result is a smaller population by 2001 on account of the slower building up of the second generation, the effects of which are likely to be felt well beyond the century'. Furthermore, 'most of the additional housing beyond 1996 is assumed to cater for the needs of natural increase', and so 'using the same variables as before, the projection on this basis becomes':

Projection 3   Stevenage Population 1971-2006 (102)

1971	1976	1981	1986	1991	1996	2001	2006
67,000	80,000	92,000	114,000	130,000	137,000	143,000	149,000

Now the first thing to note at this juncture is the almost surreal effect of the mere tinkering with a few variables and gazing into the future: for example the population can be made to be either 102,000 or 154,000 by the year 2001, and so on. However, the second and more important point to note is the flimsy nature of these seemingly precise mathematical calculations, a point which cannot be illustrated better than by quoting the Corporation's following paragraph contained in Volume 3:

It must be stressed that the above calculations are *approximate* to this stage of the study.... *Any population projections are vulnerable to changes in birth rates. Further, house building rates may not be achieved in the time-scale envisaged which in turn would affect the rate of in-migration. Likewise a shortfall in employment opportunities, either by recession of industry or inability to expand would falsify the projections. All these factors could have a significant effect on the rate of population growth.* (103, emphasis added)

Page 29 commenced with the 'employment' section, and at the outset the Corporation stated that it was no longer

appropriate to talk of 'self-contained' new towns. The
Corporation continued by suggesting that 'the employment
figures for Stevenage illustrate this point', there being
'18 per cent of the employed Stevenage residents' working
outside the town, and 'about 25 per cent of the workforce'
in Stevenage coming from outside the town: 'i.e., a net
7 per cent inward movement. The town thus provides 7 per
cent more jobs than theoretically needed to support the
working population'. (104) Or put in a rather different
way, it could be argued that the Corporation was unable
to satisfy at least 18 per cent of its indigenous population's occupational needs.

The report continued to state that it was

> debatable whether the expansion of Stevenage should be
> planned to cater only for the equivalent working popu-
> lation of the town, leaving the present 7 per cent
> excess demand and any additional requirement to find
> its supply elsewhere in the region, or to assume that
> Stevenage as the major employment centre will still
> have to provide for excess demand...

> ... in the short term, there is likely to be increased
> out-commuting by the new Stevenage residents which will
> lessen the demand for jobs in the first instance. In
> the long term there *could* be a reduction, even a
> reversal, in this trend so that more jobs in Stevenage
> would be required. *It is desirable therefore that
> space is allowed so that such a demand could be met.*
> (105, emphasis added)

In other words, if in doubt think big! The Corporation
went on to say that in the past office-based firms had
been reluctant to move to new towns despite the advantages
offered. Furthermore 'it has been suggested that the
preponderance of public sponsored housing and the early
emphasis on manufacturing industry as well as a lack of
suitable housing for executives may act as deterrents',
indeed the 'experience of some moves where Corporation
housing was occupied on arrival but subsequently vacated
within a year in favour of private housing also indicates
that far more private accommodation appears to be required
if mixed employment structures are to be developed in New
Towns', and therefore this would imply that 'the Government's policy of increasing the supply of privately built
and owned housing in Stevenage would offer attractive
prospects to firms'. (106)

Next the Corporation again talked about 'diversification', a point already touched on in relation to the
housing allocation process (and a point to be examined
in depth later):

Existing firms in manufacturing industry can be expected to continue growing to *some* degree.... Expansion, with a wider opportunity for diversification
should produce a more stable employment position as
more alternative sources of employment, including the
less volatile service industries, are introduced ...
If Stevenage is deficient, it is in opportunities that
offer higher standard service employments ... a greater
variety of office jobs with a wider career spectrum and
jobs which could employ more unskilled and semi-skilled
people for whom housing could be offered if jobs could
be found for them. *The Corporation will need to be
selective so that it can pick out from the firms attracted to Stevenage those that can best fulfill these
needs.* (107, emphasis added)

Seen in relation to the Corporation's frequent utterances
about the need for diversification - and the parallel
evidence that nothing is being achieved in that direction,
the employers having consistently to look outside
Stevenage for specific 'skills', and the 15 per cent SHA
category hardly ever being utilised - it is evident that
the above points made by the Corporation were merely
mindless promises (as will be demonstrated in chapter 11,
this whole problem of lack of diversification is rooted
in the Corporation's growth obsession).

Page 36 began with a discussion of the abnormality of the
town's age structure, which essentially has a high proportion of young people and a low proportion of the elderly. The Corporation stated that 'while Stevenage continues induced growth, these features will remain', and
'if induced growth stops (because, for example, the 1966
Master Plan phasing is adhered to), normality will be
reached more quickly'. However, the Corporation was quick
to point out that there was therefore the 'risk that the
town population will work through the age bands and *go
beyond normality* to an abnormally old town'! (108,
emphasis added) It is not unreasonable to ask the
question: where does it end?

On finance, the report stated that the 'investment expected because of an expansion of Stevenage *might* be of
the order of £380 million, of which the public expenditure
share would be of about 50 per cent'. (109, emphasis
added) The report concluded that 'above all', if it was
decided that Stevenage should continue to expand, 'the
sooner a decision was made the greater the chance of
achieving housebuilding targets', indeed 'it is imperative
from this point of view that the present rundown in
building operations, as a result of the imminent cessation
of planned immigration, should be arrested and the impetus
restored'. (110) And finally:

The *precise* boundaries of the recommended expansion area *may* require refining, but the *broad* directions and extent of the recommended expansion will have the least impact on North Hertfordshire. (111, emphasis added)

The 1973 proposals in total came in the form of 4 volumes (Volume 4 being concerned with Transportation and Drainage), totalling 420 pages, 78 illustrations and 39 tables, produced by a planning team of twenty-four persons (who assisted the Consultants).

The Deputy Chairman, Mr Harold Campbell, stated - at a heated public meeting - that

Government decisions have been changed, modified or overthrown as a result of public opinion. It is the job of the people to express themselves as vigorously as possible. It is your job and we cannot do it for you. (112)

Whether in fact this is true is indeed one of the problems to which the case study is addressed. However, it is to the 'people' that attention is now turned.

7 Stevenage 1972-4
The struggle begins

> Power, indeed, is founded, in a large measure, on
> interpersonal expectations and attitudes. If business-
> men feel weak and dependent, they do in actuality
> become weaker and more dependent, no matter what
> material resources may be ascribed to them.
>
> D.Riesman (1971), p.219

PART 1

This chapter both recalls earlier stages of the protest
and continues the account of the protest, but specifically
from the viewpoint and perspective of the protest groups
themselves.
 One of the more peripheral yet catalytic organisations to
protest against the proposals was the 'Hertfordshire
Federation of Amenity Societies', whose aim was to 'co-
ordinate and assist the activities of its member bodies in
forwarding their aims in the conservation of the environment of Hertfordshire', and to 'deal with all lawful acts
or things as are incidental to attainment of the primary
objects of the Federation and so far as may be necessary
or desirable to do such things or acts in consultation
with any person, body, institution, authority or otherwise'. (1) These extracts from the Federation's constitution indicate it was a formal, legally-oriented type of
organisation, and indeed the constitution talks of the
Federation being an organisation which attempts to achieve
its objectives by 'charitable means'. The Federation's
activities in 1973 were essentially to lend its status,
and affiliate to, 'The Campaign Against Stevenage
Expansion' (CASE), as the Federation was
    against the Stevenage Development Corporation's plans
    which were unnecessary and based on the premise that
    London needed to emigrate to the New Towns. (2)

The Federation, like many of the conservationist amenity (3) societies, was rather anachronistic in outlook, and entirely opposed to change.

Another organisation active in providing status-backing, affiliation, and, importantly, the raising of finances, yet less involved in policy-making, was the 'Hertfordshire Society', which essentially was the Hertfordshire branch of the 'Council for the Protection of Rural England' (CPRE). The Hertfordshire Society was considered by local conservationists - and to a lesser extent the farming community - to be a high status organisation, particularly as it had been able to appoint Queen Elizabeth the Queen Mother as Patron. Its policy was that of the CPRE, which aimed to

> promote and encourage for the benefit of the *nation* the improvement, protection and preservation of the English countryside and its towns and villages and the better development of the rural environment. (4, emphasis added)

Of course what the CPRE really meant was that it wanted preservation not for the 'nation', but rather for conservationists and landowners.

The constitution added that it would take any 'lawful' action to promote the aims of the Council. The CPRE was, it asserted, 'an entirely independent organisation', which was 'not subsidised by Government and thus retains the freedom necessary for effective criticism', and which 'maintains a small, expert staff in London' who monitor Government proposals, legislation and debates in Parliament. Furthermore 'when legislation affecting the countryside is going through Parliament CPRE is in constant touch with MPs to seek additions, amendments or deletions designed to protect rural England'. (5) The CPRE constitution went on to say that 'the other - equally vital - job of the national office is to pass on what it learns to CPRE's county branches' (like the Hertfordshire Society), who are 'the local watchdog, each with their own team of volunteers checking the planning registers, commenting on plans', and 'keeping ceaseless vigilance over threats to the landscape and buildings in it'. (6)

The CPRE, from its various publications, appeared to be a mixture of naivety and insight when it came to planning matters. For instance, in a booklet titled 'Planning Sense', on the subject of participation in public inquiries, it is stated that:

> It is *not* a judicial proceeding and the Inspector is *not* a judge... [correct]
> The procedure of an inquiry is very flexible and is designed to help ordinary people state their cases for

or against a particular proposal... [incorrect]
The Inspector is conducting the inquiry to find out the
truth... [meaningless]
Professionals have no specific advantages... [incor-
rect]. (7)

On the other hand a much more perceptive account of the
planning process is contained in the 1976 Annual Report,
where CPRE stated that it had become

obvious that the assumptions on which post-war planning
had been based - in particular the assumptions of
continuing rising population, economic growth and
public spending - are in shreds. Moreover, the methodological assumption of the post-war planners, viz., the
prediction of population and economic trends in the
long term largely by extrapolation of a reliable trend,
is now equally discredited. There are no more reliable
trends. (8)

The Hertfordshire Society for its part intervened in the
1973 proposals by calling a meeting in Stevenage, open to
the public, to see what kind of opposition there was to
expansion. It was stated in its circular, which had been
distributed to 'interested bodies', that the Society was
strongly opposed to 'any expansion' and was 'doing everything in its power to fight it both at county and national
levels'. It added that 'the majority of Stevenage
residents, also, wish that their town could be allowed to
settle down into a real community and the facilities and
amenities improved for the benefit of the existing
residents and their children'. Most significantly, it
continued, 'it is vitally important'

that those residents who are opposed to expansion
should form themselves into a united body to fight the
proposal in co-operation with those outside the town
who hold the same opinion. It is essential that the
proposals should not be regarded as a fait accompli
about which ordinary citizens can do nothing. This
is not so... (9)

Thus the Hertfordshire Society called a public meeting
in April to see if it had sufficient support, 'at which
a plan of campaign could be discussed and at which we can
offer the benefit of our experience in such matters'. (10)
The Society had therefore realised, early on, that any
protest campaign would have to be seen as a united one,
particularly in terms of the town in relation to the
country.
The next group to be discussed has already been referred
to, namely the 'Stevenage Valley Association' (SVA), an
organisation, as one of its members put it, which 'started
in 1967 or 1969 depending on how you look at it', meaning

in fact that it was one of those organisations that started and stopped and started again, and that really only got into being when it had a major case to fight. The members of the SVA were originally geographically related, and have always been essentially middle class, with, for example, the original executive consisting of two teachers, a probation officer, and an 'aspiring postmaster'. (11)   The SVA was formed to dispute the proposed building of Road 9 as written in the 1966 Master Plan revision, and indeed the issue was the focus of the Association, for when the Road 9 plans were shelved, this was seen

> as a definite victory for the Valley Association, so
> it went into limbo even though the road wasn't stopped
> - it was shelved. It went into limbo with a positive
> air - so it was possible to resurrect it without too
> much trouble. (12)

From 1969 to 1972 Annual Meetings of the Association should have taken place, but none did. It is stated on the membership form of the Association, that 'membership is open to residents of the Stevenage area and to all others who support its aims' - the Treasurer of the SVA pointed out that, although the Association was intended to be a Residents' Association, it increasingly began to see itself more as a Stevenage-based pressure group and subsequently attempted to recruit members from anywhere, albeit with little success. (13)   The Association had six aims: (i) to work to preserve and enhance the amenities of the Stevenage area;   (ii) to vehemently oppose the 1973 expansion proposals;   (iii) to oppose any plan to build Road 9;   (iv) to continue to try to present constructive and realistic alternatives to the proposals it rejects; (v) to work with other organisations having similar goals; and (vi) to continue to assert that 'any proposal likely to affect ordinary people should require their approval before it can be acted upon'. (14)

The Treasurer of the SVA stated that in 1972 there was still a small caucus 'of us who were residually interested in what was going on, just watching', when the expansion proposals were mentioned, which in turn produced a few phone calls between members. One of the previously active members, Ken Poole, a local librarian, was taking an Open University degree at the time so he more or less decided to refrain from any possible activities, whilst another member, Bill Ware, who ran a loudspeaker van in his spare time, urged the SVA to 'take up the fight'. (15)   There was an interesting aside concerning Mr Ware, who was one of the few working-class members of the SVA, which demonstrates both the strength of feeling at the time, and

furthermore points to the possibilities concerning joint
action between members of differnt 'political orien-
tations'. The Treasurer of the SVA explained:

Bill Ware was a working-man and a neo-fascist ... some
of us were strongly into the Anti-Vietnam campaign
business and we wanted to borrow a speaker system for
something in the Town Square, and I didn't realise he'd
be pro the Yanks in Vietnam did I?, and so we went to
talk to him and said 'can we borrow your speakers?', so
he said 'yes, what's it for?', we told him and he said
'OK'. It was only when we were putting away the
speakers that he said 'I think it's bloody silly, the
Yanks ought to get in there and finish the job off'.
But purely because of his bond with the Valley Association he brought all of his equipment for nothing and
strung it all over the Town Square. (16)

The SVA decided - or rather three members of the SVA
decided - that it 'should put in observations re the expansion proposals to show that the SVA intended to
object'. (17) The Treasurer stated that at that time he
didn't really want to get too involved - 'you know a small
bunch doing all the work, and I had a lot on at the time'
- but eventually he indeed became considerably involved.
The SVA arranged a public meeting at the local college,
the purpose of which was to be 'a fact-finding meeting'.
It invited the Corporation, the Urban District Council,
and so on, to indicate that 'we were at the forefront of
the campaign', the idea being that 'if you are going to
enter a campaign you may as well enter it and appear to
be something important in it'. (18) The meeting was considered to be quite successful by the SVA, with 150 people
turning up including all the local authorities, with the
exception of the Corporation, and the Treasurer added that
'we asked for support and cash came in, but we didn't make
members as we didn't want it to appear as a propaganda
meeting', and furthermore he stated that 'we were trying
to present ourselves as an already well-established
organization'. (19)

It was difficult for both the observer and the members
of the Association to assess the actual membership of the
SVA, for as the Treasurer put it, 'it was so badly organised as an Association that it was difficult to know who
exactly were members'. The problem was that all the
members felt that it was their own responsibility to try
to make new members, and thus all the members would take
membership forms and get people to sign them and so on,
including the payment of a small amount of cash:

the cash never really went astray, but if people had
got expenses they'd pay it out of the money they col-

lected from members. These forms would never always
come in to me as Treasurer ... I didn't know how many
of these they'd got. We could trust each other as an
Executive not to squander the funds, but there were
many people who - in fact we found this latterly where
some certificates filled in for members, 15 or 20 in
fact, were still in Phil Nicolai's hands, he'd never
passed them through to me with the money but I know
for a fact he hadn't spent the money - .... So I'm
working on the assumption that we had something between
35 and 90 members, now this might sound extraordinary,
but it's very much at this level, we just don't know
how many people joined. (20)

The work that the Association did in relation to the 1973
expansion proposals was undertaken by the Chairman Ian
Cuthill, a consultant engineer, the joint secretaries
Phil and Pearl Nicolai, a skilled engineer and his wife,
the Treasurer John Hubble, a sociology lecturer, Dr Ron
Faulkner, a general practitioner, and two schoolteachers,
Chris Ashton and Daphne Partridge. (21) The SVA decided
that the first step was to obtain as much information from
the Corporation as it could, in order to see 'what they
were up against'. Subsequently the first thesis elaborated by the SVA was the one dictated by Mr Cuthill, which
argued that, first, the Corporation itself was in need of
expansion as it was spending more than it received, for
example its 'production of houses, which would show a
return was low', and the '1973 output on administration
alone was £1 million'; and, second, the Conservative
Government was keen on 50 per cent owner-occupation and
this 'was illogical as the SDC couldn't make any money out
of that', although they would 'get a few years' grace by
overseeing the building of the houses'. (22) The SVA then
proceeded to publish a document along these lines, and
distributed it 'as much as they could'.

The SVA Executive was meeting once a week in early 1973,
at alternate houses, the meetings being taken up by the
examination of press-cuttings, SDC reports, writing
letters to the press, and so on. It was decided, particularly by Mr Hubble and Mr Nicolai, that the major publicity point was going to be the question of rented versus
owner-occupied housing, and thus an attempt was made to
make a big issue out of this, however, money 'was forever
tight', and hence fund-raising tended to take a disproportionate amount of time. (23) The next step was to
print handbills, and there followed a door-to-door collection which proved quite dispiriting, and which resulted
in the recruitment of a new member (of the old SVA period)
as 'Membership Secretary', namely Robbie Roberts. The

Treasurer stated that Mr Roberts was extremely competent
at recruitment - 'he'd take out the forms and bring them
back filled in' - as he was 'an easy talker ... you felt
you could trust him ... talked like a down-to-earth
working-class man'. (24)
 However, the membership still did not reach a three-
figure total, and Mr Roberts soon linked 'with Marion
Powell (a local campaigner-cum-politico) who said she
wanted to join, but in fact she never came to any
meetings'. (25)   There was no specific membership fee to
join the SVA and indeed, as the Treasurer put it:
    It was not a specified fee, we tried to make a speci-
    fied fee of 10p, but we couldn't even agree on that.
    (26)
The next idea was to suggest that there should be a
membership fee of 10p, together with the publication of
a monthly news sheet which would be taken around to
members who would be invited to make a constribution.   The
Treasurer commented: 'It is easy to have these kinds of
ideas, but it never got anywhere, we simply did not have
the time'. (27)
The SVA's strategy was increasingly one of simply writing
letters to the press, together with arranging public
meetings.   To begin with it was particularly easy to get
letters into the newspapers, especially as the SVA's
'meetings were always successful - we took care not to run
meetings that could be disastrous - and so we got a lot of
publicity'; indeed the Treasurer added that 'we took the
press in for quite some time'.   Moreover he went on to say
that 'we certainly took the Corporation in', and 'they
were convinced that we had a larger membership than we
had'. (28)
There emerged major differences within the organisation
and particularly between Mr Nicolai, a member of the
Communist Party, and the rather conservative and techno-
cratically-minded Mr Cuthill.   However as the SVA's
Treasurer pointed out, this was not posed as a political
difference:
    It came out merely that Cuthill wanted to work with the
    professions, he saw himself as a professional, if only
    he could get the other professionals to see that they'd
    made an error they would change.   It took him years, in
    fact I don't think ... he's thoroughly accepted that
    the professionals could possibly be corrupt or that
    they could be recognising that this was not a plan with
    professional justification but was one that was politi-
    cally all that they could do.   He would say for
    instance, 'Look let's not publish this, let's just
    write them a letter and say look we've got this infor-

mation, now we know you don't want us to publish this
really, because it will obviously make you look small
or foolish, so can we talk about it, and I'm sure we
can reach an amicable decision whereby you'll be able
to change your plans without us having to show publicly
that you're wrong.' Phil would sit there aghast, and
say in this super-polite way, 'I don't really think
that that is going to get us anywhere very much apart
perhaps from getting us a writ for libel'. (29)
Furthermore Mr Nicolai was keen to try to organise
street groups, and to make the Association a many-membered
grass-roots type of organisation. He eventually agreed
that it couldn't be done, as 'the amount of work we'd have
to put into it to get membership would be disproportionate
from the pay-off from that membership'. (30) Mr Nicolai -
and this *was* a political difference - wanted to attach the
'single issue' to other issues, such as the nature of the
democratic process, unemployment and other such related
matters, to which Mr Cuthill argued that if the campaign
was 'opened up', the fight that the Association was trying
to wage specifically against expansion would lose its
force, and moreover that a discussion on unemployment
could easily be twisted into a 'yes' for expansion. (31)
The SVA received a letter inviting it to attend a meeting
on 9 May at Rooks Nest Farm, which was situated on the
northern edge of Stevenage, a meeting which had been
organised by the 'Villages Co-ordinating Committee'. This
Committee was able to form by virtue of the first mistake
the Corporation had made in its expansion proposals,
namely that of not settling immediately on its options so
as to limit the area from which the protest would come,
and instead, as it was left open, the whole area was 'up
in arms'. In a sense the Corporation's democracy had
failed them, although of course this is to take a rather
charitable view of the Corporation's politics; an alternative interpretation could be that the Corporation
had hoped to play the residents of one area off against
another. The reason, of course, why the Corporation had
attempted a large-scale participation programme was the
impact of the Skeffington Report, together with the fact
that previously the SVA had taken the Corporation to the
Ombudsman over Road 9, and although he stated that he
couldn't comment on development corporations, he had been
through the Corporation's files and was critical over the
way it had handled the SVA's submission. Hence the Corporation went overboard for consultation and participation
but was, in fact, a mere novice at it.
The Co-ordinating Committee had been formed specifically
as a result of activity by the local village of Aston, and

particularly the village's amenity society which had been
formed at the time of the 1966 Master Plan. The members
of the amenity society had noticed that the comment form
circulated by the Corporation was 'loaded', 'biased', and
that these loaded questions had the effect that 'every
intelligent person was up in arms', and consequently the
society put an advert 'about 6" x 4" in the local paper
the next week saying, "Remember you can answer no"'. (32)
The Chairman of the Aston Village Society, Tom McCombie,
a bank manager, following the advertisement received two
telephone calls from 'independent people' in Walkern (a
local village) with the suggestion that something tangible
must be done to 'muster opposition against Stevenage'.
Consequently Mr McCombie invited various representatives
of Parish Councils, villages, and a few individuals to a
meeting which he chaired. The question raised at the
meeting was 'what can we do to start the ball rolling?'.
Mr McCombie stated that he 'suggested that we should hold
a referendum within the villages, based on a 100 per cent
house to house canvass, within a very short period of
time, namely three weeks'. (33) 7,500 questionnaires were
printed with the questions carefully chosen 'to be utterly
impartial', the first and core question being 'are you in
favour of the expansion of Stevenage beyond its present
boundaries as determined by the 1966 updating?'. A physical house-to-house check was carried out in five of the
six villages concerned in the operation - 'Wymondley
didn't do it very well' - namely Knebworth, Weston,
Gravely, Walkern, and Aston, and this gave a result of 87
per cent against, 5 per cent for (presumably the Corporation's consultants who lived in the villages, like Mr
Patterson, the Landscape Architect, knowing full well that
a 'yes' would be a minority vote), while the rest 'didn't
know'. (34)

The team that carried out the 'referendum' formed itself
into the Co-ordinating Committee, and soon afterwards
received an invitation from the Hertfordshire Society to
attend a meeting it had arranged (previously mentioned).
The meeting was attended by the SBC, the SVA, and members
of the public. Mr McCombie continued the account:

The strange part of course was that at that time the
Hertfordshire Society thought it was taking the lead
in this when in fact it was only second in the field,
and the Borough Council also thought it could tell
everybody what to do, and we were in fact lectured by
Mr Davies (technical adviser to the Council) on the
difficulties of carrying out a referendum in a scientific fashion because the Council had decided to carry
out their own sample referendum at that time, and they

completely missed the point that we were not carrying
out a sample at all, we were carrying out a 100 per
cent survey and therefore there was no scientific
reason why we should do anything other than what we
were so doing.... We of course made it clear that we
were first in the field, we'd already taken some
decisions and it was decided that all interested bodies
should meet again ... [and] draw up a constitution of a
body that would fight Stevenage expansion, because the
Hertfordshire Society were rather against, for example,
taking all the onus on themselves and felt that it was
right that a separate body should be formed for this
specific purpose. In the background of their thinking
of course there was the point of finance. (35)

So despite the squabbling about 'who was first' a decision had been reached that a new and separate body
should be formed in order that the expansion proposals
be fought on a united front, and indeed the initial consequence was the meeting called for 9 May at Rooks Nest
Farm.

The meeting was in fact attended by representatives from
the villages of Aston, Benington, Datchworth, Gosmore,
Graveley, Preston, St Paul's Walden, St Ippollits,
Walkers, Watton-at-Stone, and Weston, while apologies were
received from the villages of Langley, Knebworth, and
Wymondley. The Chairman, Mr McCombie, also welcomed
Baron Dimsdale of the Hertfordshire Society, and Mr
Cuthill and Mr Hubble of the SVA.

At the outset the representative from Datchworth stated
that 'their village knew a journalist', and as another
villager was a public relations officer, he suggested that
they could be regarded as the press and publicity team,
which was agreed by the meeting. Fund raising was the
next item on the agenda, and in the first instance the sum
of £10,000 was mentioned. The next item was termed
'immediate action', which resulted in an agreement to
continue writing letters to the newspapers and MPs, to
commence fund raising and to engage in propaganda. Then,
most importantly, Mr Reid of Datchworth (and LADACAN, the
anti-Luton-airport group), (36) suggested that the present
committee was too large, and as there would be 'a short
battle of about eighteen months' the organisation for the
campaign would have to be small. (37) He further suggested that it was not a planning battle they were to
fight, but rather a political one. It was thus agreed
that the new council would consist of one representative
each from the villages, approximately six people elected
from the SVA and two representatives from the Hertfordshire Society. From this council about six people would

be elected to serve on the executive committee. Finally
a new name was given to the organisation: 'The Campaign
Against Stevenage Expansion' or CASE, as it was to become
known.

The newly drawn up constitution stated that CASE's aims
were, first, to oppose the expansion of Stevenage beyond
its present allowed boundaries, and second, to support the
various constitutional bodies in Hertfordshire in their
opposition to the concentration of new building in the
proposed expansion area. (38) Thus the 'umbrella' organisation, the united campaign as envisaged by Mr McCombie,
had been formed, although there were stumbling blocks.
For example, Mr Hubble, one of the members of the Executive elected by the SVA, considered that he himslef had
made it extra difficult for CASE to get off the ground in
Stevenage:

> I felt that CASE were trying just simply to make sure
> there was no expansion per se, and I was prepared to
> believe that there was room for some expansion, that
> the primary purpose of our objections was to prevent
> a further influx of people moved from London or moved
> from other towns. Notably ... we got some information
> from Covent Garden and other places to try and empha-
> sise that people didn't particularly want to come to
> Stevenage. And we, the SVA, were making a particularly
> strong protest over the building of houses for sale....
> We wanted to make sure CASE was going to include these
> in their programme and they didn't particularly seem to
> want to make these big issues. There was an enormous
> political gulf, and of course there was a Conservative
> Government in power at the time, and so how CASE was
> going to fight this was not clear, but I was convinced
> that they were not going to fight the housing issue.
> (39)

The SVA was still, of course, meeting and campaigning as
a separate body as well as working within CASE, and on
30 May held a committee meeting and decided that it should
distribute the booklets it was having printed, covering a
'fairly wide area', but at the same time using any opportunity to 'flood a really promising street'. However,
the Association noted that this strategy which aimed at
'drumming up mass support during June', did rely solely
on the activities of four people! (40) The SVA was also
cut down to size by CASE, as it just could not have 'them
on' as it had done the press and the Corporation. The
Treasurer of the SVA thought that CASE did in fact originally think that the SVA was bigger than it was, in fact
he was absolutely certain:

> they'd hoped we'd subscribe to the funds from our

funds, and we would say 'what funds?' and they would
say 'from your members', to which we would reply 'what
members?'. (41)

The Association considered, in retrospect, that it was a
tactical error to be so clear about what kind of an organisation it was at such an early stage.

Mr McCombie was elected Chairman of CASE, with the
Hertfordshire Society's Vice-Chairman - and joint
treasurer of the CPRE, company director, management consultant, local landowner and farmer - Simon Bowes-Lyon as
Vice-Chairman. (42) Mr Wally Emms of Knebworth was appointed Press Officer, and Mr Cuthill of the SVA was made
Secretary. Mr McCombie considered that the executive
committee, in effect, carried out all the work of CASE,
with the council which met less frequently tending merely
to be a rubber stamp. Mr McMurtrie, a 'top executive'
with a medium-sized industrial company, was put in charge
of fund raising, and as Mr McCombie observed: 'We were
greatly indebted to Mr McMurtrie because he raised around
about £2,500, without which it is doubtful if we could
have carried on.' (43) Mr McMurtrie would simply travel
round to local landowners and farmers both west and east
of the town, and ask for donations. He would receive
money from both the landowners and farmers, who would then
claim tax relief on the donation which they would describe
as a professional fee. (44) The villages to the east of
the town became involved with CASE, even though their area
was not in the 'firing line', but they did so in the event
of some possible future move by the Corporation which
might affect them, in which case they would expect the
western villages to reciprocate.

The feeling of the anti-expansionists was by the middle
of 1973 running quite high although at times a little
hysterical, as the following letter from the Chairman of
the SVA Mr Cuthill to another SVA member, Mr Hubble,
demonstrated:

> We must stop expansion. If it means washing Shirley
> Williams's boots, telling Balchin he's a good lad or
> marching round Stevenage we must do it if it will give
> us these aims,

and once again the squabbles were evident:

> We must support and try (tactfully) to dominate the
> CASE meetings.... We need not be junior partners,
> because: (a) we know more about Stevenage, the SDC,
> the facts behind this and other expansion issues,
> London, and other Stevenage organizations than they do,
> and (b) their village support is largely negative and
> parochial, and has no real ideas except that they don't
> want bulldozers in their gardens. (45)

CASE at this time was producing on high quality paper thousands of leaflets titled 'Don't let them ruin Stevenage - join CASE and fight for your life', which had sub-headings like 'do you want overcrowded schools, a poorer health service?', and 'who benefits from ex-pansion?', and so on. The leaflet ended, 'remember that Stevenage doesn't want it, the poor can't have it and the rich don't need it'. (46) CASE's membership form, 'They're PLANNING to ruin your village', stressed that 'people still matter in this country, now is the time to stop this destructive project, and this will only be achieved if *you* who care about the way you live and your way of life, are prepared to take up the fight'. It con-tinued, 'time is short, but here are the immediate steps to take if you want to protect your village: (i) sign the petition being mounted by CASE, and (ii) join your local branch of CASE'. (47)

The detailed strategy that CASE had theoretically out-lined for itself could be seen from its working paper titled 'A Public Relations Campaign For CASE'. It stated that the campaign objectives in the short term were, first, the prevention of the development from even reaching a public inquiry stage; second, if the proposals did in fact reach inquiry stage, to ensure that opposition was informed and motivated to present an 'overwhelming case'; and finally the removal in the long term of the threat of any similar development. (48) The methods CASE intended to use were related to the areas where the effort would necessarily have to be directed, namely the Govern-ment, Civil Service, interested local authorities and local inhabitants. However, CASE saw the first task 'as one of motivation':

> The townspeople of Stevenage must be made fully aware of the threat to their future. They must then be seen to demonstrate their rejection of these proposals...
> To further these ends we would recommend that some form of symbol for the campaign be adopted with which people can readily identify. This should appear on campaign buttons, car stickers and all press material and news sheets issued by the campaign committee. We propose that buttons and stickers be sold as part of the committee's fund raising campaign. (49)

In the event none of the 'motivation-raising' and symbolic buttons and stickers ever materialised.

The working paper continued with a section titled 'recruitment' which stated that as 'this is an all-party issue' it was recommended that the initial appeal should be launched through all parties, to activate members and to recruit support on a wide basis. Again nothing came

of this except that all the local MPs were canvassed.
CASE then stated in the document that recruitment was
envisaged to take place from the forum of the Town Square.
The next section dealt with public meetings, where CASE
suggested that there should be (i) a public demonstration
in the form of a march, (ii) a deputation to deliver a
protest statement to the Secretary of State, (iii) the
lobbying of local MPs, and (iv) letter writing to the
national press (50) - exactly how the final two strategies
related to public meetings is indeed a moot point.   The
document continued to suggest that MPs ought to be asked
to table questions related to Stevenage, and that the
press and the media generally be kept fully informed.   It
was at this point that Marion Powell entered.

As mentioned earlier Mrs Powell was a campaigner for
various causes and a politico, and she in fact ended up
as Co-ordinator of CASE.   The term 'ended up' is deliberately used as there was some ambiguity as to how exactly
she obtained the post.   Mrs Powell's version was that she
had attended various meetings concerning expansion, and:

> I listened to the way they were muddling through and
> towards the end of the evening I started saying a few
> things ... with the result that at the end of the
> meeting Robert Evans, one of the farmers, said 'it
> seems to me from hearing Mrs Powell speak that she has
> more organization at her fingertips than most of us
> here, and I propose that we make her Co-ordinator of
> CASE'. (51)

Mrs Powell added that within a few short weeks of working
in that capacity it seemed as if she 'was almost running
CASE'. (52)   Mr McCombie's version, on the other hand, was
that she 'was asked to join in order to make it appear
that Stevenage was adequately represented on CASE'. (53)
However she *did* join CASE, and was to become quite an
important figure in the proceedings.

CASE, at its next executive committee meeting, reported
on a public meeting held on 5 July, and stated that it had
been fairly successful with 112 signatures on a petition.
However, it was also thought that the speakers took up far
too much time, and thus it was 'agreed that any future
meetings should be better programmed, limiting speakers'.
(54)   The same meeting ironed out some membership difficulties, in that it was clarified that members of amenity
societies who joined CASE would not automatically become
members of CASE through their society, rather there must
be individual membership and such membership would form a
branch of CASE.   This kind of discussion and decision-
making was prevalent in CASE executive committee meetings,
and did appear to take up a disproportionate amount of

time. The meeting also criticised the lack of liaison
between committee members, specifically between Simon
Bowes-Lyon, Mr Hubble, and the Public Relations Officer
in relation to a television programme which had just been
broadcast and which had concentrated on CASE's activities.
It was agreed that any such future event ought to be
organised in conjunction with the Public Relations
Officer, or the Secretary, Mr Cuthill. (This television
incident will be described later in the chapter.)

Another example of the often narrow focus of the meetings
was when, at the same meeting, Mr Cuthill questioned the
legality of printing CASE's address on the petition form,
a question which produced a long-drawn-out discussion
which reached no real conclusion. Simon Bowes-Lyon informed the meeting that he was going to contact the Town
Planning Institute, in order to request them to write an
article on the expansion proposals, and also that he had
been in contact informally with a number of MPs. (55) The
meeting, a four-hour marathon, ended with Mr Hubble of the
SVA stating that:

> the SVA felt that the campaign in the town must be run
> on the issue of limiting and eliminating the building
> of private housing. Also the Road 9 issue was still
> very much alive and the SVA are going to renew cam-
> paigning on this. (56)

It was agreed by the meeting that CASE would support
these views, and that the matter would be brought to the
attention of the council meeting the following day. The
council meeting, the following evening, commenced with the
Public Relations Officer stating that CASE should now
organise a short-term and 'siege' campaign: 'the people
of Stevenage must be motivated, and there must be a physical demonstration of opposition to expansion'. A
programme was advocated which consisted of, first, continued and increased petitioning, second a march through
Stevenage to take place on 28 July, and finally a 'gum up'
of the railway station. It was further suggested that
there ought to be a massive 'write-in' to Mr Rippon. (57)
The Public Relations Officer stated that he would arrange
TV coverage for the march and the 'gum up' (which he
didn't), and further suggested the idea of 'dummy postboxes on street corners' for posting letters to Mr Rippon,
which again would receive TV coverage (again there were
to be no 'dummy postboxes'). In one last hysterical
moment he suggested a 'massive TV advertising campaign',
adding that 'we would be the first to do it'. (58)
Finally the council clarified once and for all the membership confusion: affiliated membership was open to all
organisations, and no subscriptions were laid down; full

membership was aimed at individuals, in order that
branches could be formed in centres such as villages; and
amenity societies were to be encouraged to work through
the branch in their area. Furthermore - and this was
where the procedure became somewhat bewildering - full
members could have one representative at council (presumably then this meant one member of a branch), affiliated members similarly could have one representative at
council, and finally individual members were not to be
allowed to be represented at council! (59) Not that any
of this really mattered, as the council meeting was closed
with the statement that 'regrets are expressed at the
number of absentees'. (60)

On 16 July a memorandum was issued to all CASE members
regarding the march of 28 July, a march which was to be
part of an 'integral whole called CASE DAY'. The memo
continued to say:

> It has been suggested we should ask the walkers to
> carry suitcases bearing CASE labels and that hot air
> balloons advertising CASE should be sent up in the town
> centre and Fairlands Valley. Mrs Powell has had an
> offer of a gas machine for the balloons. She has also
> had an offer of a generator to be used by a band. (61)

On the day of the march another memo was sent to all
members stating that 'the success or failure of this march
depends on you, the people', and that '10,000 people would
not be too many, there really is no limit', and finally
the memo urged the prospective marchers 'to carry a light-
weight, large, empty suitCASE'. (62)

Before the march Shirley Williams - who together with
Vivien Bendall the prospective Conservative candidate,
Tom Willis the Liberal candidate, and various councillors
was to take part in the march, and speak at the 'rally'
afterwards in Fairlands Valley - met executive committee
members of CASE together with Stevenage Councillors at the
local Old Town hotel, the 'Cromwell', in order to discuss
the various issues of the expansion proposals, the Corporation, and other related matters. According to
Mr McCombie of CASE:

> it became obvious that she ... had reservations about
> no expansion at all, and I think it would be fair to
> say that at no time did she say that she was against
> all expansion, equally she was not adverse to appearing
> in a march which advertised itself to be against all
> expansion. The same applies of course to the Council-
> lors and the Conservative member of that Council -
> James Boyd - told me that he was in favour or thought
> it would be necessary to have a 'limited expansion' in
> the future, and the other Councillors were fairly

suitably vague on the point. I went along with them
solely because I was being pragmatic, anybody who was
with me was not against me, so that was something. (63)
About 300 marchers turned up - not the 10,000 hoped for -
and were, according to the local newspapers, largely
middle-class and 'upwards', and that there were 'few from
the town's trade union and labour movement, merely token
representation from the Labour Party'. (64) Mrs Powell,
who was the organiser of the march, saw it in the
following manner:

It was a very successful march because it takes Mr and
Mrs Average a great deal of courage to march through
the streets and most people feel unable to do so, and
I saw many supporters standing by the side of the road.
However, amongst those who did turn up for the march,
it was interesting to recognise doctors, teachers, and
social workers who were opposed to expansion for the
reason of unfeasibility - they did not want to cope
with the problems such action would bring. (65)

The next event that CASE organised, again mainly through
the efforts of Mrs Powell, was the 'lighting of bonfires'.
CASE invited people who were opposed to expansion to light
a bonfire in 'their garden or in their field' at 9.00 pm
on 3 September, an invitation which made the Council
furious - 'our fire brigade already has enough to do'.
However the event did take place and the local newspapers,
who had hired a light aircraft to photograph the 'dazzling
array of bonfires', reported only a handful, although Mrs
Powell, optimistic as ever, stated that 'one farmer had
written CASE out in burning stubble which I thought was
quite an interesting exercise and shows just what pressure
groups can do'. (66)

The next stage in the protest was the breaking away by
Mrs Powell (followed by Robbie Roberts) from CASE in order
to form her own group, 'The Campaign Against Unnecessary
Stevenage Expansion', or CAUSE as it came to be known. In
Mrs Powell's account of the breakaway, she stated that she
had set up a stall for CASE in Stevenage and had discovered that the response she had received was very different from that of the villagers and farmers, for example
people would say 'if we don't have expansion where are our
kids going to be housed?'. She then thought 'if the
people of Stevenage are feeling this way and feel that
expansion is good for them, then unless we get them
realising that expansion is not for their children but in
fact for further immigration to the town, with more
children who in turn will go on the waiting list, CASE is
nothing'. Mrs Powell then attempted to argue this point
with the CASE executive committee, but she felt that Mr
McCombie 'seemed hostile towards her'. She continued:

one night I said well I'd had enough of this, this was
obviously not my scene and I resigned. Robbie Roberts
agreed wholeheartedly with me and the two of us set up
CAUSE, we said well obviously you can't have total no
expansion, there must be limited expansion as the need
arises to house the indigenous population. (67)

Mr McCombie put the matter in a rather different manner.
He stated that one night he was chairing an executive
meeting and 'I stated categorically that it was essential
that all members of the committee should work together for
the same ends, and that there could not be any deviations
from that end and that we were all answerable to each
other'. He went on to say that unbeknown to him Marion
Powell and Robbie Roberts had gone away that evening in
agreement over certain courses of action, and in fact had
decided to break away and form CAUSE. Mr McCombie then
stated that Simon Bowes-Lyon wanted CAUSE to join up with
CASE - 'you know, liaise' - because he considered that
although they'd broken away, he wanted to liaise for the
sake of Stevenage, as CAUSE was supposed to be representing Stevenage. Subsequently Mr McCombie tendered his
resignation as Chairman, because he 'refused to work with
these people who would accept one thing in committee
without a word about what they were going to do, and then
go away the same night and break off'. Mr McCombie considered Mrs Powell to be a:

person that cannot accept discipline from any source
whatsoever and I was - she wanted to be the leader -
disciplining her, and she wasn't prepared to accept it.
Roberts went with her, but subsequently broke off from
her ... (he formed another group consisting of himself
and his wife called 'Save Our Stevenage', or SOS as it
was called later)..., and of course CAUSE after an
initial flash-in-the-pan, which is somewhat typical of
her - everything she touches - also died away. (68)

Mrs Powell began her campaign by putting out thousands of
leaflets which stated the aims of CAUSE: that CAUSE was a
non-political association of local citizens dedicated to
ensuring that the future development of Stevenage took
place in accordance with the already-agreed 1966 Master
Plan. The leaflet went on to argue that if permitted the
plan would ensure the 'steady development of Stevenage as
a live-in/work-in community', and that Stevenage would
have an increasing say in 'running its own affairs including building its own much needed amenities, building
such houses as are required for its own children and those
who wish to live and work here'. Furthermore, CAUSE opposed the expansion proposals because it realised that
such proposals, if put into operation, would 'put back

the production of homes to rent', and replace such homes
'with about 1,400 private houses, which when valued at
£15,000-£19,000 must be either bought by commuters or
third and fourth house buyers, thereby neither solving the
problems of the homeless of London nor the children of
Stevenage'. Moreover, the proposals would grab large
'chunks of agricultural land', 'overload services', and
make the 'building of Road 9 a certainty'. (69)   The
leaflet, which had commenced with the statement that CAUSE
was a 'non-political association', added that if the expansion was realised 'disruption would continue with the
never-ending expansion under the autocratic authority of
the SDC: although we pay dearly for this authority we
have *no control* over it or its activities'. (70)   Finally
the leaflet concluded by stating that CAUSE was not opposed to 'natural expansion', in that the present designated area provided enough land to meet local needs into
the 1990s, and that if further development was needed it
could take place in the same way as it did in other towns:

> You were promised that Stevenage would be a self-
> contained community with slightly more jobs than
> people. It was to be built in 25 years to a population
> of 60,000. A succession of expansion plans now author-
> izes enough land to build over 8,000 homes in the
> present designated area, to house a 30,000 population
> increase. In the 1972 Updating Plans, the SDC proposed
> to build about 800 homes per year right up to its
> demise in 1975. THIS IS NOT HAPPENING. But the 1973
> Expansion will increase the population to 150,000....
> CAUSE wants the 1973 proposals scrapped, and the 1966
> Master Plan proceeded with and genuine attempts to
> catch up the lost time in building rented homes. (71)

Mrs Powell's next step was to 'get paper' and invite
people who were homeless to sign it, stating where they
were living and how long they had been on a waiting list
and if they were children of tenants, 'and in fact I got
about 100 names in a very short time'. Membership of
CAUSE was represented by those who signed the petition
regarding the implementation of the 1966 Master Plan, and
who had paid 10p for doing so. According to Mrs Powell
the membership was '*a very mixed, a very mixed group* of
people definitely ... I would say they were basically
people who had children on the waiting list, or young
people themselves I suppose'. (72, emphasis added)   Mrs
Powell here was aware that groups obtained legitimation
if perceived as receiving wide support and membership,
although the latter part of her statement suggested that
her organisation tended, in fact, to consist of similar
persons.

CAUSE claimed a membership of some 300 people, though the actual organisation to all intents and purposes consisted of Mrs Powell and Robbie Roberts, together with his wife. Mrs Powell was unemployed, whilst the other two were 'clerical workers', and all three were self-ascribed members of the 'upper working class'. (73) Incidentally, Mrs Powell was buying her house from the Corporation, whilst Mr and Mrs Roberts were Corporation tenants not purchasing property. Mrs Powell stated that although she was unemployed it didn't really relate to her motivation, in that 'a lot of these type of activities take place in the evening and at weekends'.

CAUSE meetings consisted of Mrs Powell thinking of:
> an idea, and I would communicate this idea to Roberts and say 'do you think this is a good idea?' and he'd say 'yes excellent', and then we'd get our heads together and we would just carry something through. (74)

The subscriptions 'barely paid for the paper': however CASE gave CAUSE some funds, as did the local Council. Mrs Powell's next strategy was to demonstrate for the 'rights of the second generation to housing' in the town, and these demonstrations usually took the form of her interruption of meetings, and ceremonies officiated by dignitaries, and bringing forward a 'homeless family', and particularly families with young babies. CAUSE also produced posters for sticking up in the town, such as the one which depicted a bulldozer at work in a woodland area, with a caption 'Plant a tree in '73, knock it down to expand a town'. (75) The final event CAUSE arranged was a 'torchlight procession', the idea behind which Mrs Powell explained:
> what I had planned to do on King George V playing field was to have a house of torches, a house depicted by torches raised to the sky with a queue of people going up to the front door. Unfortunately only about 36 couples turned up and it wasn't enough to make the house, let alone the queue. (76)

PART 2

There was a great deal of squabbling, manipulation, and deception taking place between the various organisations, and indeed within various organisations, and it is this aspect of the protest that will here be further illustrated.

To begin with, the organisation of CASE was flimsy and vulnerable, (77) and indeed as one member of the executive

committee noted 'much of the meetings was taken up with
talking about the structure of the organisation, how to
get the organisation going as an organisation' and so on.
(78)   Apparently CASE was not too concerned about the
problem of fund raising, 'they talked about it a lot, but
were not obsessed by it', but what CASE was obsessed with
was membership, that is the need to recruit members and
be seen to achieve membership.   According to Mr Hubble,
an executive member of CASE and Treasurer of the SVA,
CASE in its middle-class way made the same errors and assumptions which the SVA's Communist Party member Mr
Nicolai made, namely 'that you could get people really
worked up in their own areas'. (79)   CASE, according to
Mr Hubble, tried desperately to obtain membership from
Stevenage, and when it failed to do so in one particular
area, Chells, it 'despaired'.   This is of course the
reason why the Stevenage-based organisations like the SVA
together with individuals like Mrs Powell were encouraged
within CASE, but it was also the reason why the organisation slowly became divided, with eventual breakaways,
and, moreover, small caucuses could effectively be seen
to have made all the policy decisions and indeed carried
out the action.

The 'Marion Powell incident' led to the resignation of
Mr McCombie as Chairman, and eventually to his complete
withdrawal from CASE:

> I was no longer Chairman of CASE, and they asked me to
> be at least a Vice-President, and I said that I did not
> consider it was the sort of organisation that needed
> Vice-Presidents.   I told ... [them] that perhaps one
> day I would be as much use to them outside the fold as
> in it, and that as far as taking any formal part in it
> I was finished. (80)

For her part Mrs Powell was less easily put off.   She
stated that as the anti-expansion programme grew CAUSE,
although a separate body, in fact had the same aims as
CASE - although for different reasons, 'I had the heart
of the new town and they had the villages' - so 'in other
words we worked in liaison after the initial - it wasn't
exactly a quarrel, it was just a contention they couldn't
seem to understand at the time'. (81)

The reason why CASE and CAUSE *were* able to liaise was the
work undertaken by Simon Bowes-Lyon, possibly the principal actor, who initially encouraged the importation into
CASE of the Stevenage-based organisations and individuals.
Mr McCombie suggested that 'there was a fundamental
difference of approach between Bowes-Lyon and myself which
of course has never been properly aired', (82) and indeed
there was, a difference which Frank Parkin would call one
between 'expressive' and 'instrumental' politics. (83)   In

other words, McCombie would have at times been inclined to relinquish a little power in order to 'be correct', whereas Bowes-Lyon would be utterly ruthless at all times - the end would justify the means. However, it must be remembered that McCombie and Bowes-Lyon did agree on other quite major points, and that the gulf between (say) Mr Cuthill of the SVA or Marion Powell and Bowes-Lyon was greater than that between him and McCombie.

The SVA was not considered a viable proposition by CASE, particularly as represented by Mr Cuthill, for as Mr McCombie put it, 'Cuthill took things extremely seriously but had a large amount of information which he seemed quite incapable of producing at the right time'. (84) Cuthill was 'Technical Adviser' as well as Secretary of CASE, but according to fellow SVA and CASE member Mr Hubble, he was completely and utterly 'politically inept', particularly as compared with Bowes-Lyon. According to Mr Hubble, Bowes-Lyon was 'operating within CASE almost as a separate organisation'. He went on to explain:

> Simon was a smooth, a political panther, you found him where you didn't expect him, he was there in corners, and in corners in London, and corners everywhere. And he operated from the sidelines mostly. He it was who was concerned to get some kind of legal representation quite early on, but *what* it was this was never discussed at CASE meetings. I fancy that he and McCombie ... sewed this up beforehand and didn't discuss it over much at the meeting. (85)

Bowes-Lyon was extremely concerned with the impression that an organisation like CASE was going to make, and of course people like Mr McCombie - although realising Bowes-Lyon's apprehensions about CASE - were sufficiently interested in keeping him in, by virtue of his reputation and influence: he was the grandson of the 14th Earl of Strathmore and Kinghorne. In fact the balance swung in favour of Bowes-Lyon to the extent that, effectively, he led CASE. He was, of course, the Hertfordshire Society's representative on CASE and he brought with him the Society's values and posture. For example, he stated that CASE 'needed a strident side', that 'CASE had no authority', and indeed that the 'Hertfordshire Society gave CASE a measure of credibility, you know if CASE needed a solicitor they had to show their money first, but with us involved ...'. (86) Bowes-Lyon's feelings towards Mrs Powell were similar to those expressed by Mr McCombie: 'the Hertfordshire Society need protection from the Marion Powells', and this of course is probably why he was able to continue working within CASE, the Hertfordshire Society not being excessively identified with CASE, despite its covert influence. Bowes-Lyon

stated that his strategy was somewhat different from that
of everyone else:

> to put our case over I would deal through the grape-
> vine, you know, 'who is dealing with what in the DOE?',
> through other friends in the Civil Service. Then the
> common friend, the civil servant from the DOE and
> myself would meet in the Athenaeum or the Travellers'
> for lunch and discussion. (87)

According to some CASE members, Bowes-Lyon would in fact
turn up at a CASE meeting and inform them of the DOE's
next move, intentions, and other related matters. (88) It
must be remembered here that there was a lot at stake for
Bowes-Lyon both as a farmer, landowner/developer, and as
a conservationist, in that his land was situated west of
the motorway.

Mr Hubble of the SVA formed the impression that Bowes-
Lyon never ceased to attempt to create a split between
Mr Cuthill and himself, the two members of the SVA on the
CASE Executive, and for two distinct reasons. First in
order to cut the SVA down to size so that it would follow
rather than attempt to lead, and second because Cuthill's
attention had to be made to focus on problems within the
organisation, so that he would not split the town and the
villages apart 'through one of his rather frustrated and
hysterical outbursts'. Mr Hubble added:

> Bowes-Lyon would ring me up and he would be on the
> telephone for 2 hours and more, just on and on, just
> very quietly and very persuasively talking, asking what
> I felt, saying how much he wanted to help the Valley
> Association, how much he wanted to see it from the
> Stevenage point of view - 'the villagers might have to
> come to terms with the present day' - and these kind
> of things. And how much he respected my viewpoint, and
> this came out very clearly when we had the television
> cameras down.
>
> Bowes-Lyon got in touch with Anglia Television and
> asked them if they would come down and do something on
> Stevenage expansion. Well they did, they came down and
> they said that they would attempt to do it in the
> college - so in fact the camera crew and the rest of
> them arrived at the college on Saturday morning to the
> utter consternation of the caretaker who wondered what
> all this equipment was doing at the college, and
> fetched Williams the Registrar out ... who fetched the
> Principal out which was unfortunate and they all said,
> 'Mr Hubble said it was all right', and so we had this
> terrible situation in the car park. Cuthill arrived
> at the negotiating stage, by which time I had found out
> that Bowes-Lyon had arranged two interviews - one for

him and one for me (both to represent CASE). When
McCombie found out later he moaned, 'Bowes-Lyon sounds
like plums and a silver spoon combined'. Cuthill was
beside himself with fury because they were interviewing
me and not him, he said he could do a better technical
job of it. Bowes-Lyon wanted to keep both sides, the
villages and the towns, together, so he didn't want
Cuthill to talk. Cuthill could easily have split them
asunder by one of his absurd phrases. (89)
  It was necessary of course for Bowes-Lyon to mediate
between the possible rivalries between town and country,
in order that they did not become manifest, and the
minutes of CASE meetings indeed demonstrated an increasing
measure of conflict of interest between what was perceived
to be the Stevenage view, as opposed to the village view.
For example, more and more time was taken up with the
question of housing, which would split CASE into those
such as Bowes-Lyon who had realised that it was important
to go along to a great extent with the town, and others
who were 'little Englanders', whose attitude was 'why
should we accept the new town at all?'.

PART 3

In October Shirley Williams announced that in her opinion
it did appear that the Government was much less decided
on expansion than it had been just a few months previously, indeed 'they seem to be going round in circles'. (90)
CAUSE meanwhile wrote a letter to a local newspaper, and
on the subject of housing stated that it was '10 days to
9 months for Asians, 3 to 4 years for Stevenage
youngsters, no racial discrimination?', which was followed
by a letter the following week by CASE accusing CAUSE of
being a racist organisation, (91) plus adding an aside
that it was a stronger organisation than CAUSE.
  The Housing Management figures for the period which
ended 31.12.73 did indeed show a waiting time of 3 to 4
years for the JHL, but of course what Mrs Powell was
referring to was the rather exceptional measures taken in
the case of the Ugandan Asians, a measure she probably
knew would not be repeated too often in the future. The
quarterly figures showed a total of 1,337 on the JHL, 990
on the parents of tenants list, and the fact that some 447
households had left Stevenage during the year. For some
unknown reason, there were no figures available on industrial allocations.
  Housing sales had reached a cumulative total of 5,241 out
of the total housing stock of 18,708, the cumulative

surplus on General Revenue Account had reached just over
£3 million, while administration costs for the year had
totalled £1,341,715, and the Corporation had 625 persons
on its payroll. Finally there were 351 unfilled vacancies together with 496 unemployed persons, as reported by
the ERV1 and ERV returns.

The year 1974 started off where 1973 left off, with CASE
and the SVA again irritating each other. Mr Cuthill of
the SVA (and CASE) received a letter from CASE which
stated that it was irritated by the SVA's insistence on
the implementation of the '1972 Updating', as CASE was
opposed to it (one of the reasons being that the 1972
Plan deleted a school and replaced it with several houses
at the bottom of the garden of Mr McCombie, who was at the
time still connected with CASE). Cuthill decided to
reply: 'in common with yourself we wish to see the development of Stevenage along the lines of the agreed 1966
plans. However as you know there were several errors,
omissions and miscalculations in the 1966 plans, and from
our point of view the main oversight was the low density
of the building, high family size and slow rate of
building upon which the Master Plan is based.' The SVA
preferred the 'updated plan because this is more realistic
when it comes to comparing the needs of Stevenage housing
as against the dismal record which the Development Corporation are at present achieving'. The letter mentioned
the unfortunate replacing of a village school by housing
(and of course the associated roads, etc.), and concluded:
  we must all speak with one voice and I will make sure
  that your perfectly justifiable concern is taken into
  account by the Valley Association whenever the opportunity arises. (92)

On a copy of the letter, which was sent to the SVA's
Treasurer, Mr Cuthill had scribbled on the front page
that he had hoped 'that the following throws a little
reasonable oil on it without giving anything away'. (93)

On 16 January the 'Luton Evening Post' posed the
question, 'Super plans to be axed?', and indeed later that
evening Norman Tebbit MP, at Question Time in the House of
Commons, asked Mr Rippon, 'What decision have you made
about the proposal for major extension of Stevenage and
Harlow?', to which Mr Rippon replied:
  I have decided not to proceed with the present proposals for major extension of Harlow and Stevenage,
  I shall be discussing urgently with the Corporations
  *the case for expansion on a lesser scale to meet local
  needs* in these two towns. Bearing in mind that the
  studies for a similar extension at Bracknell are not
  yet complete, I am indicating to the Development Corpo-

ration that I envisage a similar limitation in this
case also. (94, emphasis added)

The decision was made no doubt for a number of reasons,
the most important one being the collapse of the private
housing market, which was due to escalated prices, scarce
mortgages, and thus a situation of builders having surplus
land instead of the more usual pattern of their 'crying
out for it'. An article in the 'Guardian' the following
day suggested that Mr Rippon's decision ought, rather, to
be seen in the context of the Government's need to cut
back on public spending, and the 'importance placed by
Mr Rippon on the needs of the inner city as well as
housing during an economic crisis'. (95)   Shirley
Williams, for her part, stated that Mr Rippon was concerned about the loss of agricultural land and the fact
that it would mean a town divided by a motorway.   Furthermore she thought that the campaigning had influenced the
Minister: 'We have now won the battle three times.   Each
time it comes up again two years later.   I hope that
having killed it three times that is the end.' (96)

Presumably Mr Rippon's decision could also be seen in the
context of the impending General Election of the following
month, of which he would most likely have been aware,
which would have meant that a 'no' to expansion could have
possibly brought in a few votes, although of course he
would still have had to talk about some expansion 'on a
lesser scale' in order to save face.

The next question to be asked and answered is, did CASE,
CAUSE, and the other protest organisations see the decision as a victory?

To begin with, the SVA was more or less non-committal in
that its major concern was Road 9, and thus the decision
had little relevance to the matter of most concern to it.
CAUSE, on the other hand, announced that '*We've* stopped
expansion' (97, emphasis added) to the local newspapers,
and indeed Mrs Powell stated, in interview, that she was
sure that it had been pressure: 'I firmly believe in
pressure groups because I've been a one-man pressure group
in a lot of ways really ever since I came to Stevenage
twenty years ago.'   To accentuate such egocentrism, Mrs
Powell made the further claim that

I believe it was November I wrote a letter to Geoffrey
Rippon and I knew his daughter had been on drugs and
I'd heard that he was very upset about it and I wrote
a very personal letter to him and I ended it by saying,
'I know you have a daughter, perhaps you can remember
when she was a little moppet who used to climb on your
knee, how would you feel if she came to you now and
said "Daddy I've got to get married", would you like

to see her walking the streets with her baby?', and I
left it there. About five weeks later he said 'no' to
expansion and I can't help feeling that my letter had
some effect on him. I opened my letter in fact by
saying I hope you will make a decision on the expansion
of Stevenage as you feel when you get to the end of
this letter. (98)

Robbie Roberts of SOS, the organisation he had formed
following his departure from CAUSE, certainly believed
that he, together with his (small) organisation, had been
instrumental in the decision:

I had a loyal band of supporters during the campaign
(including my long-suffering wife), and my feelings
are that without their help, the campaign *could never
have been so successful*. (99, emphasis added)

CASE, in a memorandum which was sent out to all members,
stated that it was not surprised at the Minister's welcome
statement, because of 'our close contacts with the Department of the Environment'. The memo continued to say that
CASE had always felt that the 'expert representations
against the expansion' put forward by the local authorities and other bodies, and 'underlined by the massive
support of the public through CASE', would have proven to
the Minister that the proposals were ill-founded.
Furthermore:

We feel thanks are due to the *thousands* of people who
formed CASE and made it the powerful weapon it was,

and,

This success is an instance where the voice of the
people, properly and resolutely expressed, achieved a
most desirable and warranted result. (100, emphasis
added)

For Mr McCombie, wearing the hat of the Aston Village
Society, it was a 'useful decision, but in no sense was
it a victory'. (101)

Did the organisations then fold up? CAUSE stated that,
like the SVA, it would never close as 'any time there is
a change of government, the thing rears its head again'.
(102) CASE for its part said that it was a little apprehensive about what the Minister meant when he spoke of
'lesser scale'. However it nevertheless believed that he
indeed meant a very small expansion, although the *siting*
could still be of some concern. On 20 January, four days
after the announcement, CASE's executive committee met and
decided on the following course of action: (i) it was
inadvisable to disband CASE at that present time, and
therefore CASE would continue as a 'watchdog', at least
until the outcome of discussions between the Corporation
and the Minister was made known; (ii) the Corporation's

'mini' expansion had been rumoured to be larger than the
updated 1966 Master Plan, would require further land
outside the designated area, and hence the situation would
have to be investigated; and (iii) it was proposed that
the funds of some £1,400, of which £1,200 was on deposit
with the Herefordshire County Council (to quote Bowes-
Lyon: 'the money is there because it gives the best
interest return') (103) be frozen, trustees appointed,
and the money held in readiness for any future expansion
proposals either at Stevenage or nearby. (104)
 Now the protest organisations had to wait for the Corporation's next move.

8   Stevenage 1974
'Expansion '74',
and the struggle continues

A principal tenet of planning faith is the priority of future over present needs. The planner is freed from the present by his commitment to the future, and his scientificality can all be poured into anchorless data the validity of which cannot be checked.

Norman Dennis (1972), p.242

The Corporation described the decision by Mr Rippon as 'the non-event of the year'. In its Annual Report it stated that after presenting recommendations on 17 April 1973, there had followed a period of nine months 'empty about the Secretary of State's intentions'. It recognised that the 'circumstances that underlay the 1972 decision to look to Stevenage to provide 1,000 additional acres of housing for private development had wholly changed', but the 'need for public rented housing, so strongly urged in the Corporation's report' had greatly increased, and it was 'hoped that on this ground alone a major expansion would have been recognised as essential and a Draft Designation Order would have been made' by the Secretary of State. (1)

It was further stated that the Corporation was as much distressed by the delay in the Government reaching a decision as by the effect of the decision itself, in that further development in the Designated Area had depended on the decision and the delay thus threatened to slow up urgently needed housing. (2) For this reason the Corporation had urged the Secretary of State to allow the full development of Sector 9 (North) - Symonds Green and Fishers Green - and also site development works in Sectors 7 and 8: accordingly, authority for this was given in March by Mr John Silkin (3) the new Minister, who had been appointed following Labour's victory in the February election. The Corporation suggested that this would now save the public housing development from being brought to a total standstill.

The Corporation, in its Annual Report, described 1973 as
'a calamitous year', with housing output (measured in
terms of either starts or completions) being the lowest
on record since 1950, and this at a time when demand was
rising because of the natural increase in population, and
the
>   resurgence of industrial growth following the re-
>   cession, bringing with it a housing demand for key
>   workers brought into the town. (4)

This statement (and demand) had to be considered and
evaluated, of course, in the light of the industrialists'
rather poor historical record of housing allocation take-
up, regardless of the 'growth' position of the time.
The Corporation continued to state that the 'housing
problem' had arisen from several causes, but particularly
important was the fact that much undeveloped land was
phased in the Master Plan for development after 1976 (it
being reserved for natural increase) with the remainder
of the land which could have been built on immediately
being either 'difficult or expensive or in private ownership'. (5)   The Corporation added that it had 'sought *rephasing* of some of the *reserved* land, but the resistance
to this course by public authorities has led to much delay
in getting Departmental approval'. (6, emphasis added)
The Corporation continued to state that Sector 9 (South)
and Sector 10 had been released in July 1972 and Sector 9
(North) in March 1974, and that together these would, it
was asserted, allow 1,800 dwellings to be built up to
1977, although together with other and smaller sites 'this
promises an annual output of only half that achieved in
1970-2 and less than half that are needed'.   Another cause
mentioned by the Corporation was that of cost-yardstick
difficulties, and finally it noted the 'collapse of the
private housing market because of high prices, rising
costs and prohibitive mortgage interest rates', which
meant that the land allocated for private enterprise
housing under the 50:50 policy had been developed slowly
or had remained unbuilt upon, although some had in fact
been recovered for public housing, 'though it has yet to
be processed or to recover the time lost by the switch'.
(7)   The Corporation illustrated the situation with a comparison of the period 1973-4 with 1970-1: (8)

	1970-1		1973-4		
	Total	Private	Council	SDC	Total
Starts	1355	41	nil	365	406
Completions	1176	119	25	68	212

The Corporation considered that the land released from the sectors by the Minister, together with the agreement that more of it would be used for rented housing, suggested that its efforts together with those of the Borough Council* would possibly make some strides towards the earlier levels of output, although the Corporation emphasised that 'restoration to that level is only possible *if a substantial expansion of Stevenage is permitted'*, indeed 'without it the Corporation does not envisage more than a 50 per cent achievement of its past records'. (9, emphasis added) Thus the Corporation had made a tentative move in the direction of a 'substantial expansion'.

To conclude the account of this particular section of the Annual Report, it can be noted that the Corporation pointed out that young couples were being forced out of the town and industrial growth was being frustrated, by virtue of the lack of housing: thus, although 'the recent land release has been vital, further acres are still needed'. The point was illustrated - comparatively - in terms of public authority housing allocations: (10)

	1970-1	1973-4
Council	68	63
Corporation	1641	498
	1709	561

On the sale of houses, the Corporation reported - not surprisingly in view of the state of the private market - that sales had almost come to a halt in 1973. In fact only 576 new requests for quotation of prices were received, and firm offers to purchase 'were actually exceeded by the number of prospective purchasers who withdrew'. (11) The Corporation further added that owner-

* Under the Local Government Act (1972), on 1 April 1974 SUDC became by charter a Borough Council.

occupation had reached a level of 35 per cent, as had been predicted in 1972.

No sites were allocated in 1973 for large industrial projects, asserted the Corporation, because of (i) the strong demand for labour from existing Stevenage industry; (ii) the acute shortage of rented housing; and (iii) the uncertainty as to the ultimate size of the town. (12) Point (i), of course, has to be disputed in the light of the industrialists' record of non-take-up of housing allocations.

There was one Board change during the year, that of Group Captain Bader, who

> found that he was unable to discharge this duty to his satisfaction because of other official appointments, notably with the Civil Aviation Authority. He resigned ... much to the Corporation's regret. (13)

It was in fact highly unlikely that the Corporation *did* regret his resignation in that he had missed ten out of fourteen Board meetings, and was therefore a little of an embarrassment.

The Chairman reported to the Board that she had seen Mr Silkin, and that accordingly the Board ought to expect the new terms of reference regarding the extension of the designated area shortly. (14) In fact the Corporation received the new terms on 11 April:

> the purpose of this letter is to ask the Development Corporation to consider and make proposals for an extension of the designated area sufficient to meet the current objectives and local needs of Stevenage for the foreseeable future - say the next 15 years. In assessing such needs the Corporation will no doubt wish to have in mind the desirability of ensuring that enough land is available to meet not only the housing requirements of the 'second generation', but also those of workers recruited - so far as possible from London - by existing employers (industrial, commercial, or public service) in Stevenage and by any new employers who may move into the town in accordance with Master Plan requirements. In addition to these main categories of people the Corporation will wish to have regard to the requirements of the other (usually smaller) categories of people, such as ex-regular servicemen and disadvantaged families, the old people from London. At this stage, the most important thing is to identify the amount of land which is likely to be needed, and how soon, irrespective of whether the houses are to be built, e.g., by the Corporation or the Borough Council, and of whether they will be to rent or for sale; but bearing in mind that the main immediate demand is for

rented houses. It will be for the Corporation, after
assessing needs, to come to a conclusion on how much
land is likely to be required for housing and ancillary
uses, such as roads ... but it seems probable that
something of the order of *1,000 acres or thereabouts*
might prove sufficient. It also seems probable that
this might be found within the area proposed by the
Corporation as an extension of the designated area, and
which was put forward only after planning studies and a
thorough public participation exercise. It may be thus
possible for your Corporation to formulate proposals
for a smaller expansion without any very elaborate
further study. Nor, if the proposals for a smaller
area fall within the area already proposed for expansion by the Corporation would there appear to be
the need for extensive public participation at this
stage. However, the Corporation will no doubt wish to
consult the local authorities directly concerned, and
to inform the public of what is proposed, before submitting proposals to the Secretary of State. (15, emphasis added)

This of course was a perfect frame of reference for the
Corporation - '1,000 acres or thereabouts' to meet foreseeable needs for 'say ... 15 years'. In fact the General
Manager of the Corporation, Jack Balchin, stated in interview that he 'more or less had dictated the letter *for* the
DOE'. (16) Whether or not, of course, this was mere
bravado on his part - (he was interviewed following his
announcement that he was to retire) - is difficult to
answer, but the point remained that the terms of reference
were quite perfect for the Corporation.

The Corporation set to work on the task immediately. The
Board, some two weeks following receipt of the Minister's
letter, decided that it was 'desirable to find the land
within the total area previously recommended to the
Minister under the major expansion proposals', and that
for a 'minor expansion it was most unlikely that development on the western side of the A1 (M) would be justified'. (17)

The protest organisations soon reacted to the Minister's
letter, with CAUSE, for example, stating that 'expansion
again raises its ugly head, this time with a different
angle - to house the children of Stevenage - what moral
blackmail'. (18) Hertfordshire County Council for its
part was angry both at not having been consulted by Mr
Silkin, and also with the suggestion in the letter from
the DOE that there would appear to be no need for public
participation in consideration of *this* proposed expansion.
Councillor Brian Hall of the SBC suggested that the ex-

pansion plan was simply a method of 'keeping the Corporation alive'. (19)

The Corporation meanwhile considered that speed was essential, as, according to its calculations, unless it was allowed to complete its plans quickly, there was a danger that all of the existing land would have been used up before any approved extension could be developed. Indeed the Chairman decided that - and informed the Board accordingly - if there was

> disagreement with the Borough Council over the basic issues of the extension proposed by the Minister then in order to save time this should be referred immediately to the DOE without the Corporation seeking by extended compromise discussion to seek a settlement. The County Council's objections should also be dealt with in a similar way. (20)

On 10 May the General Manager sent a letter to Mr Marlow at the DOE, stating that when he had been with the Borough Council's Chief Executive recently, 'he was surmising to me' that following Shirley Williams's visit to Mr Silkin, 'you would be sending the Corporation a new request to involve the Borough Council in the expansion exercise'. The letter continued, 'I would not want' you to send such a letter without full awareness of the 'extent to which the Corporation has been seeking to involve both the Borough Council and the Herts County Council'. Mr Balchin, the General Manager, added that he had been led to believe that the 'Council will be pressing the Corporation' to include Council officers in the planning team itself. However, 'to put their Officers in the planning team with them answerable not to the Consultant Planner nor to the Corporation' but rather to local authorities,

> one of whom has already voiced their strong opposition and the other yet to declare its hand would make a mockery of the whole exercise. *The Corporation could not agree to work on this basis*. (21, emphasis added)

In the event, no local authority officers joined the planning team, although whether in fact they requested to do so is not known.

Shirley Williams herself received a letter on 13 May from the Minister, in reply to a query she had previously made. In the letter Mr Silkin stressed that 'his hope is that all those concerned will work together to see that speedy action is taken to secure the building of more rented houses in Stevenage' for all those who needed them, and he further stressed that this did not simply mean the 'second generation', in that 'if houses are not provided for key workers, not only for industry and commerce, but also for teachers, hospital workers and so on, then it is

the *people* of Stevenage who will be the main sufferers'.
(22, emphasis added) Thus Mr Silkin was here once again
pressing the case for priority to key workers, and posing
a false dichotomy between certain groups of workers and
the 'people' for justification. (23)

Inside the Corporation there was mounting pressure aimed
at the securing of a good deal for the industrialists:
for example on 26 June the Chief Estate Officer sent a
memorandum to the General Manager stating that there was
evidence that the industrialists were looking outside
Stevenage for 'future growth'. He added that 'a few
months ago Kodak explored the possibility of obtaining a
site of some 20 acres from the Corporation, and it is now
known that the company have settled for a location in the
North whilst, in the meantime, they are seeking to convert
their factory interests at Stevenage into leases that
would be more readily disposable'; and similarly 'Marconi
Instruments have now reached the stage where their
existing premises are used to the maximum and they would
like to concentrate the two factories on a 10 acre site
taking their work force from 250 to 450 persons'. The
Estate Officer went on to say that 'failure to meet such
requirements may not necessarily entail the loss of the
company to the town, but it will certainly put their
Stevenage operations into a servient rather than a dominant category'. He concluded by suggesting that:

> Our inability to provide sites of such size is a major
> stumbling block, but the extent to which houses can be
> provided is just as critical, *and adequate housing
> allocations are vital to industrialists, even when
> they have no expansion schemes in hand*. (24, emphasis
> added)

Thus a situation had arisen where the Minister, the
industrialists and the Corporation were extremely aware
of the industrialists' needs, as perceived and described
by the industrialists, even though the industrialists'
past record had consisted of exaggerated claims which had
had the effect of rendering the notion of 'planning' in-
congruous, but nevertheless the planners, backed by the
Board, had 1,000 acres to play with.

In July there was a special meeting of the Board called
to discuss 'Expansion of Stevenage - Draft Report on
Current Objectives and Local Needs'. The General Manager,
always present at Board meetings as were other officers,
submitted some revised tables and relevant paragraphs of
the report stating that 'the need for this revision arose
partly from the request of the Joint Committee (SDC/SBC)
for further information about growth rates', and partly
because of 'modification in methods of forecasting which

the Consultant Planner considered should be brought before
the Corporation'. There followed a full discussion on the
new document submitted, and 'concern was expressed that
conclusions as to aggregate housing demand and residential
land-take should be *so different* from that in the earlier
draft'. (25, emphasis added) The General Manager replied,
not particularly fruitfully, that

the new figures were related to *new assumptions* which
... like the earlier ones were *provisional* being dependent on further study (26, emphasis added)

Meanwhile the Joint Committee, a formal arrangement with
the Borough Council and which met regularly, (27) was
running into difficulties. Mrs Denington, at the July
meeting of the Committee, referred to recent press reports
of Council meetings in which criticisms had been made,
unjustly in her opinion, of certain of the Corporation's
housing schemes 'with no advance warning to the Corporation which would have offered comments that could have
assisted the Council's deliberations'. She therefore
asked whether in future 'Corporation housing schemes could
be put on the private part of the Council agendas to avoid
the publicity the press tend to give of criticisms of
schemes by the Council', to which Councillor Fowler
replied, 'it was Council policy as part of the democratic
process to open meetings to the press and public but, unfortunately, the press usually only repeated one side of
any discussion'. (28) This is not necessarily to suggest
that relations between the Council and the Corporation
were particularly poor, in that where it mattered - prin-
cipally between the Chief Executive and the General
Manager - relations were not particularly adverse. As
the General Manager of the Corporation stated, the relationship obviously was one of inherent tension but, he
continued in his inimitable manner,

My personal relationship with the present Chief Executive is nothing but good, and I think he'd say the
same ... but I want to make a distinction between good
relations and a weak stance. In other words nobody
could ever call me - my wife does but she is privileged
- weak. Some would say I was provocative, but I don't
think that's right. I'm very clear headed about where
the Corporation ought to be. (29)

Another new town development corporation general manager,
Wyndham Thomas, makes a quite similar point when he states
that where councils for new town areas 'have appointed a
chief executive in place of a clerk, the general manager's
job becomes infinitely easier and, I would gather, the
whole enterprise benefits: decisions are taken more expe-
ditiously and their quality is better'. (30)

Shirley Williams, in late July, announced that expansion
would no longer be contemplated only when 'control leaves
the hands of the Corporation', while the same period saw
nearly all the protest groups demanding that the 'Corporation must go'. (31)

In August the Corporation published 'Stevenage '74:
Expansion for Local Needs: Volume 1, Preliminary Report
on Local Needs', together with an explanatory pamphlet
titled 'Stevenage '74'. The pamphlet stated that Volume 1
was a 'provisional report': it did not indicate the final
view of the Corporation on current objectives and local
needs as before it reached that particular position it
wanted to 'be informed of the views both of the public
authorities and the public generally'. Thus, the Corporation continued, it had chosen to publish the results to
date of its present studies and collect views on them,
while at the same time proceeding with the second stage
studies:

> In this way the Corporation will be armed with informa-
> tion about public opinion on this issue. It already
> possesses ... much information about the location of
> any expansion and the factors that need to be taken
> into account for selecting the expansion area. What
> is newly required is the public viewpoint about local
> needs and objectives. (32)

The pamphlet continued to state that 'forecasts over 15
years are difficult and to some extent *speculative*' (emphasis added), and that the Corporation saw the current
objectives as (i) to allow for growth of existing industry
to correspond with its potential and to ensure that employment opportunities exist for local residents; (ii) to
seek a diverse employment structure for the town; (iii)
to provide for essential housing needs and a variety of
housing for different needs; (iv) to diversify age,
occupational and social structure; (v) to continue to
make a contribution to London's housing needs; and
finally (vi) Stevenage must be set in its sub-regional
context. (33) This statement of aims seemed all too
familiar, and indeed excessively optimistic. In Volume 1,
a more detailed account of objectives and methods, it was
stated that as the assessment was to relate to a 15-year
period, 1991 was to be used as the 'terminal year of the
plan' period. Like the pamphlet it stated that much
information had already been gathered in 'Stevenage '73',
and moreover that the 1972 updating process in fact consisted of studies which

> covered a longer term and were in response to different
> orders of reference.... But they serve to emphasise
> that the new commission's shorter term forecast *must*

not lead to ignoring the requirements at the turn of
the century to which the earlier reports drew atten-
tion.   Some account should be taken of the longer term
implications. (34, emphasis added)

Could it not be reasonably asked, in this case, why
bother at all with the statement of a formal plan *period*?
Indeed the above statement does lend credence to the views
of other employees who took a more cynical view of the
Corporation, notably the Social Development Office which
stated that it was quite certain that 'the officers of the
Corporation saw this minor expansion merely as a holding
operation and that it was only a matter of time before
another major expansion took place'. (35)

Volume 1 continued with a discussion of the 'consultation' process of which there was to be both formal and
informal machinery. Because of the 1973 consultations
and the participation exercise, the Corporation considered
it sufficient to take the following steps only: (i) to
invite the public to comment on the Minister's request and
on the issues of which the Corporation should take in discharging its commission (which was done by displaying
advertisements in three local newspapers during May);
(ii) to publish Volume 1 in order that the public could
have full opportunity to comment on this aspect of the
study 'before the report and recommendations are finalised
for submission to the Minister towards the end of the
year'; and (iii) to publish the Corporation's final
report on the proposals with an 'intimation that the opportunity exists for representations to be made to the
Corporation or directly to the Minister before any Draft
Designation Order is made'. The Corporation concluded by
stating that the aforementioned opportunities were 'of
course in addition to the statutory rights of objection
once a Draft Designation Order is made'. (36)

The preliminary report presented high, low, and medium
growth options which were based on projections, and which
resulted in a variety of building programmes according to
which option was considered the most desirable. For
example: (37)

Average Annual Building Programme Required 1976-91

	1976-81	1981-86	1986-91	15-year average
High growth	1300	1200	1000	1600
Medium growth	1120	820	870	930
Low growth	870	690	590	720

Similarly the necessary land-take, and number of
dwellings to be built, would vary: (38)

Additional Residential Acreage Required by 1991			
	High	Medium	Low
Dwellings at 31.3.76	24,450	24,450	24,450
Additional dwellings to 1991	17,390	14,040	10,750
Total	41,840	38,490	35,200
Deduction of capacity of designated area	29,000	29,000	29,000
Net extra space in terms of:			
Dwellings	12,840	9,490	6,200
Acreage	1,070	790	520

Indeed, the Corporation quite rightly stated that the
extra housing land required could be 500, 800, or 1,100
acres, according to whether a low, medium or high employment growth rate was provided for. The question was, of
course, could the Corporation be in any sense accurate in
terms of its projected growth rates, given its historical
record?

Finally the Corporation discussed population growth, and
produced figures that *might be expected to correspond
with the forecasts* of occupied housing stock'. (39, emphasis added) The population estimates were based simply
on the 1971 birth rate together with the 'average' household size, and in fact produced twelve permutations, the
three most relevant being the estimated population size
in 1991 according to whether the high, medium or low
option was used: 116,500, 107,200 and 98,000 respectively. The Corporation went on to say that

it must not be assumed that the forecasts for 1991 were
the maximum the town would reach. It is estimated that
on the medium growth projection, if induced in-
migration ceased in 1991, the figure of 107,200 could
rise by natural growth to 117,000 in 2001 ... *and this
figure must be treated with caution due to the length
of the projection period*. (40, emphasis added)

The Corporation asserted that there was a need for a
'controlled expansion of modest dimensions', indeed that
this was not a case for maximising expansion possibilities
nor for minimising expansion: 'a middle course is the
proper goal for Stevenage and that is what is here pro-

posed'. (41) The volume concluded with the assertion that
the studies had up until that time been concerned solely
with objectives and needs, the achievement of which could
well be affected by shortage of building resources,
availability of land suitable for development, or traffic
or drainage problems: 'the Corporation is aware of such
difficulties and realities but has not allowed them to
dictate the outcome of the studies'. Finally the Corporation stated that the next step was to 'marshal the
information on the constraints mentioned', so as

>to establish any limits that would prevent these
>objectives being attained. In the light of this
>further study, the Corporation would then return to
>the present report and see to what extent it is feasi-
>ble to devise proposals that will meet these objectives
>and needs. To the extent that it may not be possible
>to achieve them, they will need to be reviewed again
>and priorities among them will have to be discussed and
>established. This is a task for a second report. (42)

The consultations following on from the newspaper advertisements of May amounted to a total of fifteen organisations and twelve individuals commenting in writing, including, of course, local authorities and statutory undertakers. The Corporation, reviewing the comments received,
stated that it could not accept the view that it should
delay in discharging its instructions from the Minister
until either the Hertfordshire County Structure Plan
studies were at a more advanced level, or until any
Stevenage expansion could be incorporated in the Structure
Plan submission to the Minister: 'but it welcomed the
County's invitation to join with the County Council and
the local planning authorities in Structure Plan studies
for North Hertfordshire'. (43) The Corporation therefore
proceeded to the next stage of its studies.

The second consultative period was in September, following the publication of Volume 1. In this case only
thirty-two written responses were received, only four
being from households. Once more the Corporation commented that it could not agree to any request to delay
processing, and thus 'continued to refine its preliminary
studies in the light of further research'. (44)

The SVA sent a letter to all the candidates fighting for
the Stevenage seat at the impending October General
Election, asking them the 'Stevenage election question'.
The letter began:

>we should like you to express your intentions on the
>following important local issue: (i) do you consider
>that after 27 years of constant interference from
>Ministers in London, that the time has now come for

Stevenage to again run its own affairs?, (ii) if you
consider that the time is still not right, when do you
think it will be?, (iii) what steps will you take to
assist local citizens in this matter? (45)
The SVA added that it accepted the point that to begin
with, long-term planning and autocratic control was necessary, and it commended the foresight and initiative used
in the 1950s to assist the unavoidable housing crisis in
post-war London. But times have changed, the SVA asserted, 'today London is littered with empty building
plots, empty buildings and even 30-year-old bomb sites',
and there is a 'shortage of labour for essential services
and no longer a need for a mass exodus'. Furthermore the
SVA challenged

anyone to find one important aspect of future local development which could not be undertaken by locally-
elected bodies which already exist ... [the] real problem is that the SDC cannot represent local interests as
it must be first 'all things to all Ministers', and the
Board is still appointed by the medieval process of the
Minister selecting who he wishes, when he wishes and
dismissing them when they fail to sing his song of the
moment, and to add injury to insult he does not even
pay those he appoints, we do. (46)

Indeed, the SVA concluded, when a Minister 'kindly grants
us a public inquiry, we have to raise money to fight
people who are fighting us with our money!'.
Prime Minister Harold Wilson at the same time was at
Welwyn Garden City, where he made an election 'pledge',
namely that new town housing assets would be handed over
to local authorities.
In October the local newspapers were full of anti-Corpo-
ration statements, for example the Trades Council stated
that it was 'fed up with the phoney participation', and
that 'it was about time the Development Corporation was
wound up and its duties handed over to the local council'.
(47) In the General Election, which Labour won, Shirley
Williams increased her percentage of the vote when re-
elected to the Stevenage seat, an indication of her ever-
developing personal following. On 31 October the Borough
Council issued a press release which included a statement
that 'this must be the expansion to end all expansions'
and that a decision 'must be made as soon as possible, so
that Stevenage is lifted from uncertainty and able to
become a more settled and normal town'. (48) A few days
later, after reflecting on the Council's statement (together with its attack on the proposals at a special
Council meeting of the same day), the Corporation's
Chairman retorted:

Corporation bashing has been held to be a popular sport
by the Council for many years. I believe it is thought
to be politically attractive to voters. The Corporation members and officers have broad backs but there
comes a time when enough is enough.
   ... [our] report was publicly stigmatised as a
'shambles'. It was said to be 'littered' with
'errors'. Now if, after further consideration, the
Borough Council had reason to question the figures in
the Report, would it not have been more in the spirit
of our association to have come back to us for further
consultation? ... that is what we mean by co-operation
and consultation. But now, we learn that the Borough
Council has produced a comprehensive report of its own.
Members of the Corporation have not seen it nor,
indeed, has the Corporation been consulted in its
preparation - even though our consultants have provided
helpful information to the Council's officers. Had we
acted in so churlish a fashion towards the Council
before publishing our report one could imagine the
outcry. Which prompts me to ask: does the word co-
operation have any meaning for the Council? Or is
their resentment of the Corporation too deep to allow
a proper and mature relationship between us? (49)
Indeed the Borough Council released a report titled
'Report on the Expansion of Stevenage for Local Needs and
other related matters', dated 31 October and released in
early November. The report commenced with the statement
that it

transpired that Bracknell and Harlow District Councils
were faced with fairly similar expansion studies for
local needs and, in their deliberations with these
authorities, the Borough Council came to the conclusion
that any agreed expansion should be linked with some
understanding about the future role and life of the
Development Corporation, and about the future of the
assets owned by them, especially the housing assets.
(50)

In terms of the Corporation's preliminary report, the main
difference between the Council and the Corporation, in the
Council's view, was in relation to the growth proposed for
industry. That is, the Council considered that the Corporation's approach made industrial growth a 'strategic
issue': indeed the approach, stated the Council, resulted
in 'an over-estimate of population'. (51) The Council
suggested that it was obvious that periodic feasibility
studies about expansion produced uncertainty, and furthermore that successive 'doses of approved expansion' had the
effect of prolonging the life of the Development Corpo-

ration, and, therefore, with 'the likely disappearance of
a target population the Borough Council is entitled to
have some understanding about the future life of the Corporation, and indeed an understanding that this present
exercise is the ultimate and final expansion of
Stevenage'. The Council continued to state that the
rapid build-up of a new town may well be a suitable task
for a development corporation, but a subsequent expansion
for local needs was essentially a task for a democratically elected local authority:

> In spite of this reasoning, the Borough Council accepts
> that the Stevenage Development Corporation has in
> existence a large organization which is currently
> engaged in the expansion studies, and that disbandment
> of the Corporation and transfer of their responsibili-
> ties cannot take place overnight. The Council also
> accepts that the Corporation has some financial and
> procedural advantages which could be helpful in the
> next two or three years if there is a firm decision to
> extend the designated area by about 1,000 acres. (52)

The report accordingly concluded that it was the
Council's view therefore that a decision on expansion
should be linked with an understanding that the Corporation be 'wound up at an agreed date within a period of
not more than five years and that during that time the
following steps should be implemented': (i) a new Master
Plan to cover the expansion should be prepared jointly by
the Corporation and the Council; (ii) the Council's share
of any agreed house building programme should be rapidly
increased whilst the Corporation's share should be corre-
spondingly decreased; (iii) the Corporation should accept
responsibility for any major roadworks or other capital
works that were scheduled for completion by them in the
planned expansion at last agreed, or which arose as Corporation responsibilities from any further expansion that
may be agreed; (iv) there should be a transfer of Corporation houses to the Council and some agreement reached
about the future of the industrial and commercial assets;
and (v) the balance of any remaining amenity funds in the
hands of the Corporation should be paid to the Council.
(53)

Thus the Council was not opposed to expansion, on the
contrary it appeared that it wanted to let the Corporation
continue but with the proviso that it got an increasing
slice of the action. The Council's position here must, of
course, be seen in its political and historical context,
viz., that it had not the expertise, confidence, and, most
important, the resources, to attempt to match any Corporation proposals to meet 'second generation needs' even if

it was allowed to do so. Thus the next best thing would
be for the Council to encourage the Corporation to do the
job for it, while increasingly getting in on the act in
order to learn how to handle large-scale projects.

December saw the awaited publication of Volume 2 of
'Stevenage '74', the Corporation's proposals for expansion. Mrs Denington, the Chairman, prefaced the volume
with the following words:

> The Corporation hopes that this last exercise on ex-
> pansion will be followed by positive action and not by
> yet another study. Over the past ten years it has
> undertaken six exercises of this sort. This inevitably
> creates a sense of uncertainty amongst the public, the
> county and district councillors as well as among the
> members and staff of the Corporation itself. All of us
> need some certainty about our goals in the next period
> ahead and I am hopeful that we can have a definitive
> decision by Government on this occasion. I am equally
> convinced that expansion on the lines now recommended
> by the Corporation is absolutely necessary if
> Stevenage's vitality and potentiality are to be given
> adequate expression, if the needs generated by these
> characteristics of the town are to be met, and if our
> town is to make its contribution to the economic rege-
> neration of our country. (54)

This was indeed a statement of intent.

The volume began with the announcement that following
'consultations', the Corporation had dropped both high and
low options, and had selected two employment options only,
for the purpose of its submissions to the Secretary of
State. The first, option Y, which corresponded generally
with the medium growth option in Volume 1, represented the
growth requirement if the town was to proceed to grow on
the basis which 'past trends indicate as probable'. The
second option, option Z, lay *somewhere* between the
medium and low growth options of Volume 1, and reflected
more pessimistic assumptions. (55, emphasis added) In
fact option Z assumed 'that the restrained growth of
1969-74 - a result coming from economic inertia and
planning limitations - will continue throughout the next
15 years'. The Corporation believed that

> Britain's prosperity depends on the activity and output
> of towns like Stevenage in the South East region and in
> no way apologises from adhering to option Y, but
> arising out of the officer talks between the Corpo-
> ration's officers and those of Government departments,
> it seems proper also to include option Z even though
> the Corporation considers it *less probable* in the event
> than option Y. (56, emphasis added)

Thus it was apparent that the Corporation had decided to argue for the larger option Y. (57)

On page 13 it was stated that the Corporation would not ignore London's needs, but that they would however be considered secondary to the town's needs. The Corporation stated that in its view it would not be practicable to confine employment growth and (therefore) housing demand to a rate which would be supported solely by local population: *'both its employment potential and its civic dynamism are too strong* and will still call for some inmigration and housing therefore'. (58, emphasis added) Clichés such as these were used throughout the volume to justify this or that view, and indeed were indicative of all the volumes both for the 1973 and 1974 proposals. The final *general* point that was made in the volume was that the Corporation agreed that some indication must be given of its anticipated 'life', and indeed that a point be fixed when it would be expected that the developmental services of the Corporation would no longer be required.

The new objectives, which had been arrived at following the consultations, were stated to be sevenfold: (i) to ensure that sufficient land was made available to accommodate housing and ancillary requirements for the second generations of the existing and further in-migrant populations; (ii) to provide land for housing special categories of need, e.g., displaced persons, homeless families, the elderly and the handicapped, and so on; (iii) to provide housing 'for employment needs *especially the importation of necessary key workers'*; (iv) to allow for a *'moderate* growth of existing industry' and the introduction of some new employment both for replacement and to cater for the long-term needs of the population coming available for work'; (v) *'to encourage diversification of employment opportunities'*; (vi) to ensure that the retail, cultural and leisure services for the community are met as well as other social requirements in relation to education, welfare and the public services; and (vii) to 'preserve the identity of Stevenage and adjacent towns and villages and respect the rural environment', although any expansion would take some land out of agricultural use. (59, emphasis added) Once again the old promises are repeated, specifically point (v), whilst point (iii) indicates the Corporation's priorities.

On the basis of these objectives, the assessment of local needs was undertaken in the next section of the volume, and indeed the Corporation began quite rationally:

> uncertainty inevitably attaches to such forecasts even when limited to 15 years and certainly to those going beyond that period. (60)

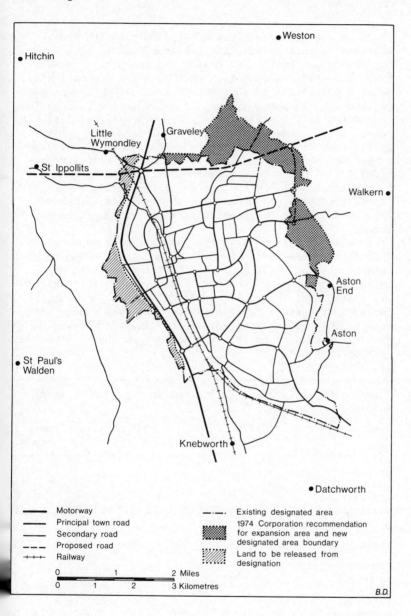

MAP 6   Recommended designated area - Option Z - 1974

This of course did not prevent the Corporation from
engaging in such forecasting, however, and in fact two
population projections were made for the period up until
1991, including in-migration to 1976: projection 1 estimated a population of some 94,100 in 1991, whilst projection 2 anticipated a total of 89,470. The Corporation
considered that 'until firmer trends in national birth
rates become evident it seems prudent to regard projection
2 as a more probable estimate over the short term'. However, the Corporation quite rightly stated that fluctuations in the birth rate would not affect the formation of
households nor indeed the growth of the resident working
population up to about the late 1980s: thus the housing
forecasts made in the particular study would not be affected.

The volume continued with the projection of household
formation in the period under consideration, using
'headship rates' (61) applied to information from population projection 2. The Corporation, again quite rightly, stated that the household formation estimates presented a situation irrespective of whichever future birth
rate assumption was adopted, as the children who would
create the second generation households up until 1991 had
already been born.

Existing Population (excluding net in-migrants to 1976) -
Household Formation to 1991 (62)

Increase	1971	1976	1981	1986	1991	Av.per annum
Second generation and married households		1,450	1,720	1,950	1,750	361
Other households		480	730	700	850	152
Total increase		1,930	2,450	2,650	2,600	513
Total households	20,070	22,000	24,450	27,100	29,700	

The Corporation concluded on this basis that an aggregate
annual requirement of about 500 for all new households,
married or 'other' seemed reasonable.

The Corporation then turned its attention to employment,
and began by stating first of all that it was 'apparent

that manufacturing firms in Hertfordshire have considerable growth *potential'*. (63, emphasis added) As always
the statement was concerned with the future, and indeed a
future seemingly unrelated to the past. However, the
Corporation saw the growth potential as related to the
favourable regional location of the area, together with
the fact that firms had a substantial proportion of their
work-force in non-production functions like administration, research and clerical work, and moreover that these
firms were therefore not quite so prone to reduction in
labour-need by automation. The Corporation added that
'this is evident in Stevenage where substantial numbers
of vacancies are reported by firms as expressing the
shortfall on desired establishments':

> If there has been recently a very limited growth in
> actual establishments, this has been partly due to the
> *short term effect of the 1971/72 severe recession and,*
> *in 'boom' periods, due to a locally acute labour defi-*
> *cit and the lack of housing.* (64, emphasis added)

In keeping with Corporation ideology, this statement was
excessively optimistic, and in relation to the assertion
that 'lack of housing' had contributed to less employment
growth, quite misleading.

'Projections of employment are invariably hazardous'
stated the Corporation, which then proceeded with its
projections. It was stated that projection Y involved the
projection of manufacturing and services of some national
significance, 'having regard to the formal estimates of
labour need *given in the Industrial Employers' Group*
survey of last July', (65, emphasis added) and that essentially the projection was equivalent to taking the
industrialists' forecasts and achieving them evenly over
the 15-year term instead of as in the Group's case, for
achieving the bulk of the growth by 1981. It can, of
course, be asked what equivalence could be achieved when
one estimate has a terminal date of 7 years whilst the
other has one of 15 years? Presumably there would be
other changes in the period between the 7- and 15-year
span on the one estimate? The Corporation concluded, however, that projection Y represented an attempt to bring
labour supply into balance with demand over 15 years, and
to slightly broaden the job base of the town. Projection
Z on the other hand was said to use much more modest
growth rates of manufacturing industries than that based
on SIEG's survey. It involved the continuation of 'the
small growth trend for recent years 1966-72 for manufacturing industries and assumes existing industrial
vacancies will be filled'. The projection allowed some
expansion of existing employments, but 'diversification

of employment would come only from the normal growth of
service industries':

> It has to assume - as projection Y does not - that
> further attraction of firms to the town *to diversify
> employment* is entirely excluded, that Stevenage in-
> dustries have already diversified their products suf-
> ficiently to avoid the consequences of over-special-
> ization, and that in the sub-region a sufficiently wide
> variety of manufacturing job choice exists. The Corpo-
> ration does not think this point has yet been reached
> or is in early prospect and fears that if economic
> history turns out as projection Z forecasts, some of
> the problems of the town's present employment structure
> due to lack of diversification will be with the town in
> 1991. (66, emphasis added)

This of course was sheer blackmail. To begin with the
arguments were based on the premise that when firms were
attracted to the town they diversified employment - that
that indeed was their function - and, moreover, the Corporation had talked about this very same point, lack of
diversification, for well over a decade and yet had done
little about it as was evident from the relations between
the ERV1 and ERV returns (this is discussed in detail in
chapter 11).

The Corporation proceeded to outline four alternative
'planning strategies', based on estimated land requirements under employment option Y, and added that strategy A
(out of A,B,C, and D) was preferred. In strategy A, under
option Y, the land demands would require 'an extension of
the built-up area up to but not engulfing the village of
Graveley, and would incorporate Aston End into a new development area'. Under option Z, the strategy would
require development to extend just beyond the northern
extremities of the present designated area, to the south
of Graveley, and would in fact exclude Aston End except
for the construction of a distributor road:

> All other aspects of strategy A are common to both
> options and the same designated area would be appro-
> priate to both options. The areas not to be developed
> would be shown as 'white land'. (67)

Strategy A in fact involved the need to provide approximately 9,500 additional - above the capacity of the
existing designated area estimated at 29,000 - dwellings
(under option Z, 7,500) by 1991 involving up to 1,000
gross acres of residential land 'of which approximately
300 acres could be made available within the present
designated area'. In overall terms, 'this means that with
the inclusion of fringe woodlands and the exclusion of
land available within the present designated area, the

additional land-take would be 1,000 acres'. More specifically the Corporation suggested that some 385 acres
within the existing designated area should be excluded
from it, namely 370 acres west of the A1 (M) together with
a little land around the village of Aston, and that in the
expansion sectors the new designated area would embrace
some 620 acres to the north and 460 acres to the east, and
thus the net land requirements would be in the order of
700 acres. (68)   Interestingly the Corporation went on to
say that if in the future

further expansion is contemplated, it is recommended
that further eastern and north-eastern expansion should
be wholly excluded from consideration. (69)

This of course could be interpreted, rather cynically, as
a long-term play at land, as before, west of the A1 (M).
The volume was concluded with the Corporation's recommendation that if a 'yes' was to be given to expansion,
the sooner a decision was made the better, in order that
the chances of achieving the necessary house-building
targets were improved. The Corporation continued to state
that if there was any risk of delay in consideration of
the Designation Order, 'a further *advance authority* to
build housing on Sectors 7 and 8 and also to start site
development on Sectors 4,5, and 6 will become imperative',
and without this 'not only will building activity dry up
but a *new* crisis over inadequate housing will arise'. (70,
emphasis added in both cases)   Thus the Corporation wanted
an early decision provided that the answer was 'yes' to
expansion: if there was a delay it wanted an early release of land in advance of phasing, and who knows what
it wanted if the answer was 'no'.

The Annual Report for the year began to show the increasing influence of the Deputy Chairman Harold Campbell,
who was intimately involved with the housing association
movement, when it was announced that three associations -
including, for example, the Guinness Trust - had been
given sites totalling nine acres. The Report also indicated yet another dismal year for house sales, with their
being limited to a total of forty-one for the year (these
were sitting tenants to whom the Corporation had a commitment to sell at the time the DOE withdrew its general
authority to corporations in this matter). Stoically the
Corporation suggested that there

is still a demand for purchase despite high mortgage
interest rates and the Corporation hopes that you will
soon be ready to allow the resumption of some house
sales ...,

yet it continued:

We regret to have to record that high mortgage interest

> rates and domestic circumstances have led to requests
> for the Corporation to repurchase properties with
> reversion to tenancy and a total of 46 dwellings have
> been repurchased. (71)

The Corporation simply did not seem to relate these two
statements to one another. It was further stated by the
Corporation that owner-occupation had risen to 35 per cent
of the total housing stock, and, still on housing matters,
that there were to be rent increases in April 1975
averaging 50p per week.

The year saw the cumulative surplus on General Revenue
Account rise from £3 to £6 million, and the ERV1 and ERV
returns demonstrated that there were 449 unfilled vacancies together with 412 unemployed persons. Housing
Management figures demonstrated the important point that
the industrialists had not taken up 91 of their allocation
of 326 houses, and showed a JHL of 1,360 with a waiting
time of

> less than two and a half years, due to the tardiness
> with which employers appear to be taking up nomina-
> tions. (72)

9 Stevenage 1974-6
The public inquiry

> The power position of all officials rests ... on
> *knowledge*, which is of two kinds: first, specialised
> knowledge gained through specialised training, which
> can be called 'technical' in the widest sense ...
> secondly, official knowledge, that is concrete infor-
> mation relevant to his performance, which is available
> only to the official through means of the administra-
> tive apparatus.
>
> Max Weber (1958), p.340

PART 1

Tom McCombie was, by late 1974, back in CASE's fold. When
he read Volume 2 of the Corporation's proposals, he realised that the new campaign against the Corporation would
have to be waged in an entirely different manner from the
earlier one. As he himself put it:

> The earlier one was an emotive drum-banging organisa-
> tion, this one we had really got to do our thinking
> about.... Sooner or later the crunch would come and
> we would have to prepare a case based on facts. (1)

The next *formal* stage in the consultation and participation process was that the Corporation published at the
same time as Volume 2 in December, a 10-page summary of
the report together with a descriptive leaflet and comment
form,* and 25,000 copies of the leaflet were distributed -
courtesy of the Boy Scout movement - in and around
Stevenage.

The Corporation stated that it would welcome *any* comments, but that particularly welcome were comments as to
the size of the expanded area, and the direction of ex-

---

* Reproduced in appendix 7.

pansion. The Corporation requested that comments were
returned by 28 February (as in 1973, the return postage
was pre-paid). In all, 340 comment forms were returned
to the Corporation, six letters without comment forms were
also received from individuals, and ten letters were re-
directed by the DOE. (2) Additionally, twenty-three
letters were received from various associations, societies, and interest groups.

The Corporation's analysis demonstrated that the majority
of comments entered 'a plea for no expansion', although a
few welcomed expansion 'particularly in relation to
housing and employment'. (3) On the subject of public
participation, most respondents who mentioned the topic,
according to the Corporation, believed 'that the public's
comment is not really taken into account, that the Corporation will do as they please, and that the decision has
probably been made already about expansion'! (4)

The following eleven responses - not a representative
sample - indicate the feeling aroused at the time:

More houses mean more work - carry on.

All I ask is for a house, for when I get married in
September 1976, please. I am all for the Stevenage
expansion in any way as a lot of young people like
myself require homes for when we marry and it will
bring more jobs into the area.

I agree with expansion because it means PROGRESS and
progress means good living for everyone. Good luck in
your attempts.

It is time the Corporation cleared out.

The bigger the better! I am sure this is the view of
the 'silent' majority. Don't listen to the smug
middle-classes living on their farms and profiting
from the rising value of land.

The town as it stands at the present time does not cope
with the wants and wishes of the population at present
resident in the town. It would seem logical to firstly
provide the amenities required for the town as it now
stands, the shopping facilities at present available
are inadequate, the selection atrocious, and the
quality poor. I think to any honest person living in
the town at present, expansion is as welcome as a pain
in the ASS.

I think something is wrong when people can be housed in

2-3 months when nominated by a local firm (they do not necessarily come from London) when a child of a tenant must wait up to 3 years, although he has lived in Stevenage 20 years and worked in local industry all his working life.

The whole thing is plain bloody mad. In all conscience Stevenage is plenty big enough. In any case in another 20 years it will be just one big slum. You get this 700 acres then how long will it be before you want to eat more of the countryside, you are like a huge mouth shovelling land in, never satisfied and who gets the rake off, certainly not we of the villages. All we get is your hooligans playing hell around.

Please! Stop inviting interference from amateurs and let the professionals get on with their job.

This form seems completely irrelevant. It seems that whatever the public views on expansion, you as the Corporation will put the plan *you want* into operation and ignore hundreds of people who are, like myself, against the town expanding.

No expansion whatsoever! Stevenage is already an over-populated area, the new town resembling nothing more than a human rabbit warren. The present planning is friendless, faceless and has no character or thought for those living in the homes other than to separate the people from the road traffic. For many, Stevenage is a place where they exist, rather than live. (5)

The SVA was meeting again more regularly, but as usual the attendance was at a minimum: for example the three meetings in February produced a total turn-out of ten. CASE, on the other hand, was enjoying well attended council meetings together with a 100 per cent executive turn-out. At its council meeting on 13 March, CASE con-sidered two strategies in relation to the new proposals, viz. that it should either follow 'alternative C' in the Hertfordshire County Council's Structure Plan, which stated that there should be no expansion beyond the present designated area and with the second generation being housed elsewhere in North Hertfordshire, or compro-mise by liaising with the Borough Council who were pre-pared to listen to suggestions. The meeting unanimously agreed that 'CASE should oppose all expansion outside the designated area, no compromise'. (6) It was therefore agreed that CASE members should do everything possible to encourage the Structure Plan, by answering the question-

naire, voting for 'alternative C' and so on, and furthermore that members should make approaches to MPs during the
forthcoming 'New Towns debate'. The Chairman of the
meeting, Bowes-Lyon, informed members that he considered a
public inquiry 'extremely likely', and that accordingly
the Hertfordshire Society had already retained Junior
Counsel. He concluded the meeting by stating that CASE's
finances were virtually as they were at the Annual General
Meeting, namely £1,200 lodged with the Herefordshire
County Council at 12 per cent. (7)

 As things turned out, a new element was suddenly introduced into the whole proceedings. The DOE requested the
Corporation to produce new boundary proposals for a
revised designated area which confined the expansion area
strictly to the Z option, to provide for the possibility
that the Secretary of State might prefer that lower
option. Thus on 9 April the Corporation submitted to the
Minister a new estimate and plan of land requirements on
a Z option basis. This in fact corresponded broadly to
the December 1974 proposals but required less land, and
thus adjusted and contracted the earlier boundaries somewhat. In essence the new net land requirement outside the
designated area became 865 acres whilst still excluding
the 385 acres from the existing designated area (i.e.,
land west of the A1 (M) and land adjoining the village of
Aston). Thus the net extra land sought in the revised
option Z expansion scheme became 480 acres instead of the
700 previously proposed. On 9 April the new letter was
sent to the DOE and included the following remarks: 'It
will be recalled' that the Corporation

> expressed a preference for option Y as more likely to
> fulfil the needs of so dynamic a town as Stevenage.
> However it has looked at the matter again in the light
> of further discussions with the County Council, the
> Borough Council and your officers. In view of the
> progress made with the County Structure Plan *and the
> facility under that plan, or its subsequent review, to
> cater for Y if initially provision were made for Z, the
> Corporation would be content to see the smaller pro-
> vision being made now.* (8, emphasis added)

 It was now plain that the Corporation had been told to
forget its option Y, and was therefore both trying to make
the best of it, and attempting to ensure that it would get
it in the long term anyway. With the new recommended
boundary the Corporation felt entitled to ask the Minister
to proceed with the publication of a 'Draft Designation
Order as a matter of urgency'. (9) The urgency, according
to the Corporation, had arisen because until a final decision was made and any revised Designation Order opera-

tive, house-building would fall steeply, with the Corporation foreseeing a housing crisis similar to that which
was experienced in 1973-4. In particular the Corporation
was referring to the fact that permission had been granted
by the Ministry for the Corporation to commence site works
in Sectors 7 and 8: however house-building could not
commence until the proposals for expansion had been determined. Furthermore, the Corporation stated that the
preparation of an area plan for Sectors 4 and 5 - the
final area of housing land existing in Stevenage under
the approved 1966 Master Plan - had commenced, and that
it was

> essential that the detailed planning of this area be
> pursued so that approval may be obtained to allow
> infrastructure schemes to be put in hand in time to
> prevent any hiatus between housing completion in
> Sectors 7 and 8 and production in Sectors 4 and 5. The
> northern half of Sector 5 is affected by expansion pro-
> posals, particularly in regard to the routing of the
> proposed north-south main distributor road. Your de-
> cision on expansion will, therefore, vitally affect
> this sector of development. (10)

The Borough Council's position was clarified somewhat in
June 1975, when in its magazine it stated that 'the whole
subject of future expansion had been raised on many oc-
casions in the past ten years, and the Borough Council,
despite reservations, have always been aware that an expansion of approximately 1,000 acres is necessary to meet
local requirements'. (11) So it was now clear that provided some kind of arrangement could be made regarding
future ownership of assets and a terminal date for the
Corporation's life, the Borough Council would be giving
the Corporation's proposals a thumbs up.

In October the General Manager addressed himself to the
Board on the topic of current housing allocations. He
stated that as a result of 'the downturn in the economy',
demands from employers had been lower than provided for.
He went on to say that taking the date of 1 October, for
example, a total of 387 nominees had been expected to
register from 1 April, but in fact only 216 applications
had been received. Furthermore none of the town's major
employers had recently requested any addition to their
original allocation, and therefore a general redistribution among employers of the housing allocations had not
been suggested. He concluded:

> There would seem little alternative but to allocate
> houses and flats available in excess of employers'
> requirements to the general waiting list of Joint
> Housing and Parents of Tenants applicants. It has

> been necessary therefore to *once again* use the Joint
> Housing and Parents of Tenant lists as a regulator to
> prevent houses standing empty for long periods. (12,
> emphasis added)

Or to put it another way, the Corporation had once again
been unable to formulate a *consistent policy* towards its
second generation's needs, because of the uneven demands
of the town's employers.

The General Manager's report of the following month made
it clear however that the industrialists would be able to
continue with their behaviour for as long as the Corporation was in existence. His report was concerned with a
draft paper from the DOE (which eventually became Circulars 445 and 460) which made proposals for changes in the
rules governing the allocation of tenancies in London New
Towns, and accordingly the Corporation was asked for its
observations. The General Manager commenced by saying
that the DOE had played down the extent to which employers' nominees were given priority, and indeed that
the Corporation questioned the Ministry's assumption that
employers did *not* have a permanent pre-emptive right to
tenancies for replacement workers. The General Manager's
argument was that what was necessary to maintain viable
the manpower situation of the employers turned on a number
of factors relating to the housing constitution in the
town and its relationship to other areas of employment, or
to London itself; and in Stevenage a substantial proportion of jobs were of a highly skilled nature, but the
tenure distribution of the town was such that it meant
that virtually all rented housing was in the monopoly
ownership of either the Corporation or the Borough
Council. Thus, the General Manager continued, there were
no other rented houses available for newcomers, and if,

> when skilled craftsmen are lost to a firm, it cannot
> find them within the town's own labour force it is im-
> perative, if the process is not to be affected *and the*
> *less skilled are not to be jeopardized,* that the Corpo-
> ration ... should be able to provide essential housing
> for such key staff. (13, emphasis added)

Thus the Corporation's message was the same as before -
key workers were to receive priority, even though such a
policy resulted in a haphazard overall housing allocation
process - but the justification was new. Why would the
less skilled be jeopardised if key workers were not given
priority?

The Annual Report for the year of 1975 stated that in
pursuit of its policy of encouraging owner-occupation, the
Corporation had set aside land for private development,
and furthermore that, in accordance with the Minister's

direction, there had been no sales of Corporation houses.
However, the report continued, the recent rent increases
of 60p a week scheduled for 1 April 1976 had led to
further enquiries from tenants as to whether they could
purchase their property, and thus the Corporation hoped
that it would not be too long before some resumption of
house sales to sitting tenants would be allowed. The
Corporation concluded, *as if this were unrelated,* that
nineteen properties were repurchased in the year! (14)
The Corporation also stated that it was continuing its
policy of encouraging housing by housing associations,
(15) and that - albeit an unrelated point - there were
113 unfilled vacancies in the town at the time, although
the ERV1 returns (not used by the Corporation) in contrast
showed a figure of 379!
On 22 December notice was given that the Secretary of
State for the Environment,

> in exercise of his powers under Sections 1 and 53 of
> the New Towns Act 1965 and of all other powers enabling
> him in that behalf, has prepared and is about to con-
> sider the draft of an order which in part varies and in
> part revokes the Stevenage New Town (Designation) Order
> 1946 as already varied by the Stevenage New Town
> (Designation) Amendment Order 1965 by:
> (i) adding areas of land totalling approximately 865
>   acres (350 hectares) on the north and north-eastern
>   boundaries of the designated area, lying within the
>   districts of North Hertfordshire and East Hertford-
>   shire in the administrative county of Hertfordshire,
>   and
> (ii) deleting areas of land totalling approximately 362
>   acres (1471 hectares) in the west of the existing de-
>   signated area and approximately 15.5 acres (6 hec-
>   tares) in the east of the existing designated area all
>   lying within the borough of Stevenage. (16)

The DOE statement also added, statutorily, that should
there be any objections, the Secretary of State proposed
to hold a public local inquiry on 30 March 1976 into any
objection duly made and not withdrawn.
Reaction was swift. A memorandum was sent to all CASE
council members on 4 January, stating bitterly that the
original threat of the large expansion, although now in
abeyance, could in fact be realised by 'piecemeal attacks
on us in the manner now before us', and furthermore that
this present proposal, if effected, would 'enable the SDC
to remain in existence for a further unspecified period'.
(17)
A few days later, in the rather different environment of
the Corporation boardroom, the General Manager produced

his report on the programme for Sectors 4 and 5, and with
it statements which seemed to indicate a fait accompli.
He stated that the Board knew that one of the understand-
ings reached between Dame Evelyn Denington* and Mr Silkin
was that the Corporation should get on with its Master
Plan studies in parallel with Designation Order processes
'so that if and when that Order is confirmed there will be
no time lost in submitting the Master Plan'! (18)   The
General Manager went on to say that the urgency of the
work was due to the fact that a Master Plan for the expanded area was found to impinge on those areas within the
existing Designated Area including Sectors 4 and 5, and
that if the Corporation was to prevent a major hiatus in
housing production, it must push on with the Area plan and
Section 6(1) proposals for areas 4 and 5. So the Corporation was thus engaged in four operations in parallel:
preparation for the public inquiry; preparation of the
Master Plan; preparation of the Sectors 4 and 5 Area
Plan; and preparation of the Section 6(1) schemes for the
two areas. The General Manager then went on to discuss
the programme for Sectors 4 and 5, and included a proposition congruent with his attitude towards public participation:

> *We must establish* groups of interested public to look
> at the proposals in more detail. (19, emphasis added)

Once again the Corporation itself wanted to determine who
should participate, let alone how they should participate.
The General Manager concluded by suggesting that his programme was the very best possible, and that delays associated with the Designation Order or the Master Plan, as
well as delays in the submission of the Area Plan or
Section 6(1) applications, could jeopardise it. He continued:

> So could opposition by local authorities, public indi-
> viduals or voluntary organizations. The fact that the
> Secretary of State confirmed the compulsory purchase
> order for land still to be acquired in these sectors is
> helpful in that subsequent arguments cannot be about
> residential development as such but only about the form
> of development. And finally, any results must turn on
> whether the Secretary of State confirms the Designation
> Order. *The trouble is we cannot wait to see if he does
> before getting on with this task.* (20, emphasis added)

January also saw Shirley Williams and Councillor Brian
Hall state that 'the proposals were just what we wanted',
(21) indeed Shirley Williams a little later stated that
she was 'frankly frightened' about what might happen 'if

---

* DBE conferred in 1974.

there was a successful objection to this *last* expansion',
and that it would 'throw the whole thing back into uncertainty and we might find ourselves once again faced
with proposals for a very much larger expansion in a year
or two's time'. (22, emphasis added) This of course is a
far different posture from the one she adopted at the time
of the earlier expansion, when she had lauded public protest, and does lend credence to CASE's attack on her - and
on the Borough Council - which amounted to an assertion
that the Borough Council and Mrs Williams were not wholeheartedly against even the major expansion: they were
merely playing a political game - that is, a Conservative
Government was in power and the expansion was for increased owner-occupation. (23)

 CASE met again on 23 January and Simon Bowes-Lyon
informed the meeting (of the council) that the Hertfordshire Society had reserved Lord Colville (a personal
friend of Bowes-Lyon's) (24) who had represented groups
before, for example in the 1964 Inquiry. It was unanimously agreed at the meeting that CASE should take action
at the forthcoming Inquiry, and that a letter should be
sent to the Secretary of State listing CASE's objections.
A dispute occurred at the meeting in regard to the relations between CASE and the Hertfordshire Society in
terms of legal representation. Mr McMurtrie, CASE's fund
raiser, suggested that it had always been intended that
the Hertfordshire Society would reserve Counsel, whilst
the organisation of the campaign would be CASE's responsibility. Others, however, disagreed. In the end the
meeting agreed that a working party be formed within CASE
to liaise with the Hertfordshire Society, that the working
party should discuss with Lord Colville the general situation, and if subsequently it was felt that CASE could not
accept the brief presented to Lord Colville then an
emergency Council meeting would be called to appraise the
situation. It was further agreed at the meeting that
'expert' witnesses must be called in farming, planning,
industry, airport expansion and so on. The meeting then
turned to CASE's constitution, and in accordance with rule
14 of this document (which related to alterations to the
Constitution), made one amendment, to Clause 2a:

     Delete: 'To oppose any expansion of Stevenage New Town
     beyond the Designated Area at the date of adoption of
     this Constitution'.
     Substitute: 'To oppose the extension of the Designated
     Area of Stevenage New Town'. (25)

The meeting concluded - following a lengthy discussion,
in retrospect, wondering whether or not the change in the
Constitution *really* meant anything! - with Bowes-Lyon
noting that:

Lord Colville's fee would be £1,OOO for three days,
plus solicitor's costs and expert witnesses.   There
seemed to be no financial difficulties therefore. (26)
With the announcement of the Inquiry the SVA also began
to move itself.   The Treasurer stated that Mr Cuthill, the
Chairman, brought around at 2.OO am the SVA's letter of
objection - 'together with his nasty dog' - which had to
be in to the DOE later the same day.   The SVA really got
involved, recalled the Treasurer,

> later on when the Minister wrote back, parried a
> fulsome reply, pointing out how foolish Cuthill was in
> two or three cases where he had been very foolish in
> the letter, we got involved then because we had to do
> something about resurrecting the credibility both of
> the organisation as well as, if we were going to
> object, objecting in a way which was going to make the
> work worthwhile. (27)

The SVA was informed by CASE that it could use CASE's
solicitor at any time and at CASE's expense, if the result
would be to strengthen the overall objection.   CASE's next
meeting, on 20 February, again discussed the issue of
legal representation.   The Treasurer of CASE queried the
sufficiency of funds in hand, and enquired what amount
would be contributed by the Hertfordshire Society.   This
apparently had not yet been decided, but Mr Bowes-Lyon
thought that if extra money was required over that in
hand, then CASE would be the best organisation to raise
it, rather than the Hertfordshire Society.   The Public
Relations Officer disagreed, and suggested that it was
more difficult for CASE to raise funds than the Hertfordshire Society, and particularly so after the Inquiry was
over.   A resolution was proposed which stated that 'this
Council resolves to make its funds available to the
Hertfordshire Society in due payment of any expenses
raised at the forthcoming Inquiry';   the Hertfordshire
Society would then be left to underwrite the balance, if
any.   This was generally agreed upon, but a further discussion took place, however, when Mr Powell-Davies, from
Wymondley Parish Council, stated that this was clearly a
joint venture, and in any event the Hertfordshire Society
would have obtained representation and thus would have
become liable for a certain charge, therefore the
Hertfordshire Society ought to make a contribution towards
fees.   Mr McMurtrie for his part had understood that the
Hertfordshire Society had instructed Counsel on CASE's
behalf, but this was denied by Mr Bowes-Lyon who stated
that Counsel had been retained by the Hertfordshire
Society with the possibility of CASE joining in.   The
meeting, following a heated discussion, agreed that the

working party must investigate the situation in consultation with the solicitors, and the amended proposal by Mr
McMurtrie to which all agreed read that, 'this Council
resolves to make available to the Hertfordshire Society
its funds as at this date'. (28)

Mr Bowes-Lyon proposed at this point a new joint working
party, with four people from CASE and two from the
Hertfordshire Society, and that every assistance should
be given to the party which would in fact have powers of
co-option for necessary witnesses, etc., and would work
with the solicitors. The meeting unanimously agreed, Dr
Warner-Smith of Graveley Village then asked Councillor
Johnson (a Borough Councillor on the Council's Planning
Committee, and an executive member of CASE) where he
stood, as he believed it was important that CASE put its
views strongly. Councillor Johnson replied that the
amendment to the Constitution made it easier for him to
stay with CASE (indeed it seemed as if the amendment was
of use to him solely) and he would not be in any difficulty with the Council. He went on to say that the
Borough Council did not agree with the Corporation on all
points, particularly about absorption of areas outside the
designated area. Councillor Johnson stated that the
Borough Council had objected to the DOE, although it had
decided - just the previous evening - not to employ
Counsel at the Inquiry, and thus would not be represented.
Councillor Johnson was then questioned more directly as to
the possible divergence of interests, to which he replied
that there might indeed be a slight divergence in that the
Borough Council had an interest of its own, but he would
however find no difficulty in serving on the working party
because the majority of points CASE would make, would be
the ones where the Borough Council was opposed to the
Corporation. (29)

A further resolution was passed by the CASE council which
stated that the 'members of the working party shall have
executive powers to dispose of the funds of CASE up to the
current balance of today'. However, it further agreed
that any decisions to spend money should not be taken by
the working party without all four CASE members being in
agreement. The financial position was given by the
Treasurer, who stated that the deposit account stood at
£537, that there was £1,200 with Herefordshire County
Council which could be recalled at any time, and that
there was a small working sum in the current account. Mr
McMurtrie then raised the question of 'insurance risk',
namely the possible injury or illness of the Inspector or
Counsel which might either lengthen or postpone the
Inquiry, with the possibility of extra costs being in-

curred. It was agreed that the working party look into
the matter. The meeting came to an end with a member of
CASE stating that he knew of an 'expert' witness on
planning matters who could be available at the normal
planning consultants' fee of £70 per day! The meeting
decided to decline the offer.

Volume 4 of 'Stevenage Expansion '74' was published on
4 March, just twenty-six days before the Inquiry was due
to start, and this was the volume which actually contained
the planning proposals around and upon which the Corporation had woven its tissue of planning criteria. The
Hertfordshire Society noted that the

> Corporation with their large staff took fifteen months
> to prepare this report, but gives the public somewhat
> less than one month to acquaint themselves with its
> contents and to formulate opinions. (30)

It could well be argued that such an action is against
natural justice. For example, as far back as 1932, it was
stated in the 'Committee on Ministers' Powers Report' presented to the Lord High Chancellor, that:

> *No party ought to be condemned unheard; and if his
> right to be heard is to be a reality, he must know in
> good time the case which he has to meet.* (31)

Volume 4 began with a foreword by the Consultant Planner,
who asserted that 'whatever decision' was made eventually
about expansion, a revised Master Plan would be required
to lay down guide lines for development over the next
fifteen years, and the information contained in Volume 4
would therefore provide a good base for a new plan. He
concluded by stating that 'some of its contents *will need
updating* and a greater emphasis will be placed on policies
for implementation'. (32, emphasis added) It can be noted
here that the planners had ensured a considerable amount
of planning work for the future regardless of the expansion decision, and furthermore it could well be asked
why the information in Volume 4 should need updating in
such a short time? Suffice it here to say that Volume 4
was certainly no clearer or, indeed, less ambiguous than
the other volumes. For example in relation to the discussion on the occupational structure of the town, it is
stated that information about occupational structure can
only be derived

> from the Stevenage Industrial Employers Group whose
> membership includes *most* of the manufacturing firms
> in the town. This provides a *fairly* representative
> source of information for this sector of employment.
> (33, emphasis added)

At the next CASE meeting on 11 March it was reported that
Mr McCombie was busily engaged with Mr Summers (of the

Aston Village Society and the Hertfordshire County
Council's Planning Department) in preparing technical
evidence for the Inquiry. Mr McCombie was not finding
this task an easy one:

> I went with some others to Lord Colville's chambers,
> taking the best part of a day off from my work to
> discuss ways and means. The Hertfordshire Society were
> taking a purely simple line, and he more or less said
> at that meeting that if CASE was merely going to say
> that everybody connected with expansion were a load of
> bastards and that was the end of it, we could do it but
> he couldn't represent us. I took the message, which
> I had already anticipated, that he would only represent
> us if we produced a reasoned argument against ex-
> pansion, which wasn't easy, as I had no information
> available except that produced by the Development
> Corporation. (34)

Mr McCombie was being aided by Mr Summers, who with his
more appropriate knowledge analysed the Corporation's
volumes from the planning point of view, and gave him a
'valuable line to attack the SDC and I attacked them from
a slightly different point of view' namely 'criticising
every element of the Corporation's arithmetic and figures,
which I am perhaps well fitted to do'. (35) He was
spending every evening after returning from work reading
through 'every aspect of the documents', and then he had
to show Lord Colville his rough draft in order to have it
approved by him, and then have it typed. (36)

At the CASE meeting on 11 March Councillor Johnson
pointed out that there had now arisen within the Borough
Council some conflict as to his position in CASE, and for
him to remain might prove embarrassing to the organisation. He offered to assist, however, in any way that he
could.

The working party reported that it had been agreed with
the solicitors that Lord Colville would be instructed on
behalf of the Hertfordshire Society, supported by CASE,
with the Hertfordshire Society as the client calling
witnesses from various areas.

It was reported at the meeting that the 'Letchworth
Naturalists' Society' was to make a representation at the
Inquiry, and the CASE council accordingly hoped that it
would put a much needed 'emotive appeal to the Inquiry'.
Mr Ian Stewart, MP for Hitchin, had also been contacted
by CASE and had informed them that he had it in mind to
apply for an Adjournment Debate in the House after the
Inquiry. The Treasurer announced that the Hertfordshire
Society were sending out 300 appeal letters for funds to
be paid direct to the solicitors who had opened an ac-

count. He had personally been approached by two Parish
Councils with offers of donations, and he had suggested
to them promissory letters rather than cash at the present
time, thus avoiding the possibility of refunding.

The Aston branch of CASE was running a petition from
residents of Stevenage, not of Aston, and the meeting
agreed that this was significant and asked therefore that
the petition be presented to Lord Colville for him to
decide how best it should be used. Finally the meeting
closed with members being asked to encourage people to
attend the Inquiry even if just for a short period, and
it was suggested that an attendance register be taken at
the Inquiry and handed in to the Inspector at the end of
the proceedings. The Aston Village Society agreed to
organise it. A week before the Inquiry Mr Silkin, whilst
moving the second reading of the New Towns (Amendment)
Bill, pledged an end to the 'divided towns'.

PART 2

The Inquiry was held in Stevenage's most recently-built
hotel (1973), the 'Grampian', which is awkwardly situated
in a far corner of the town's - equally awkwardly situated
- main shopping centre. There were no signs placed
outside the hotel directing people to the Inquiry, and it
was not until the first floor was reached (and the Cale-
donian suite) that it was apparent that *anything* was
taking place. It was held in a large hall, enclosed by
numerous blow-ups of the plan and the affected areas, with
the Inspector's desk at one end, the public at the other,
and in between an enormous amount of space reserved for
the advocates, officials, consultants, together with the
necessary entourage. (37)

At the opening at 10 am the public numbered twenty-four
(although a local newspaper claimed an exaggerated
hundred), massively outnumbered by the 'middle men', and
as the day proceeded the members of the public dwindled in
number until at the close at 4 pm they numbered five.

On the opening day the proceedings were marred by the
loud noise of extractor fans, building work which was
being carried on outside, a microphone which did not work
until 2.45 pm (a recurring problem), and a telephone which
rang in an adjacent room at regular hourly intervals, and
which was regularly unanswered for 20-minute intervals!
The Inspector, Hugh Gardner, Under Secretary at the MAFF
from 1953 to 1970 and now retired, stated that on two days
per week the proceedings would have to terminate early, as
there would be bingo - which needed setting up - in the
hall on those evenings.

Apart from the representatives from the DOE, together
with the Corporation officers and consultants, the pro-
expansion benches consisted of representatives from the
Borough Council and SIEG. Protestors numbered representatives of the Hertfordshire County Council, two
District Councils, four Parish Councils, the NFU, the
Hertfordshire Society, CASE, CAUSE, SVA, and a few individuals. (38) The Inspector, on the opening day, also
read out letters from protestors, most of whom were concerned with the effect the proposals might have on 'Rooks
Nest', the childhood home of E.M.Forster. Mr Gardner said
little throughout the Inquiry: on opening the proceedings
he stated that 200 objections to the proposals had been
received, and hence he expected the Inquiry to be a
lengthy process. He quite rightly stated that the Inquiry
was - theoretically - an 'administrative process and not a
judicial process' (39) and went on to say that he was a
'totally independent man', indeed a 'retired man with no
axe to grind'. Furthermore he had come to the Inquiry
'with an entirely open mind', that he had 'read all the
documents' and that his job was to 'report the evidence'.
He concluded that the Inquiry was a 'genuine opportunity
for the public to participate in decision making'. (40)
Of course in one sense he *was* an independent man, but in
another extremely important sense he could not be so - in
the sense of socialisation - (41) because of his expectations and values learned and reinforced as a civil servant
for over seventeen years.

The first document read out at the Inquiry was the DOE
statement made on behalf of the Secretary of State, the
purpose of which was to offer comment generally upon
written objections. (42) The DOE representative, James
Marlow, stated that the grounds on which objections had
been made could be divided into five broad categories: a
convincing case had not been made for expansion; the
possible adverse effect of expansion upon the surrounding
countryside; the implications of expansion for the South
East and Hertfordshire; the effect of expansion on the
existing new town; the fear that expansion would lower
the value of properties (particularly farming property)
and could seriously affect farmers' livelihoods. (43) The
statement then proceeded to elaborate some of the points.

Regarding the first point, namely that a convincing case
had not been made for expansion, the DOE statement asserted that the Secretary of State had to consider the
position of existing employers in manufacturing industry
in Stevenage, many of whom were attracted to the town by
the promise that adequate housing would be available for
their key workers:

provision made in the expansion proposals for incoming
industrial workers is directly related to the *future*
needs of those employers who are unlikely to be able
to recruit locally all the key workers they will
require for some years to come to cope with the planned
expansion of their activities. (44, emphasis added)

So here was the DOE in agreement with the Corporation,
thus lending credence to the SIEG projections of what they
might need in terms of manpower in future years, and doing
so despite the industrialists' systematic miscalculations
and exaggerations which had, as previously mentioned, led
to the Corporation carrying out an uneven policy towards
housing allocations. The statement continued, rather
illogically, to assert that the Secretary of State considered that as the present situation in Stevenage had
arisen as a 'direct result' of Government action, it was
therefore in the 'national interest' that a satisfactory
solution be reached. Now, first, it was a highly contentious point to make that the situation - namely that
of a growing second generation without adequate housing
provision - was a *direct* result of Government action. It
was in the sense that the town was originally designated
by central Government, but the *actual* direct causes were
(i) the policies of the Corporation towards industrial
recruitment and housing allocation, and (ii) the Corporation's miscalculations in the 1966 Master Plan as to
the future size of households. Second, what could really
be done at Stevenage which would *then* result as beneficial
to the 'nation'?

Regarding the third objection, the DOE made a similar
justification, namely that local needs could not be
defined 'too locally' in that existing industrialists had
to be able to recruit elsewhere if need be.

In relation to the fourth point - that expansion could
have deleterious effects on the existing town - the justification was again related to employment, and was couched
in terms not exactly alien to the planning ideology:

the proposed expansion is related to forecasts of
future labour requirements and ... *future development
would be monitored in the light of the circumstances
prevailing at any particular time*. (45, emphasis added)

The effect of the DOE's statement was to produce an angry
response from nearly all of the objectors, and particularly in relation to two fundamental points. First, as Mr
Hellard, Counsel for the NFU suggested, it might have been
thought from the way in which the Secretary of State had
arranged an Inquiry into the objections and then sent a
representative to knock them down, that the whole matter
was cut and dried. Similarly, Lord Colville stated that

he hoped that Mr Marlow's comments on the written objections carried no implication that the Secretary of
State had pre-judged the issues before the Inquiry. (46)
Second, as the SVA pointed out, nowhere do the categories
of objections selected

> concede that objections to the indefinite extension of
> the period of control have been received nor do they
> concede that objectors have asked why any small ex-
> pansion which is needed, cannot be met by other means
> such as local authority action. We know that this As-
> sociation is not alone in objecting to the proposed
> open ended timescale or failure to consider other ways
> than a Development Corporation. (47)

The SVA went on to say that the DOE's omission appeared
to be a deliberate act of misinformation about a key
factor.

The second day began with the circulation of a copy of
the GLC's consultative paper 'Planned Growth Outside
London', together with a subsequent press release on the
document by the Corporation, and copies of a paper by the
South East Economic Planning Council on the document.

The GLC's paper (later to be endorsed by the GLC's
members) was critical of new towns, particularly in terms
of their being inadequate tools of housing policy. The
GLC's arguments were that only one half of the new town
housing product went to Londoners and of this only a
quarter to cases of real housing need. Thus the new town
contribution to the solution of the London housing problem
was small because the stock, and indeed new provision in
new towns, contained only a small proportion of small
dwellings, and they did not therefore contribute to the
small household categories which featured on the London
waiting lists. New towns creamed off residual skilled
labour from London because the employment category had
greater priority than housing need; in national cost
terms new towns had to create infrastructure and give rise
to new services that made housing costs as high as in
London, where the high land costs were offset by the
existence of services, and thus the new towns were not a
cheaper provision: when resources were limited it made
more sense to use them on the rehabilitation of urban
areas in London than to use them in new areas, the development of which eat into the limited amount of agricultural land. (48) Indeed Sir Reg Goodwin, leader of the
GLC at the time, stated that:

> We very much value the important contribution played by
> New and Expanding Towns in the past, but in view of the
> changed situation that faces us today, we must act in
> the best interests of London and be more cautious in
> our attitude to development outside the capital. (49)

In fact the Greater London Development Plan, which had taken seven years to prepare, and which was finally published on 26 August 1976, was already being amended to bring it more into line with current thinking which was, essentially, the need to stem the loss of jobs and population. (50)

The Corporation's answer to the GLC's comment was, first, to admit that 'because offer of house is linked with offer of job and that the employer must have the last word as to whom he will employ, requisite skill takes precedence over housing need in tenant selection', and, second, to state that the GLC should address itself rather to the difficult task of constraining the unplanned out-flow 'which surely stems from London's unattractive environment driving out the people who have the resources to move out'. (51)   The South East Economic Planning Council - of which Dame Evelyn Denington was a member - made a similar point, stating that it considered that restricting the movement of people from London to the new and expanding towns would have no marked effect on industrial decline since only 7 per cent of the decline of manufacturing employment in London can be attributed to firms moving to these areas. (52)   The Inspector noted the debate.

Also on the second day there was a 'demonstration'. Mrs Powell and a colleague from CAUSE pushed prams, with placards attached and babies inside, around the Inquiry hall whilst Lord Colville was engaged in the cross-examination of Mr Marlow of the DOE. The Inspector was unaware of what had happened - 'Unfortunately I was so busy taking notes that I only looked up and became aware that something unusual was happening when the demonstration, having completed a circuit of the hall, was on its way out'. (53) Interestingly, Mrs Powell gave an account of the origins of the incident:

> I arrived to hear the opening speeches and there was a photographer there and he came up to me - there were about four actually - and he said 'are you going to do a demonstration, Mrs Powell?' and I said 'I will if you like' and he said 'yes please', so I said 'OK', so he said 'when?' and I said 'tomorrow morning if you like', because it was no effort for me to go out and find a homeless couple somewhere you see, and I had two on my hands at the time so I just did the demo for him. (54)

This incident was to be recalled later at the Inquiry.

The third day of the Inquiry, April Fool's Day, was described by a local newspaper as the day 'Lord Colville was tossing figures at Leonard Vincent, John Balchin and David Rixson, who like seasoned performers were juggling with them and throwing them back', and indeed day three did see

the two planners and the General Manager of the Corporation produce figures as if out of a hat, with Lord
Colville doing the same, to the utter bewilderment of
many. As expected, much of the Inquiry turned around the
validity of figures and diagrams, with petty squabbles and
bickering rampant. The figures in fact were never *really*
questioned, in that what tended to occur was that one
person would, for example, say 'the correct figure is
1,005' whilst another would state '1,200'. and subsequently the numbers were just left, and there would be no discussion about the relations between such figures, as it
was simply a case of 'here are my figures - where are
yours?'. In a sense it was plain why such discussions
never took place, in that it was readily apparent that
the figures were tendentious to say the least and were
based on shaky and ambiguous foundations. The following
is an example from the General Manager of the Corporation:
'The method adopted in assessing housing required over the
15 years to 1991 has been first to describe and delimit
the category of need and then to quantify it.' He continued:

> In the latter task it has been necessary to produce a
> series of demographic projections relating to popu-
> lation, household formation and working population and
> to lay alongside these *certain pragmatic inferences*
> based on past experience as to the demands to which
> these factors give rise and estimates of those other
> categories of demand that do not derive from demo-
> graphic exercises. (55, emphasis added)

So what was really important was that figures had to be
produced, even if incorrect or irrelevant: that is, it
was the ritual of figure-presenting that was necessary.
Day four saw the planners engaging in discourse unknown
to the majority present in the hall. David Eversley sadly
stresses that the incomprehensibility that planning discourse produced in many planning inquiries was due to the
planners' increasing technical competence, (56) but this
does seem rather implausible in that the last decade's
opposition to planning is as much concerned with *incompe-
tence* as it is with democracy. Indeed in Stevenage's own
case, the Corporation's Social Development Officer, while
discussing the work undertaken by the Consultant Planner
(who was also the Corporation's own Chief Planning
Officer), stated that 'most of the major contracts they've
had with the Corporation have gone wrong and the Corporation has had to pay'. (57)
An example of the planners' specialised language was
given by Mr Boddington, the Corporation's Agricultural
Consultant, who talked of a soil - as if this were common

knowledge - being a 'Swaffham Prior Association, whose
land use capability classification is 3gs. grade 3,
average'. (58)   However, possibly the most illuminating
example was offered by Mr Patterson the Corporation's
Landscape Consultant, when he talked of an 'annual process
of beating up trees'.   When cross-examined by Lord
Colville - 'did I hear you correctly?' - he expalined,
rather sheepishly, that this meant an annual process of
replanting trees! (59)

Such 'technical' language dominated much of the Inquiry,
and importantly it excluded certain participants in such
a way as to suggest that it was in fact *they* who were in-
competent.   The corollary of this domination by 'technical
language' was the lack of legitimacy the non-technical
language received.   For example, protestors would talk in
terms such as, 'it will be a tragic end to a charming
rural area', or that the 'nightingales will no longer sing
in Weston', or pleaded for 'Weston's rare orchids'.
Statements like these were appreciated with 'thanks'
together with an implicit appreciation for the respite
such statements gave from the 'real business'.   For
example, Mr Ogden, QC for the Corporation, after hearing
a long personal statement of a man's fifty years in a
village, stated that he had thought it a 'very interesting
paper'.   Unfortunately such participants tended to thank
Counsel for taking them so seriously.

Putting aside the point that there was injustice when
certain people were effectively excluded from the proceedings because of the language used, there was also the
fact that much of the technical language - as has already
been hinted at - was irrelevant and indeed pseudo-scien-
tific, whilst conversely much of the non-technical
language was meaningful.   For example, the Corporation's
Agricultural Consultant, when cross-examined by the NFU's
Counsel, responded tersely by talking about the 'inevita-
bility of the farmers getting the nudge', and then, when
asked how many farm jobs would be lost if expansion proceeded, he replied 'fifteen to twenty, I think'.   And
finally, when asked if fifty yards would be enough for a
tree barrier, he replied 'well, we'll just have to find
out'. (60)   Conversely, the following is the non-technical
proof offered by the representative of Aston Parish
Council:

> we feel there is a real danger that the additional
> amount of traffic generated in the villages, as a
> result of the expansion proposals, will lead to our
> roads having to be 'improved', in the interest of road
> safety. (61)

A better, more direct account of the 'escalation process'
inherent in the planning process would be hard to find.

Day four closed with the Borough Council's Chief Executive reading out the Council's views, which were 'broadly
in agreement with the proposals of the Corporation'. The
Council, following discussions with the Corporation, he
stated, did however make some stipulations. First, the
Council demanded that any decision on expansion be linked
with a firm decision about the future life and role of the
Corporation, and indeed the Council envisaged the Corporation being wound up by about 1980, and itself doing more
in terms of housing in the residual years of the Corporation, and so on. Second, the Council's specification of
'local needs' differed slightly from that of the Corporation, in particular it was the Council's view that the
development of industry should be directly related to the
needs of the second and subsequent generations, and, in
this context, new industry should be service industry.
Third, the Council agreed that the land west of the A1 (M)
should be zoned for agriculture in any new Master Plan,
but saw no good reason why the land should be released
from the designated area (which coincided with the
Borough). Finally, the Council made the point that
although the issue was, in fact, outside the Secretary of
State's present terms of reference, the Council was still
opposed to the building of Road 9. (62)

SIEG gave its support to the proposals on day five, and
although the Inspector stated in his (later) report that
SIEG's evidence was presented by Mr Bailey of the British
Aircraft Corporation, it was, in fact, presented by the
Chairman of SIEG, Mr G.L.Hughes, who was also a member of
the Corporation Board.

SIEG's proof was titled 'Statement of the Views of
Industry', an incorrect statement in that it was solely
the views of the employers, but that fact seemed not to
perturb anyone. Mr Hughes opened by saying that the Group
'represents' forty-four Stevenage firms totalling 18,000
workers, yet consisting of units employing as few as
fifteen persons to as many as 7,000. He went on to say
that the Council of the Group, the Chairman and all the
officers 'are elected from *responsible* senior officials
of member firms on an annual basis'. (63, emphasis added)
Mr Hughes added that in view of

the *major* and far-reaching nature of what is proposed,
the Group is particularly conscious of its responsibility to the present Inquiry - and to the people of
Stevenage and its environs - to give a *realistic
assessment of its members' needs* and to place them in
context. (64, emphasis added)

Thus SIEG was certainly aware that the 'minor' expansion
was not quite so minor. But, of course, it could not be

expected of SIEG to produce a 'realistic assessment of
their needs' in view of their historical record of
exaggeration. Indeed Mr Hughes went on to say that the
Group wholeheartedly supported the proposals for expansion, particularly as the industrialists in the town
expected to enjoy a significant improvement and expansion
in the next decade 'provided the conditions for that expansion are maintained'. He added that one of the key
conditions necessary to preserve industrial confidence
was the expectation of an increase in population sufficient to create a larger supply of labour, and thus
without such confidence industry could face a situation
of contraction which could 'in the long term affect the
work prospects and the quality of life in Stevenage far
more seriously than any transitory recession'. There
followed a little blackmail:

> *All the evidence* shows that where their expansion plans
> are stultified, industries will be forced to look at
> development areas more amenable to their needs, and
> there is no reason to suppose that the position would
> be any different in Stevenage should new house building
> be restricted to prevent the full maturity of existing
> investment encouraged over the last 25 years. Despite
> the current surplus in labour, by far the more frequent
> trend has been shortage, and industry will respond by
> greater investment to a better long term balance. (65,
> emphasis added)

When cross-examined by Lord Colville about the 'evidence'
concerning the more 'amenable' development areas, Mr
Hughes was unable to draw any such evidence to the
Inquiry's attention.

 Mr Hughes, not surprisingly, then stated that however
good the training, industry could not absorb the numbers
of school-leavers known to be forthcoming in the town
without some additional personnel. He next drew the
Inquiry's attention to SIEG's 1976 employment survey,
which in fact was a survey of 65 per cent of SIEG's
membership. The survey, among other things, showed that
there were at that time 249 vacancies, of which 209 were
in the occupational category of managerial/administrative/
technical/clerical; for example there were recruitment
difficulties in the following occupations - systems
engineers, digital electronic engineers, camera mechanics,
accountants, to mention but a few. What was interesting,
of course, was that, first, the list of occupations with
recruitment difficulties was illustrative of the point
that the GLC - and others - made, viz., that the new towns
creamed off the more skilled workers, and also had few opportunities in the towns for the unskilled, by virtue of

the industrial structure. Second, though the survey
stated that there were 249 unfilled vacancies at the time
(in terms of 65 per cent of their membership), this was a
gross exaggeration in that the ERV1 returns - a more
reliable source - showed a figure of merely 113 for the
same period, and that figure was for the total established
labour force.

Mr Hughes concluded with two more extremely contentious
points. First, he informed the Inquiry that existing
industry felt that there would indeed be ample capacity
for extra labour

> as the national economy *resumes its buoyancy in the
> 1980s,* with or without diversification. (66, emphasis
> added)

Finally, after this unwarranted assertion by SIEG, he
humbly stated that

> Industry in Stevenage does not pretend to have a
> monopoly of wisdom, *yet it can claim the benefit of
> experience* and of a knowledge of its own future
> potential given the right conditions. (67, emphasis
> added)

What SIEG was indeed experienced in was the use of scare
tactics and miscalculations in relation to the Corporation
who found the arrangement to its benefit also, in that an
uneven policy of housing allocations was a cheap price to
pay for an influential pro-growth lobby.

Day six saw the Hertfordshire County Council give its
proof to the Inquiry. The points it was to make were
predictable in that its strategy would simply be one of
obtaining as much planning control for the County as it
could. Thus its arguments were the arguments of an
authority with a lot at stake, and it in fact kept its
arguments simple, albeit somewhat repetitive. Essentially
the County Council only produced one argument, the rest
being quantitative squabbling - namely that the proposals
for Stevenage could only be properly evaluated in the
light of the examination in public of the 'key issues' of
the Structure Plan later in the year. Further, 'if the
town needs more land for expansion it should be in accordance with the Structure Plan, like every other town
in Hertfordshire'. (68) What else could it say?

Day six also saw Miss Cynthia Wood give evidence on
behalf of the Aston Parish Council, and she concluded with
the following remarks which produced the Inquiry's first
cheers and applause.

> Ten years ago the Development Corporation showed they
> could accommodate their projected population within the
> designated area. Today they produced fresh figures to
> show why they could not do so. There could be no con-

fidence that they would not produce a further set of
figures in a few years' time to justify a still further
expansion. (69)

Even the Inspector was led by this statement to mutter
'figures do seem to be used in the most peculiar way'.
On the seventh day Mr Ogden, QC for the Corporation,
stated that in the event of the Inspector deciding that
the proposed expansion area was too large, the Corporation
would release from the programmed area 214 acres around
Chesfield Park. Dame Evelyn Denington was at the Inquiry
on the seventh day and, of course, had heard this remark
by Counsel, and at the following Board meeting mentioned
it and suggested that the remark was unfortunate as the
Corporation was in danger of being deprived of essential
housing land. The General Manager attempted to placate
her by stating that the remark was an answer

to a hypothetical question put by the Inspector. The
Corporation was pressing for approval of the full
extent of the enlarged Designated Area and when
Counsel delivers his final speech this point will be
made. (70)

The Hertfordshire Society and CASE then took the floor on
the seventh day. Lt.Col.Thomson for the Hertfordshire
Society outlined the constitution of the Society and proceeded to say that its objections to the proposals were on
amenity grounds, namely the extensive loss of countryside,
and the fact that the proposals if implemented would bring
the threat of coalescence of North Hertfordshire that much
closer. He concluded his evidence by stating that his
Society did not suggest that Stevenage could never expand,
indeed it was evident that the town might one day have to
expand: however, the Society's argument was that the
Corporation ought to first of all use up the present undeveloped land, and any expansion ought to be related to the
needs of the time and not projected forward for more than
half a generation. (71)

Mr McCombie for CASE started well, suggesting that the
future could bring a situation in which the Corporation
'alternatively, proposes an increase in population to fill
an area, and an increase in area to accommodate the population'. (72) He went on with assurance to state that in
spite of the volume of print which the Corporation had
issued, packed with data, statistics and argument, CASE
could find no conviction that the expansion was justified
in that so many assumptions had to be made in such large
areas: for example the time required for recovery from
the economic recession of the day, the type of labour
required by industry in the future, the number who would
marry each other and the number of children that they

might have, and so on. The point was, he continued, that
a number of small errors in the assumptions could well
produce the wrong answer. (73) Unfortunately Mr McCombie
then himself got engaged in a quantaphrenic exercise, produced his set of figures from out of nowhere, juggled them
to produce new calculations, and then concluded by
stating, for instance, 'and so the total land requirement
is therefore 258 acres'. (74) This strategy of CASE's of
fighting figures with more figures simply made the Corporation's Counsel's job that much easier. As Mr McCombie
later stated, he was cross-examined on documents he had
not even seen, was faced with a battery of professional
people 'who had spent their whole lives leading up to
this particular thing' and was made to look 'rather
silly'. He continued:

> when I was under cross-examination, I was forced to
> give the impression that I was stalling. This was
> because I was being examined on a document which had
> been issued by the County Council which I had not seen
> and on elements of that document that were irrelevant
> to a large extent to my evidence ... for example,
> Counsel would take a statement at the end of a page
> and ask me to look at it and then asked me whether I
> didn't agree with it. I, who had never seen that docu-
> ment before, had noticed that at the top of the page it
> began with a premise that I didn't accept. Now if I
> accepted the bottom of the page I accepted the top of
> the page. But he knew according to my evidence, that
> I didn't accept the top of the page at all, so what he
> was really trying to make me do was to agree to some-
> thing which, in fact, I had already given evidence that
> I did not agree with. And this therefore I did not
> consider was fair interrogation - I thought it was
> extremely unfair, because he was just trying to catch
> me, and it proved nothing at the end of the day. (75)

Indeed Mr McCombie was made to look a little muddled, and
the QC was just trying to 'catch' him out, but this was
easy for Counsel to do as the Corporation, with two shorthand writers, junior Counsel and so on, was well equipped
to deal with any discussion at the level of figures.

Lord Colville concluded the day with his final address
which took three hours, at which time the Inspector himself ponderously took it down in longhand!

Day eight began with an individual contribution from an
ex-Corporation engineer, Mr Dearman. He began by stating
that he would confine himself to statements of fact and
would avoid any expression of opinion, and added, much to
the amusement of the Inspector, that in order to speak as
a member of the public he had to sit beside a label marked

'objectors' which implied that he was either for or
against, 'black or white'. The matter was not as simple
as that, he continued, in that between black and white
there were infinite shades of grey and on either side of
this grey band there were infinite numbers of all shades
of the rainbow. He elaborated this rather pedantic point
for a number of minutes and then proceeded to his main
point which concerned the 'falling population'. He outlined the restraints operating to limit the growth of the
population, and then more concretely stated that the
killing of 181 foetuses in Stevenage would mean that some
60 less houses would be required for natural growth at
some time in the future. There was a roar of laughter.
But Mr Dearman went further, and concluded that

> it means more than this since any nation which kills
> its young before birth will suffer not only a decline
> in the population but also meet the risk of ultimate
> decay through the destruction of moral standards. This
> will reduce the population still further. (76)

Mr Dearman was thanked by the Inspector for his contribution amidst a hush.

Mrs Powell of CAUSE then gave her evidence which like Mr
Dearman's was full of opinion ('there is a Jamaican family
I have heard about'), although she had begun by stating
that she 'only worked on fact'. Mrs Powell began cynically, by saying that she was the least yet, paradoxically,
the most concerned. She stated that she did not live in
a pretty village which could be engulfed, that she was not
a farmer who could lose home, land and livelihood, that
she was not a Corporation employee who might lose employment, and not a planner who had sights set on secure
employment for the next fifteen years. But she had been
a strong campaigner for 'other people's rights' since the
age of nine. (77)

The most interesting aspect of Mrs Powell's presence
concerned her cross-examination by the Corporation's
Counsel, who began by simply mentioning that he had been
surprised earlier in the Inquiry when she had pushed a
pram around the hall. He then proceeded to ask:

> Mrs Powell, you sent a letter objecting to the pro-
> posals in March, to the Minister, and you mentioned
> coloured immigrants, why not now? On the placard you
> had with the pram you mentioned British, why? Are you
> motivated mainly by racialist tendencies? What party
> do you belong to? ... Ah, the National Front. I need
> add no more. (78)

This, of course, gave an impression of criminal proceedings, let alone merely a court of law, and was willingly
accepted by the Inspector and other participants. The

effect of this was to affirm the belief that all the other
participants were honest, their interests 'good', and that
they were 'playing the game', and so on. Moreover, such
a cross-examination ignored Mrs Powell's evidence which
was left uncontested and which was duly reproduced in the
local newspapers as if it were true. For example, she
talked of the proposals to build another 17,980 houses
when the actual number was 15,960, 'with preference being
given to people wherever they come from' (untrue), and
that 'wherever there is a dense population, crime always
flourishes' (in need of qualification). (79) Most importantly, the Inspector felt able to leave her evidence
uncontested when his primary role at the Inquiry was to
evaluate *all* the evidence.

Mrs Powell, in fact, spoke again the following day and
reiterated her points of the previous day, while also
making a complaint about Counsel. She was able to return
because she had telephoned the Corporation's Public Relations Officer and told him:

> If I don't get a chance to reply ... I intend to come
> to the rest of the Inquiry and I shall sit there every
> day and I shall insist that every person who is cross-
> examined gives their political interests. (80)

Day nine included an amusing incident which concerned a
Mrs Franklin who insisted repeatedly that she did not farm
a particular estate, while the Corporation's Agricultural
Consultant repeatedly informed her that she did. It also
saw the East Hertfordshire District Council's Director of
Planning, Mr R.Beacham, point out one of the important
points to be made, and indeed one that had been mentioned
earlier in the text, namely that the existing Master Plan
proposed a population growth of the same order as the
present expansion proposals, and the need for the present
proposals was clearly because the land-use requirements
of the Master Plan were not predicted in sufficient accu-
racy, and there was nothing to show that the present predictions were any more accurate. (81)

Day ten was 'farmers' day', beginning with the NFU's
Counsel Mr Hellard, who outlined the NFU's national policy
towards new towns at that time. He drew attention to a
NFU memorandum dated 2 February 1976, titled 'Updating and
Development of the "Strategic Plan for the South East": a
statement of the views of the National Farmers' Union', in
which the NFU stated that as the SPSE's population projections were revised, an increasing reliance was placed
on London as the provider of the key elements for growth.
The NFU did not believe that it was ever the intention of
the regional strategy that the decanting of London's resources should be the sole or the major reason for pro-

moting growth in any of the areas indicated as suitable
for growth either within the South East or those areas and
towns on the periphery of the region. However, the memorandum continued, as the growth area strategies had been
developed and new town corporations had put forward expansion schemes this had increasingly been the case, and
this had occurred in the face of the increasing realisation that the outward movement of people and jobs had not
improved the situation within London. The NFU asserted
that the SPSE could not have envisaged that this exodus
of resources from the city would have been mirrored by
the movement of public and private capital and investment
out of the city to follow the people to the attractive
growth areas, and certainly did not foresee the situation
which resulted, that London, faced with increasing costs,
fewer resources and the undermining of its economic viabi-
lity was unable to deal with growing socio-economic and
physical problems and was thus in deep decline. (82) Thus
the NFU called for a firm statement on the role of London,
and more restricted and controlled development even in the
growth areas. Mr Hellard then recalled an earlier memorandum, 'New Towns in England and Wales', dated 1975,
which more correctly outlined the NFU's general policy to
towards the new towns:

> We endorse the aim of providing decent housing in a
> pleasant environment ... *[however]* we feel that in many
> cases new town development has meant that an urban
> population is uprooted and dropped unprepared into a
> rural setting, leaving the less privileged and less
> able urban inhabitants in the existing urban centres.
> (83)

A generous statement indeed, but the NFU then moved more
to the point when they stated that new towns covered more
than 200,000 acres, much of which had been taken out of
agricultural land which was itself problematic, let alone
the 'urban fringe problems' that the new towns created.
(84) The memorandum then pointed out that the NFU represented farmers and growers who produced over half of the
home food requirements, and that despite improved agricultural and horticultural technology, *land* remained the
basis of food production. Furthermore the NFU, it was
stated, considered that new towns must be considered
within the regional planning framework much more than at
present, and that they feared that

> Development Corporations have a limited aim - that of
> developing their new towns. This can easily become a
> self-sustaining function, isolated from local needs and
> realities. In the long run we suggest that Development
> Corporations may hinder rather than assist the assimi-

lation and consolidation of new town development.   In
particular, we feel strongly that the life of Development Corporations should not be artificially extended.
We suggest that control and management of new towns
should be vested in elected local authorities at the
earliest opportunity. (85)

The memorandum concluded with the assertion that farming/
Corporation relations were poor, and possibly a way in
which to improve these a little would be for each new town
corporation board to contain at least one agricultural
nominee. (86) Mr Hellard, before calling local farmers
to give evidence, rested his case with the suggestion that
Mr Marlow of the DOE had tried to minimise the agricultural objections with his suggestion that compensation
was the main answer: the NFU still firmly objected to the
loss of agricultural land and the disruption and continued
blighting of farm businesses.

Mr R.Warner-Smith was the first local farmer to give
evidence, and he began by informing the Inquiry that at
the time of the 1946 Designation Order the total agricultural unit of his (family) farm was 959 acres. Since
that time 322 acres had been lost (307 to the SDC), and
now the farm was in danger of losing another 281 to the
Corporation, which would leave a balance of 354 acres.
(87) Mr Warner-Smith stated that he was not comforted
by the Corporation's suggestion that

the family might prefer to move away from the area
entirely and set up on a new farm elsewhere, 'their
land being transferred to other farms affected by the
proposed expansion'. (88)

Interestingly, he continued to say how surprised he was
that nobody had made any survey of the loss of production
which would be caused by the expansion. Mr Warner-Smith
noted that Mr Boddington, the Corporation's Agricultural
Consultant, had stated that the land was unsuited to
intensive arable cropping: 'as I understand the meaning
of intensive arable cropping that is exactly what we use
the land for and, in our opinion, very successfully'.
Moreover, he continued, Mr Boddington had stated that
there had been considerable consultation with local
farmers but he for one had certainly 'not been asked about
a lot of the points raised in his survey - I have certainly never been asked for the level of capital investment -
and I cannot recall that we were ever asked to fill in a
form either'. He concluded his evidence with a couple of
interesting observations. First, he informed the Inquiry
that if the land proposed was taken from his farm then an
employee would certainly have to be dismissed, 'which
might not sound much to the outside world but to the man

himself and to his family it is clearly an extreme situation and particularly in the present economic climate'. Second, and in conclusion, he stated that he hoped that the Secretary of State would listen to his Cabinet colleague, the Minister of Agriculture, who had been calling for increased home food production, and as a result decide not to confirm the expansion proposals. (89)

Now this call for increased home food production was, in fact, in the form of a white paper titled 'Food from our own resources' (Cmnd 6020, 1975) which was itself rather an interesting document, in that its thrust was that there ought to be increased production achieved from diminishing resources. What was also interesting was that the Secretary of State for the Environment at that time was Mr Silkin who within a matter of months had left to become Minister of Agriculture, and perhaps was in a good position to consider the difficulties of inter-departmental conflicts and other associated problems:

> Of course, different Government departments have
> different priorities and ideas. But we have worked
> out, as between planning and agriculture, a way of
> living together in which the needs of agriculture, par-
> ticularly in relation to Grade I and Grade II land,
> must be fully taken into account. I think this is the
> best one can do but it is inevitable that the depart-
> ments should look at it from different points of view.
> (90)

The position of tenant farmers was the final element of the NFU's case in the form of evidence on behalf of the Allen family, tenant farmers who would lose their livelihoods if the expansion took place. It was pointed out that whereas an owner-occupier farmer could use his compensation money to buy himself another farm to replace the one of which he had been dispossessed, a tenant farmer had no such recourse, in that what he would lose was a right to occupy land and that was irremediable unless he could obtain a tenancy of another farm. And, it was concluded, opportunities of attaining a tenancy of any farm in England occurred so infrequently as to be an inconsiderable possibility, and furthermore the chance of anything becoming available in a farmer's own area was even less. (91) On that dour note the NFU concluded.

Day eleven was to be the day when 'individuals' could have their say: however, the proceedings had to be adjourned because of lack of interest. This is, of course, hardly surprising in view of the general acceptance by the public at large of the division of labour - 'it is the planners' and politicians' business' - together with difficulties of dialogue, and the fact that the Inquiry

was held in a quasi-judicial environment from 10 am to
4 pm on weekdays. (92)

Day twelve saw the SVA present its case, which was interesting yet catastrophic for the Association. The SVA's
arguments were similar to those of CASE - and similarly
were to a great extent quantitative to excess - but the
SVA also had what it considered an 'expert' witness,
Professor R.S.Scorer who would be, it was considered, a
tour de force.

Professor Scorer gave evidence on the problem of nitrogen
pollution. He considered that to increase the population
of the lower Thames-Lee area (which included Stevenage)
would be a 'strategic error of considerable magnitude',
as this would certainly increase the risk of nitrogen
pollution. He went on to say that if the water supply
(which would have to be increased to meet the needs of
the proposed extra population) contained above 11.3 mg of
nitrogen (which in 1972 the River Lee did contain),
bottle-fed babies could develop methaemoglobinaemia, or,
as it was more commonly known, the 'blue baby symptom', a
condition which required hospitalisation. He further
stated that the adult limit was unknown. (93) The representative of the Thames Water Authority present at the
Inquiry more or less agreed, and stated that there were
indeed two unknown factors which related to the problem,
namely the infiltration of storm water and the possible
effect of development to the south of Stevenage. He
stated that as to the former, investigations as to what
happened in 1974 had not made much progress, in that it
was still not known where the storm water had gained
access to the outfall sewer, and as regards new development, draining to the Mimram sewer was already nearly at
full capacity and new developments at Welwyn/Hatfield
could increase the problems there, let alone possible new
development at East Hertfordshire, Harlow and Stanstead
Airport. (94)

So the Corporation's case here seemed to be in some
doubt. The QC's way of handling the situation was simply
the strategy of 'divide and rule'. He harassed Professor
Scorer into answering questions about his relationship
with the SVA - 'are you a member?', 'do you live locally?', and so on - which had the effect of Professor Scorer
stating quite correctly that he had been merely invited by
the SVA to give evidence on nitrogen pollution. This fact
- that he was not a member of the SVA, and that his contribution was that of an individual - had the further
effect of making his evidence less potent, in that he was
not intimately concerned as the SVA was, and thus his
evidence was basically an academic argument to discuss
and digest.

The SVA's own evidence, presented by the Chairman Mr
Cuthill, was vague to say the least, and badly presented.
The Treasurer of the SVA stated (later) that its case was
practically ad lib in parts, and was totally unrehearsed
as nobody was really prepared to spend the time. 'We
didn't have a strong *organisation,* we couldn't get hold
of all the information we required', and 'Cuthill took it
upon himself as the technician, the leader' to just go to
the Inquiry and tell the Corporation that they were wrong
- indeed he thought

> he was addressing a group of executives in a small-time
> fish shop, and telling them how well they should run
> their business. (95)

Ironically, the Treasurer added, what Cuthill overlooked
in his 'megalomania' was the fact that all the Inquiry was
interested in was paper evidence. Two incidents particularly stood out of the SVA's case at the Inquiry. First,
the SVA just could not keep up the 'membership myth': it
was asked by the Corporation's Counsel the number of
members the organisation had, to which Mr Hubble (who
answered that particular question) replied, 'I can't
remember how many people attended the AGM but I could find
out', and 'I think the actual number of members is eighty-
seven.' In fact the AGM, which had been held a fortnight
before the Inquiry, attracted three members. The SVA was
not placed into the embarrassing position of having to lie
about the AGM as it was not called again for evidence,
particularly so following the second incident which completely discredited the SVA. Mr Cuthill stood up at the
Inquiry and read out a list - which turned out, in the
light of illustrative evidence, to be totally incorrect -
of planning errors of the Corporation in terms of the
existing town, which increasingly became a list of errors
(and indeed non-errors) of the most pedantic kind. For
example Cuthill would say that the Corporation had left
one square metre of concrete next to a grass verge, or
that a lamppost was one inch out of skew and so on, which
brought not only a rebuttal on 'technical' grounds but
also a comment from the Inspector to the effect that
Cuthill was 'wasting the Inquiry's time'. Mr Hubble, the
SVA's Treasurer, remembered the incident vividly:

> I was taking Scorer back to the station, and I must
> confess I took longer than I need have done as I
> couldn't face any more of it. I'd seen Cuthill writing
> this, and I thought, 'you can't be serious, I know the
> points you're going to make, you just can't read those
> out, you just can't', and he did. (96)

The final two days were taken up with the final ad-
dresses, a few letters were read out - for example, one

from Ian Stewart, MP for Hitchin, who talked of the possibility that expansion could 'lead to contamination of the villages' and that there was a 'danger of damage by children to the trees' - and finally, with the Inspector, who closed the proceedings.

The Inspector wound up the Inquiry by stating that anyone could suggest sites for him to see in his three-day walkabout, and finally concluded by stating that he would not have taken the job on if he thought for one moment that his report would be ignored. Indeed, he went so far as to say that if the 'Secretary of State differs from my opinion he will need to say why - and I flatter myself, he will find it difficult'.

The Inquiry had lasted fourteen full days together with a site inspection which lasted four full days. The Corporation's case had - in its five volumes of 606 pages with 146 tables and 99 illustrations - been fully presented but only partially discussed, and the average attendance by the public for the fourteen days was nine per day. (97)

One interpretation of the Inquiry could well have been that it was merely a ritual, in that the Corporation's Counsel appeared to be omnipotent and that there was generally throughout a sense of a fait accompli. And of course this was reinforced by both the Inquiry's procedural rules and the various status demarcations, including the crucial linguistic one.

Now came the wait for the Inspector's report and the Minister's subsequent decision.

10 Stevenage 1976-7
Confusion abounds

The uneasiness, the malaise of our time, is due to this
root fact: in our politics and our economy, in family
life and religion - in practically every sphere of our
existence - the certainties of the eighteenth and nineteenth centuries have disintegrated or been destroyed
and, at the same time, no new sanctions or justifications for the new routines we live, and must live,
have taken hold.

                              C.Wright Mills (1956), p.xvi

Shortly after the Inquiry Shirley Williams, in a lecture
given to SIEG, stated that Stevenage industry would increasingly have to find its skilled workers among the
people of the town, particularly when the system of nominated housing was phased out. Certainly the ERV1 and ERV
returns of early 1976 gave no encouragement to the procedure which, it could be argued, had resulted in there
being a total of 113 unfilled vacancies together with a
total of 1,244 unemployed persons. The Corporation itself
was also ailing a little, with the cumulative amount on
the General Revenue Account falling from a surplus of £7
million in 1975 to one of £4,500,000 in 1976, while its
administrative costs had risen to an annual amount of £2
million.

The General Manager, in an interview just before his
retirement, stated that expansion was inevitable:

You cannot put a new town in a strategic position and
then expect to restrain it. Its industrial structure,
its very newness, its reputation and the age of the
people will demand it. (1)

The new General Manager, Mr Jack Greenwood, was appointed
in July: he had been Chief Finance Officer since 1967,
and Deputy before that. In his report to the Board in
October, he continued from where his predecessors had left
off with respect to industrial housing allocations by

stating that continuing national problems concerning the
economy had affected Stevenage employers, and consequently
employers' requirements for housing had been lower than
provided for. He illustrated the point by stating that
by 1 October, 229 nominees from industry had been expected
to register but in fact since April and up to that date,
only 117 nominations had been received. The General
Manager further stated that the Housing Manager's action
on this matter had been to approve further allocations to
the second generation. Finally he said that with regard
to allocations to the employers, it was proposed that the
Housing Manager should abandon the procedure whereby
employers were asked in advance for their requirements in
order to determine their individual quotas, as

> *over the past two years* their forecasts have been in-
> accurate - albeit unintentionally - which has resulted
> in the overall allocations being reversed in mid-year.
> It is considered preferable *during this period of un-
> certainty* for the Housing Manager to set aside an over-
> all allocation ... to employers collectively, who could
> then request the right to nominate selected employees
> throughout the year ... until the quota had been used.
> (2, emphasis added)

It is hardly necessary to point out that it had not been
just the past two years in which the employers had acted
in an uncertain or inaccurate manner. In its Annual
Report the Corporation pointed out to the new Secretary
of State, Mr Peter Shore, that a decision on expansion had
not been made by the end of the year and such a delay had
caused problems of 'continuity', and indeed a significant
decline in the output of dwellings. It was crucial, it
added, that the Corporation obtain Section 6(1) approval
as soon as possible for the area plan for Sectors 4,5 and
6, if a serious hiatus in the housing programme was to be
avoided. (3) The Corporation further stated that the uncertainty that confronted the property developer continued
to delay the construction of the proposed office block of
94,000 sq ft at Swingate (town centre). The Corporation
also stated that the work on expansion together with the
cost of the Public Inquiry had totalled £160,000, whilst
Bracknell Development Corporation also engaged in an expansion scheme, announced that its total costs had
amounted to £110,000. (4)

In November both the Corporation and the Council issued
a statement asserting that if the Hertfordshire County
Council's Structure Plan was adopted, it could end any
chances of school leavers obtaining employment. The
Corporation itself particularly felt that key workers
could be disbarred from arriving in the town - indeed

key workers who were to ensure the future training of
apprentices - whilst the Council suggested a similar situation when it stated that it feared that a curb on factory
expansion could mean less money to train school leavers.
(5) It was of course predictable that the Council would
think this way in that it could see - in the not too
distant future - the assets of the Corporation falling
into its hands, and therefore it was already falling in
line with the plausible-sounding ethos of the Corporation,
namely that 'growth equalled solved problems'.

In December the Corporation's 'household survey' was
published which, like the previous surveys of 1966 and
1971, consisted of a 10 per cent sample. (6) Of the more
important things to come out of the document - the survey
was always carried out by the Engineers' Department as it
had a computer, and consequently much of the document
concerned itself with facts about transportation and so
on - were two quite important, although hardly original,
conclusions. First, there was a very large increase in
the number of school leavers who were likely to require
employment during the period terminating in 1986, and a
comparatively small number of people who seemed likely
to retire; and, second, the continuation of the trend
towards more commuting to work outside the town:

> The main changes which have occurred in the past 5
> years are in the destinations of workers. Outward
> commuting has increased from 18.4 per cent in 1971
> to 26.6 per cent which suggests that the numbers
> entering and leaving the town for work purposes each
> day are probably more nearly equal than previously
> supposed. (7)

This of course simply meant that about 25 per cent of
people were having to look outside the town for employment, and that the town's industries needed to draw in 25
per cent of their work-force from outside the town: an
indication that a town planned to be self-contained had
failed in regard to that particular goal. Thus 1976 came
to a close with no sign of a decision on expansion, and
indeed no sign of the Inspector's report.

It became apparent at the beginning of the new year that
the likelihood of expansion was beginning to recede daily:
there was first the crisis in London which was greatly
publicised, and second - and most important - the Government had an economic problem which demanded, in the traditional view, a cut in public expenditure amongst other
measures. Unemployment was running at 6.1 per cent in
January 1977, with 1.5 million unemployed, as compared
with 3.5 per cent when the Draft Designation Order was
made in April 1975. (8)

On 5 April, one year after the Public Inquiry and two
years since the Order was issued, the decision came. Mr
Peter Shore issued a statement titled 'The Future of the
New Towns' to the House of Commons, stating that he had
> decided not to make extension orders for [Stevenage and
> Harlow]. The normal growth of the towns, especially
> for second generation families will be matters for the
> local authorities concerned to deal with under other
> legislation. (9)

He went on to say that it was his intention that 'subject
to the necessary consultations' the corporations of
Stevenage, Harlow, Bracknell, Basildon, Corby, Runcorn,
Redditch and Skelmersdale be wound up within the next five
years. A letter from the DOE which the Corporation received the following day added more to the statement. The
letter stated that Mr Shore had come to his decision in
the light of his reappraisal of the new towns programme -
in the London new towns case, this simply meant any
measures which might help an ailing capital - and that it
seemed more appropriate to look ahead for a shorter period
than the fifteen years which had been in mind when the
Draft Order was published. The letter added that it was
clear from paragraph 9.32 of the Inspector's report -
which had at last come to light - that there was sufficient land allocated for residential development in the
existing designated area to meet Stevenage's needs for
several years, and if there was a need for more houses
beyond the end of this period (a period not specified),
provision to meet any such need should be made through
the operation of the town planning and housing legislation, and if necessary by the local authorities, but
not by means of the New Towns Act. (10) Another letter
the following day from the DOE continued the story. It
stated that the Minister had also indicated that the New
Towns Commission was to be retained to secure the orderly
winding up of the Corporation, and further that the Commission would then have a management role for the commercial and industrial assets. The letter went on to say
that as

> far as Stevenage is concerned our discussions should
> proceed on the basis that rented housing will be trans-
> ferred to the District [sic] Council on 1st April 1978.
> Responsibility for the residual house-building pro-
> gramme in the period between housing transfer and the
> dissolution of the Development Corporation needs to be
> established with full regard to the part the private
> sector can play. There are strong arguments for pro-
> ceeding on the basis of a degree of *certainty* and it is
> the Department's *preliminary* view that the Stevenage

Development Corporation should be wound up in 1980.
(11, emphasis added)

So it seemed as if the Corporation would terminate its
activities in 1980, although it must be remembered that
this was a preliminary view.

Ironically the Inspector had in fact recommended that the
Draft Designation Order be made, albeit with a suggestion
that there should remain open the possibility of excluding
certain areas. (12) His report was dated 13 July 1976,
and ran to a total of 73,000 words. The paragraph
referred to by the DOE in relation to Mr Shore's decision
simply stated that the Corporation had calculated a total
housing need of 36,500 in 1991 of which 29,000 could be
found within the planned residential areas of the existing
designated area. His most important observations were
contained in paragraphs 10.03 and 10.04, where he stated
that the question whether the existing designated area was
adequate for the objectives of the 1966 Master Plan no
doubt first arose when the Corporation had sought permission to develop land ahead of schedule. He added that
the permission to do so could not of course be rescinded
and indeed the work on Sectors 4 and 5 was in hand

but it *pre-empted,* to some degree, the issue the
Inquiry was called on to consider. In retrospect, it
might be argued that the time to consider whether expansion was needed ... was when it first appeared
necessary to depart from the time-scale of the 1966
Master Plan. But the opportunity was not then taken;
and one must accept the consequences, which include the
fact that the Corporation is running out of land....
An inevitable conclusion at this point in time is that,
in consequence of past decisions, some expansion of the
designated area is now necessary. (13, emphasis added)

Thus the Inspector considered that the Corporation had a
prima facie case for expansion, but unfortunately for him
the Minister later found it quite easy to disagree. The
point that the Inspector made that the expansion should
have been contemplated in 1966 was correct, but of course
from the Corporation's viewpoint such an action was at the
time impossible as it had just had its 1964 major expansion proposals turned down, so 1966 was hardly the
right time to try again.

Dame Evelyn Denington informed the April Board Meeting
that although there would now be no expansion, the embargo
on building in Sectors 7 and 8 had been lifted at once,
while the Consultant Planner informed the meeting that
provided there were no undue delays, the land in Sectors
4,5 and 6 should be sufficient for about five to six
years. (14) Dame Evelyn's attitude towards the decision
was a rather stoic 'it could have been worse':

Stevenage remains a fine town and will not be marred by this turn of events. The alternative machinery to cater for local needs will be fully exploited. The two authorities are convinced that those needs shall be met and that the future well-being of Stevenage is assured. (15)

Shirley Williams was reported to have already spoken to Mr Shore about the possibility that additional land might be needed in a few years' time if the second generation - particularly those aged up to 16 years of age - were to be housed. She expected to explore at a further meeting with Mr Shore the procedures by which some extra land might be acquired if essential for local needs. (16) Similarly, SIEG accepted the decision with 'regret and concern'. (17)

CASE, on the other hand, were naturally extremely pleased with the decision. Mr McCombie stated that the Hertfordshire Society (who had possession of CASE funds, as well as its own) was approximately £1,000 short at the end of the Inquiry, so CASE members were canvassed and £500 was raised, to which the Hertfordshire Society added £500 from its own funds. So in total CASE had spent £2,500 fighting the expansion proposals. (18) In retrospect Mr McCombie considered that the Inspector had gained a tremendous amount of support and respect from the opposition (note that he stated this after the Minister's decision), especially in the way he did his walkabout, 'he looked at every aspect, he even looked at the village notice board'. However, Mr McCombie continued, the Inspector obviously considered that CASE's arguments were not valid, and indeed he had not seemed to take much cognisance of them at all, but CASE felt that at the Inquiry it had put up the best possible opposition, in that never before had the Corporation been faced with an organisation which had been prepared to dissect its statements of fact or opinion: indeed the Corporation 'got a considerable shock'.

What of the future of CASE? The organisation had, according to Mr McCombie, been virtually disbanded. However, he continued, when the decision to disband was taken it wasn't clearly appreciated how near 'we might be to having to start up again, but I'm afraid that if we did have to start again it could very well be the case that we could not put up an effective opposition - we simply shall not have the money'. (19)

According to the SVA's Constitution, the Association lives on, but according to its Treasurer the Association is dead 'in terms of any kind of reality'. As for CAUSE, who really knows? Following the Inquiry, Mrs Powell once

again turned her attention to more traditional politics,
and in so doing decided to leave the National Party
because of its 'connections with the Ku Klux Klan', (20)
so she then formed her own party called the 'United-
Conservative-Labour Party', which failed to make members,
and blaming such a failure entirely on the choice of name
she gave to her party, she immediately formed another one,
the Brittania Party.

In May of 1977 the General Manager reported on the
current state of the Corporation's 'employment/unemploy-
ment' research and asserted that

> if it were not for the continued expansion in employ-
> ment by BAC, the local employment situation would have
> been a good deal worse. The qualification has to be
> made though, that the occupational requirements of BAC
> are not such that they can readily be met from the
> local pool of unemployed or school leavers. And,
> because the rest of local industry as a whole has been
> contracting, the consequence has been that the *manu-
> facturing base of the town has become more, rather than
> less, dependent upon the fortunes of one firm*. (21,
> emphasis added)

Thus it is to the industrial structure of the town, and
particularly the British Aircraft Corporation (BAC), that
attention is now focused.

Part three

11   Stevenage
Constraints on the urban managers

it is plainly false to postulate a major shift towards
'middle' and higher-paid jobs, when the bulk of the
labour force are in essentially wage-earning jobs, however those jobs are conventionally designated;   and
when many white-collar employees are now merely semi-
skilled operatives in the world of office work.
J.Westergaard and H.Resler (1975), p.73

Part Three is concerned with the relationship between
theoretical perspectives relating to planning, planners,
industrialists, politicians and the public, and empirical
material, notably the case of Stevenage. Attention will
be focused particularly, although not exclusively, on the
notion of 'urban managerialism'. However, before proceeding to a specific discussion of urban managerialism
it is the intention here to indicate immediately the constraints on the actions of urban managers, and moreover
to do this through an examination of the industrial base
of Stevenage.

 Harloe, in another context, describes the nature of such
constraints in the following manner:

   The urban functionaries, far from being an 'independent' variable, clearly acted within constraints
   determined by the wider economic, political and ideological structures of their society. Forces, particularly economic power, over which they had little or no
   control appeared to be far more crucial determinants
   of urban patterns and processes than the managers. (1)

 Similarly Mellor suggests that 'planners, along with
other professional groups, have a certain responsibility
as executives of government, but the options are implicit-
ly foreclosed by the requirements of industrial investment
and the demands of the corporations'. (2)

 The key to the understanding of many of the unusual
patterns of development in Stevenage since its designation

in 1946 can be found in the nature of Stevenage's industrial base.   In summary what has already been suggested is the following:

(i) right from the early days of the town there had been a reliance on a limited type of industry, namely electronics, computers, and arms production;

(ii) although the Corporation had recognised this fact - for instance there had been an annual call for more diversification - it was unable or, more likely, unwilling to do anything about it;

(iii) this lack of diversification had produced a situation where out-commuting was increasing as the skills the industrialists required were not necessarily available in the town (what must be noted here of course is that the lack of skills available for high-technology industry would not in itself lead to out-commuting: however what is crucial is the occupational mismatch of labour supply and demand - a shortage of skilled workers of certain types, a large number of unemployed persons who are unskilled, inexperienced, or have the wrong skills.   In the early years of the town, the process of 'key worker' housing produced a good 'fit' between labour supply and demand in occupational terms.   Skilled males were brought in to fill skilled vacancies so therefore a high level of self-containment was achieved.   What has happened since then, though, is that the second generation do not have the same skills and aspirations as their 'working-class Tory' fathers, but nevertheless industry has remained largely unchanged and still requires the same type of skills.   So, despite growth in the service sector, the occupational structure of the labour force is moving out of line with the labour requirements of industry.   The 'key worker' housing policy has contributed to this skill mismatch by allowing firms to import skilled labour while neglecting to offer training programmes for the locals.   Point (v) reinforces this: why go to all the expense of training 'ungrateful, longhaired, undisciplined' youngsters, when every single skilled worker can be housed quite easily);

(iv) this has resulted in industry looking outside of the town for a considerable proportion of its work-force;

(v) but often exaggerating the need, in that they were never able to take up all the allocations that they were given, even though these allocations were less than the number that the industrialists had asked for in the first place;

(vi) this led to the Corporation being unable to formulate a housing allocation policy for its second generation residents;   and

(vii) finally led the Corporation consistently to state
that land was short and that 'growth' was the only
answer.

Now obviously the Corporation would have to benefit -
apart from its own growth obsession - in some way from a
situation where it was consistently being let down in
terms of housing allocation take-up, and indeed there was
a benefit to the Corporation which can, however, only be
understood when the industrialists of the town are seen
both as a group and as individuals. In essence the argument is that the Corporation, and consequently Stevenage
itself, have been excessively dependent on one firm, BAC,
and to a lesser extent on a few others. Now this dependence, although inevitably a factor of vulnerability,
is at the same time a factor of security in this particular case, in that BAC has never really appeared to be in
any difficulties and has consistently continued to grow,
whilst other firms have simply not done so. BAC has
itself always taken up fully its quota of houses whilst
the other employers have been unable - to a startling
degree - to take up theirs. This has consistently put
the Corporation in a difficult position. It could not
begin to discriminate against the employers in comparison
with (say) the second generation housing needs, in that
its 'staple diet', BAC, was an employer. On the other
hand it could not discriminate between the employers at
the risk of reducing confidence in the Corporation and
possibly creating conflict, and furthermore the Corporation itself had to have trust in employers other than
BAC in case that particular company failed. So in a sense
the employers, and notably in the form of SIEG, had the
Corporation 'over a barrel'.

Before continuing it must again be noted that the history
of non-take-up of key worker housing allocations ought to
have enabled the Corporation to meet second generation
needs, but the Corporation so mismanaged its house
building programme in the 1970s, that house building rates
plummeted just when the Corporation had a chance to catch
up and recover from its over-generous key worker housing
policy of earlier years, in order to concentrate on truly
local needs.

STEVENAGE: THE INDUSTRIAL BASE

To begin with it must be remembered that in the formative
years of the town, and because of the nature of the population movement, the Corporation had to look for predominantly male-employing industries with a relatively low

demand for juveniles, and in so doing it was always confined by government constraints such as the IDC process
(although not in the very early years), which in times of
economic stringency favoured firms producing for the arms
programme or export markets.

1 Unemployment

It can be observed from figure 1, that unemployment in
Stevenage was for the most part well below that of the
region in the earlier years, but much closer to the
regional average in the more recent period. (3) A sharp
peak in the early months of 1963, which was more marked
in Stevenage than in the region as a whole, was the result
of a bout of particularly severe weather which put several
hundred building workers out of work for some weeks, and
of course at that time building workers in Stevenage represented an abnormally high proportion of total employment as the Corporation was reaching its developmental
peak. Longer-term trends can quite easily be discerned

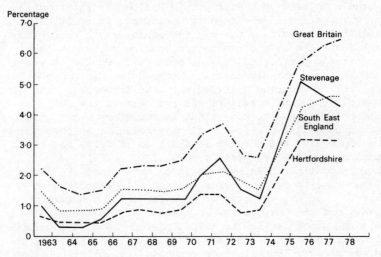

FIGURE 1 Unemployment rates 1963-77: monthly average for
each year

from figure 1: for example the effect of a three- or
four-year economic cycle can be seen. But in addition it
becomes clear that the town had moved from a position of
relatively low unemployment to one of parity with the
region and indeed well above the rates for Hertfordshire,
and moreover there are indications that fluctuations in
employment conditions in Stevenage were more marked than
in the region as a whole.

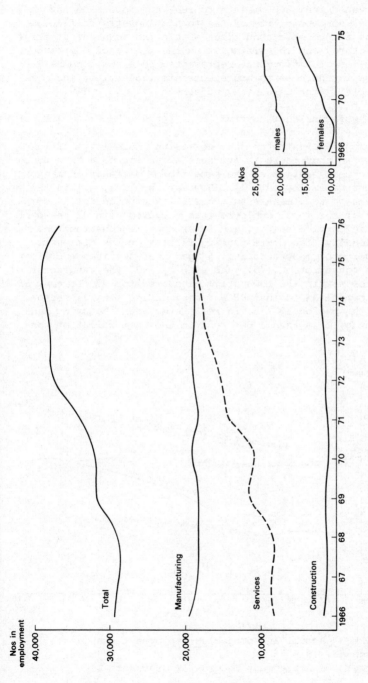

FIGURE 2   Employment in Stevenage, 1966-76
Source: DE Records

It would seem appropriate to seek the source of any ab-
normal susceptibility of the town's industry to fluctuations in economic conditions within the town's industrial
structure, and in particular in the degree of dominance,
in terms of employment, represented by a small number of
firms in engineering and electronic industries, and more
especially the aerospace industry.

2   Manufacturing industry

Figure 2 demonstrates the increasing 'normality' of the
town, in that there is evidence of an increase in service
employment, whilst at the same time a decrease in manufacturing employment. (4)   However, by 1971, within the
Stevenage EEA, manufacturing still accounted for 54 per
cent of the total employment as compared with 42 per cent
in the service sector, and 3 per cent in construction.
Nationally, the corresponding figures at the time were
36 per cent manufacturing, 54 per cent services and 6 per
cent construction. (5)   And even by 1975 the manufacturing
sector within the town still accounted for 47 per cent of
employment as against 48 per cent in the service sector.
For the period 1971-5, in real terms, manufacturing had
risen by less than 1 per cent in the town whilst at the

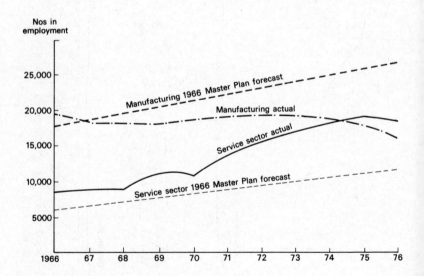

FIGURE 3   Actual and projected employment changes in
Stevenage, 1966-76
Source: DE Employment Records II Stevenage EEA

same time service employment grew by over 32 per cent.
During that time manufacturing employment in Great Britain
fell by 7 per cent and service employment rose by 10 per
cent. (6)   These figures are not particularly exceptional
in themselves except when set beside the Corporation's
forecasts about growth and the consequent growth policies:
for example see figure 3 on actual and projected employment changes.   Similarly it is interesting and informative
to note SIEG's report on growth in manufacturing employment which suggested that an extra 1,000 jobs a year were
needed from 1970 onwards, and that there was therefore a
need to step up key worker housing availability and to
refrain from industrial diversification. (7)

Table 2 is concerned with the maximum and minimum employment levels of Stevenage's 'top 11' manufacturers, in the
period 1961-76.   It can be seen that nine of the employers
achieved their highest employment levels during the 1960s,
and for five of them it occurred in 1966 or before.   The
most probable reason for this, of course, is the fact that
during their 'build-up' period they were over-optimistic
and so engaged labour forces which they consequently could
not sustain, and indeed it can be seen that the majority
of the major industrial employers in the town have been
shedding their labour force for the last seven to ten
years.

Profiles of the town's 'top 10' manufacturers are included in appendix 8, therefore only BAC, Hawker Siddeley
Dynamics and Kodak will be examined in a little more
detail here.

The British Aircraft Corporation - originally English
Electric Limited - came to Stevenage in 1955 following a
government decision to relocate the company to the town
in order to relieve the pressure upon labour in the Luton
area. (8)   Only one sixth of BAC's market is British, with
the other five sixths being almost totally absorbed by the
Middle East.   Stevenage is the headquarters for the
company's Guided Weapons Division, a division which earned
a £19.2 million profit after tax in 1976, and this compared with merely £3.8 million just four years earlier.
(9)   The products of the division are essentially those
of the Rapier anti-aircraft missile and the Swingfire
anti-tank missile, with a major contract with Iran for the
Rapier being of particular importance.   There are three
particularly important structural questions to be asked in
connection with BAC:

(a) The nature of the Arms Economy.   Kidron states the
traditional view of the relationship between the arms
economy and employment:

So far, the weight of the arms economy has been on the

TABLE 2   Maximum and minimum employment levels of
Stevenage manufacturers, 1961-76

Company		Max.emp.	Yr	Min.emp.	Yr
BAC					
1961	4225	6103	1975	3852	1968
1976	5979				
Kodak					
1961	1596	1934	1966	1405	1963
1976	1636				
Mentmore					
1961	647	1187	1974	643	1962
1976	859				
Geo.King					
1961	1776	2058	1962	551	1974
1976	704				
ICL					
1961	658	1895	1969	692	1974
1976	771				
ICI					
1961	449	1180	1969	499	1976
1976	499				
HSD					
1961	1571	1898	1963	939	1976
1976	939				
ESA					
1961	757	764	1962	510	1976
1976	510				
Taylor					
Est.1962	77	1211	1969	783	1964
1976	927				
Ether					
1961	506	1023	1965	287	1976
1976	287				
Bowater					
1961	-	815	1969	466	1976
1976	-	-	-	-	-

side of stability, charging and recharging the more
immediate causes of high employment, and well-being.
(10)

Similarly in a special CIS-CDP report, there is the
following argument:

The powerful defence lobby, the profitability of the
defence contractors, the deliberate attempt to export
arms to the middle east, and the long term nature of
Defence expenditure are all factors that ensure that
there will be no significant cuts in the (£4.5 billion)
spent here. (11)

Bill Warren, on the other hand, argues against the proposition inherent in the two previous arguments that full
employment (as we more or less have come to define it)
depends upon state arms production. He states that the
proposition usually is that arms production represents an
industry which raises demand without causing public/
private enterprise competition. However, he states that
'defence expenditure as a proportion of GNP declined from
over 10 per cent in 1952-53 to over 7 per cent in 1960
without any significant effect on unemployment rates'.
(12) Now BAC has managed to find its markets, but how
stable are they? Furthermore, with only the precision
products division at Stevenage having a commercial basis,
what alternative could BAC seek? Indeed it does face competition, as the following Stevenage Constituency Labour
Party observation (resolution) demonstrates:

Stevenage CLP expresses concern that the proposed
purchase by NATO of 27 Boeing Early Warning Aircraft
for an estimated cost of £1,400 million is a further
threat to the European aerospace industry, especially
that of the UK. (13)

(b) Nationalisation. BAC, together with Hawker Siddeley
Dynamics, were nationalised under the Aircraft and Ship-
building Act (1977), vesting on 29 April 1977. In 1976
BAC donated £10,000 to the Conservative Party in order to
'support the opposition which they were providing to those
dogmatic approaches of the Labour Government which we
considered to be contrary to the best interests of British
industry and of the United Kingdom as a whole'. The BAC
statement continued:

Those responsible in Parliament for bringing about
this change in ownership for doctrinaire political
reasons will have created additional and unnecessary
burdens for the management of the recently established
British Aerospace, burdens which can only be successfully borne by professional managers with ingenuity
and resourcefulness of the highest order. It is to be
hoped that they will not only be able to master these

new problems but will maintain or even better the
progress made in the world's highly competitive markets
by the industry under private ownership. (14)
It will of course be quite some time before it is known
how BAC (and HSD) fare under the guidance of the nationalised British Aerospace, which will inevitably attempt some
restructuring of the aerospace industry.

(c) New town privileges. As has been indicated in table
2, BAC has gone from strength to strength whilst other
employers have not done so. Of course its growth in
Stevenage has been due primarily to the fact that it had
the right product available at the right time, viz.,
weapons for the Middle East. (15) However what must also
be taken into account is the realisation that the Development Corporation has bent over backwards in order to meet
BAC's needs, both in terms of housing and infrastructure.
This is evident from the way in which the Corporation has
consistently refused - until quite recently - to rearrange
the allocation procedure in spite of the continued disap-
pointing performance of the town's employers. The reason
being, of course, BAC's continual high demand which both
the Corporation and BAC in turn met in terms of allocations and allocation take-up: this one, and extremely
crucial (as noted earlier), exception to the employers'
norm was sufficient for the Corporation to continue with
its policy despite its deleterious effects on the second
generation residents. The question to be asked here is
what would happen to BAC's 'key workers' if the local
authority - though this is unlikely - phased out nominated
housing, and BAC had to look to the local labour force
which invariably would not have the exact and particular
amount of skills the company needed?

Hawker Siddeley Dynamics, like BAC, export the majority
of their products although they do have a systematic programme for the production of guided weapons for the Royal
Navy and the Royal Air Force. In the company's 1976
Annual Report it is stated that over 60 per cent of their
products are exported, these being essentially guided
missiles and guidance systems, satellites, electro-optics,
and so on. HSD shares the same problems as BAC, but to a
lesser extent.

The Stevenage plant of Kodak is the company's third
largest, with on average 1,630 employees. However there
is not a particularly certain and optimistic future for
the plant:

We have been enabled by union agreement to continue the
slimming process that will secure employment at a point
consistent with our future needs.... Stevenage production volume declined again in 1976 due, primarily,

227 Chapter 11

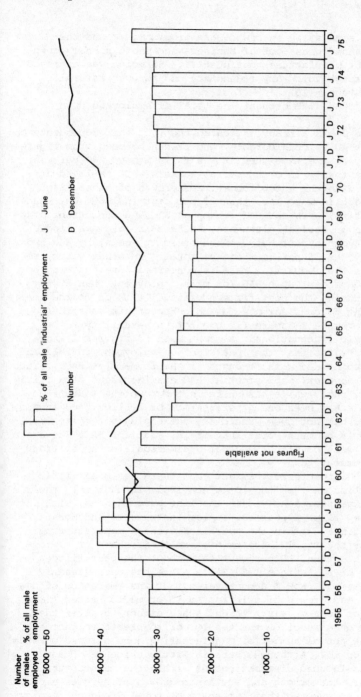

FIGURE 4 BAC male employment: number, and as a percentage of all male 'industrial' employment

to some delay in new camera programmes; and the
planned phase-out of business and professional equipment manufacture continued.... Slimming was achieved
through voluntary redundancy and through natural
wastage. (16)

And indeed 1978 brought the total of employees down to
1,100.

Table 2 has already indicated the fact that dependence on
BAC is quite considerable, and it can be seen from figure
4 that at the time when it was fully manned, 40 per cent
of the town's male industrial workers were employed at
BAC. With the establishment and growth of other firms
this declined to less than 23 per cent in 1968, but since
that time, with renewed growth at BAC and concurrent stagnation or decline elsewhere, BAC's share of male 'industrial' employment has climbed steadily again, by the end
of 1975 to 35 per cent of the total. In other words, so
far as the industrial base is concerned, Stevenage is now
more dependent upon BAC for male employment than at any
time during the past fifteen years. It is of course important to consider how far this factor has contributed
to Stevenage's apparently greater vulnerability to
economic fluctuations. A comparison of figures 1 and 4
demonstrates that the 'peaks' of unemployment in 1963 and
1968 coincided with 'troughs' in employment at BAC. Since
1968, however, employment at BAC has increased at a fairly
steady rate, while elsewhere in the town the industrial
picture has been one of stagnation or decline, and indeed,
if BAC had not been expanding, the employment scene locally would be much worse than it is. But for BAC, Stevenage
could well be either another Skelmersdale or a dormitory
or commuter town.

Table 3 points to the fact that there has been little
variation in the 'top 10' since 1961, in that only their
relative positions within the list have changed, with only
two new firms appearing, Taylor Instruments and Bowater
Packaging. Within the overall Stevenage manufacturing
sector the top 10 have maintained their share of employment at around 80 per cent throughout the past fifteen
years or so. Since 1967 BAC's share has been steadily
increasing. Row C demonstrates that the emergence of new
firms and growth of existing small or medium-sized firms
has not been on a sufficient scale either to alter the
basic dependence on the top 10, or to create an increase
in the actual number of manufacturing jobs offered outside
the top 10. Although there is little evidence of any
growth-induced diversification within the manufacturing
sector, the strong and sustained growth of service employment has ensured that the share of total Stevenage employ-

TABLE 3 Employment in the ten largest manufacturing employers in Stevenage, 1961-76

Rank order by numbers employed	1961	1964	1967	1970	1973	1976
1 BAC	4,225 BAC	4,450 BAC	4,045 BAC	4,629 BAC	5,531 BAC	5,979 BAC
2 King	1,776 King	1,720 ICL	1,984 ICL	1,809 Kodak	1,717 Kodak	1,636 Kodak
3 Kodak	1,596 Kodak	1,596 Kodak	1,895 Kodak	1,696 ICL	1,497 HSD	939 HSD
4 HSD	1,571 HSD	1,302 HSD	1,476 King	1,566 Mentmore	1,178 Taylor	927 Taylor
5 ESA	757 ICL	911 King	1,416 HSD	1,421 King	1,063 Mentmore	859 Mentmore
6 ICL	658 ICI	877 ICI	1,036 Taylor	1,103 Taylor	1,047 ICL	771 ICL
7 Mentmore	647 Mentmore	789 Taylor	923 Mentmore	1,065 HSD	952 King	704 King
8 Ether	506 Ether	786 Mentmore	883 ICI	1,058 ICI	848 ESA	510 ESA
9 ICI	449 Taylor	783 Ether	748 Ether	701 ESA	687 ICI	499 ICI
10 Marconi	355 ESA	741 ESA	739 ESA	668 Bowater	592 Bowater	466 Bowater
A Total	12,540	13,955	15,145	15,716	15,112	13,290
B BAC's share of all top 10 jobs	34%	32%	27%	29%	37%	45%
C Top 10 as % of total manufacturing jobs in Stevenage EEA	84%	79%	82%	82%	80%	82%
D No. of manufacturing jobs in Stevenage EEA not in top 10	2426	3814	3387	3480	3896	2912
E Top 10 as % of total employment in Stevenage EEA	56%	51%	53%	50%	40%	38%

Source: CES Industrial Employment Returns and ERIIs for calculating percentages of total employment in EEA, except 1976, which uses CE survey totals.

TABLE 4 Employment changes in Stevenage's 'Top 10'
companies 1971-5, compared with Great Britain.
Changes for equivalent MLHs

1971-base year 100. All other figures % of 1971

	BAC MLH 383		HSD MLH 383		Kodak MLH 351	
	GB	BAC	GB	HSD	GB	Kodak
1971	100	100	100	100	100	100
1972	95	108	95	84	95	96
1973	92	113	92	72	97	102
1974	96	115	96	74	97	102
1975	97	124	97	85	94	99

	Mentmore MLH 495		Geo.W.King MLH 337		ICL MLH 366	
	GB	Mentmore	GB	King	GB	ICL
1971	100	100	100	100	100	100
1972	97	106	97	77	100	84
1973	97	120	98	80	92	79
1974	101	121	100	41	88	37
1975	94	116	98	54	86	50

	ICI MLH 496		ESA MLH 472		Taylor MLH 354	
	GB	ICI	GB	ESA	GB	Taylor
1971	100	100	100	100	100	100
1972	103	84	105	101	95	88
1973	111	86	114	99	99	92
1974	115	70	107	94	96	90
1975	103	57	104	76	92	-

	Ether MLH 354		Bowater MLH 482	
	GB	Ether	GB	Bowater
1971	100	100	100	100
1972	95	82	101	99
1973	99	79	102	104
1974	96	80	107	105
1975	92	76	100	90

Company totals refer to employment at the Stevenage plant.

ment accounted for by the top 10 (Row D) has decreased
steadily since 1967.

Table 4 is concerned with the MLHs that Stevenage's major
companies come under (appendix 9 gives a summary of SIC
and MLH orders). Most of the major companies come under
an MLH which has either gained employment or only decreased slightly in national terms between 1971 and 1975.
Only MLH 366 (electronic computers) has shed more than
10 per cent of its employment nationally over the five
years. Three of the MLHs in which firms appearing in the
top 10 are found, have actually increased employment in
the period 1971 to 1975, while the remainder have lost
between 2-6 per cent of the 1971 totals. In other words,
Stevenage's major manufacturers are in very strong sectors
of the national economy. However, against this there is -
with the exception of BAC, Kodak and Mentmore - the fact
that the Stevenage plants have not even maintained employment levels in line with the national situation. Moreover
ICI, ICL, King and ESA have all reduced employment by over
40 per cent, and with the exception of ICL these companies
are in MLHs which in national terms have increased employment over the five years. Thus the often repeated tale of
Stevenage's dynamic and expanding employment base is so
much nonsense. Certain local factors can be used to
explain part of the problem, for example, the removal of
an operation by ICL, the take-over and subsequent rationalisation at King, and a large fire at ESA. However, one
fairly consistent feature does emerge from table 4, namely
that several of the companies in Stevenage which show
marked and exceptional reductions in employment could be
described as 'branch plants' of national or international
companies, for example ICI, HSD, ICL, King and Pye Ether.
It has long been a feature of the operations of such
companies that branch plants tend to be the most vulnerable in rationalisation programmes or recession. By
contrast BAC, for which Stevenage is the headquarters and
major production plant for the Guided Weapons Division,
has moved from strength to strength. To emphasise some
of the previous points, figure 5 compares employment
totals between Great Britain and Stevenage by SIC order
within the period 1971-5, and what is apparent is the
number of SIC orders which declined faster in Stevenage
than in the country generally. What is even more striking
is the fact that these declines have occurred in industrial sectors which cannot be considered as being particularly susceptible to labour shedding in Great Britain as a
whole. Stevenage has not had to confront the problem of
a legacy of 'traditionally' declining industries such as
heavy engineering, textiles, mining, and so on. Thus the

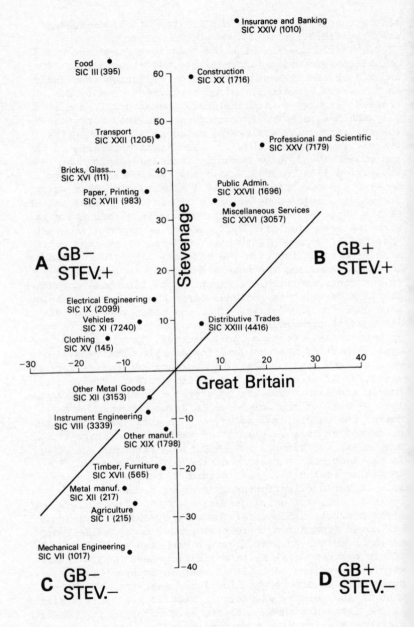

FIGURE 5 Comparison of GB/Stevenage, SIC orders, percentage change in total employment 1971-5. (Figures in brackets show Stevenage employment in 1975.)

loss of jobs in supposedly 'dynamic' sectors of industry
at a disproportionate rate must give cause for concern
over long-term employment prospects in the town.
 Using data from the 1971 Census, together with the
results of the Corporation's 1976 'Household Survey', the
Corporation's Social Development Office has analysed the
occupational structure of employed residents in the town
at 1976, (17) an analysis which can be considered as complementary in terms of findings to that of the analysis
of the manufacturing base. The two occupational groups
(appendix 10 gives the orders for socio-economic and occupational groups) with the highest proportion of workers
were clerical workers (Group XXI) and professional and
technical workers (Group XXV), both with 19 per cent in
each group. Group XXV contained the highest proportion
of males with 22 per cent of all employed males, Group VII
(engineering and allied trades workers) coming second with
20 per cent. 34 per cent of all employed females worked
as clerical workers, whilst 22 per cent worked in
services. In terms of socio-economic group analysis, 24
per cent of the total work-force came under the category
of junior non-manual, with 22 per cent in the skilled
manual and 11 per cent in the semi-skilled category. The
highest proportion of males were in the skilled manual,
and of females in the junior non-manual categories. The
analysis added that manufacturing industrial concerns do
in fact have large numbers of clerical and secretarial
staff, 'often larger than one would expect'. (18) The
analysis continued:

> a large number of skilled manual workers are employed
> outside of Stevenage. 2,320 skilled workers live in
> the town and work outside, whereas 3,910 of them live
> and work in the town.... Why? ... the predominance of
> aircraft establishments in the surrounding areas means
> that similar skills are required by firms in different
> towns. (19)

However, what must again be asked is why do so many
skilled manual workers commute out when there is supposed
to be a severe shortage in Stevenage of such workers, as
SIEG never miss an opportunity to inform the Corporation.
The reasons are threefold: (a) Wages: there have been a
number of industrial disputes concerning wages over the
years, in 1978 at BAC, Bowater Packaging, and Mentmore;
(b) Wrong skills: the narrow high-technology base requires extremely specialised skills; and (c) Lack of
jobs: the high-technology companies, for example ICL,
have shed just as many workers as other companies. The
analysis concluded with the important observation that
when an employer lost a worker the Corporation did not

gain a house, but rather merely received increased demands
from employers for more housing.

3 Service sector

The service sector of employment can be analysed in terms
of the basic service together with the non-basic service.
(20) Basic service employment is functionally related to
either a regional or national population level, and is
relatively autonomous of locality, whilst non-basic
service employment is functionally related to the local
population and locates in relation to that local population.
 Table 5 gives the aggregate growth in the service sector
employment between 1971-5, and with the minor exception of
the slight decrease in the numbers employed in SIC order
XXI (gas, electricity and water; refer to appendix 11 for
an elaboration of the service SIC orders), the overall
picture of service sector employment is one of almost un-
interrupted sustained growth. SIC order XXV (professional
and scientific, accountancy, education, law, etc.) accounted for nearly half the growth in the service sector
and nearly all of this was of a non-basic type. SIC order
XXIV (finance, banking, insurance, etc.) experienced the
most rapid growth rate over the five years and here it was
basic service employment which contributed the bulk of the
increase. Between 1971 and 1975 the overall picture was
one of non-basic sector growth of 34 per cent and basic
sector growth of 26 per cent. Furthermore it is quite
clear that even during the recession the service sector
had not been subject to the kind of large-scale 'one-off'
labour cut-backs which have been a feature of manufacturing employment in the town in recent years.
 Table 6 shows that Stevenage is represented by every
single non-basic service except MLH 864 (advertising and
market research). Similarly, table 7 shows that only MLH
811 (wholesale distribution of petroleum products) could
be considered absent in the town (in national terms MLH
811 accounts for less than 3 per cent of all employment
in SIC order XXIII, thus the 'loss' of employment to
Stevenage is insignificant). In 1971 the three major
employers of the basic service sector were research and
development, wholesaling, and national government which
between them accounted for 2,180 out of 2,439 (89 per
cent) basic service jobs. In 1975 these three activities
still provided some 80 per cent of basic service jobs.
(21) Thus by and large the growth of service sector employment has been satisfactory, although the major contribution has come from the public sector, for example health

TABLE 5   Basic and non-basic service sector employment growth in Stevenage, 1971-5

SIC	1971	1972	1973	1974	1975	Numerical change 1971-5	1975 as % of 1971
XXI Basic	-	-	-	-	-	-	-
Non-basic	96	96	87	85	88	8	92
Total	96	96	87	85	88	8	92
XXII Basic	198	199	207	230	212	14	107
Non-basic	622	725	703	822	993	371	160
Total	820	924	910	1,052	1,205	385	147
XXIII Basic	723	753	729	651	775	52	107
Non-basic	3,318	3,453	3,620	3,794	3,641	323	110
Total	4,041	4,206	4,349	4,445	4,416	375	109
XXIV Basic	61	232	232	354	409	348	670
Non-basic	533	522	592	700	601	68	113
Total	594	754	824	1,054	1,010	416	170
XXV Basic	897	881	862	827	929	32	104
Non-basic	4,069	4,655	5,758	6,067	6,250	2,181	154
Total	4,966	5,536	6,620	6,894	7,179	2,213	145
XXVI Basic	-	-	-	-	-	-	-
Non-basic	2,304	2,288	2,581	2,980	3,057	753	133
Total	2,304	2,288	2,581	2,980	3,057	753	133
XXVII Basic	560	577	662	649	758	198	135
Non-basic	706	837	893	964	938	232	133
Total	1,266	1,414	1,555	1,613	1,696	430	134

	1971	1972	1973	1974	1975	Numerical change 1971-5	1975 as % of 1971
Basic	2,439	2,642	2,692	2,711	3,083	644	126
Non-basic	11,648	12,576	14,234	15,412	15,568	3,920	134
Grand Totals	14,087	15,218	16,926	18,123	18,651	4,564	132

Boxed figures indicate a decrease in employment over the immediate preceding year. 1971 cells have been compared with 1970.

TABLE 6   Non-basic service employment, Stevenage EEA, 1971-5

SIC	MLH	1971	1972	1973	1974	1975	1975 as % 1971
XXI	601	51	47	48	45	43	84
	602	not available					
	603	45	49	39	40	45	100
XXII	702	217	216	177	166	195	90
	708	396	500	514	496	548	138
	709	9	9	12	160	250	2777
XXIII	820	880	930	911	978	1052	120
	821	2438	2523	2709	2816	2589	106
XXIV	860	145	136	515	132	119	82
	861	209	234	243	270	277	133
	862	25	19	17	12	25	100
	863	14	6	26	18	14	100
	864	-	-	-	-	-	-
	865	140	127	155	268	166	119
XXV	871	35	31	40	75	46	131
	872	2785	3025	3089	3310	3379	121
	873	74	94	111	49	101	136
	874	292	527	1447	1569	1787	612
	875	15	15	18	16	19	127
	879	868	963	1053	1048	918	106
XXVI	881	2	8	6	31	37	1850
	882	149	131	144	132	217	146
	883	22	33	26	28	47	214
	884	157	115	174	161	176	112
	885	119	121	119	108	103	87
	886	282	310	327	310	314	111
	887	37	44	40	40	41	111
	888	101	111	116	118	213	211
	889	125	134	127	111	118	94
	892	8	7	6	4	3	38
	893	30	55	24	28	27	90
	894	495	476	540	519	504	102
	895	2	2	1	4	7	350
	899	775	741	931	1386	1250	161
XXVII	906	706	837	893	964	938	133

TABLE 7 Employment in basic services in Stevenage EEA, 1971-5

SIC	MLH	1971	1972	1973	1974	1975	$\frac{1975}{1971}$x100
XXII	701	147	161	150	174	149	101
	703	51	38	57	56	63	124
	704	-	-	-	-	-	-
	705	-	-	-	-	-	-
	706	-	-	-	-	-	-
	707	-	-	-	-	-	-
XXIII	810	190	237	227	139	236	124
	811	-	-	-	-	-	-
	812	327	320	324	321	339	104
	831	125	126	98	109	111	89
	832	81	70	80	82	89	110
XXIV	860	-	-	-	137	154	-
	866	61	232	232	217	255	418
XXV	876	897	881	862	827	929	102
XXVII	901	560	577	662	649	758	135
Total		2,439	2,642	2,692	2,711	3,083	126

(the Lister Hospital) and education, and so Stevenage could hardly fail. On the commercial side, the town is noticeably less successful, and in comparison with other London new towns Stevenage is deficient in head offices (basic services).

4 Population variables

As has been indicated, there lies within the nature of the town's employment base the seeds of unemployment, in that the skills required are not necessarily readily available in the town - hence the continued importation of 'key workers'. In other words a mismatch has arisen between the occupational structure of labour demand in the town and available labour resources.

The problems which result from such a mismatch are only just beginning to appear, but the next few years will be particularly problematic by virtue of Stevenage's population spread. Figure 6 shows an annual 'crude' birth rate per thousand resident population, thus including an allowance for the increasing size of the population. Ig-

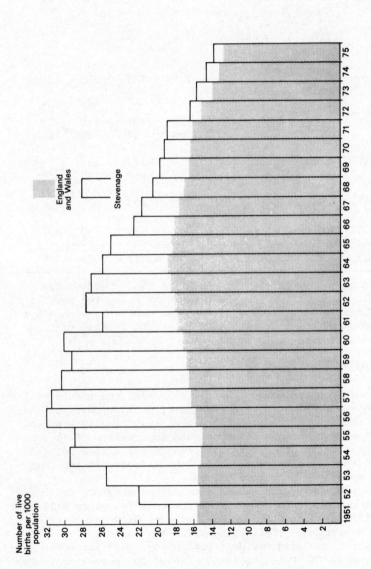

FIGURE 6 Stevenage, compared with England and Wales: 'crude' birth rate from 1951

noring fluctuations from one year to the next, the pattern is seen as a sharp increase until 1956, followed by a more or less steady decline thereafter, until in 1975 the 'crude' birth rate was less than half that of twenty years earlier. However, one of the 'age bulges' in the town is that of the 10 to 14-year age group, and the relatively high birth rates in the early 1960s have led to even greater numbers in this group. This group is now leaving school and looking for employment. The 10 to 14-year group contains 900 more children than the next younger age group, and 1,200 more than the 15 to 19-year age group.

There is, of course, as has already been mentioned, the long-term difficulty of finding unskilled jobs for school leavers due to the occupational structure of the town's industry, but there is further the tendency of employers to fill vacancies with married women rather than school leavers, believing these to be more stable employees; and there may be an increased number of married women looking for employment, especially if their husbands have been made redundant. For the age group 16-18 years, the following example is illustrative of the situation they have to face, and of course the example is further illustrative of what the 10-14 group can expect.

Young Persons Aged 16-18 Years

July 1974	209 unemployed	27 unfilled vacancies
July 1975	235 unemployed	28 unfilled vacancies
July 1976	643 unemployed	112 unfilled vacancies

Source: DE (Stevenage Office).

Although with each year after 1976 the numbers of young people requiring jobs will increase, the year in which the number will rapidly rise is 1978, and the figure will then remain at a high level until 1982, after which it will slowly decline.

5 Summary

The Social Development Office of the Corporation in a study titled 'The Role and Scope of Unemployment Studies in the Master Plan Review' (June 1977), stated that Stevenage was

dominated by large companies, themselves vitally affected by international politics, law and finance, but

what of life's necessities do they produce; missiles,
computers? (22)

Indeed so, and as has been illustrated the town is dependent on a few large companies. Foy suggests that the
unemployment problem is not likely to be solved by large
companies, in that 'if they are inefficient they are ultimately going to create more unemployment, not less, in
competitive market places'. She goes on to argue that:

If they are efficient they will aim for higher pro-
ductivity which means in essence, that at best the same
number of employees will be able to produce more
goods.... Growth in employment must come, then, from
new companies, or the established small to medium-sized
ones who have room to create new markets and new products. (23)

Parsons, in his study of 'giant' manufacturing corporations in the South East and the West Midlands, suggests
that according to his findings the policies and geographical distributions of private, large manufacturing corporations are not wholly compatible with 'balanced regional
growth'. (24)

The irony here, as far as Stevenage is concerned, is that
as can be seen from table 8 the small manufacturing firms
have tended to perform consistently well. Furthermore the
Social Development Office of the Corporation calculated
that fifteen manufacturers who employed 50 employees or
less in June 1973 totalled between them 244 employees, and
by June 1977 the same fifteen together with four similar
new firms employed a total of 554. (25)

An original hypothesis was that the manufacturing bias,
and particularly extreme dependence on one large firm - or
at best a few such firms - constituted *the* source of vulnerability in the town's employment structure. However it
has been demonstrated earlier in this chapter that by
virtue of the rapid growth of the service sector, unemployment must have other sources. It is therefore
suggested here that Stevenage suffers from a difficult-
to-define 'Stevenage factor': firms which should do well
(in employment terms) according to national and regional
indicators do not, with the exception of BAC. The exceptional growth in service employment has disguised the
serious weaknesses within manufacturing. This is of
course not to underestimate the 'lack of diversification'
problem which indeed does create a source of instability,
as well as producing an occupational mismatch. For as
Manners et al. note:

Where new town manufacturing is particularly special-
ized ... dependence can be dangerous. For example,
manufacturing employment in Hatfield, over 70 per cent

TABLE 8   Stevenage Manufacturing Firms with less than 100 employees

	6/73	12/73	6/74	12/74	6/75	12/75	6/76	12/76	6/77
Acton and Borman	33	39	28	28	35	34	40	41	42
Amoco	19	19	19	22	21	21	23	25	23
Berrick Bros	51	57	58	58	64	72	80	83	86
BICC	28	28	29	29	30	28	31	34	34
Hodge	25	17	26	26	16	26	32	18	14
CPI						6	21	47	91
Liquid Packaging						67	66	66	79
Mechatron	9	11	11	11					
Murphy	16	16	12	13	10	10	9	9	13
Pearce	18	16	20	97	94	15	19	17	22
Printech	15	51	17	64	18	15	18	15	16
Tatra			43	43	43	43	51	58	61
Warren Point					22	9	17	15	30
Stevenage Knitting	30	26	26	27	24	25	27	28	28
Alrox							20	17	15
Total	244	280	289	418	377	371	454	473	554

of which was in aircraft manufacturing in 1960, actually declined by 9 per cent between 1960 and 1966, because of difficulties in this industry. On the other hand, manufacturing in Basildon and Harlow, which is more diversified yet oriented to growth industries, expanded by no less than 13 thousand (130 per cent) and 6 thousand (50 per cent) workers respectively over the same period. (26)
And of course the same can be said of Stevenage with its reliance on Guided Weapons and computers. It could of course be argued that this problem is not unique to new towns; for example Stoke-on-Trent has a total of 34 per cent of employment in ceramics, Luton has 32 per cent in vehicles, and Sheffield has a total of 30 per cent of em-

ployment in metal trades. (27) However the important
point to remember is that new towns are first and foremost
planned environments.

It is quite easy to imagine what could occur in Stevenage
if the markets for missiles and computers disappeared;
for example there could be a repeat of the situation that
occurred at Skelmersdale New Town, where 2,400 jobs were
lost in 1976 with the Thorn Colour Tubes factory closure
together with the Courtaulds mill closure, with the result
that an area of optimism quickly became one of depression.
(28)

To summarise the problems of the industrial base, it can
be argued that:

(i) The fundamental problem affecting Stevenage employment
is an occupational mismatch of labour supply and demand,
that is, there is a shortage of certain categories of
skilled labour and a surplus of semi-skilled and unskilled persons.

(ii) Even if the occupational supply and demand situation
were better balanced, there would still be an absolute
shortfall in the number of jobs available in Stevenage,
and jobs are particularly needed in the manufacturing
industries.

(iii) The 'industry mix' of Stevenage's manufacturing
sector may no longer be operating in the town's best
interests. The product range appears to make it abnormally susceptible to economic recession, and the labour
demands, with a high proportion of skills needed, present
difficulties now that in the not too distant future
skilled labour will no longer be so easily imported.

(iv) The school leaver bulge means 'excessive' numbers of
young people seeking employment, a trend in no way coun-
tered by the number of retirements expected over the same
period.

(v) Evidence of the shortage of job opportunities in the
town is to be found not only in the unemployment totals,
but in the increasing numbers of Stevenage residents
commuting out of the town. Although out-commuting helps
to relieve local pressures in the employment situation,
it is time-consuming and increasingly costly, especially
for the less skilled who cannot expect high earnings.

Of course with the local authority ultimately 'taking
over' the town, and particularly with its increasing control from 1 April 1978 over housing policy, the future
relationship between employment and housing provision as
independent variables operating in 'harmony' to achieve
rapid population growth will be radically altered. Additionally, labour supply - either numerically or in terms
of skill - will have to be found predominantly from local

sources, subject to 'conventional' in- and out-migration patterns. Labour demand is unlikely to be boosted by the attraction of new companies to the town, as they will not be able to be lured by the offer of housing incentives.

A meeting organised by the Borough Council, with representatives from the Corporation, SIEG, Education Departments, Trades Council, and so on in attendance early in 1977, gave a glimpse of what the future main actors might have to face (the 'future' is the subject of chapter 14).

Shirley Williams considered that the industrial training schemes in the town were not working satisfactorily, and that local employers had by and large failed to respond adequately to training and incentive schemes supported by central government. However this was not the main concern of SIEG, who stated that

> the standard of educational attainment displayed by
> potential young employees and apprentices was poor.
> Whilst they did not expect school leavers trained in
> industrial skills and understanding, employers sought
> competence at the '3 Rs'. This they were not getting.
> (29)

The Council disagreed generally, but did consider that there was too much of an arts bias in schools. The Divisional Education Officer apologised for the situation and stressed the difficulties of 'changing the school curriculum overnight to meet new demands' by the industrialists. The Trades Council stated that the problem lay with the historical error of placing too much emphasis on imported 'skilled' labour, which had resulted in a failure to provide training facilities in order that vacancies could be filled by the local population. However, as always, SIEG managed to get in the last word, with the suggestion that

> local teachers and representatives of education
> authorities should 'talk quietly together'. (30)

12 Urban managerialism

> The reason why knowledge about politics ... will not
> lead to better solutions of social problems is that the
> impediments to such solutions are as a result of dis-
> agreement, not lack of knowledge.
>
> Edward C.Banfield and James Q.Wilson (1963), p.3

This chapter both describes and discusses the thesis of
urban managerialism, and furthermore does so in the light
of the Stevenage case study.

Ray Pahl puts the managerialist position in the following
manner:

> The managers of the urban system exert an *independent*
> influence on the allocation of scarce resources and
> facilities which may reinforce, reflect or reduce the
> inequalities engendered by the differentially rewarded
> occupational structures. (1, emphasis added)

Peter Norman puts the matter in a rather different and
more specific manner when he suggests that urban managerialism can be understood as asserting the overriding importance of local government in the allocation of resources and facilities in localities. (2) Norman Dennis
amplifies this theme when he talks of the effect of
'authoritative allocation of resources' in contemporary
society. (3) He states that a crucial question to be
asked in urban sociology is how far should one look beyond
the processes of bureaucratic allocation to explain them
in non-bureaucratic terms. He considers that 'one view
appears to be that the process of authoritative allocation
is in some sense an unreal or secondary, epiphenomenal expression of other types of allocation which we call capitalist'. Arguing against this view, Dennis goes on to
say:

> There is in our society a very rapid growth in the rate
> at which people's lives are affected by the decisions
> of persons and groups who are not motivated by profit

but rather by bureaucratic and professional concerns,
for example by the notion of service or vocation and
by the notion of desirability of conformity to rules.
(4)
Robert Moore describes a similar process, albeit with a
different focus:

Urban politics is not the politics of the workplace,
and the contenders are not labour and capital ... the
fact that most town dwellers, qua town dwellers, are
the clients and dependents of large bureaucratic organizations like local authorities, building societies and
insurance companies seems to have generated very little
interest among sociologists. (5)

Thus, in summary, the managerialist position argues for a
considerable degree of autonomy of the urban system in relation to the wider system of labour and capital, and
argues accordingly that the allocation process can be
studied by an examination of bureaucratic or professional
authority.

There have been of course numerous criticisms of managerialism, and general criticisms include for example the
assertion of Newton, who in his study of local government
politics states that much of the current literature on
officer-member relations overestimates the power of
officers while underestimating that of members. (6) The
more traditional criticism is similar to that of Alford,
who asserts that bureaucratisation is indeed a technological requirement for the necessary co-ordination and
administration of a class society, but nevertheless the
elites manning the bureaucracies, he continues, seldom
'challenge the premises of the institutional allocation
of the social product'. (7)

Harloe, reviewing managerialist urban sociology, makes
five points in commenting on what he considers to be its
weaknesses. First he suggests that it has been elitist,
in that the focus of concern and attention has been on the
planners and not the people affected by the plans. (8)
Second, it has been technocratic, which is to say that it
has been directed to the self-designated urban managers
whose solutions to the problems of cities are phrased in
technological terms. Third, such sociology has been
liberal pragmatic, in that it has responded to the
pressures of immediate circumstances, and reacted expe-
diently and not with any sense of an order of priorities.
Fourth, Harloe suggests that it has been social democratic: (9) redress has been sought within the conventions
of the institutions of British political life. Finally,
managerialist urban sociology is characterised as being
positivistic in method. (10) However, the most sustained

criticism of managerialism within urban sociology is that
undertaken by Marxist-structuralism. This position
refutes the theoretical standing of the urban as an independent variable. Abrams, in another context, puts the
argument well:

> The material and especially the visual presence of
> towns seem to have impelled a reification in which the
> town as a physical object is turned into a taken-for-
> granted social object and a captivating focus of
> analysis in its own right ...
> The town, then, is an explanandum, not an explanans.
> (11)

More specifically, Marxist-structuralist (12) investigations of urban problems are at the same time more general
investigations of the Capitalist State, as it is claimed
that 'the state plays an enabling and cushioning role by,
for example, supporting the giant corporations of "monopoly capitalism" by providing basic infrastructure and
consumption facilities as well as by providing special
development grants, tax relief and other forms of direct
state subsidy'. (13) The argument then is that the state
invents, plans and organises in order to develop the
interests of the dominant class as a whole, and it is this
essential development and expansion of state intervention
that is seen as an inevitable part of the continuing accumulation and exploitation inherent in the capitalist
mode of production. The assumption is that the state is
working against the interests of the subordinate class,
and that the 'urban' is a new focus for contradictions
and conflict.

The Marxist-structuralist perspective within urban sociology has developed within the theoretical debate undertaken by Marxists on the nature of the Capitalist State,
and shares with it both strengths and weaknesses. The
debate has been rather protracted and in many senses
somewhat circular, (14) and in fact began with the recognition of the empirical reality of an increasingly inter-
ventionist Capitalist State, together with the inability
of traditional Marxist theories to provide a satisfactory
analysis. The ensuing debate, according to Strinati, produced two distinct tendencies - economism and politicism -
which have proceeded to dominate the present theoretical
situation. Strinati himself turns to work of the kind
undertaken by Claus Offe whose analyses are considered
important because

> they attempt to relate the role of the state to the
> specificity of capitalism in a non-reductionist manner,
> to account for historical changes in the forms of state
> intervention and to pose the problem of the mediating

institutional links between economic processes and
state policies, including an assessment of the significance of political structures. (15)

Although this is clearly an improvement of analysis as
compared with the economism and politicism that Strinati
notes, it is difficult to see how the mere posing of the
'problem of the mediating institutional links' is going
to lead necessarily to theoretical advance. Indeed in a
sense it is hardly further forward than the Marxist-
structuralist conceptualisations of 'relative autonomy'
(16) and 'in the last instance'.

Another response has been that of 'Corporatism', a thesis
represented by, for example, the work of Pahl and Winkler,
and Crouch. (17) Pahl and Winkler assert that the essence
of Corporatism as an economic system is 'private ownership
and state control', while they describe it as 'fascism
with a human face', and define it as a

comprehensive economic system under which the state
intensively channels predominantly privately owned
business towards four goals ... Order, Unity,
Nationalism and 'Success'. (18)

Thus the corporatist argument is that 'there comes a
point when the continuing and expanding role of the state
reaches such a level where its power to control investment, knowledge and the allocation of services and facilities gives it an autonomy which enables it to pass beyond
its previous subservient and facilitative role', and subsequently that the state 'manages everyday life less for
the support of private capital and more for the independent purpose of the state'. (19) Pahl goes on to say that
contemporary political economy is increasingly about com-
promises, bargains, and the ambiguities of a more or less
liberal pragmatism. (20) The full theoretical position is
reached when Hindess asserts that the choice for Marxism
is quite clear:

Either we effectively reduce political and ideological
phenomena to class interests determined elsewhere
(basically in the economy) - an economic reductionism
coupled perhaps with an acknowledgement that things are
actually more complicated.

Or we must face up to the real autonomy of political
and ideological phenomena and their irreducibility to
manifestations of interests determined by the
structure of the economy. (21)

Now it is evident, as previously stated, that the
Marxist-structuralist perspective within urban sociology
has developed within this debate, and thus shares with it
both strengths and weaknesses.

Pahl considers that the very great merit of Castells and

others working within the Marxist-structuralist perspective is that they have focused the attention of urban sociologists on central problems. He suggests that while there may not be clarity concerning the 'links between "the state", "the urban" and "consumption", at least there is now agreement that the urban question is an issue in political economy'. (22) Indeed it is apparent that recent work has certainly revitalised urban sociology and made it a relatively concrete focus for more general problems of political sociology. However this does not deny that the weaknesses of the recent work are profuse. The most important and wide-ranging weakness is concerned with the idea of the 'urban' being dependent on, and determined by, the 'state'. For example, Lojkine states that the subordination of urban policy to the economic - 'big firms strategies' - is necessarily mediated because of contradictions arising from sources such as competing fractions of capital (monopoly, medium, local, etc.), institutions, and so on. (23) Statements like these fail to confront questions like, 'how far is urban policy subordinated to the economic?', 'how is the process mediated?', and others of similar nature.

Pahl, while discussing recent Marxist-structuralist writing on the role of the state in urban development, suggests that such writing was unclear, tautological, and difficult to apply to the concrete analysis of specific situations. An example of tautologous writing, argues Pahl, is the claim that state actions 'were repressive, merely serving the interests of capital (or a dominant fraction) or when they appeared less directly repressive, were simply concessions to the power of organized labour which would probably be short-lived and would ultimately revert to being a form of domination'. (24) Again following a similar criticism, Pahl considers that it is not made clear how far spatial forms and the production and maintenance of the 'urban' in advanced capitalist societies are entirely due to the capitalist mode of production, and how far they are due, at least in part, to general features such as scarcity, the limitations of centralised organisation and planning or whatever. (25) Furthermore, in another paper Pahl suggests that the likelihood is that local autonomy will increase with devolution of central state powers due to populist, ethnic, nationalistic and other pressures resulting thereby in increased urban and regional planning by local technocrats. (26)

Harloe makes the point that perhaps the crucial question concerns the assumption that there is a particular relationship between urban development/policies and the nature of capitalist, and not merely advanced, industrial society. He notes the observations of 'the existence of patterns and mechanisms of urban inequality in Eastern Europe which seem similar to those in the West', and the suggestion that:

the Weberian concern with the effects of growing bureaucracy and rationality is a more likely explanation of this than the Marxist concern with the capitalist mode of production. (27)

Another criticism of the approach is that of the crucial problem of the relationship between theory and research, and even though Castells, for example, states that the Marxist-structuralist perspective is advanced only through empirical research 'which simultaneously attempts to understand certain urban political problems as they exist as well as to verify some more general hypotheses about the nature of emerging contradictions in advanced societies', (28) the actual research is not particularly in evidence. Dunleavy, in a review of the study of Roanne by Biarez et al., states that the more serious problem raised by the study is the relationship between structuralist theory and empirical research. He states that the authors of the study were clearly concerned to maintain the theoretical relevance of their research, but their method of doing so, he suggests, entailed considerable costs: for example there is assertion rather than fact, excessive use of jargon, extrapolations made which were illegitimately done, evidence scattered around by the theoretical subdivision of the subject-matter in a way which becomes anecdotal at points, and, most important, not nearly enough empirical evidence. (29) Similarly Dennis claims that he would like to know

a great deal more about how international investment decisions affected events in Sunderland but he did not have much confidence that he would be able to do detailed empirical work on this. To investigate these higher order phenomena successfully one would need to be able to find out a great deal about how the day to day decisions were taken. (30)

A further evaluation of the term 'urban' and its dependent or independent status, both adds criticism to the Marxist-structuralist position, and - more importantly - indicates how complex an investigation of the urban question has to be.

Ruth Glass states that the adjective 'urban' is merely a term of dubious convenience, and that it does not refer to a universal, clearly identifiable category of settlements, institutions or conditions. However, she does add that once established, a pattern of urban grouping and concentration adds a new dimension, and 'can have a momentum of its own', though of various kinds and with various consequences depending upon its context and scale. (31) Similarly Rex states that however correct Marxist-influenced sociology is in emphasising the primacy of market and power factors in urban society, any politico-economic structure results in a spatial distribution of buildings, and this built environment constitutes the setting and the set of constraints within which new power struggles are carried on. (32)

There is of course the strictly Weberian argument of Rex and Moore, which asserts that any market situation, and not only the labour market, can lead to the emergence of groups with a common market position. On this basis Rex and Moore have argued that 'there is a class struggle over the use of housing and this class struggle is the central process of the city as a social unit'. (33) They attach crucial significance to the role of housing allocation policies in determining the social composition of different areas.

Baldwin and Bottoms in their study of the 'urban criminal' suggest that the 'specifically urban and areal dimensions' of the social processes that are connected with crime have been seriously understated in much recent criminological work, (34) while Gill, in his study of the 'creation of a delinquent area', re-examines the relationship between the urban process and delinquent behaviour, and in so doing makes connections between the 'organization of housing provision and the production of officially registered delinquency'. (35)

Husbands, in his study of right-wing movements, makes the observation that:

> An examination of the support of at least two recent examples, the AIP in America and the National Front in this country ... shows a micro-ecological or idiosyncratic spatial aspect in their support that must be incorporated into any theories of right-wing politics which attempt to build on any past theorising about Nazism. These particular movements have developed electorally as part of a reaction by some voters *within a specific urban context* either to a real or perceived encroachment upon their own neighbourhood by an ethnic group that is regarded as a competitor in some sense or else merely to the apparently increasing local presence of this other group. The hostilities that are shown by one ethnic group towards another within a situation imposed by the evolution of the spatial location of populations within a city are frequently related to levels of support for these movements. (36)

He adds that for a complete explanation of the support received by a movement such as the National Front or National Party, it is necessary to include a 'locational dynamic that reflects the processes of political economy determining the evolving ecological organization and land-use patterns' of at least certain types of city in contemporary western societies. (37) More generally, and more importantly, Mollenkopf argues that there is a prevalent view of cities as epiphenomena: 'once economic forces reach a certain level, they argue, urban agglomerations are made possible. Agricultural technology makes food plentiful and cheap, factories require steadily larger workforces, and willy nilly cities develop'. (38) Mollenkopf states that in fact the opposite is true. He argues that the city is a device for concentrating and controlling political power, and it is this capacity which makes concentrated economic activity possible, not the reverse. He adds:

> But if concentrated urban power is necessary for more intense development, it does not follow that urban social and political structures always smoothly encourage and reinforce it. As with societies as a whole, urban institutional arrangements which originally promoted economic development can evolve along their own logic and become impediments to further growth. (39)

All of the previous examples illustrate the tendency of what for convenience is called the 'urban', to interact with, relate to, and at times dominate the 'economic'. It is obvious that clarification of the concept of the 'urban' will proceed through empirical research focusing on the relations between the 'urban' and the 'economic', and particularly on specific historical transactions between the two areas.

Perhaps in summary it has to be said that the reorientation of urban sociology, as attempted by Castells et al. in terms of the reduction of the area of enquiry to the problem of the reproduction of labour power for capitalist production, is fruitful but not exhaustive of everything that is of interest and worthy of study within the 'urban' arena. Of course it could be argued that Gill, Husbands, and so on, are talking merely of the consequences of actions and structures which relate to problems of reproduction. However, this is mere reductionism, and poor Marxism. (40) Indeed there are problems which can be approached through a Marxist perspective which does not reduce all phenomena in an essentialist fashion to political economy; and moreover if all that is done is political economy and not urban sociology, there remain issues

such as what makes landlords tick, Glasgow gangs do what
they do, and the inauthenticity of so-called democratic
public forums in planning, which are not adequately appreciated by Marxist-structuralism. (41)   Pickvance aptly
argues that
     historical materialist approaches in urban sociology
     open up new avenues of enquiry, which possess a unity
     of their own, but which are not exhaustive of the space
     occupied by urban sociology. (42)
In order to relate the empirical findings of the case
study to the theoretical perspectives, it must be appreciated that there are (at least) four models of urban resource control and allocation - although only two so far
have been discussed in any detail - and that all four have
to be related to, first, new towns policy, and second, the
Stevenage case study, in order to arrive at a relatively
clear and complete set of findings.
     Pahl, in 'Whose City?', suggests four models of urban re-
source control and allocation, models which might provide
answers to the important question of 'who allocates what,
how, to whom, and in whose interests?'. (43)   To begin
with he states that there is the 'pure managerialist
model' which posits that control rests solely with the
professional officers concerned, hence allocation will
presumably be in the interests of those professions, as
they interpret them, and accordingly any conflict will be
inter-professional.   The 'statist model' assumes that
control over local resources and facilities is primarily
a matter for the National Government and that local professions or managers have little room for manoeuvre.   Thus
allocation will presumably depend on how the National
Government sees its interests or ideology best served, and
any conflict will be within National Government between
civil servants and politicians, and between politicians
themselves.   The third model posits 'control-by-capitalists' which assumes that at either national or local
levels, resources are allocated primarily to serve the
interests of private capitalists.   The role of government,
both local and national, is presumably to maximise the resources available and any conflict will be between capitalists in the scramble to make the most of those resources.   The 'pluralist model' assumes a permanent
tension between national bureaucracies, committed to obtaining and distributing larger resources, and the interests of private capital manifested through the economic
pressures of 'the City', private industry and the political party representing the dominant class.   Here conflict
is part of the model itself: different public and private
interests negotiate for positions, and the situation is

inherently changeable. It may be possible at any one
point in time, Pahl suggests, to say in whose interests
a particular policy is intended to and actually does operate, but at any moment, unlike with the other models, the
situation can change. (44)

These models can now be applied to new towns policy. (45)
The managerialist thesis assumes that new town development
corporation managers may attempt to 'net' the most
successful firms they can in order to maintain the growth
and 'success' of their towns. Similarly housing managers
of the development corporations may strenuously resist
receiving 'non-respectable' residents such as one-parent
families or the homeless. It can also be argued that the
statist model has considerable theoretical relevance to
new towns policy, for it is normally in the interests of
a 'democratically' elected National Government to ensure
that goods and resources can be seen to be distributed
more or less equitably over space. At the same time
National Government has to ensure that the actions of
local government do not distort national efforts towards
equity and territorial justice. As far as new towns are
concerned they can be seen therefore as part of a national
effort to resolve, through overspill policies, some of the
locality-specific problems of urbanisation, and at the
same time alleviate the problems of regional economic imbalance through the concentration of growth in the new
towns which, it is hoped, will act as economic multi-
pliers. In this case National Government can be seen to
pursue the twin goals of urban overspill and economic
equity between regions: local government and new town development corporations simply execute these policies.
Thus, according to this model, bargaining at local level
over how far the policy should cater for either overspill
or growth pole needs, merely amounts to an interpretation
of nationally laid down policies. The crucial allocators
operate at national level, and the resources they allocate
go both to those in housing 'need' in overcrowded cities,
and to the unemployed workers in the less well-off authorities and regions.

The control-by-capitalists model is one that has been
specifically applied to the new towns by Castells, who
argues that the entire new towns policy was

    a response to the urban crisis in the London region,
    whose origin is to be found in the over-concentration
    of industry produced by the technical and economic de-
    velopment of English Capitalism.... The individual
    interest of each firm, seeking to maximise its profits
    is (thus) in contradiction with the equilibrium of the
    whole, in that such a spatial concentration of activi-

ty, left to itself, produces a whole series of contradictions within the urban system of the London region,
while at the same time accentuating the imbalance
between regions. (46)

Thus, Castells argues, central government intervened to
regroup industry in a way that gave firms collectively
more opportunity to grow. But, as is the nature of
capitalism, its fatal flaws were only temporarily as-
suaged, and all the problems reappeared still more acutely
during the 1960s. The argument is, then, that the original conception of the new town policy fits this model.
However it might also be argued that the actual operation
of the policy fits it as well, for as Deakin and Ungerson
suggest:

It is clear that the system of incentives provided for
firms to move, involving removal grants and the provision of relatively cheap all-round factory accommodation in the new towns, is a handsome resource for
private industry; it is also clear ... that policies
for allocating new town housing are geared to the needs
of industry, in the sense that development corporation
dwellings for rent are almost entirely restricted to
those who have jobs in the new town's firms. Since,
on the whole, only those who constitute 'suitable
labour' (as opposed to suitable *tenants*) are able to
move to a new town, it is a moot point ... as to
whether national or local government intentions to use
new towns as a means of alleviating housing need can
ever counterbalance the needs of industry for particular kinds of labour. (47)

Deakin and Ungerson also suggest that the pluralist model
has the 'least direct relevance to New Towns policy',
since it posits continuous competition and tension between
three types of institution: 'national bureaucracies',
'private capital' and 'local authorities'. This they
consider to be not a suitable way of analysing new towns
policy, rather, they assert, it is 'more relevant to state
that the policy is characterized by tension between at
least three types of *goal*, which are mediated by institutions of all three kinds'. (48)

Now it is intended here to relate the theoretical positions and models to the case of Stevenage, both generally and in terms of the case study. To begin with it is
necessary to remember the arguments and observations of
the previous chapter which demonstrated quite clearly the
fact that urban policy, and particularly the housing allocation policy (and process), was determined by the 'needs'
(demands) of the industrialists. However, the important
questions to be asked are, 'how did the Corporation's own

ideology and policy preferences relate to those of the
industrialists?', and, more generally, 'how constrained
was the Corporation in policy making matters?'.

It was earlier noted that the Corporation seemed unable
or unwilling to alter the situation where there was a
distinct lack of diversified industry, which in turn led
to housing and land-use policies being followed according
to the sole criterion of industrial 'need'. What must be
remembered is that the Corporation here was in a position
where the industrialists would not be swayed on this
matter: As Geoffrey Hughes, Chairman of SIEG, put it:

> I've maintained all the way through, 'who wants di-
> versity?', the employer doesn't want it because he
> wants to feel that there are other skills similar to
> his own in the area, so that he can - not poach - swop
> labour. (49)

In the early days of the town the Corporation, under-
standably, seemed to be far more autonomous in its decision making and policy. For example in 1950 the Corporation allowed Messrs Geo.W.King Limited to extend their
factory premises in Stevenage to the extent they had proposed, despite Councillor Ireton's protestations that the
Corporation was responsible for the decentralisation of
industry from London, and it was therefore not right for
a local factory to be allowed to expand even though they
would bring labour from London. Another example that may
be cited concerns the housing allocation process, when in
1954 and in reply to the Trades Council, the Corporation
stated that its responsibility

> *did not extend beyond providing accommodation for*
> *anyone coming from London who could find employment in*
> *Stevenage.* Once a house had been occupied, the tenant
> would not be moved provided he was satisfactory as a
> tenant. Where he chose to work was not the concern of
> the Corporation, although they would prefer that he
> worked in Stevenage. (50, emphasis added)

Yet only four months later, when the Corporation was asked
by SIEG if industry could recruit certain tradesmen from
outside Greater London - without SIEG proving that such
action was necessary - the Corporation immediately replied
in the affirmative. (51)

What must be taken into account, when discussing managerialism in relation to the Stevenage Development Corporation, is that the managers are by no means a homogeneous
group of decision makers, and it is important to delineate
the demarcations within the management group. To begin
with there is the distinction between the members (of the
Board) and the officers, similarly the difference between
one department and another (to be examined in the next

chapter), and again differences within the Board membership itself. For example, Evelyn Denington argues that
the whole Corporation is essentially a cohesive team:

> We have unity of purpose here, we have no politics you
> see, I won't have any politics here, politics never
> comes into our discussions here in the Corporation.
> Although Ken McKechnie has just got up in Pin Green -
> Ken as you know is a Tory - over lunch we rib him and
> tease him and all that. Then I have Geoffrey Hughes,
> then we have the chap who is in Hawker Siddeley, what
> their politics are I don't know, they are just good
> blokes on that side of industry and so on. I don't
> know what they are but we don't have any politics here,
> we don't waste our time taking up postures you see, we
> take the thing and we discuss it on its merits and it's
> a small group and we sit round, and the officers sit
> round the Board table, I mean we're a team, we work
> together as a team, we make our decisions as a team.
> (52)

However the minutes of the Corporation Board demonstrate,
time after time, how Councillor Ireton stood alone on
certain matters and attempted to change Corporation
policy, with his disagreements invariably being of a
'political' nature. Similarly the distinction between
the officers and the members, in the Corporation's case,
has to be drawn. The officers - particularly the officers
who were members of the Planning Team - certainly influenced the development and policies of the town, and the
Board, with only a few exceptional incidents, appeared to
argue its policies totally (and necessarily) in terms of
information produced by the officers, information which
the Board could not, and at times would not, view critically. For example in 1970 the Board announced that it
was concerned that a housing hiatus might develop, as
there had been objections by the Urban District Council
to the Section 6(1) proposals for Sectors 9 and 10. The
Board stated that the Council had objected 'because of the
Corporation's proposals to complete houses on land intended under the 1966 Master Plan for natural expansion
owing to lower occupancy rates than anticipated'. (53,
emphasis added) Now the Board seemed totally unconcerned
about the officials' miscalculations per se, a little more
concerned about the effect such errors might have on its
housing 'policy', but most concerned about whether or not
the situation which had arisen from the miscalculations
could provide a base for launching into an expansion
effort, and indeed in April 1972 Evelyn Denington made an
appointment (the initiative was the Corporation's) with
the Minister to discuss the possible enlargement of the
town.

As stated earlier the crucial questions to be asked are,
'how did the Corporation's own ideology and policy preferences relate to those of the industrialists?', and 'how
constrained was the Corporation in policy making
matters?'. To being with, and in relation to the industrialists' exaggerations and miscalculations concerning
their housing need and growth potential, it is obvious
that it was in the Corporation's own interest to support
a pro-growth lobby, as pro-growth meant the 'need' for
more land which in turn meant an extension of the Corporation's 'life'. As the Corporation's Social Development
Office put it,

> the Corporation has played along with SIEG, partly
> because it was in its own interests to have this fairly
> high status group to cart along to public inquiries and
> to the Minister and say, 'now look here, we need this
> expansion because industry is clamouring for houses,
> and if it doesn't expand they'll have to shut down or
> move somewhere else', and so on. (54)

In answer to the question, 'how constrained was the
Corporation?', three factors are prominent. First, there
is the evidence of the previous chapter which suggests
that following a relatively autonomous period for the
Corporation - in a sense the pre-BAC period - the decision
making process has been largely determined by industrial
'needs' (demands: as defined by the industrialists).
Second, there is the question of the industrialists' relationship with the Board, or in other words, the nature
of the influence of Geoffrey Hughes, Chairman of SIEG and
Corporation Board member. SIEG was initially developed
in opposition to the Corporation, and indeed Geoffrey
Hughes stated that the basis on which the group came about
was simply that 'we've got to beat these boys somehow'.
However, quite quickly - he noted - the group began to
recognise that it could pursue its objectives a lot better
by discussion and it thus 'developed a very close relationship' with the Corporation. (55) Mr Hughes, in
answer to the question 'how much influence has SIEG had on
the town's affairs?', commented that it has had a 'considerable degree of influence, but of course not in the
public eye, a good deal of discussion has gone on inevitably as between landlord and occupier, and this has spilt
over into employment projections and that sort of thing.'
(56) Mr Hughes of course was very much in a 'two-hatted'
position, but he felt perfectly able to handle this. For
example he stated that he had 'powerful approaches from
members of the group' concerning issues and problems that
might have been embarrassing for the Corporation, and
indeed he added that he had been 'pressurised from both

sides as it were, but I saw that as part of the function
of doing the job, and if you don't like the heat well
don't stay near the fire'. (57)   He concluded:

> Oh yes, I've been wearing two hats most of the time
> I've been living in Stevenage. I think it's a personal
> problem one has to come to terms with. Perhaps I'm
> lucky, I've never found it particularly embarrassing.
> There have been occasions when I have had to be parti-
> cularly careful because I had knowledge of one side and
> the other which it was not possible to do so, but I
> think that this is one of the success stories that we
> can show from this country - whether it is exportable
> or not I don't know - but we do seem as a nation, to be
> able to employ people on this 'two-hatted' basis, and
> I'm a great believer that the Corporation's structure,
> which inevitably means two hats for most of them, has
> been an extremely successful venture. (58)

Finally, the third factor to consider in terms of the
'how constrained was the Corporation?' question, is the
historical composition of the Board. Appendix 2 gives
precise details of Board membership, but suffice it to say
that the majority of members, whether they were of Labour
or Conservative persuasion, had interests more akin to
those of management, ownership, and professional life than
to those of employee interests. Thus the optimistic, confident, and laissez-faire attitude of the industrialists
was quite congruent with most of the members' own attitudes.

An examination of the genesis of the various expansion
proposals further indicates the complexities of the evaluation of the four models of resource control and allocation, and particularly their interrelationships. To begin
with it must be appreciated that the expansion situations
were in part created by the simple inexperience of the
early new town planners - the urban managers. As Bull
suggests in his discussion of the plans of the later new
towns of, for example, Peterborough, Washington, Ipswich
and Northampton, all these studies made 'allowance for
future population increase after planned immigration has
ceased. This is a considerable advance on the earlier new
towns which were designed for finite populations. These
new towns are experiencing difficulties now that the population has grown beyond that for which they were designed.' (59) The situation in Stevenage was compounded
by miscalculations as to the future household size in 1966
(at the Master Plan review), but of course this miscalcu-
lation must be seen in the context of a 'cautious' Corporation having but two years previously seen its expansion
proposals turned down by Crossman, the Minister. Whilst

on the 1964 expansion issue, it can be noted that in terms
of planning ideology the Corporation was not alone: for
example, the Ministry, in informing the Corporation of
Crossman's decision not to expand the town, stated that:

> In reaching this conclusion the Minister notes the
> Inspector's view that the town thus enlarged could
> provide for a population of 91,000. *But this he thinks*
> *needs further study*. (60, emphasis added)

The 1973 proposals were a result of two factors.   First,
the Corporation approached the Minister with a request for
an expansion of the designated area because of its belief
that only 'growth' could solve its problems of housing
policy (and possibly a realisation that if the Corporation
was to further its 'life', a move would soon have to be
made);   and second, a receptive Conservative Minister
Mr Peter Walker, keen to encourage owner-occupation in new
towns.   Indeed he talked of 1,000 acres of private housing
development and an attempt to reach a 50:50 ratio of
rented and owner-occupied dwellings.   That the initiative
came from the Corporation is open to little doubt.   The
General Manager of the Corporation from 1969 to 1976, Jack
Balchin, stated that 'it was a multiple effort', but that
the Corporation's contribution however 'was not insignificant'. (61)   Councillor Ireton, a member of the Corporation since its inception, put the case more strongly:

> On all expansions some people see it as the Corporation
> wishing to keep themselves in office, both members and
> staff, and there is always a tendency of course to do
> this although we've been in existence now nearly twice
> as long as we anticipated when we started.   Some people
> with vested interests think that the thing should go on
> for ever, who would never wind the Corporation up....
> It's mostly the Ministers under pressure all the time
> by all Corporations when they get to the end of their
> life, to expand. (62)

What is important to understand here is the symbiotic
relationship in Stevenage of industry and the Corporation.
That is to say, although it is clearly evident that the
Corporation wanted an extension of its own 'life', this
was made possible by the industrialists urging for more
housing (for the future) and therefore land, together with
an industrial structure which effectively reduced the
Corporation to a position of handmaiden.   The 1973 proposals demonstrate the Minister's planning ideology:

> The Secretary of State invited the Corporation also to
> consider whether more land within the existing desig-
> nated area can be brought into use for private develop-
> ment while the extension of the area is being pursued.
> *He recognises that much of this residential land has*

been phased for development after 1980: but this provision for later years could be amply made good in any
enlarged area which was eventually designated. (63, emphasis added)

The 1974 proposals were, when first proposed by the Conservative Government, more of a 'face saving' nature than
anything else, in that the Government had stressed the
prima facie case for increased owner-occupation and then
had to withdraw its case, thus something - indeed anything
- had to be done, and be seen to be done. Before continuing it must be noted here that as the new towns are a
National Government concern, there are obviously areas of
support for the statist model. For example in 1952 Sir
Frank Lee, Permanent Secretary at the Board of Trade,
refused GEC permission to erect a factory in the town and
instead directed them to Portsmouth. Interestingly, this
direction from the Ministry allowed the Corporation to
offer the English Electric Company a wider choice of site
and some completed design work, an indication that there
is indeed room for more than one explanatory model. Again
in 1964, and concerning the proposals for a west-of-the-
motorway expansion of 1,450 acres (1,550 acres in total),
the Minister at the time, Richard Crossman, seemed to have
little difficulty in deciding against the proposals put
forward by the previous administration.

The Labour Government inherited the 1974 proposals but it
similarly had to withdraw them in deference to the more
pressing problems of London, together with problems of the
national economy. It must also be remembered that there
was another pro-expansion lobby in the 1972-4 period,
namely groups with the opportunity to gain financially
from the project. For example, although it is often reported that there is little to be gained financially in
the new towns, in Stevenage's case there were two particularly strong exceptions to this rule. First there was the
Consultant Planner to the Corporation who was also the
Corporation's own Chief Planning Officer, a dual appointment which put him in a monopolistic position, and moreover in a position where his best interests lay in the
continuation of the town. Second was the 'giant' private
building firms. Benington, talking specifically of local
authorities, states that these firms grew within a largely
public sector, (64) and Stevenage New Town is no exception, with the majority of its building work being
undertaken by the 'giants' (see appendix 12 for an analysis).

The pluralist model posits continuous competition and
tension between three types of institution: 'national
bureaucracies', 'private capital', and 'local authori-

ties'. This model appears to manage the data quite well
providing it is borne in mind that the interrelationships
involved - which are of course crucial to the model - are
not necessarily relationships of comparable strength. For
example, in the Stevenage case, the dominant institution
has been that of capital (industrialists), but the infer-
ence cannot be made that, a priori, capital will (in this
context) be in all instances the determining institution.
  The pattern of Stevenage's development could thus be
formulated as follows, with the introduction and resolution of the expansion issues being part and parcel of that
development:

(i) The Corporation's refusal to acknowledge the long-
term, consistent, and structural inability of the industrialists as a whole to take up their housing allocation (with the industrialists at the same time grossly
exaggerating their needs by means of a constant reference
to the future);

(ii) the implication of this was that in part the industrialists were controlling the Corporation;

(iii) a Corporation unable to meet the needs both of the
parents and children of tenants - that is the second
generation residents - as it both influenced and was influenced by a housing allocation system in which priority
was given to suitable labour rather than the needs of the
indigenous population; and

(iv) a Corporation eager to perpetuate its own 'life', an
eagerness which found expression in and was expressed by
its optimistic and futurological ideology, together with
certain planning miscalculations.

(v) The above scheme can be contextualised with the addition of another element, namely that of National
Government's inability to produce and maintain a consistent 'Stevenage policy', it being constrained essentially
by other government functions and priorities.

  Thus a summary comment would point to interrelationships,
and particularly of the symbiotic relationship of
Stevenage industry and the Corporation.

  Perhaps before moving on to the final set of constraints
on urban managers - the 'public' - it is important not to
undervalue, none the less, the role and influence of such
managers. As Pahl puts it:

> Since the urban managers are the central mediators
> between urban populations and the capitalist economy
> and since they also serve to generate and maintain the
> ideology of Welfare-Statism, their role remains crucial
> in the urban problematic. (65)

13   Public participation in planning
Illusion or reality?

I can only suggest that he who would combat false
consciousness and awaken people to their true interests
has much to do, because the sleep is very deep.
                                    Erving Goffman (1974), p.14

PART 1

In this chapter attention is focused on the constraints
placed upon the Corporation by the public, and furthermore
there will be an examination of the specificity of the
public's role in terms of protest. To begin with there
will be a discussion (following on from chapter 1) of
public participation in general, followed by a look at the
theoretical literature on protest and specifically the
notion of 'urban social movements', concluded by an examination of the empirical material contained within the case
study.
 Bell quite rightly observes that 'participation can mean
everything or nothing', and furthermore suggests that in
general, administrators and professionals remain uncon-
vinced of the benefits of consumer participation. Even
more, she continues:
    rising consumer expectations in the welfare state are
    producing demands for greater efficiency, higher
    standards of professional service and correctness in
    administration. This accelerates the trend - at
    present, very marked - towards stronger internal man-
    agement. But this is not easily reconciled with
    stronger participation. (1)
This observation highlights the fact that discussions of
participation are complex and general, and, furthermore,
wide-reaching. Thus in order to begin to discuss the
area, a note on the nature of political participation,
that is, 'democracy' will be necessary.

Carole Pateman, in her discussion of democratic theory,
(2) describes and evaluates what she terms the 'contemporary theory of democracy'. She states that there are two
versions of this theory, the first one being the empirical
version which focuses on the operation of the democratic
political system as a whole, and is grounded in the facts
of present-day political attitudes and behaviour as revealed by sociological investigation. Second there is
the 'theory' version which states that 'democracy' refers
to a political method or set of institutional arrangements
at national level. She describes the implications of such
a model. To begin with, the democratic method becomes the
competition of leaders (elites) for votes, and indeed
elections become crucial. Political equality becomes
defined in terms of universal suffrage, and participation
becomes participation in the choice of leaders. (3)
Pateman then argues that the function of participation in
the theory, therefore, is 'solely a protective one; the
protection of the individual from arbitrary decisions by
elected leaders and the protection of his private interests. It is in its achievement of this aim that the
justification for the democratic method lies.' (4)
Pateman states that there are thus certain conditions
necessary to keep this particular democratic system
stable. For example, the level of participation by the
majority should not rise much above the minimum necessary
to keep the democratic method (electoral machinery)
working: 'that is, it should remain at about the level
that exists at present in the Anglo-American democracies'.
(5) Similarly for the democratic method a consensus on
norms is also required.
 Pateman's criticism of the contemporary theory provides
an entrance to a more specific discussion on participation
in urban planning. She states that proponents of the contemporary theory have consistently misunderstood 'classical theory', the theory which the contemporary theory was
designed to replace, in that they have refused to accept
that classical theory was a normative theory as well as a
descriptive one. Furthermore, she adds, the revisionists
have themselves fundamentally changed the normative significance of democracy:

> The critics, then, are right in their contention that
> the contemporary theory not only has its own normative
> content but that it implies that we - or, at least,
> Anglo-Saxon Westerners - are living in the 'ideal'
> democratic system. (6)

The 'ideal' of classical theory (7) on the other hand, is
of rational, active and informed men. Pateman suggests
that the major contribution to democratic theory by the

'classical theorists' has been to focus attention on the interrelationship between individuals and the authority structures of institutions within which they interact. She concludes:

we do learn to participate by participating and ... feelings of political efficacy are more likely to be developed in a participatory environment. Furthermore, the evidence indicates that experience of a partici- patory authority structure might also be effective in diminishing tendencies toward non-democratic attitudes in the individual. If those who come newly into the political arena have been previously 'educated' for it then their participation will pose no dangers to the stability of the system. (8)

It is within this context that the issue of public par- ticipation in planning has developed, and indeed Sewell and Coppock, in answer to the question 'how much partici- pation is possible and desirable?', state that the 'central question of how far it is possible (or desirable) to move from the present system of representative demo- cracy to a system of participatory democracy remains'. (9) Similarly Thornley points to the dilemma of balancing ef- ficiency with democratic demands which has been a major source of concern in all the official documents on par- ticipation in planning since 1968. (10) He points to two factors that in his opinion have contributed to the general popularity of the participation idea. To begin with Thornley considers that the planning profession jumped on the idea as a means by which it could improve its tarnished public image: 'it was hoped that a closer relationship between the planner and the planned would help the public understand the difficulties and complexi- ties that the professional planner has to resolve'. (11) However this does introduce the possibility, as Thornley points out, that participation could be manipulated in order to educate the public into viewing their own prob- lems through professional or technocratic eyes (this is a point which has already been touched on and will be returned to). The second factor Thornley considers to be important is that the 'public also were taking a greater interest in their environment'. (12) This is again true, and importantly what particularly occurred was the spread of planning from inner city problems out into the fringes of the towns, with the result that large numbers of articulate social groups were being affected, and sub- sequently responded by protest.

Before commencing to note some of the specific problems of the participation process, it must be remembered that participatory approaches have to be introduced into a

situation in which power and influence are already uneven-
ly distributed, and in such circumstances it is clearly
not sufficient to argue for increased local control.   In
David Harvey's words, this 'will simply result in the poor
controlling their own poverty while the rich grow more affluent from the fruits of their riches'. (13)

Some of the problems associated with the participation
process have already been described in chapter 1, for
example the tendency towards 'information control', therefore the focus here will be on four interrelated issues:
the tendency towards technocratic domination;   the acute
problem of the 'apathetic public';   problems associated
with 'representativeness';   and, finally, an outline of
what may be termed 'participationism'.

To begin with it has to be noted that since the
Skeffington Report and the relative popularity of the
participation idea, the Government has been far less en-
thusiastic about participation, as is evident from Circular DOE 52/72, which was essentially the Government's (be-
lated) views on Skeffington. (14)   This Circular takes a
much more restrictive view of participation and indeed
drops the idea of Community Development Officers.   The
general result of the Circular is to give greater flexibility to local authorities on how they interpret the requirements of Skeffington and the Town and Country
Planning Act (1971).   As Thornley sums up:

> The general tone of the circular is far less enthusi-
> astic about participation than the Skeffington Report.
> This no doubt results from a realisation of the politi-
> cal complexities involved and the continuing central
> government desire for speedy plan production. (15)

Norman Dennis comments that behind the disappointment
with the low level of public participation 'lies the un-
warrantable assumption that techniques such as town-plan-
ning exhibitions carry an intrinsic virtue which somehow
will overcome these formidable obstacles and enable them
to raise popular participation to a high level'. He adds
that the assumption is that if 'they fail to do so, the
fault lies with the public, not with the device'. (16)
And of course there *is* the possibility that planning
authorities will manipulate the participation process -
consciously or otherwise - to their particular technocratic 'definition of the situation'.   For example
Lambert, Blackaby and Paris, in their study of a neighbourhood association, noted that the association's negotiations with planners were negotiations about 'maps and
drawings and lines and hatchings', whose relation to
actual resources proved extremely difficult to see. (17)
Again the crucial public inquiry stage of a participation

process is such that it is almost only comprehensible to someone acquainted with, and used to, technical documents, technical arguments, and the 'professional style'. As Levin puts it:

> The formal nature of the objection procedure and of the inquiry itself - conducted on an adversary basis, chiefly among highly-paid lawyers and experts, in a semi-judicial atmosphere in a large hall on weekdays between the hours of 9.00 am and 5.00 pm (although one evening session may be arranged) - would seem to have a direct influence upon the range of participants that appear before the Inspector. (18)

The tendency towards technocratic domination of the participation process is, of course, one of the chief explanations of the low level of interest taken by the 'public' in planning matters in general, and participation programmes in particular. As Dennis points out, participation will tend to occur only when plans more clearly 'identify effects in the foreseeable future which touch in some discernable way the well-being of the potential participant'. (19) Another reason which can be given for the low level of participation is the acceptance by the public of a division of labour. That is to say, members of the public, knowing full well both the extreme differentiation between occupational strata and the technocratic nature of the planning process, will - rather than attempt to participate - tend to view planning matters as an area best left to 'those who know about such things'.

Yet another explanation, of course, is that for participation to occur there must be present the possibility that it will indeed have some effect, and in this respect history offers few salutary examples. As mentioned previously, the system of representative democracy, as it operates, does not lend itself to a commitment to participation either in terms of a moral imperative, or in the manner in which the institutions of such a democratic system operate. In summary and in a general manner, Dennis puts it well when he argues that:

> At its most general the explanation of apathy may lie in a basic feature of the life-style of the individual wage-earner ... he is on the whole, more 'passive' than say, the salaried professional man. The world presents the working-class family with situations to which it must adapt. The middle-class family is more likely, by comparison, to view any situation as something amenable to its control. The difference of approach is carried over into dealings with public authorities. The working-class family has a low expectation that it will be influential in any negotiations. The middle-class

group is likely to be more knowledgeable about and
active in the pursuit of opportunities for self-
protection. (20)
A question which arises out of, and is integrally related
to, the low level of participation, is that of the representativeness of those who do participate, for as the
Skeffington Report implies, the views of the 'non-joiners
and inarticulate' are as important as those of the
'actively interested and organized'. Cullingworth rightly
notes that American experience demonstrates that citizen
participation can lead to strong demands to (say) keep an
area 'white', to exclude public authority housing, and to
safeguard local amenities at a high cost to the larger
community. He concludes with the argument that not every
community is best placed to assess its needs in relation
to a wider area. (21) (This important question will be
examined further in the chapter, within the discussion of
protest.)
This particular section will be concluded with a note on
the most radical criticism which, for want of a better
term, may be called the critique of 'participationism'.
This is of course an extremely general criticism, and one
which suggests that participation can only mean social
control. Coit develops the critique by first drawing a
distinction between citizen participation and local
action, arguing that the former is organised by 'above'
(the state) while the latter is organised autonomously at
the grass-roots level. (22) Coit suggests that occasion-
ally some citizen-participation organisations develop a
political consciousness together with conflictual strategies, but normally the vast majority fall into the category of participationist in terms of their lack of independence, their basic ideology, and the limited scope of
their action which prevents them from having more than
token power. Coit further argues that local action organised at grass-roots level, with no official ties, offers
more possibility for 'meaningful social change'. (23)
Coit develops the argument with the suggestion that the
root cause of the failure of 'participation to work' is
the
   ideology of *participationism*. For even if the citizen
   participation of [Arnstein] worked and became what she
   calls 'citizen control', without other fundamental
   changes in the political and economic system, the
   results would be the reintegration of marginal elements
   and the bolstering of the status quo. (24)
Citizen participation is characterised by Coit in the
following manner. To begin with it tends to eliminate the
notion of antagonism between the working and ruling class,

and furthermore it encourages compromise and conciliation
in order to obtain minimum concessions. Moreover participation is often used to keep troublemakers off the streets
and put them into less threatening occupations, and finally Coit suggests that participation agencies tend to skim
off the local leadership from the community by employing
them. On the other hand, 'local action' is characterised
in terms of 'three directions' in which local action
groups ought to direct their actions. Such groups should
work to develop a class consciousness and critical analysis of capitalism: 'they should relate the privations
of daily life to some of their fundamental causes, such as
the priority given private property over human rights and
predominance of the profit motive in real estate markets'.
(25) Second, such groups ought to work out methods of
self-management in groups, where leadership is shared
rather than hierarchical, and develop methods whereby
'inhabitants can creatively take part in making the decisions concerning their neighbourhood and homes'. Finally, Coit suggests that such groups should develop a strategy that is truly conflictual rather than pseudo-con-
flictual. (26)
  It is now appropriate to turn to the literature on
'protest', and more specifically to the notion of 'urban
social movements'.

PART 2

The importance of the work of Castells et al. on 'urban
protest', and more specifically on 'urban social movements', is that it recognises, and points to, the fact
that processes of social change may be initiated by specific 'urban' contradictions, and moreover that it is the
urban protest movements (which develop out of such contradictions), and not the planning institutions, which are
more likely to be the real instigators of change and innovation. Castells himself, however, does add that
    It remains to be seen if there is any possibility of
    urban change without general social change; in other
    words, total political change. The question cannot be
    treated abstractly nor in isolation but only by study-
    ing, over time, the articulation and interaction of
    protest movements that are linked to production, urban
    protest movements and political movements. (27)
  Castells argues that the study of urban politics can be
broken down into two analytical fields 'which in reality
are indissolubly linked', namely urban planning in its
various forms, and urban social movements. (28) An urban
social movement is defined as

the system of practices resulting from the articulation
of a conjecture of the system of urban actors and other
social practices, such that its development tends ob-
jectively towards the structural transformation of the
urban system or towards a substantial change in the
balance of forces within the political system as a
whole. (29)

Castells adds that an urban social movement emerges when
there is a correspondence between the fundamental structural contradictions of the urban system and a 'correct
line within an organization formed from the crystalliza-
tion of other practices'. (30) Now what is important is
the fact that it is the inadequacies of Castells's attempt
to theorise and locate the notion of urban social movements, together with the subsequent critiques of his approach, that develops the articulation of urban protest
and urban movements. It is of course to Castells's merit
that he has opened up a new area of enquiry, an area only
previously explored - systematically - by American political science.

There is an immediate problem raised by Castell's definition of urban social movements as those which enable
the 'structural transformation of the urban system or
towards a substantial change in the balance of forces
within the political system as a whole'. Now as Husbands
points out, these criteria in Castells's definition -
success and left-wing character - either individually or
together, rule out from substantive interest in the subject a large amount of the content of contemporary social
movement study. (31) Importantly, Husbands continues to
make the point that

Some of the responses to this logic of urban development under capitalism may be regarded as in some
general sense left-wing (e.g., certain community action
groups, tenants' associations). However, the opposite
response of backlash and anti-immigrant sentiment does
raise the urgent question of when, why and among whom
a right-wing reaction may also occur. (32)

Dunleavy, in an important paper, attempts to modify the
structuralism of Castells et al., in order to take account
of two central points made by the 'neo-elitist' (33)
writers, namely the need to recognise the capacity of the
state apparatus and other dominant groups to suppress or
deflect hostile political developments, and the consequent
'analytical necessity of studying political inactivity or
quiescence in addition to overt political action'. (34)

Dunleavy begins by discussing the structuralist account
of protest, and notes that for structuralism what determine the development of protest groups and their

success (or failure) are the contradictions around which
they arise, together with the organisation of the protest.
He then notes three important arguments put forward by the
structuralists concerning protest. First, Dunleavy notes,
the structuralists argue that protest movements based on
economic contradictions will be more likely to secure
fundamental changes of the system. Second, it is argued
that protest which is worker-dominated is more likely to
be confrontational in tactics and goals, while protest
movements with a social base cutting across class lines
will tend to acquire middle-class leadership and be inte-
grative or co-optive in function. Finally, the point is
made that protest organisations, to be effective, need to
take what Castells calls a 'correct line between fragmented failure to link contradictions (reformist ideology) and
fusing them together in a single totalizing opposition
(revolutionist utopia)'. (35) Dunleavy goes on to note
that in the structuralist literature there is an assumption that decision makers will make no concessions unless
forced to by protest movements. He comments:

> The *non-achievement* of urban or political effects or of
> reforms in turn reflects the deficiencies of the pro-
> test or urban social movement according to structural-
> ist analysis; for example, it could reflect the
> pursuit of an incorrect line, or the failure to develop
> around fundamental contradictions or to link contra-
> dictions effectively. (36)

Dunleavy asserts that the assumption of uni-directional
influence reduces the study of protest to a very simple
stimulus-response model in the structuralist view, a view
which ignores the fact that the *actions* of the state
apparatus and other dominant groups may also have a
crucial influence on protest failure. He points to neo-
elitist theory which had, he argues, demonstrated how many
resources dominant groups can deploy to prevent the accurate perception of their interests by the powerless, and
to inhibit mobilisation, organisational development and
protest success. He adds that the structuralist literature 'makes no reference to this body of theory and in
persistently locating the source of failure within the
protest movement itself, it seems to me extraordinarily
conservative in its conclusions'. (37)

It is clear from the mere cursory discussion of the
structuralist position on urban social movements outlined
above that there are two fundamental problems of the
model, which are intimately related, namely the refusal to
see the possibility of change coming from 'dominant institutions', and problems associated with the notion of the
'correct line'. These two problems can be reformulated

into three convenient and interrelated areas: (i) protest
group culture, (ii) strategies, and (iii) institutional
change.

i Protest group culture

Olives, arguing from a structuralist position, asserts
that urban and political effects (changes) will not occur
without organisation, nor without a social base, and,
moreover, that given the presence of *organization-type of
action and social base, it appears that it is the size of
the stake which is decisive ... in determining whether
urban or political effects are obtained or not*. (38) Now
the role of organisation, in the process of mobilisation,
is important within the structuralist position, as organisations are seen as the means by which social forces develop and contradictions expressed and linked. However,
as Pickvance argues - and this is where there *is* divergence from the structuralist emphasis - organisation plays
a greater role in social movements than simply permitting
the linking of contradictions. He suggests that the
  survival and success of such movements depends on the
  resources they are able to obtain, free or through
  social exchange, from organizations in the community,
  from higher levels of hierarchies, and from the personal networks and multiple positions of their members.
  (39)
There has been little examination by the structuralists
of the organisational resources necessary or sufficient
for urban social movements (or protest groups) to be
'effective'. However, Pickvance examines the question of
how a 'social base' becomes a 'social force', or to put it
another way, how a population affected by an urban issue
becomes mobilised, (40) and in so doing he illustrates the
weakness of the structuralist approach in not making such
an emphasis. He argues that before a 'social base' can
be used as an element in 'sociological analysis of urban
protest', attention must be paid to the social structure
and 'value-orientations' of the social base, and not
merely to its demographic characteristics. (41) For
example, what has to be discovered is whether or not informal groupings exist, and whether there exist inter-
class and inter-ethnic relationships, and only by doing
so can it be determined to what extent a social base is
likely to act in a 'united way or is likely to act in a
fragmented way along class or ethnic lines'. (42) Similarly the value-orientations which relate to motivations
for participation in protest activity, cannot be ignored.
Pickvance points to the importance of recognising the

possible existence of 'alternative forms of consciousness', which could well prevent the transformation of a
social base into a social force. He cites the work of
John Rex and in particular his work on 'housing classes',
where it is demonstrated that there are clear alternatives
to housing (and social class) consciousness, namely forms
of consciousness based on 'the urban value system' and
'ethnic identity'. (43) Pickvance summarises by arguing
that organisation around an issue takes place when competing forms of consciousness are absent, the issue is
clearly identified, and the organisational means are
available. He adds that to

> complete an account of participation in protest move-
> ments, however, we need to pay attention to (a) other
> influences on participation besides the salience of the
> issue itself, and (b) the effect of the organization in
> which individuals join together to protest. (44)

Pickvance points to the fact that most membership will be
a leisure-time activity, as such membership necessarily
would be in competition for resources of time, money and
commitment with other social roles, and particularly work
and domestic roles: 'these roles affect the *amount of
time* (e.g., due to overtime working or coping unaided with
young children), and *timing of its availability* (e.g., due
to shift working)'. (45) Another constraint on membership, he points out, is when an association demands a fee
for membership and thus becomes more selective. Low fees,
Pickvance argues, are more common in organisations where
extent of membership is 'an end in itself, e.g., to legitimate pressure group action', than in more 'expressive'
associations where social selectivity may be deliberately
sought. He continues to add that the 'amount of *commitment* entailed by protest organization membership is likely
to vary from very little to very much'. (46, emphasis
added) This of course includes those people who literally
view organisation membership as a 'way of life'. Given
the time, money and commitment to engage in protest activity, a potential member may still not join an organisation because the implicit 'terms of entry' could make
it unattractive to him. By 'terms of entry' Pickvance
means the obligations - especially the two fundamental
obligations of, first, the acceptance of the *form* of
organisation, and, second, the acceptance of association
with the other members - that a person has to accept in
order to pursue a protest goal. (47) Pickvance proceeds
to make the crucial point, particularly in relation to
urban protest movements, that there appears to be an
'elective affinity' between the middle classes and formal
modes of organisation. That is, those organisations which

emphasise verbal and reasoning skills, 'planning activities, taking initiatives, following procedures, keeping
records', and so on. He adds that, in other words,
> the skills such associations demand and the inter-
> mediate rewards they offer (in terms of correct exe-
> cution of procedures, rather than attainment of ulti-
> mate protest goals) make them particularly attractive
> to the middle class who possess the required skills and
> have jobs where bureaucratic procedures are a daily
> reality. (48)

Thus the form of an organisation, in pursuit of a protest
goal, will deter from membership those who find it unacceptable, and thereby in so doing limit the organisation's
potential support.

Similarly Pickvance asserts that the obligation to interact with other members will prevent the full mobilisation
of the social base. For example, there could be differing
value-orientations, socio-economic backgrounds, political
attitudes and so on, and Pickvance notes that what is
important is not particularly uniformity, as that is impossible, but rather to what extent 'potential participants in a protest organization are willing to tolerate
interaction with those of divergent views in pursuit of
a given goal': 'in other words, to what extent built-in
tendencies to fission can be held in check'. (49)

ii Strategies

The reason for pointing to the need to examine more
thoroughly protest groups' strategies, is the inadequacy
of the structuralist notion of the 'correct line'.

The structuralists fail to theorise the 'correct line'
and instead prefer to assume that a correct line would be
simply a left-wing strategy: they fail to recognise the
complexity of the problem. A most useful heuristic
device, one which enables a fuller understanding of the
nature of the exchanges between (say) protest organisations and 'dominant' institutions, is that of the idea
of the 'rules of the game'. This idea, coming from the
field of political science, is essentially concerned with
the more subtle measures and forms of social control.
Wahlke et al. state that the 'rules of the game' offer a
means of 'avoiding certain types of open conflict among
group members in order to permit collective actions by the
group for purposes upon which the members are basically in
agreement', and further that they permit the maintenance
of 'the working consensus essential to legislative performance'. (50) Of course the 'rules of the game' idea
is only a more specific and particular example of a gener-

al process, namely, that of ideological domination.
Parkin puts the matter well when discussing 'dominant
values', stating that

> what is essentially an *evaluative* matter can be trans-
> formed into an apparently *factual* one by virtue of the
> legitimating powers of the dominant class. (51)

Now in order for a protest group to formulate aims and
strategies, with a view to effecting the changes it requires, it must be aware of, and understand, the rules of
the (game) that will order its exchange with the re-
spective authority. Levin, in a discussion of public
inquiry procedures, states that in order to achieve any
prospect of success, the advocates of a particular interest are likely to have not only to demonstrate its merits
but to comply with two conditions, namely those of
'legitimacy' and 'reasonableness'. For example, the
'reasonableness' condition, argues Levin, may 'militate
against the success of objectors (or their advocates) who
make personal criticism of officials or planners, and
possibly even against the success of objectors who criti-
cize the planning process'. (52)

Saunders, in his study of pressure groups in the London
Borough of Croydon, observed that the most successful
groups were those whose aims and strategies came to be
regarded by decision makers as 'helpful' and 'responsible', and furthermore that such groups invariably shared
the 'interests and preferences of decision makers'. (53)
Saunders goes on to say that opponents of the status quo,
'representing interests with which decision makers do not
identify', may well be routinely 'excluded' from participation in the political process by virtue of the strategies they are obliged to adopt. (54)

Mason, in his study of the Halliwell Residents' Action
Group (of Manchester), notes that their ability to
organise an orderly meeting of 300 people in the middle
of a clearance area was one of the reasons which 'served
to convince the local authority that the committee was an
effective mobilising force and thus, as Bonnier says, it
was given its "certificate of representativeness"'. (55)

Another rule that has to be recognised and understood -
in order to attempt an appropriate response - is that concerned with the representativeness of the membership of
protest groups. If a group is perceived as only representing its own interests, it could well be disregarded,
despite the merits of its case and the fact that the institution 'in authority' will equally be partisan in some
way or another. For example, the City Architect of
Coventry, following Coventry's public participation
exercise in 1961, stated that it was essential that

pressure groups were not assumed to be representative of
public opinion. He added that pressure groups may
> make representations to expedite action which may be in
> the interests of one particular locality, or one parti-
> cular element in environmental planning; but when such
> action is viewed within a total programme of priorities
> for the city as a whole, it may be premature or com-
> pletely unjustified. (56)

Now it may be argued that this particular rule is completely illegitimate in that, for example, not all middle-
class involvement has been directed towards the protection
or extension of self-interest; for instance, Broady
points to the Child Poverty Action Group, a middle-class
organisation which presses for a redistributive policy.
(57) However, the point remains that recognition of the
rule is crucial, regardless of its merits, in order that
aims and strategies are formulated.

Saunders, in his previously cited study, states that
there have been examples of successful pressure-group
campaigns mounted by groups whose interests and goals have
diverged from those of the political elite - for example,
campaigns for increased day nursery provision. He observes that such campaigns have invariably 'involved careful choice of strategies (e.g., petitions, peaceful and
well-regulated demonstrations, protest letters, etc.)',
whereby the charge of 'irresponsibility' has been avoided.
He adds, however, that they
> have rarely challenged the more fundamental aspects of
> council policy, and their eventual success has in large
> part been attributable to the willingness and ability
> of their members to incur high personal costs in terms
> of time, money and energy over a long period. (58)

Dunleavy's observations of the Beckton Residents' Committee (of the London Borough of Newham) who were involved
in a rehousing issue, admirably demonstrate the importance
of an understanding of protest group culture and strategies. He states that part of the reason why the Beckton
protest (against the policy of rehousing in system-built
high flats) failed, was its general weakness and lack of
resources, and argues that an 'organizational base did not
exist' which the protest could utilise:
> hence the leadership's desperate search for support -
> at a National level from the Ministry and their MP,
> both of whom declined to intervene, and locally from
> the local party branches, ending with the involvement
> of the local Conservatives, who sought throughout their
> brief association with the movement to control and
> 'moderate' their demands and tactics. (59)

Dunleavy observes that effectively the protest was iso-

lated except for the fairly extensive coverage it received
from the local press, 'coverage which led nowhere in terms
of influence'. He then turns to the strengths of the
Beckton group, and states that for quite a period of time
it was remarkably strong in terms of its ability to carry
out protest activity, that is, its ability to mount demonstrations, hold public meetings and mobilise its membership. Dunleavy adds that although the leadership pursued
a hopelessly 'incorrect line', the movement, without ex-
ternal help, did develop (in the period 1968-70) into a
viable collective organisation 'radically contestatory in
outlook, realistic about the use of force and based firmly
on self-protection issues associated with clearance and of
major importance in the lives of Beckton's residents'.
(60) In ideological terms the movement never developed
class consciousness, but this would have been 'extraordinarily difficult in what is virtually a one-class locality
run by, or apparently run by, the Labour movement', but
'to their credit the Beckton residents always rejected the
bogus technicalism of the Council and its officers'. (61)

iii Institutional change

Dunleavy makes two important points about his study,
points which introduce, appropriately, the discussion of
'institutional change'. He asserts that the constraints
on the exercise of local authority power are very few,
'particularly in Newham where the Labour Party has completely dominated local politics since the 1930s', and,
further, that 'no accurate analysis of this protest movement would be possible without data on local authority
decision-making'. (62)
 Now structuralists, Pickvance argues, emphasise the
actions of movements at the expense of the actions of the
'authority', and, moreover, take as axiomatic that 'authorities will not grant changes which threaten the stability
of the mode of production'. (63) He adds that government
institutions cannot be dismissed as sources of minor
changes, but that the role of authorities in initiating
changes is an empirical question, requiring analysis of
policy formation within government institutions:
    It is only by studying processes of policy-formation
    within authorities (i.e., establishing their degree of
    autonomy) that one can correctly estimate the relative
    importance of social movements, on the one hand, and
    factors internal to the state, on the other. (64)
He describes, for example, the work of Muchnik who discusses the role of community councils in urban renewal in
Liverpool. Muchnik describes the conflicts between the

different departments in the local authority, suggesting
that community councils were encouraged by the Planning
Department in its struggle with the Housing Department,
'since they would put forward pressure (and hence provide
legitimacy for) the comprehensive redevelopment policy
sought by the Planning Department'. (65)

Pickvance summarises the position well when he argues
that the structuralist view which asserts that urban
social movements are the exclusive sources of change,
'ignores the pressures exerted by other urban actors
(e.g., land-owners, financial institutions) and ... fails
to recognise that local authorities have their own policy
preferences which result from the clash between departments (and groups of professionals), local-central conflicts, the goals of the controlling political party,
etc.'. Pickvance concludes that:

> It is only when particular local authorities are made
> the subject of study ... that it will be possible to
> attribute the 'urban effects' in particular cases to
> the actions of urban social movements, authority policy
> and other urban actors. (66)

Returning finally to Dunleavy's study, he makes the point
that the most interesting aspect of the local authority
response to the Beckton residents, was that the protest
activity never really affected it, and in many ways it was
scarcely directed at the protestors at all. He argues
that the Beckton residents' movement had no leverage on
the power of the public housing apparatus, and that even
if the protestors had influenced the decision making, they
would not have done so because they forced the authority
to take notice of them, but rather because actors in the
authority were willing to be influenced. His final comments on the matter are worth being reproduced in full:

> The fact that these actors *did not want to be influ-
> enced* is indicative of the strength of the structural
> forces tying the locality into the general development
> of public housing policy. The basic tendency of this
> development, towards the reproduction of an unequal
> status quo with the inner city working class at the
> bottom of the pile, was far too strongly entrenched
> to be capable of alteration either by the protest
> movement or by the local authority.' (67, emphasis
> added)

PART 3

Ray Pahl makes the point that the claim that the development of urban social movements could lead to radical

changes in the nature of urban society would find difficulty in getting empirical support from British experience. (68)   It is the intention here to look at the nature
of the protest movements of Stevenage, and most importantly to examine whether they were a constraining influence
on the urban managers, the Development Corporation.

To begin with, it must be remembered that the case has
already been made for explaining the abandonment of the
two expansion schemes, in terms of institutional change,
rather than as a response to protest. That is, the
abandonment of the 1973 proposals has been seen to have
been due mostly to the collapse of the housing (and associated) markets, and similarly the abandonment of the
1974 proposals appeared to be a direct result of a Ministerial 'rethink' of the new towns policy, which was neces-
sitated by the problems of the inner city. Another point
to be noted is that the new towns are an instrument of
central government, and thus the potential for local
pressure to be effective is a priori limited to quite a
considerable degree.

The Corporation did, of course, attempt to shape (and
repress) the protest: for example, there were the problems associated with the 1973 comment form; the statements to the press, which suggested (inaccurately) that
views were, at that time, split 50:50; the fact that
Volume 4 of 'Stevenage Expansion '74', the planning
report, was only published twenty-six days before the
public inquiry, and so on. Moreover, there was the structure of the 1976 public inquiry, which the protestors did
not quite manage to adapt to. (69) However, what is important is that the Corporation behaved in the same manner
when it was not responding to protest. That is, the Corporation was using a variety of methods of information
control, as a matter of routine in the more stable years,
and hence did not have to alter its modus operandi for the
'protest years'.

The difficulty in evaluating the strengths and weaknesses
of the protest groups is due mainly to two factors. To
begin with, it has already been asserted that the abandonment of the schemes was due to institutional pressure, yet
the two main protest groups, CASE and CAUSE, disagree.
For example, in relation to the 1973 proposals, CAUSE asserted that *'we've* stopped expansion' (emphasis added),
while CASE talked of their *'massive* public support' (emphasis added), and argued that 'expert representation
assisted us'. (70) The second factor is of a more general
and theoretical nature, and is associated with the perspective - which is implicit throughout this work - which
denies structural explanations of outcomes, explaining

them rather in terms of power. As Lukes puts it, such a
perspective necessarily makes counterfactual claims to the
effect that 'some specified agent or agents could have
acted (that is, had the ability and the opportunity to
act) in a certain way'. (71) He argues that there can be
an appeal to empirical evidence in such cases, which is
obviously of an indirect nature, and that in particular an
appeal can be made to evidence 'of the same agent acting
differently under relevantly similar circumstances, or of
relevantly similar agents so acting'. (72) He concludes
that such an appeal to evidence and argument 'concerning
counterfactuals is quite central to the explanatory enterprise'; however, 'by the nature of the case, it must
always be indirect and ultimately inconclusive, but it can
be more or less plausible'. (73)

Geoffrey Hughes, Chairman of SIEG (and Corporation Board
member) in fact puts the matter rather well in relation to
the 1973 proposals, when he argues that the protestors
ultimately faced poor prospects of 'success':

> no Minister is going to make a Designation Order, or
> something like that, without having made fairly de-
> tailed enquiries through, what I might call, official
> channels. He's not going to simply wake up one morning
> and say 'What a damn good idea to double the size of
> Stevenage'. Even if he does have an idea like that
> he's going to put it through his mechanism and say,
> 'Look, what's the effect of my saying this', and so
> it's not a wilful decision. It's taken with clear
> advice and probably consciousness of the *risks* and dis-
> advantages, so that unless one comes to the conclusion
> that the whole Ministry set-up and Ministers are com-
> plete fools, or so bigoted that they're just going to
> blazen their own thing through - which I don't accept
> for any party - then it must mean that there's a good
> deal of basic reasoning before that stage is reached
> and therefore the chances of the local community being
> able to reverse it are, I would have thought, very
> small. (74, emphasis added)

Now what is important to note here is that, first, the
1973 proposals *were* reversed; second that it has been
argued, however, that it was not due to protest activity;
and third that what must be kept open as an option is the
possibility that (a) protest activity *could* be directly
instrumental in the reversal of proposals made by authorities, (b) protest activity *could* be instrumental in the
modification of proposals, and (c) protest activity, together with institutional changes, *could* be instrumental
in either the modification or reversal of proposals.

One acute problem to be faced, in relation to counterfactual claims concerned with the actions of protest groups, is the realisation that authorities are likely to be reticent about disclosing the specific reasons concerning policy changes (e.g., policy reversals), and particularly so if such changes *have* been brought about solely - or in connection with other forces (like institutions) - by protest groups. Thus evidence 'of the same agent acting differently under relevantly similar circumstances, or of relevantly similar agents so acting', will be extremely difficult to find.

What can be attempted here is a discussion of both the 1973 and 1974 expansion proposals in relation to the protest groups' actions, relating the material to the earlier discussion on group culture (and thus reiterating some of the points made earlier in chapter 7), strategies, and institutional change.

Table 9 is a representation of the groups' culture and strategic outlook, which are viewed positively or negatively, in respect of the 'rules' governing their exchanges with the Corporation: namely, the need for the protestors to be 'reasonable', to have a knowledge of what can and cannot be achieved by them (as defined by the Corporation), to be 'representative', and so on.

It has to be remembered here that although CASE acted as an 'umbrella' organisation, each of the other protest groups did, nevertheless, continue with additional individual campaigning. Furthermore, it is not intended in the tabular representation to describe all of the aspects of the groups' culture, consciousness, and strategies, but merely to point to the more salient features involved.

It is important to understand the nature of the Corporation (and its stance) at the time of the 1973 proposals, and the first point to recognise in this connection is that, as throughout the past decade, there has - at officer level - been a working consensus, with the sole exception of the Social Development Office. This department carried out social research on the town, but, most importantly, provided the 'raw data' for the Planning Team on the crucial matters of population and (un)employment. The reason for the continual disagreements between the SDO and the rest of the Corporation (which invariably included the Board members), as noted throughout the text, was the fact that the Planning Team consistently ignored, or modified, the data and advice provided by the SDO. (75) The other departments of the Corporation tended to look uncritically at developments, like the expansion proposals, particularly if it meant, potentially, a 'longer life' for the Corporation and its staff. The 'for expansion' stance which - with the exception of the SDO, which sided with

TABLE 9 Protest groups and the 1973 expansion proposals

	organisational form	consciousness	strategies
CASE +	resources: 'sufficient in terms of persons, knowledge, contacts, and time	high commitment; not overtly political; conservationist	good on linking the town/country issue
CASE −	internal problems: leadership squabbles and personality clashes	too technical	not technical enough; naive; poor publicity
CAUSE +	resources: 'sufficient' in terms of knowledge; good leadership	anti-bureaucratic	good at publicity seeking; reasonably effective 'demonstrations'
CAUSE −	resources: few material and financial resources; tendency towards 'personality cult'	too political	not technical enough; naive; too broad in issues
SVA +	reasonably well established and tight-knit	liberal-democratic; technical	good at reaching SDC directly
SVA −	essentially one-class membership; financial problems; general lack of organisational skills	lack of commitment	could not make up its mind on issues (e.g. to 'broaden the struggle' or not?; 'grass roots members'?, etc.)
Herts. Society +	excellent resources, especially in terms of contacts and finance	conservationist	successful at initial co-ordination; good at recognising the need for a 'united front'
Herts. Society −	too ready to allow itself to be co-opted	not political enough	too conservationist; too concerned with its own status

the protest - the Corporation officers and members took,
was legitimated by the Corporation stating (formally,
quite correctly) that it was merely acting as the Minister
requested. Thus the protest groups were up against a
Corporation quite determined in its position.

Table 9 summarises comments already made in chapter 7
(for example, on the internal squabbles which created
difficulties for CASE) but it takes the analysis further
and in so doing demonstrates the complexities of the
issue. For example, it is argued that, in relation to
the 1973 proposals, CASE's consciousness (of the problem)
was, as well as being conservationist, essentially too
technical, although its strategies were, on the contrary,
not technical enough.

In terms of organisational form, all the groups had quite
difficult problems which were never really recognised, let
alone remedied. CASE, as was noted in chapter 7, had
internal problems which related both to leadership
squabbles (McCombie v. Powell), and to differences in
approach (McCombie v. Bowes-Lyon). CAUSE had a quite
different problem, namely that as it was, essentially, a
sole-membered organisation, its aims and raison d'être
became too identified with the leader's own aims, and
indeed with the leader's personality: Mrs Powell's own
individual characteristics encouraged this process. The
SVA had problems associated with being essentially a one-
class organisation, but these were, however, overshadowed
by the problems caused by the sheer lack of organisational
skills, particularly evident in terms of finance. The
Hertfordshire Society has to be evaluated rather differently, in that it was never completely apparent how it saw
itself, and how it saw its role in the protest; for
example, was it to be merely a co-ordinating body. Similarly, it was never particularly clear how strong its
feelings were about the issue. However, what is clear is
that it seemed too ready and willing to be co-opted into
the umbrella organisation of CASE, despite its own excellent resources, although this can be partly explained by
its 'consciousness', which despite being conservationist,
was not nearly political enough.

It has to be noted that all the groups had 'sufficient'
(in context) resources, proportionate to status, either
in terms of finance, contacts, or time. Again, and
thinking particularly counterfactually, individual roles
within the organisations were crucial; and specific to
individuals rather than to structure. To take but one
example, CASE was dependent in terms of particular resources on the 'skills' of two individuals, namely Mr
McMurtrie the fund-raiser, and Simon Bowes-Lyon, who had

numerous important contacts. CASE, without these two particular members, could well have been a very different
organisation altogether.

In terms of 'consciousness' it can be seen from table 9
why the groups encountered so much difficulty in relating
to one another. CASE was able to integrate the Hertfordshire Society rather easily, as both were conservationist
in outlook, not overtly political, and the differences
between Mr McCombie of CASE and the Hertfordshire
Society's representative, Simon Bowes-Lyon, were not so
great as to be dysfunctional. Mrs Powell (CAUSE) was un-
manageable in CASE, particularly because she was against
the bureaucracy of the Corporation (amongst other things),
which she found also in the structure of CASE, and further
because of her more directly 'political' line. The SVA,
on the other hand, caused problems of interrelationships
by virtue of its 'technical' outlook, together with the
fact that its commitment was forever on the wane.

As was stated earlier, consciousness did not always
translate directly into the 'appropriate' strategies. The
strategies undertaken by the groups were all 'reasonable'
ones, and the strategy of uniting the anti-expansion
support of the town and the villages was of crucial importance. However, the strategies, which obviously at
times related more to the feeling aroused at particular
times than to reasoned analysis, were inappropriate. The
Corporation made the case for expansion both on 'technical' grounds, and on the fact that there did not appear to
be mass opposition to the proposals. The groups made inappropriate responses; first, despite CASE's technical
consciousness, it engaged little in technical analysis, as
did CAUSE. The SVA, the organisation best equipped to
undertake technical analysis, failed to do so, due mainly
to its indecision as to the appropriate strategies, a
situation which was caused by the disagreement between
Phil Nicolai, who wanted to 'broaden the struggle', and
Ian Cuthill, who wanted to keep to a purely technical approach. The second inappropriate response was that of
engaging in an emotive 'drum-banging' protest, as this
confirmed the Corporation in its view - for instance, the
march only attracted 300 persons - that the protest was
not particularly widespread or representative. Another
point was that as the Hertfordshire Society was extremely
concerned about its own status, it refrained from too
readily joining in the 'drum-banging' protests.

However, although it is extremely plausible to argue that
the groups did not engage in the appropriate strategies in
this particular case, the proposals were, nevertheless,
abandoned, although the reasons for this, it has been

argued, were concerned with the collapse of the housing market, together with a 'need' to curtail public expenditure, and an increasing recognition of the 'needs' of the inner city. It has already been noted that the groups - and particularly CASE and CAUSE - saw their activity as instrumental in the abandonment, although the reasons given for this action, together with an appreciation that the groups engaged in the inappropriate strategies, demonstrate that this was not so.

The 1974 proposals came at a time which Councillor Ireton (of the Corporation Board) considered was fortunate

> for *some* of the objectors, but was an unfortunate time for *some* of the Corporation. It came at a time ... when it co-incided with all this pressure from the GLC and other Metropolitan Counties, about inner city redevelopment. (76, emphasis added)

The positions of the protest groups, and the Corporation, were extremely similar to those of 1973, with a few minor but not too significant changes. For example, both the SVA and CAUSE were not opposed completely to a minor expansion for local needs, provided it was minor, and was for local residents. Similarly, the SDO of the Corporation saw such a proposal as sensible in relation to a housing backlog, although the department retained its cynicism towards the ability of the Corporation's planners. The General Manager of the Corporation, on the other hand, believed that a major expansion was more appropriate: 'You cannot put a new town in a strategic position and then expect to restrain it'. (77) Presumably the planners and the majority of the members of the Corporation thought along similar lines. However, with the Corporation being told by the Ministry to trim down its already 'minor' proposals, it was both quite confident and determined that it would receive a final 'yes' to expansion, and this attitude on the part of the Corporation in turn made the protest groups more resolute in their opposition.

Table 10 illustrates the protest groups' characteristics in relation to the 1974 proposals, and indeed indicates a few changes. To begin with there were fewer internal problems for CASE to deal with, mainly due of course to the CASE/CAUSE split. The internal problems of CASE were reduced not only by the split, but also by the fact that there was generally less commitment generated by the groups together with reduced membership (and of course, the proposals were not as major as the 1973 ones).

The interesting points to be raised by table 10 concern the strategies utilised by the groups. Tom McCombie of CASE was correct in assuming that the 'new' campaign

TABLE 10   Protest groups and the 1974 expansion proposals

		organisational form	consciousness	strategies
	+	resources: 'sufficient' in terms of persons, knowledge, contacts, and time	low commitment; not overtly political; conservationist	good on linking the town and country issue
CASE	−	fewer internal problems	too technical	too technical; poor publicity
	+	resources: 'sufficient' in terms of knowledge; good leadership	anti-bureaucratic	good at publicity seeking; reasonably effective 'demonstrations'
CAUSE	−	resources: few material and financial resources; tendency towards 'personality cult'	too political	not technical enough; naive; too broad in issues; inappropriate 'demonstration'; too political
	+	reasonably well established, and tight-knit	liberal-democratic; technical	
SVA	−	fewer members; financial problems; general lack of organisational skills	little commitment	poor technical case; 'Scorer incident'
	+	resources: excellent especially in terms of contacts and finance	conservationist	successful at initial co-ordination; good at recognising the need for a 'united front'
Herts. Society	−	too ready to allow itself to be co-opted	not political enough	too conservationist; too concerned with its own status

against the Corporation's proposals would have to be waged
in an entirely different manner from the earlier one:
'sooner or later the crunch would come and we would have
to prepare a case based on facts'. (78) What was particularly significant about CASE's realisation that the need
existed for a different type of campaign was that this
followed what it considered to be its 'success' in the
'drum-banging' protest of 1973. However, although the
groups understood the new 'rules' of 1974, they did not
particularly achieve much success during the important
confrontation of the 1976 Public Inquiry. Up until the
Inquiry, CASE and the Hertfordshire Society had worked
hard at acquiring both the appropriate legal representation and the 'technical' knowledge necessary for the confrontation. When the Inquiry unfolded, however, it was
apparent that although CASE did in this instance choose
the appropriate strategy, it simply could not carry it
out effectively. The structure of the Inquiry (process)
proved to be too difficult for CASE to understand and
utilise fully, with such inadequate preparation. As Mr
McCombie put it, he was faced with a battery of professional people, who had spent 'their whole lives leading
up to this particular thing', and indeed was made to look
'rather silly'. (79) The SVA's technical case proved to
be almost disastrous, and it was further discredited when
'played off' against Professor Scorer. Mrs Powell, of
CAUSE, both presented a 'political-type' argument instead
of a purely 'technical' one, and also was the first pro-
testor to break the 'rules', notably the rule of 'reasonableness', when she demonstrated with the pram.
  The abandonment of the 1974 proposals indicates further
the complexities of analysis. It has been argued here
that the reason for the abandonment was simply a fundamental rethink on new town policy, in the light of the
recognition of inner city problems. However, although the
groups engaged in this instance in the appropriate strategy, namely on a technical front, they both achieved little
success at the Public Inquiry where their strategy was put
to the test, and did not convince the Inspector, who (in
his Report) considered that the Corporation had a prima
facie case for expansion: nevertheless the Minister ignored the Inspector's recommendations.
  It is a temptation, in conclusion, to suggest that the
participatory process, and in particular the struggles of
the protest groups, was merely ritualistic in that it
seemed that, whether or not the groups utilised the appro-
pritate strategies, however organisationally sound or
otherwise they were, whatever recommendation the Inspector
made (re 1974), and however forcefully the Corporation put

its case, Central Government would make a decision based
solely on its own priorities (and problems). And of
course, as indicated earlier, this is in some measure accurate, and to be expected. However, it is more constructive to draw three conclusions from the study (regarding public participation), conclusions of a less grand
nature, but none the less important.

To begin with, it was obvious that the groups, despite a
misplaced belief in their own influence (in 1973), knew
that certain situations required different strategies.
That is, the change in strategy from an emotive 'drum-
banging' approach to an approach based almost wholly on
technical analysis was significant in terms of political
sophistication. However, the second conclusion which
follows on from the first is less salutary, and is that
it seems plausible to argue that the groups' 'failure' was
due, in part, to the fact that they *did* play completely to
the 'rules'. The groups agreed to the rules readily, and
in so doing rendered themselves less effective. Both of
the expansion proposals were important to the Corporation,
who operated the rules, whose purpose was to protect the
Corporation's interests which in this case were the realisation of the proposals: perhaps in relation to more
minor issues the protest groups could have 'played and
won'. Of course, 'breaking the rules' in this instance
would have meant a more contestatory, conflictually-
oriented, and politically motivated protest.

The final conclusion again follows on from the previous
two, and is that if it is true that future conflicts in
society will increasingly be focused in terms of 'urban
issues', then the assumption that such conflicts will produce a united front of protest (of middle-class conservationists, 'ecologists', and the working class), or indeed
a united working-class response, does not gain much support from these particular findings. This is not to say
that other 'urban situations' cannot produce such an
effect, although it is hard to imagine how the powerless
involved in rehousing schemes (or slum clearance), for
example, could be such a force, but simply that for
'Stevenage and the two expansion proposals', two points
stand out. First, that the difficulties of organising
together diverse groups (classes) of persons remain, and
second - and more important - that for the working class
of Stevenage 'urban issues' appear divorced from both
their work life and their everyday conflicts.

14   Prospects for the new urban managers?

Politics is a matter of boring down strongly and
slowly through hard boards with passion and judgement
together.

Max Weber (1978), p.225

As noted in chapter 10, the DOE's intention (albeit quite
a preliminary view) was that the Corporation should be
wound up in 1980, with the New Towns Commission being retained to manage the commercial and industrial assets.
Rented housing was to be transferred to the Borough
Council on 1 April 1978, and the 'normal growth of the
town', Mr Shore added, especially in relation to second-
generation families, was to be the responsibility of the
'local authorities concerned', and was to be dealt with
'under other legislation'. (1) This final chapter will
consider the prospects for the 'new urban managers', the
Borough Council (the role of the New Towns Commission will
not be discussed), and in particular will consider its
prospects in relation to the industrialists who, as has
been demonstrated, placed considerable constraints on the
Corporation's actions. However, to begin with, two more
general and theoretical aspects will be discussed briefly,
first, the nature of the relationship between new town
corporations and elected councils, and second, particular
aspects of local government.

Richard Crossman's observations on the strained relationships between new town corporations and elected councils,
described in chapter 2, illustrate quite vividly that the
problem, together with the problem of the 'ultimate future
ownership' of the towns, has been central to new town development. Booth, in a survey of (new town) councillors'
attitudes towards new town development corporations, (2)
gave councillors a series of options concerning future
policies (the survey was undertaken before the 1976 Act)
they would favour. Booth comments that:

The option that almost every councillor chose was the
immediate abolition of the development corporation and
total transfer of all functions and assets to the local
authority. (3)

He adds that the Conservatives were split, but that the
majority were against a take-over by the local authority,
while the Labour councillors were clearly in favour of a
complete local authority take-over. (4) A typical comment
from a Labour councillor was that the present situation
was 'remarkably similar to the Colonial administration of
the 1950s - well meaning but sure that the natives are not
really ready to look after themselves'. (5) Booth also
asked the councillors for their attitudes about development corporations as they operated at that time, as opposed to their attitudes towards future policies. He
found that, in general, the Labour councillors were in
favour of the principle of the development corporation,
but wanted a revision to make them more democratic and
accountable to the local authority, 'mainly because these
labour councils have pressing housing and other social
needs which the development corporation can do nothing to
remedy, even though they have the resources, because it is
beyond their terms of reference'. On the other hand, he
noted that the Conservative councillors tended to be
against the idea of a development corporation, as it meant
the compulsory purchase of property, often threatened
small traders through redevelopment, and because it
'swallowed up' rural areas. However, Booth adds that the
Conservative councillors were in favour of corporations in
practice, 'partly because with a development corporation
in control, local Labour controlled councils have less
power to pursue partisan policies'. (6) Booth sums up
the 'problem' by stating that in

the haste to get the new towns off the ground after
1946, the need for co-operation with the local authorities was considered of secondary importance. Today the
climate of public opinion has changed and in many areas
of public life individuals and elected representatives
have demanded and achieved the right at least to be
consulted at an early stage about any decisions that
affect them. (7)

The specific case of Stevenage illustrates all of these
tendencies. Up until quite recently the Borough Council
has - of necessity - played a rather minor role in its
relationship with the Corporation. However, the past few
years have seen the Council assert itself more within the
relationship, due to the fact that (i) it has had to learn
some of the skills necessary to develop and 'manage' a
town such as Stevenage, in the knowledge that it would one

day have to undertake such a task; (ii) more committed
councillors have been recruited, resulting in a stronger
political leadership; and (iii) a slightly more participatory culture has developed (this is related to the
previous point). Attitudes of some of the Stevenage
councillors illustrate the development of a more positive
attitude on the part of the Council (as well as reiterating some of the attitudes found in Booth's survey).

In a survey (8) of Stevenage Councillors - a survey with
a poor response rate - ten out of eleven considered that
the Corporation was efficient, yet also considered that
its non-democratic nature was not a good asset. Similarly
nine out of eleven considered that its achievements had
been considerable, but that it was however time for the
Corporation to be wound up. (9) In answer to the
question, 'what are your feelings about the Corporation
being wound up?', the general response was summed up by
one councillor who stated: 'very pleased, but it should
have gone twelve years ago'.

Perhaps the most interesting comments were those in response to the question, 'what (if any) do you think are
the difficulties of an "elected" councillor serving on an
"appointed" board?'. Only four out of the eleven considered that it would be difficult to serve two masters. A
Labour Councillor, who was at the time on the Corporation
Board, suggested that he had found no difficulties,
'because the general relationship between Council and
Corporation is good (perhaps because there are three
Councillors on the Board)'. Another Labour Councillor
considered that it was not at all difficult to serve two
masters 'if the person was genuine'. Some critics of the
Council have suggested that one of the reasons why the
Council had remained relatively submissive to the Corporation for such a long time was because of the process of
co-optation. That is to say, it was suggested that
members of the Council had been appointed to the Board
and that had subsequently the effect of tempering potential conflict, whilst at the same time other Councillors,
in waiting for a possible place on the Board, had been
somewhat subdued. One Stevenage Councillor points to the
difficulties in the role:

> I have noticed some difficulty experienced by Council-
> lors who are on the Development Corporation. For one
> thing they are often accused of taking sides - e.g.,
> one side or the other at the wrong time - and also the
> appointed members often show irritation with elected
> members because of the democratic procedures they are
> obliged to go through and their reluctance to commit
> themselves immediately. (10)

Another Councillor, however, goes beyond the discussion
of the difficulties of the role and hints, quite clearly,
at a possible co-optation process: 'they wear two caps.
But it works if the local council ensure that Board
members do not chair any committee. This was not so in
Stevenage, much to my regret.' Particularly important,
it could be argued, has been the chairmanship of the
Housing Committee in the 1970s by Board member Councillor
Mick Cotter.

Councillors are, of course, by no means the only element
in the local authority structure, indeed as Cousins
claims,

> the most accurate model, descriptively, is that based
> on the officers as being policy makers, related to the
> community via pressure groups, with the councillors
> playing only a minor role ... this view also fits with
> the belief that local authorities exist primarily to
> provide services, with elected representatives forming
> a sort of consumer consultative council. (11)

Cockburn, in an important work on the structure and
function of Lambeth Borough Council, (12) takes the argument further, by suggesting that a local council is part
of a structure which, as *a whole and in the long term* has
other interests to serve' than those of the local community. (13) She argues that a local authority is deeply involved in *reproducing* the local labour force, (14) and
cites the case of Lambeth, which though is not itself an
all-purpose authority, none the less runs housing and
social services, leisure and recreation facilities.
Cockburn adds, rather deterministically, that Lambeth pays
a 'higher authority (the Greater London Council) to educate its children; the Metropolitan Police to control
them; and it collaborates with the Area Health Authority
to keep them fit'. (15)

Cockburn's arguments concerning the relationship between
officers and members are particularly interesting, and are
especially pertinent to the discussion of Stevenage. She
argues that the 'sharp distinction' made (both in theory
and practice), between officers and members, is a misin-
terpretation of both their positions, particularly as it
implies that 'if one could just put more power into the
hands of the elected members and weaken the officers' grip
on policy, all would go very much better for working-class
interests'. (16) She states that

> Many 'officers' are also 'workers' and identify as
> such. Conversely, it is far from evident that all
> elected members are politically distinct from senior
> officers in the bureaucracy. (17)

Cockburn concludes that the Lambeth study has demonstra-

ted a close partnership between 'senior office holders of
the two sides', drawn even 'closer through the mechanisms
of corporate management'. (18)

It is in relation to the previous discussion that the
prospects for the new urban managers have to be evaluated.
In a sense it is an evaluation of a new political phenome-
non, in that a consideration of the Stevenage Borough
Council has to take into account the following features:
(i) the nature of the Council as it has evolved in relation to the Corporation;   (ii) a Council which has control and authority, but, however, without control of commercial and industrial structures and assets;   (iii) a
Council which contains officers (albeit merely a handful),
previously employed by the Corporation;   (iv) a Council
which has relied more than is usual on officers in order
to compete with the highly 'professional' Corporation;
and (v) a populace which has certain expectations: for
example, the Corporation was able, at certain times, to
shorten the waiting time for housing.   The joint updating
of the Master Plan exercise, together with the formation
of the 'Employment Consultative Committee', offer insights
into the development of the Council, and - most important
- its relation to the industrialists.   However, before
actually discussing these two events it is necessary to
update the case study, and describe other related events
of 1978.

In November 1977 the Corporation's Consultant Planner
asked the Social Development Office for information and
comment on a firm which was likely to be allowed to set up
in the town.   The firm in question was Du Pont (UK)
Limited, the wholly-owned subsidiary of the American
multinational chemical company, Du Pont.   The company
wanted to come to Stevenage with a two-phase development
plan, the first being the consolidation and expansion of
its photo products department, while the second phase was
to be the decentralisation of certain office activity from
London.   In phase 1 the initial employment requirement was
to be 110, with half of the positions being for skilled
workers who would transfer to Stevenage and would require
housing.   Phase 2 would produce an employment need of 140,
with 57 vacancies becoming available in the town.   Following these two phases, there would be an additional land
requirement, or, as the Consultant Planner put it, 'upon
completion of both phases it is necessary for the site to
be capable of further expansion by at least 50 per cent'.
Among the comments the Social Development Office offered
was that in common with much
    of Stevenage industry the Du Pont (UK) operations are
to be in specialised high technology sectors.   Although

nominally a chemical company, Du Pont (UK)'s operations
in Stevenage will have a sophisticated electronics
bias. No effective diversification of the industrial
base can be expected from this development. (19)
Thus, after over twenty years of claiming to be concerned
about the need for diversification, it was evident that
such a consideration was still far from the Corporation's
mind, and indeed it could well be argued that it was now
impossible to diversify.
Problems associated with employment and unemployment were
prominent in early 1978. Mr Overton, Planning Officer for
Hertfordshire County Council, stated in January that there
was 'every indication that things are going too fast' in
terms of employment and housing in Hertfordshire, while
at the same time rumours were rife that much of the
'space' work undertaken at Stevenage would be moved to
Bristol, to fill a gap left by the completion of Concorde.
The management of British Aerospace in Stevenage denied
this, and stated that the 'future was healthy', and that
the only problem the management was having, was in 'attracting skilled workers'. (20)
The final week in January saw the announcement by Mr
William Rodgers, the Transport Minister, of the 'cross-
country Ml link'. This was the plan - mentioned earlier -
to link the Al (M) at a point near Stevenage with the Ml,
and then on to Oxford and Swindon for an east-west route.
Where exactly the new route from Swindon to Stevenage was
to be constructed had yet to be decided. Mr Rodgers
stated that it could be done either by updating existing
routes, or by building new trunk roads and by-passes. (21)
The month ended with an announcement that Stevenage continued to be the town 'worst hit by unemployment' in the
county, with 1,475 people jobless, which was an increase
of 67 from the previous month. (22)
It was reported in the 'Guardian', in early March, that
the 1,400 work-force of Kodak Limited at Stevenage would
have to be cut by at least 300, in order to 'reduce overheads which were making the plant unprofitable', while
locally it was announced that one of the first firms to
move into Stevenage, Shunic Limited, was 'in trouble'.
The Managing Director of Shunic was Mr Geoffrey Hughes,
Chairman of SIEG, and member of the Corporation Board.
(23)
Two interesting observations were made in the later weeks
of March: to begin with it was argued in the TCPA's
journal that unemployment together with housing shortages,
could well lead to an 'exodus of second-generation families from the older new towns', while Frank Allaun MP, in
a letter to the 'Guardian', noted that 'bit by bit, evi-

dence is emerging that the Defence Ministry is undertaking preliminary research on the Cruise missile'. He added that the Government, in reply to a Commons question, had admitted that 'contracts have been placed with British Aerospace and a number of other firms for further limited studies'. (24)

The Corporation itself had spent much of the earlier part of 1978 engaged in 'intensive work' on the preparation of the transfer scheme, as required by Mr Shore's direction, under Section 3(1) of the New Towns (Amendment) Act (1976), on 5 April 1977. (25)   In May 1977 the Corporation had given notice, both in the local press and by letters to all the occupiers of property concerned, that the Secretary of State, in accordance with the aforementioned section of the 1976 Act, had directed the Corporation, in conjunction with the Borough Council, to submit to him a transfer scheme for the transfer to the Council of the Corporation's interest in its housing stock and related assets.   The scheme was approved, with minor modifications on behalf of the Secretary of State, on 14 December 1977, and had the effect of vesting in the Council as from 1 April 1978 the following (summarised) list of Corpora-tion property: (a) residential property, consisting of about 14,500 dwellings and 7,000 garages, at present let by the Corporation, and the freeholds of Corporation-built houses sold on lease;   (b) housing infill sites and other open land within residential areas to be transferred; (c) all shops and workshops in neighbourhood centres; (d) certain neighbourhood community and youth premises, and tenants' meeting halls;   (e) all neighbourhood public houses;   (f) all neighbourhood petrol filling stations; (g) Corporation offices and depots concerned with the management, maintenance and landscaping of transferred property;   (h) doctors' and dentists' surgeries in neigh-bourhood areas;   (i) electricity sub-stations within areas to be transferred;   and (j) all woodlands and tree belts in or adjacent to transferred areas. (26)

The Corporation 'recorded with regret', in 1978, that as a result of the transfer scheme 52 members of staff (44 non-industrial and 8 industrial), were unable to obtain posts in the reorganised establishment of the Borough Council, or in the 'residual establishment of the Corpo-ration', and consequently would become redundant on 30 June.   The Corporation noted that of the redundant staff, 28 were not 'unduly distressed' at being made redundant, but the remainder would become redundant 'against their wishes'.   The Corporation concluded by stating that a total of 274 Corporation staff (99 non-industrial and 175 industrial) had secured posts with the Borough Council. (27)

Thus the Council in 1978 was engaged in two projects with the Corporation, namely the preparation of the transfer scheme, and the updating of the Master Plan. It is now possible to discuss the updating exercise, the formation of the 'Employment Consultative Committee', together with general employment issues, in order to attempt to provide an answer to the crucial question: 'how far will the Council be constrained in its actions, in the housing and planning field, by the industrialists?'.

It was agreed, following the abandonment of the 1974 expansion proposals, that the Corporation should (within the provisions of the New Towns Act, 1965), update the 1966 Master Plan in consultation with the Hertfordshire County Council, Stevenage Borough Council, and the North and East Herts District Councils. The updating was to broadly reflect the objectives of the County Structure Plan, with particular reference to its 'policy for Stevenage'. The document that resulted (in September 1978, and confidential), was 'Stevenage '78: Updating of the Master Plan 1966 (summary of proposals for consultation), 3rd Draft', (28) written by the Consultant Planner. On page 1 it was stated that it had been agreed that it would be advantageous to examine and quantify Stevenage's requirements over the plan period, 1976 to 1991, so that land needs could be ascertained at an early date, and that local authorities concerned could be made aware of Stevenage's long-term requirements, with their possible impact on district plans:

> The update would also provide a basis for subsequent district plans which would be the responsibility of Stevenage Borough Council. (29)

In fact the Borough Council decided that it *did* want to use the updated Master Plan, as a basis for the district plan, but only if Road 9 was excluded. Evelyn Denington,* Chairman of the Corporation, agreed, and thereby, single-handed, completely overturned Corporation policy. (30) The remainder of the document was concerned mainly with aspects of employment and population, (31) and demonstrated a continuing tradition. On page 2 was the statement that Stevenage's population was numerically stable, but that there was evidence of a decline, due primarily to migration:

> One of the undesirable features of emigration at present is that the young, *skilled,* marrieds are leaving the town due to lack of employment opportunities. (32, emphasis added)

---

* Formally introduced into the House of Lords on 19 July 1978, now Baroness Denington of Stevenage.

Thus, taken in conjunction with the earlier statement by
the management of British Aerospace that its only problem
was 'attracting skilled workers', it is clearly evident
that either the document does not convey accurate information, or the skills required by Stevenage industry are
particularly specific. (33) Issues of employment and unemployment were covered in the document on pages 8 and 9,
and to begin with it is noted that like other towns
throughout the UK Stevenage had been seriously affected
by the economic recession 'and consequent unemployment',
which since 1975 had reached an 'unacceptable level', and
in fact 2,000 jobs were lost between 1975 and 1976. However, it is then noted that between December 1977 and
June 1978 there had been an increase of about 600 jobs
in the industrial areas, and thus there was 'evidence for
an improvement'. The statement continued with the assertion that there was merit in 'Stevenage' making attempts to provide at least a sufficient number of jobs
for its economically active population, and accordingly
that in the short term 'the forecast shows' that some
1,000 new jobs a year would be required, split between
the manufacturing and service sectors:

> However it is hoped that this figure will be reduced in
> view of some recent success by the Corporation in at-
> tracting new employers to Stevenage *as well as expan-*
> *sion of existing firms*. (34, emphasis added)

Now this is simply a repeat of the trend of delusion, the
'growth obsession', or simply deceit, in that at the same
time that the document was being written it was announced
that Stevenage's Pye Ether Limited would be closed down by
April 1979, with a consequent 200 redundancies, and similarly it was reported that 'more than 1,000 Stevenage
workers are facing a week of worry about their jobs after
an announcement that Kodak's Chairman and Managing Director, Jim Moorfoot, is to meet union officers next Wednes-
day'. (35) To reinforce the opinion that the document was
not to reverse the earlier tradition, the same page continued with the following statement:

> One of Stevenage's main employment problems is the
> occupational mis-match of skills; it is therefore very
> important that *diversification of employment opportuni-*
> *ties is promoted* to reduce the mis-match. This means
> that there is an urgent need for more jobs for the un-
> skilled and school-leavers. (36, emphasis added)

Yet less than four months earlier it had been announced
that a large Letchworth-based computer firm was to be
moving to Stevenage. (37)

Service employment was dealt with, the argument being
that 'a campaign to attract "basic services" (head

offices, etc.) to Stevenage should be launched immediately as the service sector is likely to provide more opportunities for the unskilled'. The question that has to be asked here is simply, 'do office jobs necessarily meet unskilled needs?'. (38)

The document is summarised in the following manner. In the first place it was argued that in order to meet labour supply needs approximately 1,000 new jobs per year in manufacturing and service employments would be needed for the next three years. It is then argued that if the employment policies are to be successful about 400 new dwellings per annum from 1981 to 1991 would be required. Finally, it was stated that

> If the proposed employment growth and house building rates are achieved *additional residential land will be required outside the designated area* so that housing completions can begin in this area in 1985. (39, emphasis added)

The 'lead time' required for this operation, from acquisition, provision of infrastructure and the first house completions, it was added, was approximately five years. The document concluded with the statement that acquisition procedures should therefore begin sometime in 1980 and that the site chosen for this purpose, was 150-160 acres immediately east of Chells, in the Chells Manor area. (40)

It would be a mistake to consider that the ideology of the updating exercise was in the sole possession of the Corporation. To begin with the updating was a joint exercise, and furthermore as early as November 1977 Mr Ray Davies, Director of Technical Services for the Council, stressed the need for a small expansion and stated that he hoped that the

> Council will do everything in its power to see that the potential of every firm in Stevenage is realised even if it means giving them more land. If we stop firms growing we could be responsible for driving them elsewhere and that could be disastrous. (41)

The Social Development Office of the Corporation, for its part, was of the opinion that the 'growth obsession' continued, but that the mantle had shifted from the Corporation to the Council. The Office noted that the Council had gone for a 'maximum' housing output - 550 houses per year, as opposed to the figure of 400 (the 'minimum' in the updating plan) - which *did* make quite a case for going outside the designated area. (42)

An examination of the formation of the 'Employment Consultative Committee', where the Council had primacy over the Corporation, again demonstrates the development of the Council and its policies.

In June 1978 the Council received a memorandum from the
DOE titled 'The Responsibilities of Local Authorities on
the Dissolution of New Town Development Corporations',
(43) which stated that, in relation to industrial development, the New Towns Commission would have the power to
promote or assist the setting up, or extension of, business in the town, 'by any means'. Nevertheless, the memorandum continued, 'the Government's view is that the local
authorities should be primarily responsible for planning
and promoting future growth in a town after dissolution
of its development corporation, with the Commission playing a supportive role'. (44) The following month Councillor Nobby Clark told a meeting of the Borough Council that
in his opinion:

the Corporation made a mess of the industrial set-up in
this town. They had too rigid a policy and delegated
an unhealthy amount of authority to officers.

The Council are planning to set up their own 'Employment Consultative Committee' and we are attempting to
liaise with local industry and the Department of Trade.
We are now beginning to make ourselves felt in this
area. It seems an anomaly that as we have gradually
taken more and more concern and interest in this town's
affairs we have been kept out of this one area, and
it's not for the want of trying. (45)

The Council had earlier agreed that it would continue a
key-worker allocation system, and would continue to offer
housing to retired parents of residents, (46) but of
course its relationship with Stevenage industrialists
would not be exactly the same as that which the Corporation had. Geoffrey Hughes, Chairman of SIEG, points to
a fundamental difficulty:

Industry could talk to a Development Corporation quite
freely; let's be honest, it didn't tell us all of its
hopes and fears but it could go a long way towards
that.... It's much more difficult now. We're moving
to the stage of talking to the Local Authority because
it's invidious to put a local councillor in the position of giving him information, which would be helpful
in the overall picture, but which would clearly be
highly dangerous if he used it in open council meetings
because then it gets in the press and for that reason
industry has had to be a little more cagey about what
it says and we're still trying to develop - in fact,
it's going on right now - a mechanism for being able
to have confidential discussions without breaking the
obvious necessity of a local councillor operating fully
in public. I think the Council have come to recognize
this difficulty and are working hard to find means of

doing this because they want that information, they
must have, anyone trying to plan ahead has got to get
that sort of confidential thing. They know they won't
get it unless they provide a protective mechanism for
the information that is given to them in confidence.
(47)

Indeed the 'Employment Consultative Committee' was to be
just that protective mechanism. The Council decided to
set up the Committee 'having regard to the urgent need to
revitalise the employment situation in Stevenage', (48)
with the purpose of reviewing both policy and strategy in
regard to the employment situation and related matters.
The Committee's status was of an advisory and exploratory
nature, and accordingly it would be submitting reports to
the Council via the Planning and Works Committee. The
membership structure of the Committee was quite revealing:
7 members of the Borough Council; 3 officers of the
Hertfordshire County Council; a member of the Corporation
(and subsequently, the New Towns Commission); 10 *employ-*
ers from industry and commerce (6 and 4, respectively);
2 representatives from the *employees* (i.e., Trade Union
representation); and a member each from the Hertfordshire
Working Party on Unemployment, and the Employment Services
Agency, making a grand total of 25. (49) It must be
further noted that employees of British Aerospace are
strongly represented among Labour members, and 'they are
not, any of them, industrial militants'. (50)

An explanatory paper on the role of the Committee, (51)
stated that although several officers would be concerned
with the work of the Committee, a senior officer from the
Technical Services Department would be designated for
easily accessible contact on industrial or employment
matters. (52) The impression must not be given that the
Council's members (as compared with officers), would be
necessarily prominent on the Committee, despite the vo-
ciferousness of Councillor Nobby Clark together with the
structure of the Committee (although here it must be noted
that the Committee included ten employers as compared with
seven Council members). For instance, there is a revealing letter sent by the Council's Chief Executive, Mr
Dick Hughes, to the General Manager of the Corporation,
Mr Jack Greenwood, following a statement made by the
Leader of the Council which included the sentence: 'It
is abundantly clear to the Council that the employment
aspect has had not sufficient thought and attention during
recent years.' (53) Mr Hughes, who had in fact drafted
the statement, referred to the sentence in his letter and
stated that 'you may feel that it is a criticism of the
Corporation, but I did word it so that it could also be

taken to imply criticism of the Borough Council'. (54)
The letter continued with Mr Hughes stating that whilst
on the subject of future development he wanted to draw
Mr Greenwood's attention to Minute 149 of the Planning and
Works Committee (19 April 1978) which stated that: 'the
Development Corporation be asked as an immediate step to
involve the Chairman of the Committee (or in his absence
the Vice-Chairman) and the Director of Technical Services
in all discussions concerning the industrial and commercial development of the town'. Mr Hughes adds:

> You will realise that our members make some of the
> running on these matters without prior guidance, *and I
> am wondering whether there would be merit in an officer
> discussion before you involve your Board*. (55, emphasis
> added)

In another paper, endorsed by the Council, Mr Hughes
repeats statements made by the Corporation consistently
over the years, and most recently in the updating plan:

> There is a shortage of skilled workers to fill the
> skilled jobs which become available in the existing
> firms, and this 'mis-match' increases with the increase
> in second generation residents. There remains a need
> for more diversification, and for encouragement of
> small firms. The teenager 'bulge' will worsen, and
> job opportunities - although being created - have
> little immediate effect. (56)

Yet a report submitted to the Council's Planning and Works
Committee at the same time points out, quite unwittingly,
how much more serious and complicated the situation was.
For example, table 3 of the report, which was concerned
with the age and duration of unemployed adult males at
July 1978, demonstrated the problem not only of the 'teen-
age bulge' and the 'second generation', but that also of
the 25-44 age-group: for periods of unemployment of up
to 4 weeks, there were 118 in the 18-24 bracket, 71 in the
25-44 bracket, and 44 in the 45-64 bracket. However, for
periods of unemployment over 26 weeks, there were 43 in
the 18-24 bracket, *113* in the 25-44 bracket, and 32 in the
45-64 bracket. (57)

Thus the evidence from both the updating exercise and the
formation of the 'Employment Consultative Committee' suggests that the Council is not commencing its new role in
a manner any different from that of the Corporation over
the past thirty years.

The Council is being forced to work, of course, in a
context which has evolved at first haphazardly, but later
in a much more systematic manner. Moving from an early
position of relative autonomy in its actions, the Corporation has come to be dominated (and determined) - in the

crucial areas of land-use planning and housing allocations
- by the industrialists of the town. Such a situation is
not, of course, completely the result of intention, although, as has been demonstrated, the Corporation's
'growth obsession' (fuelled by the Planning Team) has
neatly fitted into the evolving pattern. Rather, it is
the structure, both of the industrial base and the Corpo-
ration/Stevenage industrialists' relationship, that sets
and determines the present context. For example, the
'present' situation of the fundamental occupational mismatch of labour supply and demand is something that simply
cannot be easily altered, either 'individually' or through
collective intention. The relationship between Stevenage
industry and the Corporation, as was argued in chapter 12,
evolved to eventually become one of symbiosis. The Corporation, eager to perpetuate its own 'life' (together with
its 'growth obsession'), found advantage in aligning
itself with a growth-motivated set of industrialists.

Now of course this symbiotic-type structure has - as has
been earlier demonstrated - resulted in a certain pattern
of development for the town. Briefly, to recapitulate the
argument, the following points can be made:

(i) The town has been dominated by a few high-technology
industries, requiring specialised skills. This has resulted - with the onset of second generation labour - in
an occupational mismatch of labour supply and demand,
that is, there is a shortage of certain categories of
skilled labour, and a surplus of semi-skilled and unskilled persons.

(ii) Historically the industrialists have always exaggerated their housing 'needs', in order to 'play safe' (together with an optimistic-cum-growth ideology) in case
the Corporation began to discriminate in favour of the
indigenous second generation residents.

(iii) The result of the aforementioned pattern has been
that the Corporation has never formulated a housing
policy, particularly in relation to the competing claims
of 'key workers' and the second generation residents.

(iv) A solution to the 'problem' has been to attempt to
expand the town, in that such an expansion would satisfy
both the growth-motivated industrialists and the Corporation, and the second generation residents. However,
for a variety of reasons, no expansion has taken place.

(v) The 'present' situation is one fraught with difficulties: there is an increased second generation, on
the look-out for housing; there is an industrial structure which 'requires' key workers, who cannot necessarily
be found within the town (and the second generation);
land is being used up quickly; and, at this particularly

difficult juncture, the Corporation is to be dissolved, with the relatively 'inexperienced' Borough Council to take over.

Now, there might not be the same mutual advantages to be gained from the Council/Stevenage industry relationship, as there was with the earlier relationship of the Corporation and the industrialists. For example, the Council *is* an elected body and has to make some kind of attempt at representation of interests, which might result in friction in its relationship with the industrialists (whose demand for 'key worker housing' will continue). Similarly, although the public participation and protest, in the 1970s, was relatively minor in its nature and influence, the Council would not be able to hide behind a 'we are merely servants of the Minister' type of justification for any expansion it might propose. And this again could lead to difficulties in its relations with the industrialists (let alone public protestors).

However, the crucial question is not whether, in fact, the Council *wants* to reverse or modify the aforementioned pattern and structure of development, but rather will it, if it so desires, be able to? For the case study demonstrates, quite clearly, the fundamental constraining influence of the industrialists, on both the structure and action of the urban managers. Urban managers have to both create and co-ordinate jobs and houses, and it is in this connection that the industrialists' influence is pervasive; and, unfortunately for the Borough Council, land just cannot be acquired and developed as and when it pleases.

Appendices

APPENDIX 1   Methodological note

INTERVIEW SCHEDULE

The following persons were interviewed, the interviews
taped and later transcribed (with the exception of the
Bowes-Lyon interview).

Jack Balchin (SDC)	15. 2.76
Simon Bowes-Lyon (Hertfordshire Society)	8.12.77
Charles Burr (SDC)	10. 5.77
Evelyn Denington (SDC)	18. 5.77
Steve Halls (DE: local office)	6. 5.77
John Hubble (SVA)	2.6.77 and 10. 8.77
Geoffrey Hughes (SIEG)	29. 9.78
Philip Ireton (SDC)	24. 5.77
Ian Johnson (Conservative Party)	29. 4.77
Ernest Lenderyou (SDC)	18. 2.76
Tom McCombie (CASE)	31. 8.77
Marion Powell (CAUSE)	28. 4.77
Shirley Williams MP	1. 4.77
Cynthia Wood (Aston Parish Council)	1. 8.77

'STATISTICAL' INFORMATION

The following sources have been used extensively for some
of the statistical material in the text:
Bailey, R. (1977), 'The Homeless and Empty Houses',
Penguin, Harmondsworth.
Building Societies Association (1976), Facts and Figures,
'Quarterly Bulletin' No.7.
Butler, D. and Sloman, A. (1975), 'British Political
Facts: 1900-75', Macmillan, London.
Chamberlain, C.W. (1977), Attitudes Towards Direct Politi-
cal Action in Britain, pp.164-202 in C.Crouch (ed.)
(1977), 'British Sociology Yearbook' vol.3, Croom Helm,
London.

Community Development Project (1976), 'Whatever Happened to Council Housing?', Community Development Project, London.

Craig, F.W.S. (1971), 'Britain Votes 1: Parliamentary Election Results 1974-77', Political Reference Publications, Chichester.

ERVs and ERVls, obtained from the Department of Employment (Stevenage Office).

Haseler, S. (1976), 'The Death of British Democracy', Elek, London.

HMSO, 'Social Trends', HMSO, London.

Stevenage Development Corporation, 'Purpose', the quarterly magazine of the SDC.

Town and Country Planning Association (1953-78), Annual Digest of New Town Statistics, TCPA, London.

Personal communication from Mr C.Spratley, Chief Finance Officer of the Stevenage Development Corporation, regarding information on the General Revenue Account and other related financial matters.

APPENDIX 2   SDC board members: brief profiles

The following are brief profiles of most of the SDC
members (I could not obtain information on a few members),
together with a brief analysis. The data is derived from
personal communications with E.Lenderyou and P.Ireton, and
'Who's Who?', 'Directory of Directors', and Registers of
Architects, Accountants, Bankers, Solicitors, and Sur-
veyors.

Abbreviations: L - Labour Party, C - Conservative Party.
Chronological Order from 1946.

F.D.Campbell-Allen (C): was in management at John
Lewis's.
Hinley Atkinson (L): was assistant editor at the 'Daily
Herald'.
Sir Clough Williams-Ellis CBE,MC,JP,FRIBA (L): was an
architect in private practice, and member of the TCPA
Council.
Alderman Frank Corbett JP (L): was a member of the Wood
Green Council.
Philip Ireton JP,CBE (L): first freeman of Stevenage;
member of Hertfordshire County Council 1946-77, and
Chairman in 1974; member of the SUDC and SBC 1946-76;
member of the TCPA Council; clerical worker, British
Rail; Chairman of the Stevenage Labour Party 1938-45;
member of the SDC's Estates, Planning, and Establishment
Committees.
Elizabeth McAllister (L): was a freelance writer of books
on town planning; Council membership of the TCPA.
Monica Felton PhD (L): was an academic; member of the
LSE Senate; first woman clerk of the House of Commons;
member of the Reith Committee; Chairman of Peterlee
Development Corporation 1948-9.
Alderman W.J.Grimshaw JP (C): was a Middlesex County

Councillor; Alderman of Hornsey; member of the Metro-
politan Water Board 1942-8.
Sir Thomas Gardiner KCB,KBE,GCB (C): retired Chief of the
Post Office; Government Director of the Anglo-Iranian Oil
Co. 1950-3; member of the Royal Commission on Scottish
Affairs 1952-4; Vice-Chairman and acting Chairman of the
National Dock Labour Board 1949-51; member of the Forces
Medical/Dental Services Committee 1953-6.
Alderman the Rev.C.Jenkinson MA,LLB (L): was Leader of
the Leeds City Council.
J.Corina (L): was involved in the Co-operative Movement.
Sir Thomas Bennett KBE,FRIBA, FRSA (C): was an architect
in private practice; Chairman of Crawley Development
Corporation 1951-60; Director of Bricks 1940; Director
of Works 1940-4; Controller of Temporary Housing 1944-5.
W.Winson (L): was Manager and Director of SPD Limited, a
subsidiary of Unilever Ltd.
C.T.Every (C): was a Chartered Surveyor.
S.Gestetner (L): was head of the Gestetner firms.
Baroness E.Denington CBE,DBE,Hon.FRIBA,Hon.MRTPI (L):
Chairman of the GLC 1975-6, member 1964- ; member of the
LCC 1946-65; was a journalist and teacher, and General
Secretary of the National Association of Labour Teachers
1938-47; member of St Pancras Council 1945-59; Chairman
of the Housing Committee of the GLC 1964-7; Deputy Leader
in opposition GLC 1967-73; member of the Central Housing
Advice Centre Committee 1955-73; member of the SEEPC
1966-77; Chairman New Towns Association 1968-77; member
of the Sutton Dwellings Housing Trust 1976- ; member of
North British Housing Association 1976- ; Council member
of the TCPA.
Colonel J.A.Davies OBE,MI Mech.E,AMIEE (C): was a
Director of Hollerith Tabulating (now ICI).
Lt.Gen.Sir Charles King KBE,CB (C): retired Army;
Engineer in Chief at the War Office 1941-4.
J.A.F.Watson FRICS,JP (C): was a Chartered Surveyor;
member of the Reith Committee; published books on penal
reform.
S.Jackson (C): accountant.
Major A.G.Howard MBE,JP (C): retired Army; accountant;
connected with one of the Unit Trusts; Chairman of the
SUDC 1947-52; ex-Head of Stevenage Home Guard.
Sir Roydon Dash DFC,Hon.LLD,FRICS (C): was a Chartered
Surveyor; member of Bracknell Development Corporation;
ex-Chief Valuer of Board of Inland Revenue.
P.Pryor (C): local farmer; Director of Trumans
(brewers).
G.L.Hughes (C): Director of Shunic Ltd (Stevenage);
SIEG: Chairman of SDC's Finance Committee.

A.F.Tuke (C):   Chairman of Barclays Bank 1973- ;   ex-Scots
Guards;   Chairman of Committee of London Clearing Banks
1976- .
The Rt Rev.E.W.B.Cordingly MBE,AKC (C):   ex-Chaplain to
the Queen;   ex-Rector of Stevenage.
Sir Arthur Rucker KCMG,CB,CBE (C):   Private Secretary to
successive Ministers of Health 1928-36;   member of Common-
wealth War Graves Committee 1959;   Honorary Treasurer,
Oxfam.
Cmndr P.B.Martineau OBE,RN rtd (C):   solicitor.
S.H.Clarke CBE,MSc (L):   worked for the Ministry of Home
Security;   Director of Warren Springs Research Laboratory,
Stevenage 1958-63.
Co.Cllr Hilda Lawrence (L):   SBC Councillor;   Secretary of
the Stevenage Residents Association in the 1950s;
journalist;   member of the Annan Committee.
Co.Cllr M.Cotter (L):   SBC Councillor;   factory worker
(Kodak).
Harold Campbell (L):   Chairman of (i) working party of
Housing Co-operatives, (ii) Housing Associations' Regis-
tration Advisory Committee, (iii) Co-operative Planning
Ltd 1964-74, (iv) Co-ownership Development Society Ltd
1969-76, (v) Sutton Housing Trust, (vi) DOE working party
on New Forms of Housing Tenure 1976-7, and (vii) Hearing
Aid Council. Member of Enfield Borough Council 1959-63;
Director Co-operative Housing Centre 1976- ;   Director
Enfield Highway Co-operative Society Ltd 1965- ;   Deputy
Chairman of the Housing Corporation 1969-73;   General
Manager of the Newton Housing Trust 1970-6;   Secretary of
the Co-operative Party 1964-7.
J.D.Crane FCA (C):   accountant with Hawker Siddeley
Dynamics and Director of Hawker Siddeley Dynamics;
Director of Aircraft Research Association Ltd;   Director
of Eurosat SA (Geneva);   member of Eurospace Council.
Cllr K.C.McKechnie (C):   Transport Manager at Bowaters.
Gp Captain Sir Douglas Bader CBE,DSO,DFC (C):   member of
Civil Aviation Authority since 1972;   Director of
Trafalgar Offshore Ltd.
P.Metcalfe (L):   ex-Labour Party agent in Stevenage;
works-study at Bowaters.

Thirty-six people have been appointed to the Corporation
Board since 1946, the political membership being 19 Conservative and 17 Labour. Not surprisingly, in the early
years there tended to be Labour appointments, followed by
a period of Conservative appointments, and in the later
years a reversal to Labour.

Chronological list of appointments and terminations (I am not distinguishing between those members who resigned, and those whose term of office had ended).

1946   Ellis, Felton, Campbell-Allen, Atkinson, Corbett, Grimshaw, Ireton, Gardiner, and McAllister.
1948   Corina and Jenkinson. Termination: Ellis.
1949   Jenkinson died in August.
1950   Every, Winson, Davies, Gestetner, and Denington. Terminations: Campbell-Allen, Atkinson, Corbett, Grimshaw, and McAllister.
1951   Bennett.
1952   King, Howard, Jackson, and Watson. Terminations: Corina, Felton, Winson, Davies, and Gestetner.
1953   Dash.
1956   Pryor and Hughes. Terminations: King, Howard, and Watson.
1959   Tuke. Termination: Every.
1960   Cordingly. Termination: Pryor.
1962   Martineau and Clarke. Termination: Cordingly.
1965   Lawrence and Cotter. Termination: Tuke.
1967   Campbell.
1970   McKechnie and Crane. Terminations: Jackson and Martineau.
1972   Bader and Metcalfe. Termination: Clarke.
1974   Termination: Bader.

There was a much higher 'turnover' in the early years, as can be clearly seen. The only really significant 'political' appointments were those made by Richard Crossman in 1965, when he nominated two Stevenage Councillors to the Board, and again in 1966 when he appointed Mrs Denington as Chairman.

Chronological list of Chairmen, together with duration, and attendance record.

Ellis	5.12.46-August 1947	84 per cent attendance (calculated from the SDC minutes).
Gardiner	10.10.47-10.10.48	100 per cent
Jenkinson	11.10.48- 3. 8.49	60 per cent (due to sickness).
Felton	26.10.49-10. 4.51	88 per cent
Bennett	10. 7.51-10. 5.53	88 per cent
Dash	26. 5.53-13. 3.62	99 per cent
Rucker	14. 3.62- 7. 1.66	99 per cent
Denington	13. 1.66-	98 per cent

Chronological list of Deputy-Chairmen, together with
duration, and attendance record.

Felton	5.12.46-30. 4.48	90 per cent
Corina	12. 5.48-10. 1.52	88 per cent
King	11. 1.52-10. 3.56	98 per cent
Rucker	11. 3.56- 7. 1.62	90 per cent
Martineau	23. 3.62-31.12.67	84 per cent
Campbell	1. 1.68-	99 per cent

All the other members have an attendance record of
between 90 and 95 per cent, with the exceptions of Ireton,
95+ per cent, and Bader, 30 per cent.

L.VINCENT

In partnership with R.Gorbing until 1977.
The headquarters of the practice is at Stevenage with
branches (in association with Tempo Graphics) at Bristol,
Manchester, and Norwich.
Local authority housing contracts: Halifax; Hatfield
Development Corporation; North Bedfordshire District
Council; Stevenage Borough Council; Stevenage Develop-
ment Corporation; Wandsworth; Welwyn District Council;
and Welwyn Garden City Corporation.
Private housing for Bovis, Laing, Lovell, and Rialto.
Old peoples' housing: Anchor Housing Association;
Guiness Trust; and Hanover Housing Association.
Industrial buildings: for example, in Stevenage, Amoco,
BAC, Dixons, and Flexile.
Central Area Redevelopment: Camberley, Luton, and
Manchester.
Leisure Centre for the Stevenage Borough Council.
Planning Consultancies: Basingstoke; Bridgend;
Colchester; East Herts. District Council; Glamorgan
County Council; St Albans; and Stevenage Development
Corporation.

S.BOWES-LYON

Eton, and Magdalen College, Oxford.
Farmer, accountant, Investment Manager, and Director of
(at a minimum) six firms, including: Electro Pneumatics
(a subsidiary of Cosmopolitan Assurance Co Ltd, registered
in Nassau); Financial Assurance Ltd; Manchester Creosote
and Storage Co Ltd; and St Paul's Walden Bury Estate Co
Ltd.
(Information obtained from Companies House, Cardiff.)

APPENDIX 4   Building societies and the SDC's owner-occupation scheme

The following Building Societies were involved in the 70 per cent/30 per cent mortgage scheme:
   Alliance
   Abbey National
   Cheltenham and Gloucester
   Leicester
   Nationwide
   Woolwich

STEVENAGE EXPANSION, 1973 – COMMENT FORM – CONFIDENTIAL

YOU ARE INVITED

To help the Corporation to reach a decision on the Expansion Area to be recommended to the Secretary of State for the Environment.

PLEASE: (1) Read the Corporation's Summary of the Feasibility Report.

(2) State your first three preferences of expansion area by putting 1, 2 and 3 in boxes below:

	Feasibility Study	M	N	P	Q	R
	Your Priority					

(3) Say if you think there is another "strategy" of choice that is better:

(4) Answer the following particular questions on which the Corporation would like your views:

	Please circle your choice:		
	Yes	No	Don't Know
(a) Do you agree that both to live and work in Stevenage is better than to live here and travel to work outside?	1	2	3
(b) Do you think that more, and more varied, jobs are required in Stevenage? Circle 'NO' if you think them sufficient.	1	2	3
(c) Do you think there are sufficient shops in Stevenage?	1	2	3
(d) Are you satisfied with facilities for recreation and entertainment?	1	2	3
(e) Is it a disadvantage for a motorway to run through a town rather than outside?	1	2	3

(f) Do you think more houses should be provided in Stevenage?

	Rent	Sale
for renting	1	2	3
for sale	1	2	3

If you reply 'Yes' to both, please circle the more important in the 'rent' or 'sale' box opposite.

(5) Put in order of importance the following factors affecting expansion:

Please put
1 2 3 4 or 5

(a) Agricultural Land: need to preserve and safeguard landscaping

(b) Housing: need to provide more land for housing both public and private

(c) Jobs: need for greater variety of job opportunities

(d) Shopping and Entertainment: need for better facilities.

(e) Villages: need to prevent urban sprawl and protect villages surrounding Stevenage.

(6) Give your general comments on the Feasibility proposals in the Report:

PLEASE GIVE THE FOLLOWING DETAILS

		AGE GROUP				Male or Female	
Under 20	20-29	30-39	40-49	50-59	60 & over	M	F
1	2	3	4	5	6	1	2

Please circle
appropriately

PLACE OF RESIDENCE

If you live in Stevenage

Please give the name of the area of the town in
which you live:

How long have you lived in the town?   years.

If you live outside Stevenage please give the
name of the town or village.

It would be helpful if you signed your reply

STEVENAGE URBAN DISTRICT COUNCIL

Survey of Public Opinion on Possible Expansion of
Stevenage

You have already received a copy of Stevenage Development
Corporation's Summary of the Feasibility Report together
with a comment form. Hertfordshire County Council and
Stevenage Urban District Council oppose expansion and a
summary of Stevenage Council's arguments against expansion
is enclosed.
   It is considered that the Corporation's comment form
does not facilitate free expression of views for or
against expansion. The Council considers it vitally
important to obtain the opinion of a fair cross section
of the community and FOR THIS REASON HAVE SELECTED YOU
PERSONALLY to read and consider all the arguments and to
complete and return (postage paid) this form to Southgate
House, Southgate, Stevenage.

QUESTION 1   The existing population of Stevenage is approx
              72,000 and is to grow by planned immigration
              to 80,000 by 1975 and then by natural growth
              to 102,000 by 2001.

              Are you in favour of additional planned im-
              migration beyond 1975 which would increase
              the ultimate population by, say:

                                    tick as appropriate

              (a) About 50,000 to a total of 152,000

              (b) About 25,000 to a total of 127,000

              (c) About 10,000 to a total of 112,000

(d) About 5,000 to a total of 107,000

(e) Not at all

If you have ticked (e) please ignore Questions 2 and 3.

QUESTION 2   If you feel there is a case for expansion do
you consider that:

(a) The majority of houses to be provided
shall be public housing for renting

(b) The majority of houses to be provided
shall be for private ownership

(c) The number of houses to be provided
shall be equally divided between
houses for renting and private
ownership

QUESTION 3   If you feel there is a case for expansion including the provision of houses in accordance
with your answer to Question 2, do you consider that it should be carried out by:

(a) A democratically elected Council (responsible to the town)

(b) A Government appointed Corporation
(responsible to the Government)

There is no need to sign this questionnaire but to help us
find out how representative is the response we receive,
please PRINT here:

(1) YOUR SURNAME

(2) YOUR ADDRESS

Comments may be made in the blank space overleaf.

COMMENT FORM USED TO INVITE PUBLIC OBSERVATIONS
ON THE PROPOSALS IN VOLUME 2

YOU ARE INVITED

to read the accompanying leaflet and/or the more
detailed reports:
(i)   Volume 2 - Corporation proposals for expansion
       £1.00.
(ii)   Summary of the Corporation proposals 10p.

to comment on the proposals contained therein

ANY COMMENT WILL BE WELCOME

particularly on the following topics:
(i)   the size of the expanded area
(ii)   the deletion of land to the west of Al(M) and
       around Aston village from designation
(iii) the direction of expansion
(iv)   the provision for homes and jobs

COMMENTS SHOULD BE RECEIVED BY 28TH FEBRUARY

and these will be analysed and included in the Corporation's report on consultations to be published in
Spring 1975.

COMMENTS (CONFIDENTIAL)

ADVERTISEMENT SEEKING PUBLIC COMMENTS ON
CORPORATION'S TASK

STEVENAGE DEVELOPMENT CORPORATION
EXPANSION FOR LOCAL NEEDS

In April 1973 the Stevenage Development Corporation submitted proposals at his invitation to the then Secretary
of State for the Environment for the expansion of
Stevenage by the addition of about 3,500 acres to the
present designated area.

In January, 1974, the Rt.Hon.Geoffrey Rippon MP, then
the Secretary of State, announced that he had decided not
to proceed with those proposals for major extension of
Stevenage, and that he would be discussing urgently with
the Corporation the case for expansion on a lesser scale
to meet local needs in the town.

The election intervened and following the change of
Government a letter was received from the Department of
Environment on the instructions of the new Minister of
Planning and Local Government, the Rt.Hon.John Silkin MP,
asking the Corporation to submit new proposals for ex-
tension of the town. The letter of April 11 reads:

EXPANSION OF STEVENAGE

I refer to earlier correspondence and discussions about
your Corporation's proposal of 1973 for the expansion
of Stevenage. The purpose of this letter is to ask the
Development Corporation to consider and make proposals
for an extension of the designated area sufficient to
meet the current objectives and local needs of
Stevenage for the foreseeable future - say the next 15
years. In assessing such needs the Corporation will no
doubt wish to have in mind the desirability of ensuring
that enough land is available to meet not only the
housing requirements of the "second generation," but
also those of workers recruited - so far as possible
from London - by existing employers (industrial, commercial, or public service) in Stevenage and by any new
employers who may move into the town in accordance with
master plan requirements. On addition to these main
categories of people the Corporation will wish to have
regard to the requirements of the other (usually
smaller) categories of people, such as ex-regular
servicemen and disadvantaged families, and old people
from London, whom the Corporation house as opportunity
offers under their present tenancy allocation rules.

At this stage, the most important thing is to identify the amount of land which is likely to be needed, and how soon, irrespective of whether the houses are to be built, eg. by the Corporation or the Borough Council, and of whether they will be to rent or for sale; but bearing in mind that the main immediate demand is for rented houses.

It will be for the Corporation, after assessing needs, to come to a conclusion on how much land is likely to be required for housing and ancillary uses, such as roads, schools, open space, shops and so on, but it seems probable that something of the order of 1,000 acres or thereabouts might prove sufficient. It also seems probable that this might be found within the area proposed by the Corporation as an extension of the designated area, and which was put forward only after planning studies and a thorough public participation exercise. It may thus be possible for your Corporation to formulate proposals for a smaller expansion without any very elaborate further study. Nor, if the proposals for a smaller area fall within the area already proposed for expansion by the Corporation, would there appear to be the need for extensive public participation at this stage. However the Corporation will no doubt wish to consult the local authorities directly concerned, and to inform the public of what is proposed, before submitting proposals to the Secretary of State.

INVITATION TO EXPRESS YOUR VIEWS

The Corporation wishes to know whether the people or organisations in the Stevenage area have any views on these matters or on any other local needs they feel may affect the future of the town.

IF YOU HAVE, WRITE TO US

Your ideas can then be studied and taken into account in arriving at the proposals which the Corporation has been asked to submit to the Secretary of State.

Write your comments under the headings given above, if possible, and send them to:

THE GENERAL MANAGER
STEVENAGE DEVELOPMENT CORPORATION
SWINGATE HOUSE, DANESTRETE,
STEVENAGE SG1 1XE

to arrive by May 31, 1974, and certainly not later than
June 8, 1974.

We would prefer you to give your name and address when
writing but if you wish your letter to be treated in
strict confidence please make this clear.

CURRENT OBJECTIVES AND LOCAL NEEDS

In defining the town's current objectives and local needs
the Corporation will consider them under such headings as
the following (there may be others) -

HOUSING	LEISURE PROVISION
EMPLOYMENT	SOCIAL AMENITIES
SHOPPING	TRANSPORTATION REQUIREMENTS
PUBLIC SERVICES	

FUTURE PROGRAMME

We shall be studying public comments in June and thereafter and aim at the following target dates:

July 1974	Publication of report of Corporation's preliminary appraisal of current objectives and local needs.
Mid-September 1974	Publication of draft proposals for scale and location of proposed expansion area.
Mid-October 1974	Formal submission to the Secretary of State.

If the Secretary of State in due course issues a Draft
Designation Order for expansion there will be further opportunity for public representations and, if necessary, a
Public Inquiry. The Corporation would later submit a proposed Master Plan and this too would be the subject of
public consultation followed by a Public Inquiry.

APPENDIX 8   Industrial profiles: the 'top 10'

There were four factories in existence before the new town came into being which were still in use in 1978: ESA Ltd (school furniture); Geo.W.King Ltd (cranes, hoists, and conveyors); Stevenage Knitting Co Ltd (knitwear); and D.Wickham and Co (mechanised plant and vehicle components).

In 1977 there were 87 factories located in the two industrial areas, plus 15 industries operating in the Corporation's unit factories.

The following are brief profiles of Stevenage's 'top 10' industries, and are presented in alphabetical order.

Bowater Packaging Ltd

Manufacturers of packaging materials and an operating unit of the Bowater Corporation Ltd, an international firm. Came to Stevenage in 1958 from London and their factory - site area: 6.88 hectares - was built by the SDC. Pre-tax profit in 1976 was £9 million.

British Aircraft Corporation (now part of British Aerospace)

Production of missiles and satellites. Came to Stevenage in 1955 from Luton. Its factory was built by the SDC on a site area of (in total) 26.30 hectares. Profit after tax in 1976 was £13.7 million (as compared with £8.7 million in 1975).

Hawker Siddeley Dynamics Ltd (now part of British Aerospace)

Came to Stevenage in 1952 (as De Havilland) from Hatfield, and is engaged in the production of guided missiles and guidance systems, satellites, etc. The total site area is 5.67 hectares, and the factory was built by Hawker Siddeley. Group profit after tax for 1976 totalled £48.4 million.

Imperial Chemical Industries Ltd

Production of polythene film. Came to Stevenage in 1953 from Welwyn Garden City, and built its own factory on a total site area of 4.49 hectares. An international firm, its after-tax profit for 1976 for the group as a whole was £279 million.

International Computers Ltd

Electronic research. Came to Stevenage in 1954 from Letchworth, its premises being jointly built by ICL and the SDC on a site area of 3.35 hectares. An international firm, whose 1976 group profit after tax was £12.5 million.

Kodak Ltd

Manufacturer of cameras and accessories. Came from Harrow in 1954 and has a SDC-built factory on a site area of 5.03 hectares. The group profit for 1976 after tax was £13 million.

Marconi Instruments Ltd

Came to Stevenage in 1953 from the Old Town (of Stevenage) as W.H.Sanders (Electronics) Ltd. Premises were mainly built by the SDC, on a site of 1.17 hectares. Profit after tax for 1975 was £428,000.

Mentmore Manufacturing Co Ltd

Manufactures pens. Came from London in 1957 and has a SDC-built factory on a site area of 2.82 hectares. Profit after tax in 1976 was £92,180 (the previous ten years showed an annual average profit of £300,000).

Pye Ether Ltd

Manufacturer of electrical and scientific equipment. Came from the Old Town (of Stevenage) in 1953 and has a SDC-built factory on a site of 1.58 hectares. Group profit after tax for 1976 was £6 million.

Taylor Instruments Ltd

A wholly-owned subsidiary of the Sybron Corporation of New
York. Production of control instrumentation. Came from
London in 1962 and have built their factory on a site of
5.946 hectares. Annual Report (1976) of the Sybron Corporation states that: 'Taylor's manufacturing unit in Great
Britain showed a profit in 1976 after 2 years of loss
operations' (p.10): however no figures are given.

The above information has been derived from the Annual
Reports of the Companies, together with material supplied
by Alan Cudmore of the Estates Department, SDC.

APPENDIX 9   Standard industrial classification (revised 1968)

Summary of Orders

Order	Description of Industry
I	Agriculture, Forestry, Fishing
II	Mining and Quarrying
III	Food, Drink and Tobacco
IV	Coal and Petroleum Products
V	Chemicals and Allied Industries
VI	Metal Manufacture
VII	Mechanical Engineering
VIII	Instrument Engineering
IX	Electrical Engineering
X	Shipbuilding and Marine Engineering
XI	Vehicles
XII	Metal Goods not elsewhere specified
XIII	Textiles
XIV	Leather, Leather goods and Fur
XV	Clothing and Footwear
XVI	Bricks, Pottery, Glass, Cement, etc.
XVIII	Paper, Printing and Publishing
XIX	Other Manufacturing Industries
XX	Construction
XXI	Gas, Electricity and Water
XXII	Transport and Communication
XXIII	Distributive Trades
XXIV	Insurance, Banking, Finance and Business Services
XXV	Professional and Scientific Services
XXVI	Miscellaneous Services
XXVII	Public Administration and Defence

Examples of Minimum List Heading
SIC order XI Vehicles

Minimum List Headings within this SIC order:

MLH 380 Wheeled tractor manufacturing
381 Motor Vehicle Manufacturing
382 Motor Cycle, tricycle and pedal cycle manufacturing
383 Aerospace equipment manufacturing and repairing
384 Locomotives and railway track equipment
385 Railway carriages and wagons and trams

It is clearly important in the Stevenage case to be able to differentiate between employment in the aerospace industry and the motor vehicle manufacturing industries, both of which fall into the same SIC order, but are identified by MLH.

SIC order XXIV Insurance, Banking, Finance and Business Services

MLH 860 Insurance
861 Banking and bill discounting
862 Other financial institutions
863 Property owning and managing, etc.
864 Advertising and market research
865 Other business services
866 Central Offices not allocatable elsewhere

APPENDIX 10   Classification of occupations 1970

Summary of Groups

Group	Description of Occupations
I	Farmers, Foresters, Fishermen
II	Miners and Quarrymen
III	Gas, Coke and Chemical Makers
IV	Glass and Ceramic Makers
V	Furnace, Forge, Foundry, Rolling Mill Workers
VI	Electrical and Electronic Workers
VII	Engineering and Allied Trades Workers n.e.c.
VIII	Woodworkers
IX	Leather Workers
X	Textile Workers
XI	Clothing Workers
XII	Food, Drink and Tobacco Workers
XIII	Paper and Printing Workers
XIV	Makers of Other Products
XV	Construction Workers
XVI	Painters and Decorators
XVII	Drivers of Stationary Engines, Cranes, etc.
XVIII	Labourers n.e.c.
XIX	Transport and Communication Workers
XX	Warehousemen, Storekeepers, Packers, Bottlers
XXI	Clerical Workers
XXII	Sales Workers
XXIII	Service, Sport and Recreation Workers
XXIV	Administrators and Managers
XXV	Professional, Technical Workers, Artists
XXVI	Armed Forces (British and Foreign)
XXVII	Inadequately described Occupations

SOCIO-ECONOMIC GROUPS

(From Classification of Occupations 1970)

Summary of Socio-Economic Groups

SEG	Description of Group
1.1	Employers in industry, commerce, etc. - large establishments
1.2	Managers in central and local government, industry, commerce, etc. - large establishments
2.1	Employers in industry, commerce, etc. - small establishments
2.2	Managers in industry, commerce, etc. - small establishments
3	Professional Workers - Self-employed
4	Professional Workers - Employees
5.1	Ancillary Workers and Artists
5.2	Foremen and Supervisors - non-manual
6	Junior non-manual Workers
7	Personal Service Workers
8	Foremen and Supervisors - manual
9	Skilled Manual Workers
10	Semi-skilled Manual Workers
11	Unskilled Manual Workers
12	Own Account Workers (other than Professional)
13	Farmers - Employers and Managers
14	Farmers - Own Account
15	Agricultural Workers
16	Members of Armed Forces
17	Inadequately described Occupations

APPENDIX 11   Basic and non-basic services

BASIC SERVICES

SIC	MLH	Description
XXII	701	Railways
	703	Road Haulage Contracting for Hire and Reward
	704	Other Road Haulage
	705	Sea Transport
	706	Port and Inland Water Transport
	707	Air Transport
XXIII	801	Wholesale Distribution of Food and Drink
	811	Wholesale Distribution of Petroleum Products
	812	Other Wholesale Distribution
	831	Dealing in Coal, Oil, Building Materials, Grain and Agricultural Supplies
	832	Dealing in other Industrial Materials and Machinery
XXIV	866	Central Offices not allocatable elsewhere
XXV	876	Research and Development Services
XXVII	901	National Government

NON-BASIC SERVICES

SIC	MLH	Description
XXI	601,602, 603	Gas, Electricity, Water
XXII	702	Road Passenger Transport

	708	Postal Services and Telecommunications
	709	Miscellaneous Transport Services and Storage
XXIII	820	Retail Distribution of Food and Drink
	821	Other Retail Distribution
XXIV	860	Insurance
	861	Banking and Bill Discounting
	862	Other Financial Institutions
	863	Property Owning and Managing
	864	Advertising and Market Research
	865	Other Business Services
XXV	871	Accountancy Services
	872	Educational Services
	873	Legal Services
	874	Medical and Dental Services
	875	Religious Organisations
	879	Other Professional and Scientific Services
XXVI	881	Cinemas, Theatres, Radio, etc.
	882	Sport and Other Recreations
	883	Betting and Gambling
	884	Hotels and Other Residential Establishments
	885	Restaurants, Cafes, Snack Bars
	886	Public Houses
	887	Clubs
	888	Catering Contractors
	889	Hairdressing and Manicure
XXVI	892,893	Laundries, Dry Cleaning, etc.
	894	Motor Repairers, Distributors, Garages, etc.
	895	Repair of Boots and Shoes
	899	Other Services
XXVII	906	Local Government Service

APPENDIX 12   Private building contractors and the SDC's
housing stock

The following is a brief analysis of the private building
contractors involved in the building of the Corporation's
housing stock.

In the years 1950-76 a total of thirty-four contractors
were involved in the building of the housing stock (the
Corporation itself did no house-building whatsoever), and
a total of 19,601 houses were built.

The 'top four firms' were Carlton Contractors, Mowlem,
Terson, and Geo.Wimpey who between them accounted for the
building of 14,637 houses.

The next eight firms were: Comben and Wakeling, Rob
Marrot, Thomas McInerney, Peplow, Rush and Tomkins, Wm
Siddall, Token Construction, and J.Willmott. These eight
firms accounted for the building of 2,615 houses between
them.

The other twenty-two firms built a total of 2,349 houses
between them.

The early years were dominated by Terson and Carlton,
followed by Wimpey, and in recent years it was Mowlem who
were receiving the majority of the contracts.

Gilbert Ash Ltd have had a near monopoly of factory
building in the town.

Raw data was supplied by Bob Sulzbach, Architects Department, Stevenage Development Corporation.

The following is a brief description of a survey I attempted to carry out with Stevenage Borough Councillors,
both past (i.e., if they were on the Council from 1970
onwards), and present. I received a response rate of 16
per cent.

  Sixty-two copies of the questionnaire, together with a
supporting letter, were sent to councillors on 30 August
1977, with a reminder (together with another copy of the
questionnaire) on 1 October. Thirty-two of the questionnaires were sent to 'present' councillors (as at 1978).
The response rate was two completed questionnaires from
'ex-councillors', together with nine completed questionnaires from 'present' councillors.

  The questionnaire included four questions from a suggested schedule in John Dearlove's 'The Politics of Policy
in Local Government'(1973), Cambridge University Press.

COPY

Questionnaire

Please try and answer as many of the questions as possible, and in as much detail as possible. If there is not
enough space for a reply to a question, please attach
extra paper.

Q1 Could you please tell me your age, sex, occupation and
    what type of accommodation you reside in. Plus the
    age you commenced as a councillor, your party, and any
    offices held in Council.

Q2 When you stand for election, do you think that the
    policies of the local party you support are important
    in determining the election outcome?

Q3 Speaking for yourself, how do you get to know about
    the needs and attitudes of the people of the Borough?

Q4   In the average month, roughly how many people in the
     area would have been in touch with you personally, as
     a member of the Council?

Q5   In general terms, what do you have in mind, and what
     do you look for, when you identify a group as
     'helpful' or 'unhelpful'?

Q6   How do you view the Development Corporation in terms
     of (i) its efficiency, (ii) its non-democratic ap-
     pointment, and (iii) 'generally', in terms of what it
     has achieved?

Q7   What are your feelings about the Corporation being
     'wound up'?

Q8   What (if any) do you think are the difficulties of an
     'elected' councillor serving on an appointed Board?

Q9   In general terms, can you tell me your feelings con-
     cerning the proposed expansion schemes of 1973 and
     1974, and the response to them by the 'public'?

(The tense was altered in the questionnaires which were
sent to the ex-Councillors.)

Notes

INTRODUCTION

1 Pahl (1975a), p.284.
2 Hindess (1973), p.45.
3 There were in fact two sets of minutes, both confidential, but one set particularly so, and termed the 'private minutes'. On 21.7.48, the Board made the decision (reported in the Corporation minutes 21.7.48 (50), p.2) to create a 'private minute book', which was to contain 'particularly confidential matters'.
4 Personal communication, reference BA/PSO/14506/77, dated 16.9.77.
5 Not, however, the 'private minute book'.
6 Dated 21.10.77.
7 Dennis (1973), p.3.

CHAPTER 1   SOME THEMES IN URBAN PLANNING

1 See, for example, Dennis (1972), Davies (1972);   see also McAuslan and Bevan (1977) and Wilson (1969).
2 Castells (1973), p.18;   cf. Scott and Roweis (1977), especially p.1103.
3 Mellor (1978), p.133.   Mellor adds:
> At all times there has been an interest in the welfare of the community, and a concern to redress the balance between groups in their access to urban resources.   In this sense planning must be seen, along with activities of government in the provision of housing, education and welfare, as part of the shift in power at the beginning of the century away from the propertied interests to the mass of the population.

Cf. Halsey (1970, p.21):   'Planning is associated with left-wing politics.'

4   Mellor, op.cit., p.135; see also Friedman and Hudson
    (1974), who discuss the knowledge status of planning.
5   Esland (1976), p.29.
6   Ibid., p.31; on 'proletarianisation', see Braverman
    (1974, p.407), who, discussing the new middle class,
    states that:
        Not only does it receive its petty share in the
        prerogatives and rewards of capital, but it also
        bears the mark of the proletarian condition. For
        these employees the social form taken by their
        work, their true place in the relations of pro-
        duction, their fundamental condition of subordina-
        tion as so much hired labour, increasingly makes
        itself felt, especially in the mass occupations
        that are part of this stratum.
7   Esland, op.cit., p.32.
8   Hughes (1971), p.288, quoted in Esland, op.cit., p.37.
9   Esland (1976), p.43.
10 Mannheim (1971), p.193.
11 Dennis (1972), p.244.
12 Eversley (1973, p.5), Habermas (1971), Mollenkopf
    (1976), and Davies (1972, p.2) who states that:
    'Planning is, in its effect on the socio-economic
    structure, a highly regressive form of indirect tax-
    ation.'
13 See Jacobs (1965) and Sennett (1970).
14 Davies (1972), pp.101-4.
15 Dennis, op.cit., p.242.
16 Taviss (1969), p.582.
17 Sklair (1974), pp.79-80.
18 MacEwen (1963), p.69.
19 Ozbekham (1968), p.210.
20 Wildavsky (1973), pp.149-50.
21 Broady (1966), p.150.
22 Eversley, op.cit., p.162. Habermas (1971, pp.63-4),
    in an essay on the relation between expertise and po-
    litical practice, discusses the technocratic model.
    He asserts that:
        The dependence of the professional on the poli-
        tician appears to have reversed itself. The latter
        becomes the mere agent of a scientific intelligent-
        sia, which, in concrete circumstances, elaborates
        the objective implications and requirements of
        available techniques and resources as well as of
        optimal strategies and rules of control.
    Habermas then discusses the weaknesses of the model,
    which he considers to be (i) the assumption of the
    immanent necessity of technical progress, and (ii) the
    presupposition of a continuum of rationality in the

treatment of technical and practical problems, which
in fact cannot exist.
23   Mills (1970), p.425.
24   Damer and Hague (1971), p.17;   on advocacy planning
     see Davidoff (1965).   Palmer (1972, p.12), makes the
     following comment on advocacy planning:
>   Unfortunately, while acting as an advocate for the
>   poor may prove to be very rewarding for the pro-
>   fessional, it effectively minimizes the necessity
>   for any of the rules of the game being changed so
>   as to include the poor themselves.

     For general accounts of public participation in plan-
     ning, see Stringer and Taylor (1974), Roberts (1976),
     and Sewell and Coppock (eds) (1977);   for a recent
     case study, see Ryan and Isaacson (1976);   and on par-
     ticipation, 'generally', see Crouch (1977a).
25   For a discussion, see Bell (1973).
26   Gyford (1976), p.144.
27   Thornley (1977, pp.36-7), describes the nine recom-
     mendations made by the Skeffington Committee, concern-
     ing public involvement in the planning process: (i)
     people should be kept informed;   (ii) information on
     the opportunities for participation should be made
     available;   (iii) participation should concentrate on
     the discussion of choices and, second, the local
     authorities' presentation of proposals;   (iv) communi-
     ty forums should be set up giving local organisations
     an opportunity to discuss;   (v) proposals should be
     publicised in the areas affected;   (vi) community de-
     velopment officers should be appointed to secure the
     involvement of those people who do not join organisa-
     tions;   (vii) people should be told what they have
     achieved by participation;   (viii) citizens should be
     encouraged to assist with the planning process (e.g.,
     by doing surveys) as well as expressing views;   and
     (ix) better education about planning should be de-
     veloped both in schools and by the public at large.
      As Dennis (1972, pp.223,231), notes:
>   What is conspicuously lacking in the Skeffington
>   Report is any sign that there might be other points
>   of view which are equally entitled to [this] sort
>   of authoritative airing when planning proposals are
>   under discussion [and] ...   In every detail
>   Skeffington structures the situation to grant
>   control of information channels to the planning
>   authority, instead of exploring methods of over-
>   coming indifference, apathy and public disbelief
>   that any influence it might have on the eventual
>   shape of the plans would repay the effort of par-
>   ticipation.

28   Levin and Donnison (1969), p.478.
29   Dennis, op.cit., p.229.
30   Arnstein (1969).
31   Dennis (1972), Alford (1973), Cohen (1975), Lukes (1975).
32   Berger (1977), p.144.
33   Dennis (1972, p.49), Jordan et al. (1975, pp.7-8); for general accounts of the process see Levin (1976, p.114) and Dearlove (1973).
34   Selznick (1952), p.135.
35   Dunleavy (1977), p.18.
36   Rose and Hanmer (1975, p.27), Dennis (1977, p.19).
37   Quoted in Hill (1976), p.193.
38   Sapolsky (1968), p.432.
39   For a general account see Lipset (1969), pp.216-18.
40   Barrington Moore (1972), pp.68-9.

CHAPTER 2   THE LONDON NEW TOWNS: AN OVERVIEW

1   See the following: Creese (1966), Heraud (1975), Merlin (1969) on comparative studies; Schaffer (1970), Osborn and Whittick (1969), Rodwin (1956), Apgar (1976), Blair (1974), Di Maio (1974) on new towns in the USSR; and Ash (1974) on new towns in Israel.
2   Goodey (1974), p.124.
3   Ibid., p.124.
4   Ibid., pp.124-9.
5   Jacobs (1965), p.28; cf. Inglis (1977), Peterson (1968).
6   Carter (1962), p.20; cf. Simmie (1976, p.9):
       as before the designation of new towns, the most
       pressing economic and social problems are still to
       be found in old towns. Sub-regional policies in-
       cluding green belts and new towns have exacerbated
       rather than improved the conditions in old towns
       particularly for those most in need. No further
       development, expansion, resources or continuation
       of these sub-regional policies should be envisaged
       until such time as satisfactory and practical poli-
       cies are funded and implemented for the relief of
       old towns.
7   See Broady (1966), Michelson (1976, pp.168-93).
8   Hirsch and Sorenblum (1973), p.19.
9   Glass (1948), pp.18,190.
10 March (1972), p.507. He also comments that:
       The new towns are the show places of British plan-
       ning endeavour. They flatter our collective vanity

for the big gesture. The tendency is to centralise
our thinking through neat designs, rather than to
find a means of decentralising it into unruly life
(p.505).

11 For a discussion and review of the different types of
new towns see Schaffer (1970). Goodey (1974, pp.
122-4), offers the following brief review: The Mark 1
new towns were those designated in the late 1940s, and
included the London ring of eight towns. Goodey notes
that the 'names for the London ring towns were all
derived from existing settlements - Welwyn *Garden City*
providing the link with the Howardian tradition'.
Mark 2 towns date from the 1960s (the only product of
the 1950s being Cumbernauld):

> In policy terms the Mark 2 towns represent a range
> of provincial experiments in housing 'overspill' (a
> delightful term to be attached to new town popu-
> lations) and providing new regional growth points.
> Base settlements were larger - those for Mark 1
> towns average 9,000 while those for Mark 2 average
> 17,000 - and projected expansions were correspond-
> ingly greater. The Mark 3 towns represented an-
> other increase in base community size and target
> population ...

12 New Towns Committee Final Report, Cmnd 6876, HMSO,
1946, p.2; see also Interim Report of the New Towns
Committee, Cmnd 6759, HMSO, 1946, p.4:

> Our responsibility is ... to conduct an essay in
> civilization, by seizing an opportunity to design,
> evolve and carry into execution for the benefit of
> coming generations the means for a happy and
> gracious way of life.

13 Castells (1977a), p.280; cf. Pickvance (1977).
14 Hudson (1976), p.136.
15 Miliband (1973), p.99; see also Saville (1957-8).
16 Miliband (1964), p.274.
17 Ibid., p.275.
18 Runciman (1966), p.138.
19 Marwick (1971), p.114; on the Uthwatt Report on
Compensation and Betterment (1942) see Ratcliffe
(1976), pp.42-3.
20 Rose (1968), p.6; Bailey (1975), p.85; Bourne
(1975), p.73; Blair (1974), p.145.
21 Deakin and Ungerson (1977), p.18.
22 Self (1972), p.5.
23 Creese (1966), p.342; Schaffer (1970, p.253) also
talks of sculpture:

> Even the small touches are not to be missed.
> There's 'joyride', the symbolic Belsky bronze of

mother and child in the famous Stevenage town centre.

24 Hall (1974), p.106; cf. March (1972, p.507):
Most new town reports show slight concern for people's preferences. The paternalism of Lord Reith ... remains a strong influence down to the present day: a nice middle-class, professional knowingness about what is, and what is not, good for others.

25 Cullingworth (1972), p.231.

26 New Towns Committee Final Report, op.cit., pp.10-11.

27 Schaffer, op.cit., p.53.

28 Sharp (1972), p.43.

29 Eric Moonman, A new deal for New Towns, 'New Statesman', 3.11.72, pp.630-2.

30 Schaffer, op.cit., p.57.

31 New Towns Act (1965), as amended by the New Towns (Amendment) Act (1976).

32 Personal communication, DOE, dated 8.8.77.

33 All the information is derived from personal communication, ref: DOE BA/PSO/14207/77, dated 25.8.77. See also personal communication, ref: DOE BA/PSO/14506/77, dated 16.9.77, p.1: 'members of new town corporations do receive the full salary even though they may on occasion be unable to attend a board meeting'.

34 Schaffer, op.cit., p.62. This section relies heavily on this source.

35 Ibid., p.201.

36 Ibid., p.227.

37 Ibid., p.228; cf. Friend et al. (1974) who make the same point.

38 Cresswell and Thomas (1972), p.71.

39 Trimble (1973), p.220.

40 Luttrell (1972), p.81.

41 Deakin and Ungerson, op.cit., p.52.

42 Cresswell and Thomas, op.cit., p.71.

43 Thomas (1969), pp.386-7.

44 This section draws considerably on Deakin and Ungerson, op.cit.; for a discussion of the 'expanded towns' see Harloe (1975b).

45 Thomas and Cresswell (1973, p.49) disagree and hold a minority opinion, that:
The Industrial Selection Schemes are lengthy and impersonal and many individuals bypass this scheme by applying directly for jobs in the new towns which they hear about through personal contacts ... In the case of the London new towns, for example, only about ten per cent of migrants go through the Industrial Selection Scheme.

46 Deakin and Ungerson, op.cit., p.45.
47 Ibid., p.46; cf. Merlin (1971, p.93) who points out
    that in Vällingby (Sweden) housing is allocated
    through a system of waiting lists without any link
    between the allocation of housing and the place of
    employment.
48 Deakin and Ungerson, op.cit., p.47.
49 Mann (1973), p.32.
50 Cresswell and Thomas, op.cit., p.68.
51 Ibid., p.68.
52 Silkin (1948), pp.431-3.
53 See Dennis (1968), p.89, who makes a similar point.
54 Sarkissian (1976), pp.231-3; cf. Evans (1976, p.247),
    who suggests that 'the reasoning behind the idea of
    social mix has usually been non-economic'.
55 Sarkissian, op.cit., p.243.
56 Cresswell (1974), Ogilvy (1968), Cherry (1972),
    Bolwell et al. (1969).
57 Heraud (1968), p.53.
58 Transcript of taped interview with E.Lenderyou in
    1976, pp.3-4.
59 See, for example, Cresswell (1974).
60 Thomas and Cresswell (1973), pp.31-2.
61 Ibid., pp.36-8. They also add (p.38) that
        were it not for the bias in the industrial struc-
        ture, London's new towns would have a deficiency of
        professional workers among the resident working
        population. Given an industrial structure less de-
        pendent on engineering, and closer to the national
        average, professional workers would be *under-repre-
        sented* among the resident population of the London
        new towns rather than slightly under-represented as
        they are at present.
62 Barr (1965), pp.5-6.
63 Berry (1974), Heraud (1966), Willmott (1962), Roderick
    (1971), Boer and Greendale (1974), Willmott (1964);
    cf. Mann (1973, p.32):
        the relative absence of unskilled workers and their
        families from the New Towns does have a rather
        serious implication for the conurbations. For it
        is the unskilled who are worst housed there.
    Eversley (1977, p.172), discussing the Inner Area
    Studies (Lambeth) 'Inner London - policies for dis-
    persal and balance', HMSO, notes that:
        the new towns are only prepared to take a trickle
        of newcomers not immediately useful for their
        technologically advanced industries.
64 Deakin and Ungerson, op.cit., p.50.
65 Ibid., p.137. In Deakin and Ungerson's study, the

conclusion is drawn (pp.136-7) that for the vast majority

> of the respondents in both the samples the move to a New or Expanding Town had been a great success. And this was despite large jumps in rent and other living expenses which over half of the major sample claimed were making the financial side of their lives a 'struggle'. Despite this, over 80 per cent of the respondents in this survey thought their move had been worthwhile - they had found a house and garden, room for their children to play, a literal breath of fresh air, and, for many, the first chance ever to live out family life without interference from over-close relatives, neighbours or landlords.

66   See Schaffer, op.cit., p.229.
67   Ibid., p.229.
68   Thomas and Cresswell (1973), p.23.
69   'Labour's Housing Policy', Labour Party, 1957, p.17.
70   Robson (1957), p.17.
71   Aldridge (1977), p.527; the reports she refers to are the Second Report from the Expenditure Committee (Session 1974), New Towns, vol.2, Minutes of evidence (HC 305-II), and vol.3, Appendices (HC 305-III), HMSO, London, 1974; and Thirteenth Report of the Expenditure Committee (Session 1974-5), New Towns, vol.1, Report (HC 616-1), vol.4, Minutes of evidence and appendices (HC 616-4), vol.5, Index (HC 616-5), HMSO, London, 1975. This material was produced after two sets of sittings of the Home Office and Environment sub-committee. The first took place in 1972-3 and 1973-4, and addressed themselves to general questions of the planning and administration of the new towns programme (vols 2 and 3). A second and briefer enquiry was concerned with the financing of new towns, nationally (vol.4). Aldridge quotes directly, from vol.1 (p.xxxiii):

> The lack of concern in the Departments of Industry and Employment for the relationship of their programmes to housing and planning programmes indicated to us that the widely held view that the New Towns are a good example of inter-departmental co-ordination is regrettably incorrect.

She adds (p.527) that:

> Indeed, the recurrent theme of witnesses and evidence is of potentially profound contradictions and conflict smothered by the private boredom of successive governments and concealed by all-party self-congratulation.

72 Mann (1973), p.3.
73 Goodey (1974), p.131. Goodey talks of the 'New Town
    Blues', or as it is sometimes called, 'Transitional
    Neurosis', and comments that it is an 'attractive and
    persistent term, a hook on which to hang stories of
    mental illness, suicide and marital problems'.
74 Orlans (1952), p.292.
75 Crossman (1975), p.126. Aldridge, op.cit., p.527,
    again commenting on local authority evidence to the
    Expenditure Committee, notes that:
      Bitterness of long standing about their impotence
      in the face of central government and the develop-
      ment corporations was revealed. For many local
      authorities this anger centred less on the develop-
      ment corporation's extensive land and property
      ownership, its apparent wealth or the scale of its
      operations than on the perceived tendency of de-
      velopment corporation staff not to consult or even
      inform local councillors and officers of the corpo-
      ration's intentions in any significant way. The
      new towns' insulation from local policial accounta-
      bility was also much resented.
76 See, for example, Crossman, op.cit., p.464:
      I am always discovering great segments of the De-
      partment where my policies haven't impacted. New
      Towns is one of them. I must get at this section
      after the election.
    Cf. the views of Sir Douglas Allen, Head of the Home
    Civil Service (1977, p.135):
      The actual relationship between politician and
      civil servant ... is ... in most cases a relation-
      ship which develops and improves as those concerned
      get used to working together.
77 Crossman, op.cit., pp.460,355; cf. Purdom (1949, p.
    456):
      the co-operation ... needs to be accepted as the
      responsibility of the development corporation.
      Whatever the difficulties, the corporation must
      overcome them.
78 Duff (1961), p.89.
79 W.Thomas (1972), pp.46-7.
80 Ibid., p.51.
81 Transcript of taped interview with Jack Balchin in
    1976, p.17.

CHAPTER 3 STEVENAGE 1945-60: BEGINNINGS

1 SUDC Town Planning and Development Committee minutes,
   17.1.45, p.2.

2   Transcript of taped interview with Philip Ireton in
    1977, p.1. Note also his comment: 'I was trying to
    get Stevenage developed on Garden City lines before
    the Abercrombie Report came out.'
3   SUDC Town Planning and Development Committee minutes,
    18.4.45, p.2, and 17.10.45, p.1.
4   Why Stevenage? The background is supplied in a
    booklet published by the Corporation in 1949, for the
    attention of the first tenants:

> At the end of the Second World War, the local
> Council were envisaging an expansion from six
> thousand to thirty thousand population. There was
> already a tendency for industry to move into the
> town. It seemed likely that Stevenage would have
> its share of the industrial development in the Home
> Counties, which had already led to rapid growth in
> other Hertfordshire towns.... Other areas in the
> vicinity had similar expectations of expansion, and
> had such plans been allowed to go forward the con-
> sequence would have been a continuous and solid de-
> velopment along the existing Great North Road
> stretching as far as Hitchin. Instead, the first
> Minister of Town and Country Planning [the Rt Hon.
> W.S.Morrison] to hold that office instructed Sir
> Patrick Abercrombie to prepare a plan for the whole
> of the Greater London area on entirely different
> lines. Instead of the unbalanced growth typical of
> the inter-war period, properly designed New Towns
> were proposed, and in the plan Stevenage figured as
> one of the sites recommended. This recommendation
> was accepted by the present Minister of Town and
> Country Planning, and Stevenage was the first town
> for which a Designation Order was made under the
> New Towns Act. (p.7)

Orlans (1952, pp.56-7), is more specific regarding the
question:

> why *Stevenage* and not another site? Of course,
> judged from the map and such data as could be ob-
> tained by preliminary surveys, the site appeared to
> Ministry planners 'ripe' for development and for
> many bombed-out London industries seeking new lo-
> cations. But so were other sites subsequently
> chosen for New Towns. In the last analysis it can
> be said that Stevenage came first simply because
> *it happened to come first;* because at an indeter-
> minate moment Abercrombie, K, or somebody else hit
> upon it, the wheels of the Ministry then began to
> turn in that direction and had not yet met a
> sizable obstacle.

Cf. the comments of a Stevenage representative on the Hertfordshire County Council, as reported in the Hertfordshire Express, on 10 November 1945: 'there had been no controversy or opposition to the satellite town at Stevenage simply because no one knew anything about it'.

5   SUDC Town Planning and Development Committee minutes, 10.4.46, pp.6-8; cf. the comments of Purdom (1949, pp.391-2):

> The London press took an active interest in the opposition, too active an interest perhaps, and an attack was made upon the minister for his high-handed action. The minister attended a public meeting, when the chairman of the urban district council presided, and the minister was heckled. The district council then took a vote of the electors, when 1,316 voted against the scheme and 913 in its favour. The high number of votes against the scheme was not surprising because many people resented the manner in which the scheme was being imposed upon them.... Had the inhabitants been approached with appreciation of their natural feelings, with the desire to persuade them that the elements of disturbance would be kept to a minimum, that compensation would be reasonable, and that the scheme was of importance in the national interest, accompanied by the invitation that they should take part in the making of the new community, a smaller number would probably have been against it.

6   Schaffer (1970), p.46.
7   Ibid., p.46.
8   SUDC meeting of the New Town Inquiry Committee, 12.7. 46, p.3.
9   Purdom, op.cit., p.393, notes that:

> Complaint was made at the Inquiry that there was no opportunity for the cross-examination of expert witnesses giving evidence on behalf of the proposal, as there were no such witnesses.

10 See Schaffer, op.cit., p.39: 'From this act of designation flow all the statutory powers - the right to buy land compulsorily, the freezing of land values, the use of Exchequer money.'
11 Schaffer, op.cit., p.46.
12 Orlans (1952), p.251; see Hirst (1976) on such Courts.
13 Lucas (1976), p.117; cf. Ricci (1971, p.187): 'A realist might validly conclude that our rights permit us to speak, but they do not oblige our leaders to pay attention.'

14   de Smith (1977), pp.541-2; see also de Smith (1973,
     pp.147-8), where he notes that:
     Statutory rules have now imposed upon Ministers who
     initiate compulsory purchase orders almost exactly
     the same procedural duties as have been prescribed
     in connection with orders initiated by local au-
     thorities: Compulsory Purchase by Ministers (In-
     quiries Procedure) Rules 1967 (S.I. 1967 No.720),
     cf. S.I. 1962 No.1424 (local authorities).
     Dennis (1972, pp.22-6), sketches in the background:
     In the late 1940s and early 1950s, however, there
     was a weakening in the tendency to see the Welfare
     State in the abstract, in terms of individual
     interests versus the public good. The question was
     raised once again: What happens when actual
     persons are confronted with the specific decisions
     of public authorities which they feel are damaging
     and unjust?.... Concern was shown at the still
     growing practice of allowing public authorities to
     determine matters within their jurisdiction without
     judicial control or scrutiny, i.e. to define more
     and more decisions as administrative decisions.
     Legislation was increasingly stating that where a
     Minister was satisfied that certain facts existed
     then he could exercise the powers specified in the
     enactment. The courts were strengthening the doc-
     trine that local authorities were to be free from
     judicial interference to decide those matters which
     Parliament considered were best dealt with them by
     virtue of their knowledge and experience. This
     doctrine was pushed further when applied to the de-
     cisions of planning authorities.... The final out-
     come of a public inquiry remained unquestionably a
     decision of policy and not a definition of law.
     Inspectors were not required to possess legal
     training; they sat alone; their report need not
     be restricted to evidence presented at the inquiry;
     the Minister was not bound to accept the inspec-
     tor's findings; and he could reach his final con-
     clusion on facts or considerations of policy beyond
     the appellant's knowledge. The local authority
     whose decision was challenged at a public inquiry
     had legal and technical experts and public funds at
     its disposal while the private appellant was often
     too poor or diffident to secure legal representa-
     tion. Even when he was able to afford a solicitor,
     he may have been at work when the public inquiry
     was held, and therefore unable to hear what was
     made of his case.

15   Quoted in March (1972), p.505;   cf. the Stevenage
     Gazette of 16.11.76:
         Thirty years ago today many residents of a small
         North Herts town (population 6,237) who took the
         Hertfordshire Express, their local newspaper, were
         reading page 8 with something like horror. If they
         had not heard the announcement on the BBC's six o-
         clock news the previous Saturday evening, or been
         told by an anxious neighbour, they were just dis-
         covering that the sleepy little market town nest-
         ling in agricultural land, was to be part of a
         massive architectural, social and economic project.
16   Purdom, op.cit., p.394.
17   Orlans, op.cit., pp.132-76.
18   Ibid., pp.176-80;   Thomas and Cresswell (1973, p.44),
     make another point concerning shopkeepers:
         Other groups may find that they have divided loyal-
         ties, particularly those who stand to gain or lose
         in a financial sense fairly heavily. Local shop-
         keepers may feel that the influx of population will
         give an enormous boost to trade. On the other hand
         if they are excluded from new shopping developments
         they may find that they are in a backwater, perhaps
         worse off than they were before.
19   Rose (1968), pp.10-11;   see also the Hook Plan, LCC
     (1961). Levin and Donnison (1969, p.478) put the
     problem quite straightforwardly: 'The future resi-
     dents of a new town are unidentifiable ...'
20   Orlans, op.cit., p.89.
21   Ibid., p.189.
22   Ibid., p.190.
23   SDC Annual Report (AR), 1948, p.76. The Annual
     Reports cover the period to the March of the year in
     which they are published: for example AR 1959 covers
     the period March 1958 to March 1959.
24   Data derived from the TCPA journal, January 1955.
25   These 'historical' facts are derived from numerous
     sources, as enumerated in appendix 1.
26   SDC minutes, 7.10.47 (32), p.1. Note that the figure
     in the bracket is the number of the Board meeting.
27   AR 1948, pp.79-80.
28   He later wrote an account of Britain's New Towns
     (Duff, 1961).
29   SUDC Town Planning and Development Committee minutes,
     15.10.47, p.298.
30   SDC minutes, 2.9.47 (30), p.2.
31   SDC minutes, 2.12.47 (36), p.3.
32   SDC minutes, 21.7.48 (50), p.2.
33   SDC minutes, 15.3.48 (44), p.2.

34   SDC minutes, 10.5.48 (47), p.3.
35   SDC minutes, 4.1.49 (63), p.4.
36   Orlans, op.cit., pp.222-3: on the town's sewerage
     problems see pp.293-9.
37   SDC minutes, 16.8.49 (78), p.1, and 30.8.49 (79), p.1.
38   SDC minutes, 13.9.49 (80), p.7.
39   Ibid., p.7.
40   On the General Manager's statement, see SDC minutes,
     13.9.49 (80), p.7, and on the Urban District
     Council's, see SDC minutes, 4.10.49 (81), p.3.
41   SDC minutes, 1.11.49 (82), pp.1-3.
42   See 'The New Town of Stevenage' (1949), published by
     the SDC. What in fact was happening was that some of
     the Corporation Board members were becoming increas-
     ingly displeased with the Social Development Office's
     ever-increasing critical stance towards the overall
     development, and it was thus decided to 'accommodate'
     the Office - see Lenderyou 1976 transcript, p.11.
43   SDC minutes, 10.1.50 (84), p.1.
44   SDC minutes, 28.3.50 (90), p.15.
45   Regarding the discussion see SDC minutes, 19.5.50
     (93), p.2, and on the decision see SDC minutes,
     30.5.50 (94), p.8.
46   SDC minutes, 13.6.50 (95), p.1.
47   SDC minutes, 11.7.50 (96), p.10.
48   For accounts of the problem see Self (1961), p.90;
     Murie et al. (1976), p.101.
49   See Orlans, op.cit., p.270; Rodwin (1956), p.166;
     Chisholm and Manners (1971a), p.18.
50   SDC minutes, 31.10.50 (105), p.13.
51   See Ireton 1977 transcript, p.2.
52   SDC minutes, 15.2.51 (112), p.12.
53   AR 1952, p.343.
54   SDC minutes, 4.9.51 (124), p.4.
55   Duff (1961), p.62.
56   SDC minutes, 13.11.51 (129), p.5.
57   SDC minutes, 29.1.52 (134), p.4.
58   SDC minutes, 8.7.52 (145), p.2.
59   SDC minutes, 23.9.52 (149), p.2.
60   SDC minutes, 6.5.52 (142), p.2.
61   SDC minutes, 9.12.52 (156), p.7.
62   AR 1954, p.373.
63   Ireton 1977 transcript, p.6.
64   Ibid., p.6.
65   SDC minutes, 12.5.53 (164), p.9.
66   SDC minutes, 9.6.53 (166), p.8, and 25.8.53 (170),
     p.2.
67   AR 1954, p.381.
68   TCPA journal, January 1955.

69   SDC minutes, 22.6.54 (183), p.9.
70   SDC minutes, 26.10.54 (187), p.8. Thomas and
     Cresswell (1973, p.50), make the following observa-
     tions:
    Strategic interactions are (also) likely to take
    place between employers and the development corpo-
    rations who will have overlapping but not coinci-
    dent objectives. Employers will want on the whole
    to operate free from restrictions whilst the new
    town planners will want to impose restrictions suf-
    ficient to achieve their aims. This may, for
    example, result in development corporations in the
    satellite new towns allowing a wide latitude for
    the definition of 'key workers', who need not be
    recruited from London through the usual channels,
    in order to get the employers to co-operate with
    the prescribed methods of recruiting for the rest
    of the workforce.
71   SDC minutes, 9.2.54 (176), p.7.
72   SDC minutes, 21.12.54 (189), p.3.
73   The data source here, and throughout the text, is the
     Department of Employment's (Stevenage area), ERV1 and
     ERV returns, which relate only, in my use of them, to
     the category of Male 18+. I have omitted the female
     category from the discussion, as there was little
     female employment (and unemployment) in the town, par-
     ticularly in the early years.
74   SDC Master Plan: Volume 1 (1966), p.12.
75   AR 1956, p.355.
76   SDC minutes, 8.3.55 (192), p.5.
77   AR 1956, p.359.
78   See 'The People', 7.10.56, article titled 'Goon Town'
     by P.Kent.
79   SDC minutes, 3.1.56 (202), p.7.
80   SDC minutes, 31.1.56 (203), p.13, and AR 1957, p.363.
81   SDC minutes, 24.7.56 (209), p.5.
82   SDC minutes, 24.7.56 (209), p.3.
83   SDC minutes, 26.5.56 (208), p.3.
84   SDC minutes, 27.11.56 (211), p.13.
85   SDC minutes, 27.11.56 (211), p.4.
86   Ireton 1977 transcript, p.10. The present Chairman of
     the Corporation, Evelyn Denington, stated that the
     procedure was as follows (1977 transcript, p.3):
    If a Minister wants changes on the Board he talks
    to me as Chairman and says 'I want you to ask X and
    Y to resign' ... yes this has happened ... when he
    says he wants X and Y to resign, and I say I like
    X and Y, they are jolly good members and I don't
    want to get rid of them, and I've so far, touch
    wood, won my point always.

87   AR 1958, p.356.
88   Ibid., p.355.
89   These minutes are attached to the Board minutes, and
      apart from a few exceptions, will be quoted without
      specifying the exact reference.
90   SDC minutes, 26.11.57 (266), p.2.
91   AR 1958, p.356.
92   Ibid., p.382.
93   Ibid., p.382. Note that the financial figures are
      derived from the Annual Reports, and from the SDC's
      Finance Department (see appendix 1).
94   SDC minutes, 7.1.58 (227), p.1.
95   SDC minutes, 11.2.58 (228), p.1. Duff (1961, pp.
      87-8), makes the following observation on the Resi-
      dents' Federation:
          the Annual General Meeting of the Stevenage
          Residents' Federation in 1958, held in the Town
          Hall and addressed by Lord Silkin, collected an
          audience of 30 from a population of close on
          30,000 ...
96   SDC minutes, 13.6.58 (231), p.4.
97   AR 1959, p.359.
98   SDC minutes, 28.10.58 (236), p.1.
99   Charles Burr, ex-Assistant Housing Manager of the
      SDC, puts it in the following manner: 'industry do
      tend to try to suggest that perhaps they want a few
      more houses than they do, they try and play it safe
      ... we have to be frank with them' (transcript of
      taped interview, 1977, p.11).
100   SDC minutes, 25.11.58 (237), p.13.
101   SDC minutes, 12.4.59 (242), p.20.
102   Both quotations from the SDC minutes, 11.3.58 (229),
      pp.2-4.
103   AR 1960, pp.344-9.
104   Ibid., pp.344,356.
105   SDC minutes, 14.4.59 (241), p.14.
106   Data derived from the TCPA journal, January 1960.
107   SDC minutes, 14.4.59 (241), p.23.
108   'Purpose', No.16 (Autumn 1959), p.3.

CHAPTER 4 STEVENAGE 1960-9: CONSOLIDATION AND
CONTRADICTIONS

1   SDC minutes, 16.2.60 (249), p.16.
2   AR 1961, p.358; Evelyn Denington (1972, p.146), made
     the following remark, much later:
         the new town worker is not tired when he arrives
         at work having had an uncomfortable, crowded and

time-wasting journey, or irritated by traffic jams, but he starts work fresh and his output is greater.

3 AR 1961, p.362.
4 Ibid., p.363.
5 SDC minutes, 23.8.60 (255), p.15.
6 Dame Evelyn Sharp, to the SDC, and reported in the SDC minutes, 18.10.60 (256), p.2.
7 AR 1961, p.365.
8 Ibid., p.371.
9 Ibid., p.372.
10 SDC minutes, 23.8.60 (255), p.1.
11 SDC (1975, written by J.Lenton), p.10.
12 SDC minutes, 21.2.61 (259), p.1.
13 SDC minutes, 17.1.61 (258), pp.2-3.
14 AR 1962, p.355.
15 SDC minutes, 12.2.62 (270), p.3.
16 SDC minutes, 10.4.62 (273), p.6.
17 Ibid., p.6.
18 Contained in SDC minutes, 10.7.62 (276), pp.2-4.
19 Ibid., p.4.
20 SDC minutes, 14.8.62 (277), p.3.
21 Resolution dated 31.7.62, reported in the SDC minutes of 14.8.62 (277), p.1.
22 Malik (1964), p.61.
23 Wedderburn (1964), especially pp.vii,1-4,9,13,20.
24 SDC minutes, 9.10.62 (278), p.4. It is also interesting to note Pahl's (1964, p.31) observations of Stevenage, the English Electric Company, and commuting in particular:

A rough check of the Senior Staff earning over £1,250 of the English Electric Company (now the British Aircraft Corporation) at Stevenage showed that a third lived in surrounding towns and villages. This company employed about 4,000 people in 1961 and at that time parking space had to be found for 900 cars each morning.

25 Wedderburn, op.cit., p.4.
26 'Purpose', No.26 (Autumn, 1962), p.3.
27 AR 1963, p.282.
28 SDC minutes, 22.1.63 (281), p.1.
29 SDC minutes, 12.2.63 (282), p.3.
30 Contained in 'Observations upon the Expansion of Stevenage', SUDC (August, 1963), p.1.
31 AR 1964, pp.313,317-18.
32 Reported in SDC minutes, 12.2.63 (282), pp.1-2.
33 AR 1964, p.317.
34 Thouless (1930).
35 AR 1964, pp.323-5.
36 For a profile see appendix 3.

37   SDC minutes, 21.1.64 (291), p.1.
38   Housing Management quarterly minutes to 31.12.64.
39   SDC minutes, 21.7.64 (298), p.3.
40   See Crossman (1975), p.66 (account dated 20.11.64).
41   Ibid., p.79 (account dated 2.12.64). Note also his
     remarks on p.80:
         and this astonishing statement was made on my
         behalf as the opening words of the Inquiry. And
         it was, though no newspaper noticed it.
42   See 'Report of a Public Inquiry into Objections to the
     Proposed Expansion of the Designated Area of Stevenage
     New Town', SDC (1965), pp.3-5,41-67,70,94.
43   Ibid., pp.38-41.
44   Ibid., p.94.
45   SDC minutes, 19.1.65 (302), p.6.
46   Letter reported in SDC minutes, 13.4.65 (308), pp.5-6.
47   Ibid., p.6.
48   Reported in AR 1966, p.361.
49   Ibid., p.361.
50   AR 1966, p.361.
51   Crossman, op.cit., p.496 (account dated 6.4.66);   cf.
     John Silkin, personal communication (1977, p.1):
         I thought that Corporation Board members ought to
         be chosen more from the District Councils in which
         the New Towns were situated, which of course does
         mean that they would be chosen on political
         grounds, although preferably the parties in the
         District Councils should both be represented on
         the corporation board. But the basis was to get
         a greater working co-operation between the corpo-
         ration and the councils than I thought there had
         been in the past.
52   SDC minutes, 15.2.66 (313), p.2.
53   New Towns Circular, No.8, May 1966.
54   Quarterly minutes, ending 31.12.66.
55   SDC minutes, 26.4.66 (317), p.1.
56   SDC, 'Stevenage Master Plan' (1966), p.105, para.
     14.10.
57   Reported in SDC minutes, 21.2.67 (326), p.2.
58   The decision of the Minister (of Housing and Local
     Government), is reproduced in appendix 2, pp.110-16,
     of the 'Master Plan' (1967).
59   Personal communication, E.Lenderyou (1978), p.3.
60   AR 1968, p.399.
61   Ireton (1977 transcript), p.3.
62   AR 1968, p.402;   on the 'yardstick' measure, see
     Community Development Project (1976).
63   Circular from Ministry of Housing and Local Govern-
     ment, 'Owner Occupation in New Towns', 19.5.67.

64 See column 10.
65 SDC minutes, 24.1.67 (325), p.8.
66 SDC minutes, 12.12.67 (335), p.5.
67 Ibid., p.5.
68 Reported in SDC minutes, 23.5.67 (329), p.6.
69 SDC minutes, 4.10.68 (344), p.7.
70 Quarterly minutes, ending 31.12.68.
71 AR 1969, p.437.
72 Transcript of taped interview with J.Hubble, Treasurer of the SVA (1977), p.1.
73 SVA (1968), pp.4-5.
74 The study was by N.Lichfield and Associates, 'Stevenage Public Transport: cost benefit analysis of alternative public/private transport modal split', SDC (May 1969).
75 SVA, op.cit., p.5.
76 Letter reference NT 260/23/13, p.2.
77 Ibid., p.2.
78 SVA press release, 4.8.69, p.1, para.1.
79 Ibid., p.1, para.1.
80 Personal communication, Lenderyou (1978), p.1.
81 This, of course, followed the study by Cullingworth and Karn (1968), on the ownership and management of housing in the new towns.
82 SDC minutes, 9.9.69 (355), p.4. This was highly un-usual, for as Timberlake (1976, p.124) points out, in another context:

> It cannot be denied that most of the Development Corporations have sought little help from building societies - nor have the societies made much spon-taneous effort to penetrate the housing market in the New Towns.

83 AR 1970, p.476; Karn (1970), in her housing survey of Stevenage, states that an overwhelming proportion of households thought that the Development Corporation should sell its houses to tenants and were also in favour of easier 100 per cent mortgages.
84 SDC minutes, 14.10.69 (356), p.1.
85 Housing quarterly minutes, ending 31.12.69, and SDC minutes, 11.11.69 (357), p.4.
86 AR 1970, p.478.

CHAPTER 5   STEVENAGE 1970-1: RUMOURS OF THINGS TO COME

1 Dated 23.1.70.
2 Ibid., p.1, para.2.
3 See the Building Societies Association's circulars 1559 (23.1.70), and 1676 (7.10.71); on Building

Societies in general see Duncan (1977); and Boddy
(1976).

4   SDC minutes, 30.2.70 (360), p.2.
5   AR 1971, p.476.
6   Ibid., p.498.
7   Ibid., pp.495-6.
8   Ibid., p.496.
9   General Report, February 1970, p.2, para.4.
10 Ibid., p.2, para.6.
11 Ibid., p.15, paras 52 and 55.
12 For an account of the creation of the Department of
    the Environment see Draper (1977), and for a review of
    Draper see the symposium in 'Town Planning Review',
    Sharp (ed.) (1978). Perhaps it is worth noting here
    the editorial comments of the Review (p.387):
        The creation of the Department of the Environment
        in 1970 was the result of a process that spanned
        two governments. The decision that a merging of
        the Ministries of Housing and Local Government,
        Public Building and Works, and Transport was de-
        sirable was made under the Wilson administration;
        a General Election which brought the Conservatives
        into power caused little more than a hiccup in the
        execution of the merger.
13 Letter by the General Manager to the Ministry, dated
    21.12.70.
14 Special meeting of the SDC, 19.12.70, p.2, paras 3 and
    32.
15 Annual average figure.
16 SDC press release, 12.1.71, p.1.
17 SVA press release, 13.1.71, p.2.
18 AR 1972, p.521.
19 Circular 206, p.2.
20 Ibid., p.2.
21 Ibid., p.2.
22 AR 1972, p.518.
23 Ibid., p.517.
24 Unpublished report, dated 1.1.71, pp.2-8.
25 Memorandum from SDO, titled 'Industrial Employers'
    Group', 25.1.71. The memorandum adds (p.2):
        the Corporation has excessively identified itself
        with the viewpoint of the Industrial Employers'
        Group, the major interest of which, apart from
        laying claim to as large a share as it could of
        the Corporation's housing programme, has been to
        restrict local competition for labour as far as
        possible.
26 Reported in the 'Luton Evening Post', 27.7.71.
27 Dated July 1971.

28 Ibid., p.5, para. O.5.
29 Ibid., p.14, para. O.5(vi).

CHAPTER 6 STEVENAGE 1972-3: 'EXPANSION '73' - THE CASE
IS PRESENTED

1 SDC minutes, 13.1.72 (380), p.2.
2 This was eventually made fully available when published in June 1972 (SDC).
3 'Social Indices', p.3, para. 3.1.
4 SDC minutes, 9.3.72 (382), p.3.
5 Ibid., p.3.
6 'Verbatim Report of Proceedings - SDC Public Meeting,
   17 April 1972', (SDC), p.3.
7 Ibid., p.8.
8 Ibid., p.27.
9 Ibid., p.27.
10 Ibid., p.54.
11 Ibid., p.55.
12 Ireton (1977 transcript), p.6.
13 Ibid., p.6.
14 Dated October 1972, p.3.
15 Ibid., p.15.
16 SDC minutes, 20.4.72 (383), p.2.
17 SDC minutes, 18.5.72 (384), p.4.
18 SDC minutes, 15.6.72 (385), p.4.
19 Reported in SDC minutes, and in 'Stevenage Expansion
   1973: Volume 1, Consultation and Participation', SDC
   (March 1973), appendix 7, p.99.
20 See, for example, the arguments of the CDP (1976).
21 Data from the Building Societies Association, see
   appendix 1.
22 For accounts of the DOE, see Sharp et al. (1978);
   Draper (1977); and Caulcott (1977).
23 AR 1973, p.575.
24 SDC, 'Stevenage '72: Updating of the Master Plan:
   Goals and Objectives', p.7.
25 Ibid., p.1.
26 Ibid., p.7.
27 Ibid., p.12, para. 1.8.
28 Ibid., p.13, para. 2.4. This is, of course, congruent
   with the traditional planning ideology, for as Dennis
   (1970, p.73) puts it:
       Purely in terms of land-use planning the least risk
       policy means decisions which err on the side of
       generosity rather than niggardliness in land-use
       allocations. The planner who plays safe with his
       population figures leaves himself maximum flexibi-
       lity in his strategy for other policies.

29   Ibid., p.13, para. 2.4.
30   Ibid., p.2.
31   See the 'Stevenage Gazette', 13.7.72, 14.9.72, and 26.10.72.
32   Ibid., 13.7.72.
33   SDC minutes, 12.10.72 (388), p.11.
34   AR 1973, p.518.
35   Ibid., p.520.
36   Reported in the 'Stevenage Gazette', 30.11.72.
37   SDC minutes, 7.12.72 (390), p.1.
38   Dated 26.11.72.
39   P.7 and p.1.
40   AR 1973, p.520.
41   Special meeting of the SDC, 11.1.73, p.2.
42   Ibid., p.3.
43   Jack Balchin reported in the 'Stevenage Gazette', 25.1.73.
44   See 'Stevenage Expansion 1973: summary of preliminary report on feasibility studies for expansion', SDC (January 1973), p.1, para. 1.3.
45   Ibid., p.3.
46   See, for example, the 'Luton Evening Post', 'Stevenage Gazette', 'Stevenage Comet'.
47   Reported in the 'Luton Evening Post', 25.1.73.
48   'Stevenage Expansion 1973' (January 1973), p.1, para. 1.2.
49   Both incidents reported in the 'Stevenage Gazette', 8.2.73.
50   Ibid., 1.2.73; and 'Stevenage Comet', 15.2.73.
51   'Luton Evening Post', 26.1.73; 'Stevenage Gazette', 22.2.73 and 8.2.73; cf. Milne (1973, p.22):
         in the case of both Stevenage and Harlow, the Corporations have found themselves up against strong local authority opposition - on strategic grounds and on the charge of almost no consultation.... All the bad blood which typified many of the original new town designation inquiries appears to have been stirred up.
52   'Stevenage Expansion 1973: Volume 1, Consultation and Participation' (March 1973), p.7.
53   SDC minutes, 15.2.73 (392), p.4.
54   Reported in the 'Stevenage Gazette', 1.2.73.
55   Lenderyou (1976 transcript), p.9.
56   'Stevenage Expansion 1973: Volume 1, Consultation and Participation' (March 1973), p.9, para. 3.7.
57   Ibid., p.13, para. 4.2.
58   Ibid., p.13, para. 4.3.
59   Ibid., p.14, para. 4.4.
60   Ibid., p.17, para. 4.12.

61 Ibid., p.17, para. 4.14.
62 Press release, undated; Rowe (1973, p.465) notes
    that:
>   The questionnaire is in itself an interesting docu-
>   ment, for those who voted 'no' (7 per cent of
>   households, against 1 per cent for) were encouraged
>   to qualify their vote by further questions which as
>   indicated earlier might be used to pre-empt their
>   position, without the substantial majority who did
>   not vote being considered as a massive vote for ex-
>   pansion.

    Boaden and Walker (1976, pp.20-1), make the following
    general observation:
>   Predetermined questions, often with a limited range
>   of structured answers, obviously restrict and may
>   direct what respondents have to say ... who contri-
>   butes, and the character of their contribution, is
>   a product of sampling and questionnaire design,
>   both of which are controlled by the planners and
>   the consultant.

63 Transcript of taped interview with Jack Balchin
    (1976), p.6.
64 Ibid., p.16; also, in response to more general
    questions about public participation, he stated that
    the public contribute to, but do not share in, the
    decisions that the Corporation make to the Secretary
    of State; that too much participation could be harm-
    ful; and that 90 per cent of the public were indif-
    ferent to what public agency builds the town, it being
    merely the results that matter to them.
65 'Stevenage Comet', 4.1.73; cf. Glasgow Media Group
    (1976, p.344): 'recent work, both empirical and
    theoretical, has stressed the agenda setting role of
    media as a clue to their importance as systems of
    social control'.
66 Reported in the 'Stevenage Gazette', 22.2.73.
67 Memorandum, SDO, 24.2.73.
68 SDO internal report, March 1973, p.1.
69 Ibid., p.3.
70 'A public opinion survey on the proposed expansion of
    Stevenage', SUDC (April 1973), p.2, para. i; cf. Rowe
    (1973, p.466):
>   Most people would think their areas underprovided
>   with employment opportunities, shops, recreation
>   and entertainment, houses for their children, but
>   few would vote for expansion if the concomitant in
>   sheer scale were exposed.

71 SDO, op.cit., pp.8-9.
72 SUDC, op.cit., p.i.

73 Ibid., p.ii, para. iv; cf. Cresswell (1974, p.7):
an investigation of the desires and feelings of
different groups involved in a new town threatens
to expose the justifications which planners may
give for their actions.... On the issue of expansion, Stevenage Urban District Council with
their own survey pre-emptively met the claim that
what was planned was what the residents wanted.

74 Quoted in 'Stevenage Expansion 1973: Vol.1', op.cit.,
p.32.

75 Ibid., p.32.

76 Ibid., p.40; see also Ambrose and Colenutt (1975) on
speculative building.

77 SUDC, op.cit., p.40.

78 Ibid., p.41.

79 Ibid., p.49.

80 Ibid., p.49.

81 Ibid., p.50.

82 SDC minutes, 22.3.73 (392), p.2.

83 Ibid., p.2.

84 Ibid., p.2.

85 See the 'Stevenage Gazette', 1.3.73 and 22.3.73, and
the 'Stevenage Comet', 1.3.73.

86 SDC, 'Stevenage Expansion 1973: Vol.2' (March 1973),
p.i.

87 Ibid., p.59, para. 7.6.

88 SDC minutes, 15.2.73 (392), p.7.

89 See Rowe's (1973, p.466) comments:
The Corporation has now decided upon expansion in
the main towards the uncanvassed west, though
whether this arises as a simple democratic response or in accordance with classic military con-
ceptions of diversionary tactics is open to conjecture.

90 'Stevenage Expansion 1973: Vol.2', pp.70-2, paras
9.13 and 9.14.

91 Ibid., p.ii.

92 Ibid., p.ii.

93 Ibid., appendix 4, pp.88-90,p.88.

94 Cmnd 5280, HMSO, 9.4.73.

95 Hansard, 17.5.73.

96 SDC minutes, 18.5.73 (395), p.4.

97 Ibid., p.4.

98 'Guardian', article by Judy Hillman, 16.5.73.

99 See for example Buxton and Craven (1976); Laslett
(1977), pp.171-3; McKeown (1976); Mitchison (1977),
pp.80-6; Reddaway (1977); Sandford (1977), pp.
115-17; Stone (1970), pp.13-28. Cox (1975, p.153),
suggests that 'a general rule for forecasts of all

kinds is that the further ahead one tries to look the more obscure the prospect', see also Dennis (1970, p.58) who makes the following observation concerning population predictions:

> They depend upon variables which change unpredictably and independently of each other. The inherent difficulties of a figure of future population which can give guidance to present decisions can be seen most convincingly by looking at variations in estimates of national population where, as compared with local projections, forecasting is simple.

100 'Stevenage Expansion 1973: Vol.3' (December 1973), p.28, para. 5.9.
101 Ibid., p.28, para. 5.10.
102 Ibid., p.28, para. 5.11.
103 Ibid., p.28, para. 5.12.
104 Ibid., p.29, para. 5.14.
105 Ibid., p.29, para. 5.15.
106 Ibid., p.30, para. 5.18.
107 Ibid., p.33, para. 5.25.
108 Ibid., p.36, para. 5.41.
109 Ibid., p.61, para. 9.18.
110 Ibid., p.87, para. 15.2.
111 Ibid., p.89, para. 15.11.
112 Reported in the 'Stevenage Gazette', 1.3.73.

CHAPTER 7   STEVENAGE 1972-4: THE STRUGGLE BEGINS

1 Constitution, p.1, obtained through personal communication with W.Emms (Secretary), 15.2.77.
2 Ibid., p.2, para. 3.
3 For a study of Amenity Societies see Barker and Keating (1977).
4 Constitution of the CPRE (revised October 1977), p.1, para. a.
5 Summary leaflet of the CPRE (1977), p.3.
6 Ibid., p.3.
7 May 1973, p.4, para. 4.
8 Annual Report (1976), p.4.
9 Letter from the Hertfordshire Society, 16.4.73, received by the Hertfordshire Workers' Educational Association.
10 Ibid.
11 Transcript of taped interview with John Hubble (1977), p.1.
12 Ibid., p.2.
13 Ibid., p.3, and membership form, p.1.

14 Hubble transcript, p.2.

15 Ibid., p.3.

16 Ibid., p.4; cf. Stretton (1976, pp.72-81), where he discusses the difficulties of co-operation between classes on environmental issues, as does Mann (1975, p.278). This incident also demonstrates that an individual's ideological structure is not necessarily, or particularly, homogeneous, but rather is an interaction of (often non-complementary) discrete elements (and is not, therefore, related merely to Ware).

17 Hubble transcript, p.3.

18 Ibid., p.3.

19 Ibid., p.3.

20 Ibid., pp.4-6; Lipsky (1968, p.1157) discusses the lack of organisational resources in protest groups.

21 Also in the SVA was Gerry Anstock, Headmaster of Pear Tree School, who in fact was 'Mr Rivers' in Brian Jackson's (1964) account of streaming.

22 Hubble transcript, p.5.

23 Ibid., p.5.

24 Ibid., p.5.

25 Ibid., p.5.

26 Ibid., p.6.

27 Ibid., p.6.

28 Ibid., p.6.

29 Ibid., p.6.

30 Ibid., p.7.

31 Ibid., p.8; cf. Hampton (1970, p.292) on the Walkley Action Group, who were opposed to the redevelopment of Walkley:

> the success of the group was based upon their parochialism ... there was no attempt ... to 'broaden the struggle'.

Coit (1978, p.303), on the other hand, argues that:

> Focusing all action on one problem such as high rents without developing a further analysis leads to an incomplete response on the part of the community group.

32 Transcript of taped interview with Tom McCombie, Chairman of the Aston Village Society (1977), p.1.

33 Ibid., p.1.

34 Ibid., p.2.

35 Ibid., p.3.

36 LADACAN, the Luton and District Association for the Control of Aircraft Noise, was set up in 1968, as was BRECCAN, the Beachwood Green Campaign for the Control of Aircraft Noise.

37 Villages Co-ordinating Committee, minutes, 9.5.73, p.2.

38   Ibid., p.3.
39   Hubble transcript, p.8; see the information sheets
     produced by the 'Covent Garden Community Campaign for
     the Future'.
40   SVA committee meeting, minutes, 30.5.73, p.1.
41   Hubble transcript, p.9.
42   See appendix 3 for some further information.
43   McCombie transcript, p.7.
44   Transcript of interview with Simon Bowes-Lyon (1977),
     p.1.
45   Undated letter, written sometime in June.
46   Undated.
47   June 1973, p.1.
48   Undated, p.1.
49   Ibid., p.2.
50   Ibid., p.2.
51   Transcript of taped interview with Marion Powell
     (1977), p.1.
52   Ibid., p.1.
53   McCombie transcript, p.4.
54   CASE executive committee meeting, minutes, 1.7.73,
     p.1.
55   Ibid., p.3.
56   Ibid., p.3.
57   CASE council meeting, minutes, 12.7.73, p.1.
58   Ibid., p.2.
59   Ibid., p.3.
60   Ibid., p.4.
61   CASE memorandum, 16.7.73, p.1.
62   Dated 28.7.73, p.1.
63   McCombie transcript, p.10; Shirley Williams herself
     commented, in taped and transcribed interview (1977,
     p.1):
          I think well of the Corporation generally, don't
          get me wrong, because I think that they have been
          a good body, but I think that like many other un-
          elected bodies they tend to get carried away with
          a feeling of their own empire building really, and
          because they made a good job of Stevenage one, I
          think they were keen to carry on without cessation
          to Stevenage two.
64   'Luton Evening Post', 8.8.73; cf. McCombie tran-
     script: 'wasn't very well attended ... it was decided
     on and organised in too great a hurry ...' (p.11).
65   Powell transcript, p.2.
66   Ibid., p.4.
67   Ibid., p.2.
68   McCombie transcript, p.6.
69   CAUSE broadsheet (1973), p.1.

70   Ibid., p.1.
71   Ibid., p.1.
72   Powell transcript, p.5.
73   Ibid., p.5.
74   Ibid., p.6.
75   Personal communication, 5.10.77, p.1.
76   Powell transcript, p.5.
77   Pickvance (1976b, p.218) makes the following point:
        organization plays a greater role in social move-
        ments than simply permitting the linking of contra-
        dictions. It is suggested that the survival and
        success of such movements depends on the resources
        they are able to obtain, free or through social ex-
        change, from organizations in the community, from
        higher levels of hierarchies, and from the personal
        networks and multiple position of their members.
     For a further discussion see chapter 13.
78   Hubble transcript, p.9.
79   Ibid., p.9.
80   McCombie transcript, p.6.
81   Powell transcript, p.5.
82   McCombie transcript, p.5.
83   Parkin (1968), p.34. He adds that the distinction is
     the same as Weber's contrast between the 'ethic of re-
     sponsibility', and the 'ethic of ultimate ends'.
84   McCombie transcript, p.4.
85   Hubble transcript, p.9.
86   Bowes-Lyon transcript, p.1.
87   Ibid., p.2.
88   Cf. McCombie transcript, p.8; and Hubble transcript,
     p.12. Cf. also Mutch (1977, p.46):
        Late in 1967 there was increased public pressure
        and speculation concerning the improvement of
        Turnhouse. The Cramond Association was told pri-
        vately by a civil servant in the Scottish Office
        that plans did exist for the new airport and that
        it might be advisable to declare the interest of
        the local people.
89   Hubble transcript, p.9.
90   Reported in the 'Stevenage Gazette', 11.10.73.
91   Ibid., 8.11.73 and 15.11.73.
92   Letter dated 8.1.74
93   Ibid.
94   Mimeo, obtained through the SDC.
95   'Guardian', 17.1.74.
96   Reported in the 'Stevenage Gazette', 17.1.74.
97   Reported in the 'Stevenage Comet', 31.1.74.
98   Powell transcript, p.9.
99   Robbie Roberts, personal communication (1978), p.3.

He continued to say that, when abandonment was announced: 'It was with no small measure of pride.'
100   Memorandum, 17.1.74, p.i, and council meeting
minutes, 9.2.74, p.2.
101   McCombie transcript, p.10.
102   Powell transcript, p.10.
103   Bowes-Lyon transcript, p.2.
104   CASE executive committee meeting, minutes, 20.1.74,
p.3.

CHAPTER 8 STEVENAGE 1974: 'EXPANSION '74', AND THE
STRUGGLE CONTINUES

1   AR 1974, p.400.
2   Ibid., p.400.
3   Silkin was severely criticised, in 1974, with regard
to his connections with Wayfeg Investments, the property speculators - see Colenutt (1975); the General
Manager of the Corporation at the time, Jack Balchin,
demonstrated while being interviewed in 1976 how
complex the political process is:
> We have much greater linkage with Mr Silkin than
> we ever did with Mr Channon the previous Minister
> ... the reason for that is that Silkin is the son
> of his father, and there is in the Jewish communi-
> ty great attachment and reverence by sons for
> fathers and this has expressed itself in John
> Silkin wanting to be as good a Minister for New
> Towns as his 'creator' father was (p.17 of tran-
> script).
4   AR 1974, p.401.
5   Ibid., p.402.
6   Ibid., p.402.
7   Ibid., p.402.
8   Ibid., p.402.
9   Ibid., p.402.
10   Ibid., p.403.
11   Ibid., p.403
12   Ibid., p.404.
13   Ibid., p.399.
14   SDC minutes, 28.3.74 (404), p.2.
15   Reproduced in 'Stevenage '74', preliminary report,
August 1974, p.4, para. 3.1.
16   Balchin transcript, p.9.
17   SDC minutes, 25.4.74 (405), p.2.
18   'Stevenage Gazette', 25.4.74.
19   Hertfordshire County Council, press release, 30.4.74
ref: E2200A; and 'Stevenage Gazette', 9.5.74.

20   SDC minutes, 25.4.74 (405), p.2.
21   Balchin to Marlow, pp.1-2.
22   13 May 1974, ref: 1826174.
23   The use of terms such as the 'people' is of course
     ideological. Similar terms are those, for example,
     which Hyman (1975, p.128) describes:
          the belief that there is an overriding 'national
          interest' which transcends the conflict of inter-
          ests between rich and poor, exploiting and ex-
          ploited; that economic life represents a system
          of free exchange between equal individuals; that
          the function of the state is to protect the weak
          and powerless just as much as the strong and power-
          ful: all these ideas serve the interests of those
          in positions of economic and social control by con-
          signing legitimacy on the social order.
24   Memorandum from Chief Estate Officer, dated 26 June,
     ref: CES/M.4/6/AC/MEF.
25   SDC minutes, 11.7.74 (409), p.1.
26   Ibid., p.2.
27   The Corporation's Committee structure was as follows:
     finance; planning; housing special cases; es-
     tablishment; appeals; joint committee (SDC/SBC);
     joint housing committee; and joint planning committee
     (ad hoc).
28   Minutes of the joint committee meeting, undated.
29   Balchin transcript, pp.18-19.
30   Thomas (1972), p.50.
31   'Luton Evening Post', 17.7.74; and 'Stevenage Comet',
     25.7.74.
32   SDC pamphlet, p.1.
33   Ibid., pp.2-3. Note that the other objectives merely
     overlapped with those stated.
34   SDC, 'Stevenage '74' (1974), Vol.1, p.5, para. 3.3.
35   Lenderyou transcript (1976), p.10.
36   SDC, op.cit., p.6, paras 4.5 and 4.6.
37   Ibid., p.40, adapted from table 19.
38   Ibid., p.42, adapted from table 21.
39   Ibid., p.43, para. 11.1.
40   Ibid., p.43, para. 11.3.
41   Ibid., p.23, para. 8.8.
42   Ibid., p.44, para. 12.2.
43   SDC, 'Stevenage '74, Vol.3' (December 1975), p.5,
     para. 2.4.
44   Ibid., p.11, para. 3.5.
45   'Election question - the future of Stevenage',
     23.9.74, p.1.
46   Ibid., p.2.
47   'Stevenage Comet', 10.10.74.

48 Press release, 31.10.74, p.1.
49 Press release, 4.11.74, pp.1-3.
50 SBC report (1974), p.i.
51 Ibid., p.24, para. 10.1.
52 Ibid., p.27, para. 11.4.
53 Ibid., p.28, para. 11.5.
54 'Stevenage '74, Vol.2', December 1974, p.i.
55 Ibid., p.10, para. 2.19.
56 Ibid., p.10, para. 2.20.
57 Jack Balchin, the General Manager, described the move
    - retrospectively - in the following manner: 'in 1974
    we proposed a peripheral expansion ... making the lop-
    sidedness of the town more lopsided' (1976 transcript,
    p.2).
58 'Stevenage '74, Vol.2', p.13, para. 3.5.
59 Ibid., p.19, para. 3.26.
60 Ibid., p.23, para. 4.2.
61 Ibid., p.25, para. 4.11:
        A headship rate is the proportion of any group of
        persons who, if given the opportunity, will es-
        tablish separate households. Headship rates vary
        within age, sex and marital status to facilitate
        reasonably accurate predictions of the future
        numbers of married households and those 'other
        households' consisting of single, widowed or di-
        vorced persons with or without children. The
        actual household formation reflects these rates,
        but it is also influenced by the degree of afflu-
        ence in a community at any time and the ease with
        which potential households can 'set up house'.
62 Ibid., p.26, adapted from table 2.
63 Ibid., p.28, para. 4.22.
64 Ibid., p.28, para. 4.22.
65 Ibid., p.28, para. 4.28.
66 Ibid., p.30, para. 4.29.
67 Ibid., p.63, para. 10.4.
68 Ibid., p.83, para. 10.9.
69 Ibid., p.85, para. 10.21.
70 Ibid., p.85, para. 10.24.
71 AR 1975, p.376.
72 Quarterly minutes to 31.12.74, p.2.

CHAPTER 9 STEVENAGE 1974-6: THE PUBLIC INQUIRY

1 McCombie transcript (1977), p.6; cf. Stretton (1976,
   p.74): 'people learnt how to pick horses for courses
   through participation'.
2 SDC, 'Stevenage '74: Volume 3, Public Consultation'
   (1975), p.14.

3   Ibid., p.16.
4   Ibid., p.21.
5   Selection of comment forms.
6   CASE council meeting minutes, 13.3.75, p.1.
7   Ibid., p.2.
8   Letter to the DOE, 9.4.75, reproduced in appendix D of 'Stevenage '74', Vol.3.
9   AR 1975, p.374.
10 AR 1976, p.388.
11 'Forum', the magazine of the SBC, Spring 1975, p.3.
12 SDC minutes, 16.10.75 (426), p.5.
13 SDC minutes, 11.11.75 (429), pp.1-2.
14 AR 1976, p.392.
15 On Housing Associations see Harloe et al. (1974), pp. 61-79; and Swann (1975).
16 Draft Stevenage New Town (designation) Amendment Order, 197 DOE.
17 CASE memorandum, 4.1.76, p.2.
18 SDC minutes, 14.1.76 (430), p.3.
19 Ibid., p.4.
20 Ibid., p.4.
21 'Stevenage Comet', 13.1.76.
22 Transcript of taped interview with Shirley Williams, MP (1977), p.9. Mrs Williams elaborated:
        there were two reasons why I was in a hurry ... one was because it didn't seem to me that the objectors were other than what you might call automatic objectors ... secondly, and equally important, I knew and the Corporation knew, and the Council knew, that if we didn't get a decision - *it didn't really matter whether it was a Z or Y decision* - quickly we would run straight back into a very long waiting list in the town for housing (p.3, emphasis added).
23 McCombie transcript, p.9.
24 Bowes-Lyon transcript (1977), p.2.
25 Council meeting minutes, 23.1.76, p.2.
26 Ibid., p.3; cf., on the financing of protest, Perman (1973) and McKie (1973), both on Cublington; 'Sunday Times' (12 June 1977) regarding the Windscale Inquiry:
        The debate could go on for months and shortly after it ends another inquiry is due to open on plans for a new fast-breeder reactor. The question for the protestors is: 'will they have the resources to fight another battle so soon?'.
    Smith (1977, p.407) makes a similar point concerning the Windscale Inquiry.
27 Hubble transcript (1977), p.13.
28 CASE council meeting minutes, 20.2.76, p.1.
29 Ibid., p.2.

30 Reported in the 'Stevenage Gazette', 13.3.76; cf.
    Mutch (1977, pp.47-8) who states, in his study of
    Turnhouse Airport, that the British Airports Authori-
    ty's (BAA) proposals were not available beyond a
    general outline, and three months' notice only was
    given of a public inquiry (1 November 1971):
        Although the objectors' solicitor asked BAA for
        details of their proposals on 22nd June, they were
        not released to the objectors until September.
        BAA's slowness in detailing their plans was very
        harmful to the objectors and their consultants, and
        it may be presumed that this was the intention.
31 Cmnd 4060, HMSO (1932), p.79.
32 SDC, 'Stevenage '74: Volume 4, Planning Report'
    (1976), p.i.
33 Ibid., p.73, para. 3.1.20.
34 McCombie transcript, p.6.
35 Ibid., p.6.
36 Ibid., p.6.
37 For a pictorial account see Mullan (1978).
38 For a complete list see SDC, 'Stevenage '74: Volume 6,
    Draft Designation Order and Public Inquiry' (1977),
    pp.105-10.
39 Cf. Shirley Williams (1977 transcript, p.7): 'he has
    every right to do as a judge should'; similarly Mr
    Cuthill (in a personal communication, 1978, p.14,
    para. 7.3), Chairman of the SVA, suggested that:
        Inquiry inspectors should be appointed by and paid
        by and only beholden to the top judiciary. The top
        judiciary should be appointed by the Crown (as
        custodians of the constitution) in accordance with
        agreed rules. These things are too important to be
        left to politicians (and what is a politician, 'a
        little man in big boots who knows the answers
        before he has even been asked the question').
40 Shorthand account of the proceedings.
41 See Milgram (1965) for a quite devastating account of
    the process.
42 Cf. memorandum M35 from the Ministry of Housing and
    Local Government (5.9.1950), in relation to procedure
    at public inquiries:
        Where the inquiry is 'into objections' it would be
        logical for the objectors to open the proceedings
        by stating their case and for the corporation to
        follow with their comment on the objections stated
        ... however ... (emphasis added).
43 SDC, 'Stevenage '74: Volume 6' (Inspector's report),
    p.1, para. 2.
44 Ibid., p.2, para. 5.

45   Ibid., p.9, para. 31.
46   Ibid., p.52, para. 5.16;   p.59, para. 6.21.
47   SVA proof at the Inquiry.
48   GLC paper 44 (No.623), 1976, p.1.
49   Foreword to the above document.
50   'Guardian', 27.8.76.
51   SDC press release, 31.3.76, p.1.
52   SEEPC (76) 35, 22.3.76, p.3:   'The Council's comments
     on the policy document "planned growth outside
     London"';   Dennis (1976, p.7), makes the following
     point:
        The cause of the decline is not primarily the
        result of manufacturing industry from London, which
        accounts for only 27 per cent of the total decline,
        but of the high rate of factory closures unconnect-
        ed with industrial movement (44 per cent).... Loss
        of manufacturing employment in London arising from
        movement is due more to unplanned movement (11 per
        cent of the total decline) than to movement to the
        Assisted Areas (9 per cent) or in the London Over-
        spill towns (7 per cent). A large part of the
        total movement (41 per cent) was by multi-plant
        companies closing in London and transferring pro-
        duction to existing plants elsewhere.
     Cf. Whitelegg (1976) and Gripaios (1977) on the same
     matter.
53   SDC, 'Stevenage '74: Volume 6', p.3, para. 1.0.9.
54   Powell transcript (1977), p.6.
55   Balchin proof, pp.2-3.
56   Eversley (1973), p.306.
57   Lenderyou transcript (1976), p.11.
58   Boddington proof, p.2.
59   Patterson proof, p.3;   cf. Eversley, op.cit. (p.306),
     who argues that:
        It is a sad fact that the more technically compe-
        tent a planner becomes, the less does his work make
        sense to others. How can one explain a Britton
        Harris concept of 'optimality' to an electorate
        which only wants decent housing, safe roads and
        access to the countryside?
60   Boddington proof, p.4.
61   Aston Parish Council proof, p.6.
62   SBC proof, pp.1-2.
63   SIEG proof, p.1, para. 1.
64   Ibid., p.1, para. 2.
65   Ibid., p.3, para. 3;   cf. Molotch (1976, p.311):
        Perhaps the key ideological prop for the growth
        machine, especially in terms of sustaining support
        from the working-class majority, is the claim that

growth 'makes jobs'. This claim is aggressively
promulgated by developers, builders, and chambers
of commerce. Such people do not speak of growth as
useful to profits - rather, they speak of it as
necessary for making jobs.

66 SIEG proof, p.6, para. 7.
67 Ibid., p.8, para. 9.
68 Hertfordshire County Council proof, p.4.
69 Aston Parish Council proof, reproduced in 'Stevenage
    '74: Volume 6', p.41, para. 5.29.
70 SDC minutes, 14.4.76 (433), p.2.
71 Hertfordshire Society proof, p.2, para. 6.
72 CASE proof, p.1.
73 Ibid., p.1.
74 Ibid., p.11, para. 25.
75 McCombie transcript, p.8.
76 Dearman proof, p.11, para. 9.
77 Powell proof, p.1.
78 Shirley Williams's view on the matter was that:
    It would be quite improper for an inspector to hold
    against somebody the fact that they belonged to a
    particular political party. The barrister is quite
    entitled to say that but the inspector should say
    'Mr XYZ, that matter is not germane to what we're
    considering. I would be grateful if you would stop
    that line of enquiry', which he has every right to
    do as a *judge* should (1977 transcript, p.7, empha-
    sis added).
79 Cf. Castells (1976, p.294):
    The theses of 'urban sociology' ... are also the
    basis for extremely important daily ideologies,
    such as, for example, the explanation of criminali-
    ty by the size of cities.
80 Powell transcript, p.9.
81 Beacham proof, p.11, para. 5.5.
82 See Hall (1976) for the idiosyncratic life history of
    the SPSE.
83 NFU (1975), p.1, para. 2.
84 Giles (1976, p.55), states that
    The post-war uptake of agricultural land in England
    and Wales for various urban and transportational
    uses has been at the rate of about 35,000 to 40,000
    acres per year - or just over one per cent of the
    national farm.
85 NFU (1975), op.cit., p.9, para. 11.
86 Ibid., p.9, para. 12; for general information on the
    NFU see Wilson (1977) and Beyron and Harrison (1962).
87 The figures are somewhat unreliable: the Inspector
    puts the figures at 912,269 and 362 respectively
    ('Stevenage '74: Volume 6', p.52, para. 6.24).

88 Ibid., p.53.
89 Warner-Smith proof, p.9.
90 Personal communication, 13.1.78, p.1; cf. Cresswell
    (1976, p.72):
> Our dependence on other countries as primary pro-
> ducers of our food supply could become a serious
> problem if the producers took a similar view and
> stand to that recently taken by the oil producing
> countries.
91 J.R.Willis, on behalf of the trustees of F.W.Allen,
    proof, p.4, para. 2.6; cf. Giles, op.cit., who makes
    exactly the same point in his case study of the re-
    lations between 'agriculture' and Milton Keynes New
    Town.
92 Cf. the comments of David Hall, of the TCPA, on the
    Windscale Inquiry ('Guardian', 25.10.77), when he
    notes that on day 81 the local authority for the
    Windscale area was made to compress its evidence into
    two and a half hours, and yet at 3.30 pm the Inquiry
    was adjourned because there were no other parties
    present to appear.
93 Cf. DHSS memorandum CMO (76) 15, 11.8.76, 'Nitrates
    in drinking water'.
94 Inspector's report, mimeo (not in 'Stevenage '74:
    Volume 6'), p.20, para.3.36.
95 Hubble transcript, p.14.
96 Ibid., p.14.
97 Volume 6 was the Inspector's report and thus not part
    of the Corporation's case. Cf. Baer (1978, p.10) who
    suggests that there 'is no question that new town re-
    sidents are active, more active socially and politi-
    cally than their counterparts in the rest of the
    country'; similarly Evelyn Denington (1977 tran-
    script, p.10) asserts that in Stevenage, as compared
    with London Boroughs
> there is a very lively community, they are an aware
> community and anybody in this community who doesn't
> like it ups and says so.

CHAPTER 10   STEVENAGE 1976-7: CONFUSION ABOUNDS

1 Reported in the 'Stevenage Gazette', 22.6.76.
2 SDC minutes, 21.10.76 (437), p.2.
3 AR 1977, p.378.
4 AR 1977, pp.396 and 62.
5 'Stevenage Gazette', 25.11.76.
6 SDC, 'Stevenage Household Survey: March 1976' (December 1976).

7 Ibid., p.14, para. 2.34; cf. Thomas (1977).
8 'Department of Employment Gazette', vol.85, No.12,
   December 1977, p.406; and vol.86, No.1, January 1978,
   p.90.
9 Mimeo, obtained through the SDC.
10 DOE, 5 April, ref: NT/5447/1/45.
11 'The future of Stevenage', DOE, 6 April.
12 See p.97 of SDC, 'Stevenage '74: Volume 6' (1977).
13 Ibid., p.95.
14 SDC minutes, 21.4.77 (444), pp.1-4.
15 'Forum', the magazine of the SBC, Spring 1977, p.2.
16 'Stevenage Gazette', 14.4.77.
17 Ibid.
18 McCombie transcript (1977), p.9.
19 Ibid., p.17.
20 Powell transcript (1977), p.11.
21 SDC minutes, 19.5.77 (445), p.2.

CHAPTER 11 STEVENAGE: CONSTRAINTS ON THE URBAN MANAGERS

1 Harloe (1975a), p.3.
2 Mellor (1977), p.159.
3 Much of the material used in this chapter derives from
   the work of the Corporation's SDO, and I acknowledge
   their assistance and guidance in helping me sort
   through it.
4 I certainly do not consider that the service economy
   in any way relates to a 'post-capitalist' society (or
   any such type of argument). Rather I share the arguments of, for example, Kumar (1976, pp.445-6), whose
   view is that:
       There is no doubt that, in all the industrial so-
       cieties, there has been a long-term tendency
       whereby the majority of the working population has
       come to be employed in the service (tertiary)
       sector rather than in the manufacturing (secondary)
       sector. We must take care not to see in this de-
       velopment some radically new turn, some unexpected
       discontinuity with past evolution. Whatever signi-
       ficance we wish to attribute to this tendency,
       therefore, we must - as the post-industrial
       theorists do not - stress the essential continuity
       in this respect of the industrial and post-indus-
       trial societies.
   Cf. Gershuny (1977).
5 See SDO, Research, Information and Monitoring Series,
   E.6, June 1977, p.3.
6 Ibid., p.3.

7   See the report by SIEG reproduced in SDC, 'Population, Employment and Housing in Stevenage: technical report' (1970, pp.68-84), p.76.

8   The Estates Department of the SDC supplied this information.

9   AR 1976 British Aircraft Corporation, p.22.

10 Kidron (1970), p.64; see also Harman (1978) for a discussion of the issues.

11 CIS-CDP (1976), p.7.

12 Warren (1974), pp.20-2.

13 Minutes of the meeting of the General Committee of the Hertford and Stevenage Constituency Labour Party, 25.3.77.

14 AR, op.cit., p.7; cf. the anti-nationalisation views, in relation to the aerospace industry, of Anthony Crosland (1963), pp.320-34.

15 It is interesting to acknowledge the fact that as BAC is heavily involved in the Middle East, it would directly benefit from the 'oil crisis' which so increased Middle East spending power, while causing deep-felt recession elsewhere.

16 AR 1976 Kodak, pp.1-2.

17 SDO RIM/E4, 'Analysis of occupations: based on household survey information (10 per cent sample)' (October 1976), p.4, para. 5.5.

18 Ibid., p.4, para. 6.0.

19 Ibid., p.6, para. 6.4.

20 See Massey (1971), for a discussion.

21 See Daniels (1976), where he discusses Stevenage office employment, and makes the point that the employment is too connected to the manufacturing industries.

22 SDO RIM/E15, 'A Planning Context: Part 2' (June 1977), p.20.

23 Article in the 'Times', 20.6.67.

24 Parsons (1973), p.223.

25 Personal communication, E.Lenderyou, 1978.

26 Manners et al. (1972), p.132.

27 See Rawstron and Coates (1973), p.13.

28 See CDP (1977), p.6, on the problems of Skelmersdale.

29 SDO RIM/E7, 'SBC Employment Meeting', (18.1.77), p.2.

30 Ibid., p.2.

CHAPTER 12   URBAN MANAGERIALISM

1   Pahl (1974), p.1. Pahl has now refined his position, and talks rather of the managers of the urban system being merely mediators between the urban population

and the capitalist economy, generating and maintaining the ideology of Welfare Statism (see, for example, Pahl, 1975a, p.284).

2 Norman (1975), p.65; for empirical studies from this perspective see Dennis (1972); Davies (1972); English et al. (1976); and Neve (1977).

3 Dennis (1975), p.219.

4 Ibid., p.220. He adds:

> In 1951 local authorities in this country disposed of about 8 per cent of the national income, so 8 per cent was allocated authoritatively. Today local authorities dispose of about 20 per cent of national income. Therefore it is an important question in itself, regardless of what lies behind the process, to understand what is happening and how these allocations are being made.

5 Moore (1977), pp.105-6.

6 Newton (1976), p.230.

7 Alford (1973), p.148.

8 In another publication Harloe (1978a, p.12) states that the same sociologists have

> scored increasingly hollow intellectual victories over the naive sociologising of architects and planners.

This seems hardly fair, in that the critique of architects and planners has demonstrated the power that such professionals have, enabling them to manipulate 'democratic' processes. See Dennis (1972), for but one example.

9 Cf. the views of Sandercock (1975, p.230), in her book on urban development in Australia:

> I can see no inherent reason why a social democratic society cannot effectively carry out a policy of redistributive social justice.

10 Harloe (1975a), p.11.

11 Abrams (1978, 1978a), pp.9 and 30; cf. Castells (1976c, p.71):

> Similarly, urban stratification refers to the spatial dimension of the theory of social stratification, and thus does not require new intellectual tools.

12 For an example of the position see Castells (1977a); Pickvance (ed.) (1976); and Harloe (ed.) (1977). It ought to be *stressed* that this particular version of Marxism is structuralist.

13 Pahl (1976a), p.18; cf. Lamarche (1976).

14 Cf. Holloway and Picciotti (1978, p.3) who state that:

> The discussion in Britain of the Marxist theory of the state has tended to become stuck in the rather

infertile rut of the Miliband-Poulantzas debate.
This debate has given rise to an illusory polarity
between the approaches of these two authors, between what has sometimes been called the 'instru-
mentalist' and the 'structuralist' approach ... a
false polarity which has done much to delimit and
impoverish discussion ... that which Poulantzas and
Miliband have in common is at least as significant
as that which separates them.

15 Strinati (1977), pp.1 and 11.
16 Interestingly, Winkler (1976, p.136), talking of
    Poulantzas, asserts that Poulantzas makes the
    relative independence of the economy and the polity
    a defining characteristic of the capitalist state.
    The basis for this autonomy is, interestingly, the
    same in the liberal and neo-Marxist theories: the
    state's ability to play off distinct sections of
    the economy against one another. For liberal
    pluralists, these are 'interest groups', for
    Marxists, classes and fractions within the dominant
    class.
17 See Pahl and Winkler (1975); Pahl (1976a); Winkler
    (1976); Crouch (1977); and, for an interesting dis-
    cussion, see Westergaard (1977).
18 Pahl and Winkler (1975), pp.31,29 and 28.
19 Pahl (1976a), p.14.
20 Ibid., p.15.
21 Hindess (1977), p.3; cf. Hirst (1977, p.130):
    It follows that the notion of *relative* autonomy is
    untenable. Once any degree of autonomous action is
    accorded to political forces as means of repre-
    sentation vis-à-vis classes of economic agents,
    then there is no necessary correspondence between
    the forces that appear in the political (and what
    they 'represent') and economic classes. It is not
    simply a question of discrepancy (the political
    means 'represent' the class more or less accurate-
    ly) but of necessary non-correspondence.
    Cf. Willis (1977), pp.174-5.
22 Pahl (1978), p.314. He adds: 'There is no new urban
    sociology: marxists are simply addressing themselves
    to questions which they had hitherto ignored.'
23 Lojkine (1975), pp.14-15.
24 Pahl (1978a), p.11, as a discussant in Harloe (ed.)
    (1978).
25 Pahl (1976a), p.2.
26 Pahl (1976b), p.12; on nationalistic pressures, see
    Poulantzas (1974); Nairn (1977); and, for a critical
    evaluation of Nairn, see Hobsbawm (1977).

27 Harloe (1978a), discussing the observations of Pahl.
28 Castells (1976), p.296.
29 Dunleavy (1977), pp.189-90.
30 As a discussant in Harloe (ed.) (1975), p.95.
31 Glass (1976), pp.349-53. For example, she suggests
    (p.353) that:
        We would hardly expect ... identical responses from
        the populations of equivalent blighted areas in
        Belfast and Birmingham; or for that matter even
        from the same Belfast locality before and during
        the turbulent period.
32 Rex (1971), p.151; cf. Pahl (1970, p.135), on urban
    constraints, as opposed to constraints related to the
    work situation:
        This pattern of constraints creates the urban
        social structure: the effect of cumulative con-
        straints is to tie certain sections of the popu-
        lation to specific localities so that it is legiti-
        mate to describe a locality social system. The
        housing market imposes some of the most severe con-
        straints on certain sections of the population: an
        incongruence between the housing market and the job
        market helps to create a distinctive socio-ecologi-
        cal system, which is the way the social structure
        interrelates with the spatial structure in a given
        locality.
33 Rex and Moore (1967), p.273.
34 Baldwin and Bottoms (1976), p.1.
35 Gill (1977), pp.1 and 3. In his 'Chicago School' type
    study, Gill makes the important observation that:
        No two neighbourhoods are the same. Differences in
        historical development, economic influences, social
        composition and physical layout continue to produce
        the character of the individual neighbourhood.
        Complex cultural influences are also at work (pp.
        14-15).
36 Husbands (1977), p.4.
37 Ibid., p.5.
38 Mollenkopf (1976), p.3.
39 Ibid., p.4.
40 One is reminded here of other reductionist debates,
    for example in psychobiology - see Kaplan and Manners
    (1972).
41 It is interesting that proponents of attempts to de-
    velop a fully social, and Marxist, theory of deviance
    (for example, Taylor, Walton and Young, 1973, and
    Spitzer, 1975) argue that political economy can only
    provide one dimension of the solution, and that
    elements of interactionism and phenomenology cannot
    be easily ditched.

42 Pickvance (1976a), p.32; cf. the comments of Harloe
    (1977a, p.19), who suggests that Castells' Althusser-
    ian theoreticism has led to a polarisation of studies
    of 'elites' (that is to say, studies of bureaucracies
    together with local struggles) and the more 'struc-
    tural' studies à la Castells. However, Harloe consi-
    ders that Castells himself oscillates between theore-
    ticism and concrete studies, indeed studies which
    depart from his theoretical framework yet genuinely
    develop the historical materialist analyses of urban
    problems.

43 Pahl (1975); for a useful outline of Pahl's position,
    see Deakin and Ungerson (1977), pp.14-16.

44 This outline has relied on Deakin and Ungerson, ibid.

45 This section also relies on Deakin and Ungerson,
    ibid., pp.16-19.

46 Castells (1977a), p.277.

47 Deakin and Ungerson, op.cit., p.17.

48 Ibid., p.18.

49 Transcript of taped interview with Geoffrey Hughes
    (1978), p.4.

50 SDC minutes, 22.6.54 (183), p.9.

51 SDC minutes, 26.10.54 (187), p.8.

52 Denington (1977 transcript), p.7; cf. Hughes tran-
    script, p.11:
        the number of times we have formally taken a vote
        around the table is very few indeed, and I was
        going to say over 20 years I can count it on the
        fingers of two hands, but that's a little small.

53 AR (1971), pp.495-6.

54 Lenderyou (1976 transcript), p.6.

55 Hughes transcript, p.2.

56 Ibid., p.1.

57 Ibid., p.5.

58 Ibid., p.6.

59 Bull (1967), p.114.

60 Letter reproduced in SDC minutes, 12.4.65 (308),
    pp.5-6.

61 Balchin (1976 transcript), p.10.

62 Ireton (1977 transcript), pp.4-7.

63 Reproduced in SDC, 'Stevenage Expansion 1973: Volume
    1, Consultation and Participation' (1973), appendix 7,
    p.99.

64 Benington (1976), p.8.

65 Pahl (1975a), p.284; cf. Alford (1973, p.155) who
    comments that in serious comparative studies of the
    state and processes of policy formation, there should
    be
        recognition of the empirical reality of the differ-

entiation of interest groups, the expansion of all
forms of state and bureaucratic activity, and also
the appropriation and control of the social product
by a small segment of the population.

CHAPTER 13   PUBLIC PARTICIPATION IN PLANNING: ILLUSION
OR REALITY?

1   Bell (1973), pp.8,9,10.
2   Pateman (1970).
3   Ibid., p.14.
4   Ibid., p.14.
5   Ibid., p.14.
6   Ibid., p.16.
7   Pateman does point out that the notion of a 'classical' theory of democracy is a myth, the term being
merely shorthand for a diverse group of participatory
theorists (p.17).   She adds:
    The point is ... that the theory of *representative
    government* is not the whole of democratic theory
    as much recent work would suggest (p.20, emphasis
    added).
8   Ibid., pp.103,105;   cf. Duncan and Lukes (1963, pp.
160,173):
    Electoral apathy, incompetence, and so on, which
    exist in most stable 'modern democracies' are now
    considered to be conditions of their successful
    functioning and are therefore taken to be the new
    democratic norms ... [and] it has nowhere been
    shown that apathy is either necessary or functional
    to democracy.
9   Sewell and Coppock (1977a), p.9.
10 Thornley (1977), p.3.
11 Ibid., p.37.
12 Ibid., p.37.
13 Harvey (1973), p.93 (quoted in Hambleton, 1978,
p.307).
14 Circular 52/72 DOE - Town and Country Planning Act
1971, Part II, Development plan proposals, publicity,
and public participation (1972);   Thornley, op.cit.,
p.39, comments on the government's response to
Skeffington:
    The report produced little action and the issue
    remained in limbo for about 3 years ... central
    government eventually published its views on the
    report in 1972 in the form of a circular (DOE
    52/72).
15 Thornley, op.cit., p.39.

16 Dennis (1970), pp.352-3.
17 Lambert, Blackaby, and Paris (1975), p.192.
18 Levin (1976), pp.113-14; cf. Wraith and Lamb (1971, p.318):

> the matters in issue become weightier, the volume of paper increases, cross-examination becomes sharper, professional representation more expert. Procedure inevitably becomes stricter and more formal and thus more intimidatory to the ordinary person.

19 Dennis (1972), pp.228-9.
20 Dennis (1970), pp.348-9.
21 Cullingworth (1972), pp.308-9; cf. Fagence (1977, p.278) who states that public meetings are particularly susceptible to domination by the articulate, the vociferous, and the well-organised.
22 Coit (1978), p.298.
23 Ibid., p.298.
24 Ibid., p.299.
25 Ibid., p.302.
26 Ibid.
27 Castells (1977), p.45.
28 Castells (1976b), p.149.
29 Ibid., p.155.
30 Ibid., p.171
31 Husbands (1977), p.36.
32 Ibid., pp.5-6.
33 For an overview of the 'neo-elitists', see Halebsky (1976), pp.182-233, especially pp.217-18.
34 Dunleavy (1978), p.1.
35 Castells (1976b), p.171, quoted in Dunleavy (1978), p.3.
36 Dunleavy (1978), pp.4-5.
37 Ibid., pp.5-6; Halebsky (1976, p.217) describes the impact of the work Dunleavy is pointing to in the following manner:

> In sum, in terms of Schattschneider's discussion of the 'mobilization of bias', Bachrach and Baratz' conception of the 'two-faces of power' and 'key' and 'routine' decisions, and their discussion of 'nondecision-making' it can be reasonably maintained that significant power and issues are to an important degree encapsulated within institutional settings and may never reach the arena of overt decision making. The analyses reviewed here suggest that the structure and distribution of power cannot be adequately perceived by relying on an examination of issue participants.

The references he makes are to Schattschneider (1960); Bachrach and Baratz (1962, 1963).

38 Olives (1976), pp.177-8.
39 Pickvance (1976b), p.218.
40 Pickvance (1977a).
41 Ibid., p.178.
42 Ibid., p.177.
43 Ibid., p.180. He refers to Rex and Moore (1967), and
    Rex (1971).
44 Pickvance, op.cit., p.181.
45 Ibid.
46 Ibid.
47 Ibid.
48 Ibid., p.182; compare the comments of Norman Dennis
    (1977, p.23):
        Influence which depends ... merely on persuading
        the authority that it has its facts wrong, or has
        misinterpreted the law, or neglected certain
        values, or overlooked the claims of certain groups
        ... hinges on the availability of the rank-and-file
        of the following three resources. The first re-
        source is the rank-and-filers' confidence in the
        validity of their own perception of the situation.
        Secondly, skills in writing and speaking, especial-
        ly skills in writing and speaking to hostile or
        indifferent authorities. Thirdly, access to the
        communication media. Characteristically, members
        of the rank-and-file in groups and communities lack
        all these resources.
49 Pickvance, op.cit., p.182; another example of the
    lack of theorising of the 'organisational form'
    question, is the nature of leadership in such organ-
    isations. For instance, although Harloe (1977a,
    p.39), states, in relation to urban social movements:
        that a key factor for Borja (as for others such as
        Mingione) in explaining the emergence of an active
        movement is 'the mediation of those active and
        dedicated individuals who constitute the most ad-
        vanced element of the population',
    there is little discussion in general structuralist
    writings, on the nature of 'leadership'. The papers
    Harloe refers to are Borja (1977) and Mingione (1977).
50 Wahlke et al. (1962), pp.145,168.
51 Parkin (1973), p.81; there are, of course, many va-
    riations on the 'rules of the game' theme. See, for
    example, Lijphart (1975, pp.122-37) on the process of
    'accommodation' in the Netherlands; Walker (1978) on
    agenda-item selection in politics; and Offe (1972,
    p.89), who describes, albeit more structurally and
    systematically, a similar process in relation to con-
    sensus formation.

52   Levin (1976), pp.116-17.
53   Saunders (1975), p.37.
54   Ibid.
55   Mason (1978), p.101, and see Bonnier (1972).
56   Quoted in Cullingworth (1972), p.311.
57   Broady (1974), p.4; cf. Craven (1978, pp.262-3), who
     makes a similar point.
58   Saunders, op.cit., p.55.
59   Dunleavy (1978), p.197.
60   Ibid., pp.197-8.
61   Ibid., p.198.
62   Ibid., p.199.
63   Pickvance (1976b), p.203.
64   Ibid., p.204.
65   Muchnik (1970), pp.76-9, quoted by Pickvance, op.cit.,
     p.206.
66   Pickvance, op.cit., p.207. He adds:
         The distinction between urban social movements,
         authority policy and other urban actors is unsatis-
         factory, since, for example, authority policy
         itself will be partly a response to pressure from
         previous social movements (e.g., for public
         housing) and other urban actors. (emphasis added)
67   Dunleavy (1978), p.201.
68   Pahl (1975a), p.273.
69   A few of these examples of the Corporation's actions
     can be categorised under the methods of 'complication'
     and 'authorities saying that they are using power on
     behalf of someone else'. For a discussion of the
     terms see Dennis (1977).
70   The SVA, of course, was basically more concerned about
     the Road 9 issue. The CAUSE statement was reported in
     the 'Stevenage Comet', 31.1.74; the CASE statements
     in memorandum 17.1.74 (p.i), and council meeting
     minutes, 9.2.74, p.2.
71   Lukes (1977), p.24; Elster (1978, p.175) notes that:
         The notion of counterfactual (or contrary-to-fact)
         propositions has recently become important in two
         unrelated disciplines: philosophical logic and
         economic history. In both cases interest in
         counterfactuals stems from a concern with causa-
         tion: with the *notion* of causality in the case of
         the philosopher, with the *evaluation* of the rela-
         tive importance of causes in the case of the his-
         torian.
72   Lukes, op.cit., p.24.
73   Ibid.
74   Hughes (1978 transcript), p.10.
75   See, for example, the contents of the RIM working

papers, El to E23, and contrast with the appropriate
sections in the planning reports. Another reason, of
course, for disagreement was the basic difference in
outlook and ideology between the SDO (social scientists, 'philosophers') and the Planning Team (engineers, economists, geographers, etc.).

76 Ireton (1977 transcript), p.7.
77 Reported in the 'Stevenage Gazette', 22.6.76.
78 McCombie (1977 transcript), p.6.
79 Ibid., p.8.

CHAPTER 14 PROSPECTS FOR THE NEW URBAN MANAGERS?

1 Mimeo, obtained through the SDC.
2 Booth (1976). Booth surveyed local councillors in new
   towns, and aimed at complete coverage in England.
   Questionnaires were mailed to all local councillors in
   new town wards, and he achieved a 50 per cent response
   rate in England. In his sample survey of Scotland and
   Wales he achieved a 46 per cent response rate.
3 Ibid., p.79.
4 Ibid. Of course the number of Conservatives in the
   survey would be extremely small, as the new towns tend
   to be Labour strongholds. For instance, note Booth's
   own comments (p.74):
       The average new town councillor is in his mid-
       forties; he has some experience of council
       working, having been at least a vice-chairman of a
       committee, and having been on the council for about
       four years; he has a well paid job, probably in
       engineering, research or teaching; he lives in his
       own home; and he is a member of the Labour Party.
5 Quoted in Booth, ibid., p.80.
6 Ibid., p.76.
7 Ibid., p.82.
8 The data has been obtained from an attitudinal survey
   undertaken in 1977, which is described in appendix 13.
9 One abstention, the sole Conservative respondent,
   stated: 'the Corporation should still run as they
   have specialist personnel ... and are non-political'.
10 This councillor, of course, had undertaken both roles.
11 Cousins (1975), p.18; Sklair (1975, p.286), provides
    a further sobering thought:
        The most important lesson of the struggles against
        the HFA [Housing Finance Act] for the structure of
        the Labour Party is therefore, quite unsurprising-
        ly, that without proper democratic controls and
        particularly the power of regular recall, council-

lors will generally choose the path of least resistance in controversial situations whether or not
this corresponds with the wishes of the people who
produced their election victories.

12 Cockburn (1977a).

13 Ibid., p.41.

14 Ibid., p.58. Note her remarks: 'The state's primary
role is continually *to reproduce the conditions within
which capitalist accumulation can take place.*' (p.51,
emphasis added)

15 Ibid., p.58.

16 Ibid., p.168.

17 Ibid.

18 Ibid.; cf. Cockburn (1977, p.9):
the power of Parliament gradually receded into the
civil service and to the Cabinet, more amenable to
the permanent interests of the state. Likewise, in
Lambeth and other local authorities power long ago
shifted from the Council chamber to committee and
thence, with the introduction of corporate management, to the top-level Policy Committee.

19 1.11.77, memorandum to Consultant Planner from the
SDO, ref: EZ/GM 'Du Pont (UK) Ltd', p.3, para. 4.0.

20 Both reported in the 'Stevenage Gazette', 19.1.78.

21 Reported in the 'Stevenage Gazette', 26.1.78.

22 Reported in the 'Luton Evening Post', 31.1.78.

23 'Guardian', 3.3.78; 'Stevenage Comet', 2.3.78.

24 Article by G.Champion, reported in the 'Stevenage
Gazette', 23.3.78; 'Guardian', 30.3.78. The Cruise
Missile, which has figured prominently in the Strategic Arms Limitations Talks (SALT) between the USA and
the USSR, is a long-range, accurate, low-flying (to
avoid radar detection) missile, which can carry large
nuclear warheads.

25 Proof of Annual Report for the period ending 31.3.78,
dated September, p.408.

26 Information from Housing Department, SDC. There are
some notable exclusions from the list: (a) excluding
flats and maisonettes in the town centre shopping
area. The scheme does not affect the rights of
lessees to purchase the freeholds of their houses
under the Leasehold Reform Act (1967), but any notice
thereunder should be given to the Council; (d) excluding the following premises - Bedwell, Broadhall,
The Oval, and 'Springfield' community centres; and
(f) excepting the Oval and Lonsdale filling stations.

27 Proof of AR 1978, p.405. The report includes the
following comment on p.393:
The number of staff in post at 31st March was 510 -

293 non-industrial and 217 industrial - but with staff 'transferring' to the Borough Council on 1st April and becoming redundant on 30th June 1978 this figure will reduce to 184 - 149 non-industrial and 35 industrial.... Your decision issued on 22nd March that the target date for the wind-up of the Corporation is 30th June 1980 means inevitably that the Corporation will face acute staffing problems during the next two years and we shall need to exercise considerable ingenuity to see that all our commitments are met on time. We hope that you will be able to alleviate our difficulties by arriving at a redundancy settlement which the remaining staff will regard as fair.

28 This is unlikely to be amended, in any significant sense.

29 SDC, 'Stevenage '78', p.1, para. 1.2.

30 Personal communication, E.Lenderyou, 5.1.79.

31 Cf. proof of AR (1978), on the updating exercise:
The principal factor identified by this exercise is 'employment', which is currently giving rise to concern over the high levels of unemployment (approximately 4 per cent at March 1978) ... [and] current demographic studies suggest that the town's population is *unlikely* to grow at the rates suggested in previous forward-planning exercises, but this situation *should* ease the strain on the limited land and financial resources. (p.406, emphasis added)

32 'Stevenage '78', p.2, para. 2.2.

33 For example, it was reported in the 'Stevenage Gazette', 13.4.78, that the space division of British Aerospace (ex-HSD), had landed a contract worth £75 million to build communications satellites: 'means more jobs for skilled technical staff'.

34 'Stevenage '78', p.9, para. 4.2.

35 Reported in the 'Stevenage Gazette', 6.8.78.

36 'Stevenage '78', p.9, para. 4.3.

37 Reported in the 'Stevenage Comet', 6.4.78.

38 There is an added problem, viz. that such a policy could face difficulties in relation to Structure Plan requirements (private communication, E.Lenderyou, 5.1.79).

39 'Stevenage '78', p.21, paras 11.2(a,ii); 11.2(b,ii); and p.22, para. 11.2(b,iv).

40 Ibid., p.22, para. 11.2(b,iv). The statement adds that this site was: 'identified in the 1974 expansion study as the right area for housing both environmentally and techically'.

41 Reported in the 'Stevenage Gazette', 17.11.77;   cf.
    the opinion of one of the Stevenage Councillors (in
    response to the questionnaire) on the 1974 expansion
    proposals:
        Expansion was the result of industrial pressure.
        After all with the houses readily available, in-
        dustry was able to poach the best labour from all
        over the UK, again defeating the idea of housing
        families from London.
42 Personal communication, G.Marsh (29.9.78);   cf. the
    views of Molotch (1976, p.310) on 'growth':
        the desire for growth provides the key operative
        motivation towards consensus for members of politi-
        cally mobilized local elites, however split they
        might be on other issues, and that a common inter-
        est in growth is the overriding commonality among
        important people in a given locale.
43 DOE memorandum dated 21.6.78.
44 Ibid., p.3, para. 7.
45 Reported in 'Stevenage Midweek Gazette', 11.7.78.   The
    article was titled 'A Stevenage Ghost Town - Fear'.
46 Personal communication, E.Lenderyou (5.1.79), p.1.
47 Hughes (1978 transcript), p.7.
48 Letter from the SBC's Chief Executive (CEO/U/2/REH/
    YLFH) to the Corporation, dated 1.9.78, titled
    'Employment Strategy: Formation of Employment Con-
    sultative Committee', p.1.
49 Ibid.
50 Personal communication, E.Lenderyou (5.1.79), p.2.
51 Titled 'Paper 1', and attached to the letter (CEO/U/2/
    REH/YLFH).
52 Ibid., p.2.
53 Letter (CEO/U/2/REH/pmh) dated 4 May 1978, p.1.
54 Ibid., p.1.
55 Ibid., p.1.
56 'Paper 3', attached to letter (CEO/U/2/REH/YLFH), p.2.
57 'Paper 4', attached to letter (CEO/U/2/REH/YLFH), p.3.

Bibliography

1   PRIMARY SOURCES

i   Publications and Reports of the Stevenage Development
    Corporation (all published by the Stevenage Development
    Corporation)

Part 1
SDC (1949), Stevenage Master Plan.
SDC (1949), The New Town of Stevenage.
SDC (1955), Stevenage Master Plan.
SDC (1965), Report of a Public Inquiry into Objections to
            the Proposed Expansion of the Designated Area
            of Stevenage New Town.
SDC (1966), Stevenage Master Plan, Volume 1: Planning.
SDC (1966), Stevenage Master Plan, Volume 2: Traffic
            Survey 1964-5.
SDC (1966), Stevenage Master Plan, Volume 3: Traffic
            Survey 1965-6.
SDC (1966), Stevenage Master Plan, Volume 4: Traffic
            Study, Technical Report.
SDC (1968), Survey of Children's Play.
SDC (1969), Stevenage Public Transport: Cost Benefit
            Analysis of Alternative Public/Private
            Transport Modal Split. A study by N.Lichfield
            and Associates.
SDC (1970), Under Five in a New Town: A Survey of Nursery
            and Playgroup Provision in Stevenage.
SDC (1970), Social Indices in Stevenage.
SDC (1970), Population, Employment and Housing in
            Stevenage: General Report.
SDC (1970), Population, Employment and Housing in
            Stevenage: Technical Report.
SDC (1971), Household Survey.
SDC (1972), Social Indices in Stevenage.

SDC (1972), Stevenage '72: Updating of the Master Plan: Goals and Objectives.

SDC (1972), Stevenage '72: Updating of the Master Plan: Consultation Document.

SDC (1972), Verbatim Report of Proceedings - SDC Public Meeting, 17 April 1972.

SDC (1972), Newcomers to Stevenage: Volume 1, The Process of Settling.

SDC (1972), Stevenage Public Transport Superbus Experiment.

SDC (1973), Stevenage Expansion 1973: Preliminary Consultation Document.

SDC (1973), Stevenage Expansion 1973: Volume 1, Consultation and Participation.

SDC (1973), Stevenage Expansion 1973: Volume 2, Proposals for Expansion.

SDC (1973), Stevenage Expansion 1973: Volume 3, Planning Report.

SDC (1973), Stevenage Expansion 1973: Volume 4, Transportation and Drainage.

SDC (1974), Stevenage '74: Expansion for Local Needs: Volume 1, Preliminary Report on Local Needs.

SDC (1974), Stevenage '74: Expansion for Local Needs: Volume 2, Corporation Proposals for Expansion.

SDC (1975), Stevenage '74: Expansion for Local Needs: Volume 3, Public Consultation.

SDC (1975), A Stevenage Chronicle. Written by J.Lenton.

SDC (1976), Stevenage '74: Expansion for Local Needs: Volume 4, Planning Report.

SDC (1976), Stevenage '74: Expansion for Local Needs: Volume 5, Transportation, Drainage and Agriculture.

SDC (1976), Stevenage Household Survey.

SDC (1977), Stevenage '74: Expansion for Local Needs: Volume 6, Draft Designation Order and Public Inquiry.

SDC (1978), Stevenage '78: Updating of the Master Plan 1966 (Summary of Proposals for Consultation), 3rd Draft.

Part 2   Reports and papers of the Social Development Office (SDO)

(a) Employment papers (research, information and monitoring series)

SDO (1976), E1: 1976 Employment Base.

SDO (1976), E2: Possible Consequences of the Structure Plan.

SDO (1976), E3: Employment Needs of School-Leavers.

SDO (1976), E3A: Employment Needs of School-Leavers.
SDO (1976), E4: Analysis of Occupations.
SDO (1976), E5: Unemployment and Vacancies.
SDO (1977), E6: Employment 1976 Situation.
SDO (1977), E7: SBC Employment Meeting.
SDO (1977), E8: Stevenage Unemployment.
SDO (1977), E9: Department of Employment, Unemployment
          Statistics.
SDO (1977), E10: Progress Report.
SDO (1977), E11: Trends in Female Employment.
SDO (1977), E12: Trends in Service Employment.
SDO (1977), E13: Economic Activity Rates.
SDO (1977), E14: A Planning Context: Part 1, Appraisal of
          Previous Stevenage Employment Studies.
SDO (1977), E15: A Planning Context: Part 2, Scope of
          Employment Studies in Master Plan Review.
SDO (1977), E16: Labour Supply 1981 and 1986, Initial
          Projection.
SDO (1977), E17: Diversification of Employment.
SDO (1978), E18: Analysis of Commuting Patterns.
SDO (1978), E19: A Planning Context: Part 3, Wider Issues.
SDO (1978), E21: Short Term Needs and Long Term
          Implications.
SDO (1978), E1P1: Youth Opportunities Programme.
SDO (1978), E13A: Economic Activity Rates, Revision of
          Projections.
SDO (1978), E16: Supplement, Labour Supply.
SDO (1978), E23: Diversification of Employment.
SDO (1978), Employment Studies: Technical Reports.

(b) Population papers
SDO (1976), P1: The 1976 Base Population.
SDO (1976), P2: Preliminary Projections of Base
          Populations.
SDO (1976), P3: The 1976 Base Population: Further
          Thoughts.
SDO (1977), P4: Fertility.
SDO (1977), P5: Mortality.
SDO (1977), P6: Projections.
SDO (1978), Population Studies: Technical Report.
SDO (1978), MC2: Employment, Population and Household
          Formation, Short Term and Long Term
          Implications.

ii Publications and reports of the Stevenage Urban
    District Council (all published by the SUDC)

SUDC (1963), Observations upon the Expansion of Stevenage.
SUDC (1969), Fairlands Valley Park and Road Nine.

SUDC (1971), Stevenage: Advisory Report to Stevenage Urban
              District Council. Prepared by Llewellyn-
              Davies and Associates.
SUDC (1973), A Public Opinion Survey on the Proposed
              Expansion of Stevenage.

iii Other sources of documentation from the Stevenage
     Development Corporation, Stevenage Urban District
     Council, and the Stevenage Borough Council (Note:
     Memoranda, letters, and press releases are contained
     in the text)

SUDC (1945-6), Minutes of the Town Planning and
                Development Committee Meetings.
SUDC (1946),   Minutes of the New Town Inquiry Committee
                Meetings.
SDC (1947-78), Minutes of the Stevenage Development
                Corporation Board Meetings, including the
                Housing Management Quarterly Minutes.
SDC (1958-68), 'Purpose', a quarterly booklet for tenants.
SBC (1975-8), 'Forum', the quarterly magazine of the
                Stevenage Borough Council.

iv Documentation from the 'Protest organisations' (Note:
    Memoranda, letters, and press releases are contained
    in the text)

SVA (1968),   The Amenity Aspect of Fairlands Valley as
                a Park.
CASE (1973-6), Minutes of the CASE Executive Committee
                Meetings.
CASE (1973-6), Minutes of the CASE Council Meetings.
SVA (1973-6), Minutes of the SVA Committee Meetings.
NFU (1975),   New Towns in England and Wales.
NFU (1976),   Updating and Development of the 'Strategic
                Plan for the South East': A Statement of
                the Views of the National Farmers' Union.

v Interview material (See Appendix 1: personal
   communications appear in the notes)

Balchin, J. (1976)
Bowes-Lyon, S. (1977)
Burr, C. (1977)
Denington, E. (1977)
Halls, S. (1977)
Hubble, J. (1977)
Hughes, G. (1978)
Ireton, P. (1977)

Johnson, I. (1977)
Lenderyou, E. (1976)
McCombie, T. (1977)
Powell, M. (1977)
Williams, S. (1977)
Wood, C. (1977)

vi   Miscellaneous

(a) Statements of proof given at the Stevenage public
    inquiry, 30 March to 26 April 1976, in chronological
    order

Mr James Marlow	Assistant Secretary, New Towns Directorate, DOE.
Mr Michael Ogden, QC	Counsel for the SDC.
Mr Charles Fay	Assistant to Mr Ogden, QC.
Mr L.G.Vincent	SDC Adviser on Town Planning.
Mr J.A.Balchin	General Manager of the SDC.
Mr D.M.Rixson	Adviser to the SDC on Town Planning.
Mr K.A.Hotchkiss	Chartered Engineer concerned with Surface Water Drainage.
Mr E.W.Crisp	Chartered Engineer, Adviser to the SDC on Foul Drainage.
Mr D.C.Hinge	Chartered Chemist for Lee Division, Thames Water Authority.
Mr J.L.Dakers	Chartered Engineer for Lee Division, Thames Water Authority.
Mr A.Morton	Chartered Engineer, Adviser to SDC on Traffic and Transportation.
Mr R.B.Lenthall	Chartered Engineer employed by SDC.
Mr M.A.B.Boddington	Managing Director of Rural Planning Services, Adviser to SDC on Agricultural Aspects.
Mr R.E.Hughes	Chief Executive Officer, SBC.
Mr G.L.Hughes	Chairman of SIEG.
Mr R.Jameson	Solicitor, introducing evidence for Hertfordshire County Council.
Mr G.C.Steeley	Deputy County Planning Officer, Hertfordshire County Council.
Mr D.A.Woolston	Solicitor, North Hertfordshire District Council.
Mr B.G.Hull	Planning Officer to the North

	Hertfordshire District Council.
Miss C.Wood	Aston Parish Council.
Mr C.Bardswell	Walkern Parish Council.
Lord Colville	Presenting evidence for the Hertfordshire Society, CASE, and the Graveley and Weston Parish Councils.
Lt.Col.J.C.Thomson	Chairman of the Hertfordshire Society.
Mr J.W.Franklin	Graveley Parish Council.
Mrs L.Pugh	Weston Parish Council.
Mr S.T.McCombie	Chairman of CASE.
Mr E.F.Dearman	Individual resident of Knebworth.
Mr J.W.J.Wallace-Jarvis	Solicitor for East Hertfordshire District Council.
Mr R.Beacham	Director of Planning, East Hertfordshire District Council.
Mr G.Rawlings	White Farm, Aston End.
Mrs M.Powell	Chairman of CAUSE.
The Rev.A.Marshall-Taylor	Rector of Graveley.
Mr R.J.Mills	Individual resident of Aston.
Mr H.W.J.Moss	Brook Hall Farm, Aston End.
Mrs C.V.Bleasdale	Individual resident of Aston.
Mr D.Hedge	Individual resident of Aston.
Councillor A.S.Joy	Welwyn Parish Council.
Mr P.Bugge	Individual resident of Walkern.
Mr E.J.Moreham	Individual resident of Aston End.
Mr Hellard, QC	Counsel for the NFU.
Mr R.Warner-Smith	Farming firm of J.W.Smith and Sons.
Mr B.Wakely	Rooks Nest Farm, Walkern.
Mr G.W.Beeson, FRICS	Evidence on behalf of Messrs Clark Bros.
Mr D.Walmsley	Solicitor, appearing for J.W.Smith and Sons.
Mr M.J.R.Willis, FRICS	Evidence for the Trustees of F.W.Allen.
Mr M.J.Hubble	SVA.
Mr I.A.Cuthill	SVA.
Professor R.S.Scorer	Department of Mathematics, Imperial College.
Mr R.J.Butcher	Solicitor for Mr W.H.Foks, Aston End.

Mr P.Perks, FRICS   Partner of J.R.Eve and Son.
Mrs P.Porter   President of Aston Women's
                          Institute.

(b) Newspapers
'Hertfordshire Express'
'Luton Evening Post'
'Stevenage Comet'
'Stevenage Gazette'
'Stevenage Midweek Gazette'

2 REFERENCES RELATED TO NEW TOWNS

ALDRIDGE, M. (1977), The British New and Expanded Towns:
Hail and Farewell?, 'International Journal of Urban and
Regional Research', vol.1(3), Oct., pp.520-31.
ALONSO, W. (1970), What Are New Towns For?, 'Urban
Studies', vol.7, pp.37-55.
APGAR, M. (ed.) (1976), 'New Perspectives on Community
Development', McGraw-Hill, London.
ASH, J. (1974), The Progress of New Towns in Israel, 'Town
Planning Review', vol.45(4), Oct., pp.387-401.
BAER, M.A. (1977), The Development of Political Interest
Groups in a Local Environment, paper presented at the
American Political Science Association meeting, September,
Washington, USA.
BAER, M.A. (1978), Social Facets of Organizational
Development in New Towns, mimeo.
BAER, M.A. (1979), Political Participation in New Towns,
in 'British Journal of Political Science', (forthcoming).
BARR, J. (1965), New Towns as Anti-Ghettos?, 'New
Society', 1 April, pp.5-6.
BOER, J.C. de and GREENDALE, A. (1974), 'Are New Towns for
Lower Income Americans Too?', Praeger, New York.
BOLWELL, L., CLARKE, B. and STOPPARD, D. (1969), Social
Class in New Towns: A Comment, 'Urban Studies', vol.6(1),
Feb., pp.93-6.
BOOTH, S. (1976), Councillors' Attitudes Toward New Town
Development Corporations, 'Policy and Politics', vol.4,
pp.71-83.
BOOTH, S. (1978), An Image Tarnished: The New Towns Now,
'New Society', 14 Oct., pp.67-9.
BULL, D.A. (1967), New Town and Town Expansion Schemes,
'Town Planning Review', vol.38(2), July, pp.103-15.
CORDEN, C. (1977), 'Planned Cities: New Towns in Britain
and America', Sage, London.
CREESE, W.L. (1966), 'The Search for Environment: The
Garden City - Before and After', Yale University Press,
New Haven, Conn.

CRESSWELL, P. (1974), 'The New Town Goal of Self Containment', Open University, Milton Keynes.

CRESSWELL, P. (1976), The Land Take of New Towns, pp. 67-86, in R.Thomas (ed.) (1976).

CRESSWELL, P. and THOMAS, R. (1972), Employment and Population Balance, pp.66-79, in Evans (ed.) (1972).

CULLINGWORTH, J.B. and KARN, V. (1968), 'The Ownership and Management of Housing in the New Towns', HMSO, London.

DANIELS, P.W. (1976), Office Employment in New Towns, 'Town Planning Review', vol.47(3), July, pp.209-25.

DEAKIN, N. and UNGERSON, C. (1977), 'Leaving London: Planned Mobility and the Inner City', Heinemann, London.

DENINGTON, E. (1972), New Towns for Whom?. pp.142-9 in Evans (ed.) (1972).

DOE (1978), The New Towns, DOE, London.

DUFF, A.C. (1961), 'Britain's New Towns: An Experiment in Living', Pall Mall Press, London.

EVANS, H. (ed.) (1972), 'New Towns', Charles Knight, London.

FIELD, D. (1968), New Town and Expansion Schemes, 'Town Planning Review', vol.39(3), Oct., pp.196-217.

GILES, A.K. (1976), The Impact of Urban Development on Agriculture: a Case Study of Milton Keynes, pp.53-66, in R.Thomas (ed.) (1976).

GRANT, W.P. (1970), Rancorous Community Conflict: A Study of Political Leaders in Two Scottish New Towns, 'International Review of Community Development', vol.23, pp.201-18.

HERAUD, B. (1966), The New Towns and London's Housing Problems, 'Urban Studies', vol.3, pp.8-21.

HERAUD, B. (1968), Social Class and the New Towns, 'Urban Studies', vol.4(1), pp.35-8.

HERAUD, B. (1975), The New Towns: A Philosophy of Community, pp.39-57 in Leonard (ed.) (1975).

HERAUD, B. (1976), The Development of Community in the New Towns, pp.87-107, in R.Thomas (ed.) (1976).

HMSO (1946), Interim Report of the New Towns Committee, Cmnd 6759, HMSO, London.

HMSO (1946), Second Interim Report of the New Towns Committee, Cmnd 6794, HMSO, London.

HMSO (1946), New Towns Committee Final Report, Cmnd 6876, HMSO, London.

HMSO (1974), Second Report from the Expenditure Committee (Session 1974), New Towns, vol.II, Minutes of evidence (HC 305-11) and vol.III, Appendices (HC 305-111), HMSO, London.

HMSO (1975), Thirteenth Report of the Expenditure Committee (Session 1974/75), New Towns, vol.I, Report (HC 616-I), vol.IV, Minutes of evidence and Appendices (HC 616-IV), vol.V, Index (HC 616-V), HMSO, London.

HUDSON, R. (1976), 'New Towns in the North East of England', North East Area Study: University of Durham.

HUSSAIN, J. (1977), Londoners who Left, 'New Society', vol.41(770), 7 July, pp.17-18.

KARN, V. (1970), 'Stevenage Housing Survey', University of Birmingham Centre for Urban and Regional Studies, Occasional Paper 10.

LICHFIELD, N. and WENDT, P.F. (1969), Six English New Towns: A Financial Analysis, 'Town Planning Review', vol. 4(3), pp.283-315.

LONDON COUNTY COUNCIL (1961), 'The Planning of a New Town: Data and Design Based on a Study for a New Town of 100,000 at Hook, Hampshire', LCC, London.

LUTTRELL, W.F. (1972), The Growth of Industry, pp.80-7, in Evans (ed.) (1972).

MARCH, L. (1972), Why Have New Towns?. 'New Society', 8 June, pp.505-8.

MERLIN, P. (1971), 'New Towns', Methuen, London.

MILNE, R. (1973), Whose Town is This Anyway?, 'Surveyor', 3 Aug., pp.20-4.

MOSS, J.A. (1968), New and Expanded Towns - Demographic Characteristics of Newcomers, 'Town Planning Review', vol. 39(2), pp.117-40.

MULLAN, R.G. (1978), Public Inquiries as Rituals?, 'Heriot-Watt Journal of Town and Country Planning', Jan., pp.4-9.

NICHOLSON, J.H. (1961), 'New Communities in Britain', NCSSL, London.

OGILVY, A.A. (1968), The Self-Contained New Town, 'Town Planning Review', vol.39(1), April, pp.38-55.

ORLANS, H. (1952), 'Stevenage: A Sociological Study', Routledge & Kegan Paul, London.

OSBORN, F.J. and WHITTICK, A. (1969), 'The New Towns', Leonard Hill, London.

PETERSON, W. (1968), The Ideological Origins of Britain's New Towns, 'Journal of the American Institute of Planners', vol.34(3), pp.160-70.

PILGRIM, B. (1969), Choice of House in a New Town, 'Regional Studies', vol.3(3), pp.325-32.

PORZECANSKI, M. de, CHEESMAN, R. and LINDSAY, W. (1972), New Towns: the Evolution of Planning Criteria, Working Paper No.64 of the Centre for Land Use and Form Studies, University of Cambridge.

POTTER, S. (1976), 'Transport and New Towns, Vol.2', Open University, Milton Keynes.

PURDOM, C.B. (1949), 'The Building of Satellite Towns: A Contribution to the Study of Town Development and Regional Planning', J.M.Dent, London.

ROBINSON, A.J. (1975), 'Economics and New Towns', Praeger, New York.

ROBSON, W.A. (1957), The New Towns: Their Future Ownership, 'TCPA Journal', Jan., pp.14-19.

RODERICK, W.P. (1971), The London New Towns, 'Town Planning Review', vol.42(4), pp.323-42.

RODWIN, L. (1956), 'The British New Towns Policy', Harvard University, Cambridge, Mass.

ROWE, A.H. (1973), Stevenage - A New Concept, 'Built Environment', Aug., pp.464-6.

SCHAFFER, F. (1970), 'The New Town Story', Paladin, London.

SELF, P. (1972), Introduction: New Towns in the Modern World, pp.1-11, in Evans (ed.) (1972).

SHARP, E. (1972), The Government's Role, pp.40-5, in Evans (ed.) (1972).

SIMMIE, J.M. (1976), New Towns Versus Old Towns, pp.7-29, in Thomas (ed.) (1976).

SMOOKLER, H.V. (1976), 'Economic Integration in New Communities', Ballinger, Cambridge, Mass.

STRANZ, W. (1977), The Education of a Secretary of State?, 'TCPA Journal', June, pp.292-5.

THOMAS, R. (1969), 'London's New Towns: A Study of Self-Contained and Balanced Communities', PEP Broadsheet No. 510, London.

THOMAS, R. (1969a), 'Aycliffe to Cumbernauld: A Study of Seven New Towns in Their Regions', PEP Broadsheet No.516, London.

THOMAS, R. (ed.) (1976), 'Perspectives on New Town Development', proceedings of a conference organised by the New Towns Study Unit and the Regional Studies Association at the Open University, Nov. 1975, Open University, Milton Keynes.

THOMAS, R. (1977), 'Commuting Flows and the Growth of London's New Towns, 1951-71', Open University, Milton Keynes.

THOMAS, R. and CRESSWELL, P. (1973), 'The New Town Idea', for the Open University, Urban Development Unit 26, Open University, Milton Keynes.

THOMAS, W. (1972), The Management Task, pp.46-54, in Evans (ed.) (1972).

TIMBERLAKE, H.L.P. (1976), New Towns and Building Societies, 'Building Societies Institute Quarterly', Oct., pp.124-6.

TOLLEY, R.S. (1972), Telford New Town: Conception and Reality in West Midlands, 'Town Planning Review', vol. 43(4), pp.343-61.

TRIMBLE, N. (1973), Industry in the New Towns of Great Britain, 'TCPA Journal', Jan., pp.219-23.

WAIDE, L. (1973), Expanded Towns: The Background, 'Built Environment', March, pp.136-8.

WEDDERBURN, D. (1964), 'White Collar Redundancy',
University of Cambridge, Department of Applied Economics,
Occasional Paper.
WILLMOTT, P. (1962), Housing Density and Town Design in a
New Town: A Pilot Study at Stevenage, 'Town Planning
Review', vol.33, July, pp.115-27.
WILLMOTT, P. (1964), East Kilbride and Stevenage: Some
Social Characteristics of a Scottish and an English New
Town, 'Town Planning Review', vol.XXXIV, Jan., pp.307-16.
WILLMOTT, P. (1967), Social Research and New Communities,
'American Institute of Planners', vol.33, pp.387-97.
WIRZ, H.M. (1975), 'Social Aspects of Planning in New
Towns', Saxon House, Farnborough.

3   GENERAL REFERENCES

ABRAMS, P. (1978), Introduction, pp.1-9, in Abrams and
Wrigley (eds) (1978).
ABRAMS, P. (1978a), Towns and Economic Growth: Some
Theories and Problems, pp.9-33, in Abrams and Wrigley
(eds) (1978).
ABRAMS, P. and WRIGLEY, E.A. (eds) (1978), 'Towns in
Societies: Essays in Economic History and Historical
Sociology', Cambridge University Press.
ALFORD, R.R. (1973), The Bureaucratization of Urban
Government, pp.263-80, in Gordon (ed.) (1973).
ALLAUN, F. (1972), 'No Place Like Home', André Deutsch,
London.
ALLEN, D. (1977), Ministers and Their Mandarins,
'Government and Opposition', vol.12(2), Summer, pp.135-50.
ALLENSWORTH, D.T. (1975), 'The Political Realities of
Urban Planning', Routledge & Kegan Paul, London.
AMBROSE, P. and COLENUTT, B. (1975), 'The Property
Machine', Penguin, Harmondsworth.
ANDERSON, S. (ed.) (1968), 'Planning for Diversity and
Choice', Harvard University Press, Cambridge, Mass.
ARNSTEIN, S.R. (1969), A Ladder of Citizen Participation,
'Journal of the American Institute of Planners', July,
pp.216-24.
BACHRACH, P. and BARATZ, M.S. (1962), Two Faces of Power,
'American Political Science Review', Dec., pp.918-48.
BACHRACH, P. and BARATZ, M.S. (1963), Decisions and Non-
Decisions: An Analytic Framework, 'American Political
Science Review', Sept., pp.632-42.
BAILEY, J. (1975), 'Social Theory for Planning', Routledge
& Kegan Paul, London.
BAILEY, R. (1977), 'The Homeless and Empty Houses',
Penguin, Harmondsworth.
BALDOCK, P. (1977), Why Community Action? The Historical

Origins of the Radical Trend in British Community Work,
'Community Development Journal', vol.12(2), pp.68-75.
BALDWIN, J. and BOTTOMS, A.E. (1976), 'The Urban Criminal:
A Study in Sheffield', Tavistock, London.
BANFIELD, E.C. and WILSON, J.Q. (1963), 'City Politics',
Vintage Books, New York.
BARKER, A. and KEATING, M. (1977), Public Spirits: Amenity
Societies and Others, pp.143-63, in Crouch (ed.) (1977a).
BATLEY, R. (1972), An Explanation of Non-Participation in
Planning, 'Policy and Politics', vol.1(2), pp.95-114.
BAUM, H. (1977), Advertisement, in 'Planners Network',
vol.9, June.
BAXTER, R. (1972), The Working Class and Labour Politics,
'Political Studies', vol.20, pp.97-107.
BELL, C. (1978), Studying the Locally Powerful: Personal
Reflections on a Research Career, pp.14-41 in Bell and
Encel (eds) (1978).
BELL, C. and NEWBY, H. (eds) (1977), 'Doing Sociological
Research', George Allen & Unwin, London.
BELL, C. and ENCEL, S. (eds) (1978), 'Inside the Whale:
Ten Personal Accounts of Social Research', Pergamon,
Oxford.
BELL, K. (1973), Disequilibrium in Welfare, Inaugural
Lecture Series, University of Newcastle on Tyne.
BENINGTON, J. (1976), 'Local Government Becomes Big
Business', Community Development Project, London.
BERESFORD, M. (1967), 'New Towns of the Middle Ages',
Lutterworth, London.
BERGER, P.L. (1977), 'Pyramids of Sacrifice', Penguin,
Harmondsworth.
BEYLE, T.L. and LATHROP, G.T. (1970), 'Planning and
Politics', Odyssey Press, New York.
BEYRON, V.H. and HARRISON, J.E. (1962), 'The Political
Significance of the British Agricultural Vote', University
of Exeter Press.
BIAREZ, S., BOUCHET, C., de BOISBERRANGER, D., MINGASSON,
C., MONZIES, M.-L. and POUYET, C. (1973), 'Institution
communale et pouvoir politique', Mouton, Paris.
BLAIR, T.L. (1973), 'The Poverty of Planning', Macdonald,
London.
BLAIR, T.L. (1974), 'The International Urban Crisis',
Paladin, London.
BLUNDEN, J., BROOK, C., EDGE, G. and HAY, A. (1973),
'Regional Analysis and Development', Harper & Row, London.
BOADEN, N. and WALKER, R. (1976), Sample Surveys and
Public Participation, 'DOE Linked Research Project into
Public Participation in Structure Planning', IRP10.
BODDY, M. (1976), Building Societies and Owner-Occupation,
pp.30-44 in Conference of Socialist Economists (1976).

BONNIER, F. (1972), Les Pratiques des Associations de Quartier et les Processus de 'Récupération', 'Espaces et Sociétés', Nos 6-7, July-Oct.
BORJA, J. (1977), Urban Movements in Spain, pp.187-213 in Harloe (ed.) (1977).
BOURNE, L.S. (1975), 'Urban Systems', Clarendon Press, Oxford.
BRAVERMAN, H. (1974), 'Labor and Monopoly Capital', Monthly Review Press, New York.
BREWSTER, B. and BREWSTER, M. (1978), Further Notes on 'the Search for Democracy': Professional Competence and Community Work, paper presented at the Sociologists in Polytechnics Conference, Newcastle upon Tyne Polytechnic, March.
BROADBENT, T.A. (1977), 'Planning and Profit in the Urban Economy', Methuen, London.
BROADY, M. (1966), Social Theory in Architectural Design, 'Arena', pp.149-54.
BROADY, M. (1974), Social Planning and Voluntary Associations, mimeo.
BROADY, M. (1975), Planning for Community and Social Justice, mimeo.
BROWN, A.A. and NEWBERGER, E. (eds) (1977), 'Internal Migration: A Comparative Perspective', Academic Press, London.
BUSFIELD, J. and PADDON, M. (1977), 'Thinking About Children', Cambridge University Press.
BUTLER, D. and SLOMAN, A. (1975), 'British Political Facts: 1900-75', Macmillan, London.
BUTTELL, F.H. and FLINN, W.L. (1976), Environmental Politics, 'Sociological Quarterly', vol.17, pp.477-90.
BUXTON, M. and CRAVEN, E. (1976), 'The Uncertain Future: Demographic Change and Social Policy', Centre for Studies in Social Policy, London.
CARLEN, P. (1976), Magistrates' Courts: A Game Theoretic Analysis, 'Sociological Review', vol.23(2), pp.347-79.
CARTER, E. (1962), 'The Future of London', Penguin, Harmondsworth.
CASTELLS, M. (1973), 'Luttes urbaines', Mouton, Paris.
CASTELLS, M. (1975), Urban Contradictions and Political Processes: A Case Study (Part 1 of a paper titled 'Toward a Political Urban Sociology'), mimeo.
CASTELLS, M. (1975a), Advanced Capitalism, Collective Consumption, and Contradictions: New Sources of Inequality and New Models for Change, pp.175-97 in Lindberg et al. (eds) (1975).
CASTELLS, M. (1976), Urban Sociology and Urban Politics: From a Critique to New Trends of Research, pp.291-301 in Walton and Masotti (eds) (1976).

CASTELLS, M. (1976a), The Wild City, 'Kapitalistate', vols 4 and 5 (double issue), pp.2-31.

CASTELLS, M. (1976b), Theoretical Propositions for an Experimental Study of Urban Social Movements, pp.147-73 in Pickvance (ed.) (1976).

CASTELLS, M. (1976c), Theory and Ideology in Urban Sociology, pp.60-84 in Pickvance (ed.) (1976).

CASTELLS, M. (1977), The Class Struggle and Urban Contradictions: The Emergence of Urban Protest Movements in Advanced Capitalist Societies, pp.40-7 in Cowley et al. (eds) (1977).

CASTELLS, M. (1977a), 'The Urban Question: A Marxist Analysis', Edward Arnold, London.

CASTELLS, M. (1978), 'City, Class and Power', Macmillan, London.

CATANESE, A.J. (1974), 'Planners and Local Politics: Impossible Dreams', Sage, London.

CAULCOTT, T. (1977), The DOE: Genesis of a Giant, 'Municipal Review', No.575, pp.237-65.

CHERRY, G.E. (1970), 'Town Planning in its Social Context', Leonard Hill, London.

CHERRY, G.E. (1972), 'Urban Change and Planning', Foulis, Henley on Thames.

CHERRY, G.E. (ed.) (1974), 'Urban Planning Problems', Leonard Hill, London.

CHISHOLM, M. and MANNERS, G. (eds) (1971), 'Spatial Problems of the British Economy', Cambridge University Press.

CHISHOLM, M. and MANNERS, G. (1971a), Geographical Space, pp.1-24 in Chisholm and Manners (eds) (1971).

CLARK, C. and JONES, G.T. (1971), The Demand for Housing, Centre for Environmental Studies, University Working Paper 11.

CLEGG, S. (1975), 'Power, Rule and Domination', Routledge & Kegan Paul, London.

COATES, D. (1975), 'The Labour Party and the Struggle for Socialism', Cambridge University Press.

COCKBURN, C. (1974), Urban Government, pp.213-42 in Cherry (ed.) (1974).

COCKBURN, C. (1977), Local Government as Local State: Its Part in Capitalist Reproduction, Centre for Environmental Studies Workshop, unpublished paper.

COCKBURN, C. (1977a), 'The Local State: Management of Cities and People', Pluto Press, London.

COHEN, A.P. (1975), 'The Management of Myths', Manchester University Press.

COIT, K. (1978), Local Action, Not Citizen Participation, pp.297-311 in Tabb and Sawers (eds) (1978).

COLENUTT, B. (1975), Behind the Property Lobby, pp.123-33 in Conference of Socialist Economists (1975).

COMMUNITY DEVELOPMENT PROJECT (1976), 'Whatever Happened to Council Housing?'. Community Development Project, London.

COMMUNITY DEVELOPMENT PROJECT (1977), 'The Costs of Industrial Change', Community Development Project, London.

CONFERENCE OF SOCIALIST ECONOMISTS (1975), 'Political Economy and the Housing Question', Conference of Socialist Economists, London.

CONFERENCE OF SOCIALIST ECONOMISTS (1976), 'Housing and Class in Britain', Conference of Socialist Economists, London.

COPPOCK, J.T. and SEWELL, W.R.D. (eds) (1976), 'Spatial Dimensions of Public Policy', Pergamon, Oxford.

COUNTER INFORMATION SERVICE - COMMUNITY DEVELOPMENT PROJECT (1976), 'Cutting the Welfare State (Who Profits?)', Community Development Project, London.

COUSINS, P.F. (1975), The Nature of Local Democracy, 'London Review of Public Administration', No.8 (Winter), pp.7-21.

COWLEY, J., KAYE, A., MAYO, M. and THOMPSON, M. (eds) (1977), 'Community or Class Struggle', Stage One, London.

COX, P. (1975), 'Demography', Cambridge University Press.

CRAIG, F.W.S. (1971), 'Britain Votes 1: Parliamentary Election Results 1974-77', Political Reference Publications, Chichester.

CRAVEN, E. (1978), Issues on Representation, pp.242-67 in Davies and Hall (eds) (1978).

CROSLAND, C.A.R. (1963), 'The Future of Socialism', Jonathan Cape, London.

CROSSMAN, R. (1975), 'The Diaries of a Cabinet Minister' (vol.1), Hamish Hamilton and Jonathan Cape, London.

CROUCH, C. (1977), 'Class Conflict and the Industrial Relations Crisis', Heinemann Educational Books, London.

CROUCH, C. (ed.) (1977a), 'British Sociology Yearbook: Vol.3 Participation in Politics', Croom Helm, London.

CROWLEY, R.W. (1977), Population Distribution, pp.255-77 in Brown and Neuberger (eds) (1977).

CULLINGWORTH, J.B. (1972), 'Town and Country Planning in Britain', George Allen & Unwin, London.

DAMER, S. and HAGUE, C. (1971), Public Participation in Planning: A Review, 'Town Planning Review', vol.42(3), July, pp.217-33.

DAVIDOFF, P. (1965), Advocacy and Pluralism in Planning, 'Journal of the American Institute of Planners', Nov., pp.331-8.

DAVIES, J.G. (1972), 'The Evangelistic Bureaucrat', Tavistock, London.

DAVIES, J.G. (1977), Inside Local Government, 'New Society', No.788, 1 Sept., pp.438-9.

DAVIES, R. and HALL, P. (eds) (1978), 'Issues in Urban Society', Penguin, Harmondsworth.

DEAR, M. (1977), Locational Factors in the Demand for Mental Health, 'Economic Geography', vol.53(3), pp.223-40.

DEARLOVE, J. (1973), 'The Politics of Policy in Local Government', Cambridge University Press.

DENNIS, N. (1968), The Popularity of the Neighbourhood Community Idea, pp.74-92 in Pahl (ed.) (1968).

DENNIS, N. (1970), 'People and Planning', Faber & Faber, London.

DENNIS, N. (1972), 'Public Participation and Planners' Blight', Faber & Faber, London.

DENNIS, N. (1973), Half-Beating City Hall: The Duke Street Story (with introduction), mimeo.

DENNIS, N. (1975), Discussant, pp.219-32 in Harloe (ed.) (1975).

DENNIS, N. (1975a), Community Action, Quasi-Community Action and Anti-Community Action, pp.143-63 in Leonard (ed.) (1975).

DENNIS, N. (1977), In Dispraise of Political Trust, pp. 15-25 in Sewell and Coppock (eds) (1977).

DENNIS, R.D. (1976), The Decline of Manufacturing Employment in Greater London 1966-74, paper read at Inner City Conference, York University, Sept.

DEPARTMENT OF THE ENVIRONMENT (1972), Circular 52/72 DOE - Town and Country Planning Act 1971, Part II, Development Plan Proposals, Publicity and Public Participation.

DIAMOND, D. and McLOUGHLIN, J.B. (eds) (1977), Progress in Planning, vol.7(1).

DI MAIO, J. (1974), 'Soviet Urban Housing', Praeger, New York.

DOMHOFF, G.W. (ed.) (1975), New Directions in Power Structure Research, 'Insurgent Sociologist', vol.V(III), Spring.

DONNISON, D. (1975), The Age of Innocence is Past: Some Ideas About Urban Research and Planning, 'Urban Studies', vol.12, pp.263-72.

DRAPER, P. (1977), 'The Creation of the DOE', Civil Service Studies 4, HMSO, London.

DREIER, P. (1975), Power Structures and Power Struggles, pp.233-44 in Domhoff (ed.) (1975).

DUNCAN, G. and LUKES, S. (1963), The New Democracy, 'Political Studies', vol.XI (June), pp.156-78.

DUNCAN, S.S. (1977), The Housing Question and the Structure of the Housing Market, 'Journal of Social Policy', vol.6(4), pp.385-412.

DUNLEAVY, P. (1977), Methodological Sectarianism in Urban Sociology, 'International Journal of Urban and Regional Research', vol.1(1), pp.185-91.

DUNLEAVY, P. (1978), Protest and Quiescence in Urban Politics: A Critique of Some Pluralist and Structuralist Myths, paper read at the Centre for Environmental Studies Conference, York University, 1977, and pp.162-202 in Harloe (ed.) (1978).

ELDREDGE, W.H. (1967), 'Taming Megalopolis' (vol.1), Anchor Books, New York.

ELKIN, S.L. (1974), 'Politics and Land Use Planning: The London Experience', Cambridge University Press.

ELSTER, J. (1978), 'Logic and Society', John Wiley, Chichester.

ENCEL, S. (1978), In Search of Power, pp.41-66 in Bell and Encel (eds) (1978).

ENGLISH, J., MADIGAN, R. and NORMAN, P. (1976), 'Slum Clearance', Croom Helm, London.

ESLAND, G. (1976), Professions and Professionalism, pp. 11-51 in Open University (1976).

EVANS, A. (1976), Economic Influences on Social Mix, 'Urban Studies', vol.13, pp.247-60.

EVERSLEY, D. (1973), 'The Planner in Society', Faber & Faber, London.

EVERSLEY, D. (1977), The Inner Area Studies: London, 'Built Environment', Sept., pp.172-4.

FAGENCE, M. (1977), 'Citizen Participation in Planning', Pergamon, Oxford.

FLETCHER, R. (ed.) (1974), 'The Science of Society and the Unity of Mankind', Heinemann Educational Books, London.

FOOT, M. (1975), 'Aneurin Bevan' (vol.1), Paladin, London.

FRIEDMAN, J. and HUDSON, B. (1974), Knowledge and Action: A Guide to Planning Theory, 'Journal of the American Institute of Planners', pp.21-54.

FRIEND, J.K., POWER, J.M. and YEWLETT, C.J.L. (1974), 'Public Planning: The Inter-Corporate Dimension', Tavistock, London.

GARRARD, J.A. (1978), The History of Local Political Power - Some Suggestions for Analysis, 'Political Studies', vol.XXV(2), pp.252-69.

GAVENTA, J.P. (1975), Power and Powerlessness: Quiescence and Rebellion in an Appalachian Valley, unpublished D Phil thesis, Oxford University.

GERSHUNY, J.I. (1977), Post-Industrial Society: The Myth of the Service Economy, 'Futures, the Journal of Forecasting and Planning', vol.9(2), April, pp.103-14.

GILL, O. (1977), 'Luke Street', Macmillan, London.

GLASGOW MEDIA GROUP (1976), Bad News, 'Theory and Society', vol.3(3), pp.339-65.

GLASS, R. (1948), 'The Social Background of a Plan', Routledge & Kegan Paul, London.

GLASS, R. (1955), Urban Sociology in Great Britain: A Trend Report, 'Current Sociology', vol.4, pp.5-19.

GLASS, R. (1976), Urban Images, pp.349-67 in Harrison and
Gibson (eds) (1976).
GLYN, A. and SUTCLIFFE, B. (1972), 'British Capitalism,
Workers and the Profits Squeeze', Penguin, Harmondsworth.
GOFFMAN, Erving (1974), 'Frame Analysis', Penguin,
Harmondsworth.
GOODEY, B. (1974), 'Images of Place: Essays on
Environmental Perception, Communication and Education',
University of Birmingham, Centre for Urban and Regional
Studies, Occasional Paper No.30.
GOODMAN, R. (1972), 'After the Planners', Penguin,
Harmondsworth.
GORDON, D.N. (ed.) (1973), 'Social Change and Urban
Politics', Prentice Hall, Englewood Cliffs, N.J.
GORDON, I. and WHITELEY, P. (1977), The Political Ideology
of Labour Councillors, 'Policy and Politics', vol.5, pp.
1-25.
GRIPAOIS, P. (1977), Industrial Decline in London, 'Urban
Studies', vol.14, pp.181-9.
GRIPAOIS, P. (1977a), The Closure of Firms in the Inner
City: The South East London Case 1970-75, 'Regional
Studies', vol.11(1), pp.1-7.
GYFORD, J. (1976), 'Local Politics in Britain', Croom
Helm, London.
HABERMAS, J. (1971), 'Towards a Rational Society',
Heinemann Educational Books, London.
HAGUE, C. and McCOURT, A. (1974), Participation and the
Public Interest, 'Urban Studies', vol.11(2), pp.143-55.
HALEBSKY, S. (1976), 'Mass Society and Political
Conflict', Cambridge University Press.
HALL, P. (1971), 'London 2000', Faber & Faber, London.
HALL, P. (1974), 'Urban and Regional Planning', Penguin,
Harmondsworth.
HALL, P. (1976), South East, 'New Society', 28 Oct.,
p.418.
HALSEY, A.H. (1970), Preface to Dennis (1970).
HAMBLETON, R. (1978), 'Policy Planning and Local
Government', Hutchinson, London.
HAMPTON, W. (1970), 'Democracy and Community', Oxford
University Press.
HARLOE, M. (ed.) (1975), Proceedings of the Conference on
Urban Change and Conflict, Centre for Environmental
Studies Conference, Paper 14.
HARLOE, M. (1975a), Introduction and Position Paper, pp.
1-30 in Harloe (ed.) (1975).
HARLOE, M. (1975b), 'Swindon: A Town in Transition',
Heinemann Educational Books, London.
HARLOE, M. (ed.) (1977), 'Captive Cities', Wiley,
Chichester.

HARLOE, M. (1977a), Introduction, pp.1-49 in Harloe (ed.) (1977).

HARLOE, M. (ed.) (1978), Proceedings of the Conference on Urban Change and Conflict, Centre for Environmental Studies Conference, Paper 19.

HARLOE, M. (1978a), The New Urban Sociology, 'New Society', 5 Oct., pp.12-13.

HARLOE, M., ISSACHAROFF, R. and MINNS, R. (1974), 'The Organization of Housing', Heinemann Educational Books, London.

HARMAN, C. (1978), Review of Mandel's 'Late Capitalism', 'International Socialism', Series 2(1), July, pp.79-96.

HARRISON, G.A. and GIBSON, J.B. (eds) (1976), 'Man in Urban Environments', Oxford University Press.

HARVEY, D. (1973), 'Social Justice and the City', Edward Arnold, London.

HASELER, S. (1976), 'The Death of British Democracy', Elek, London.

HECLO, H. and WILDAVSKY, A. (1974), 'The Private Government of Public Money', Macmillan, London.

HIGGINS, H.M. and RICHARDSON, J.J. (1971), Local Government and Public Participation: A Case Study, 'Local Government Studies', vol.1(1), pp.19-33.

HILL, M. (1976), 'The State, Administration and the Individual', Fontana, London.

HILLEBRANDT, P.M. (1977), Crisis in Construction, 'National Westminster Quarterly Review', Nov., pp.47-65.

HINDESS, B. (1973), 'The Use of Official Statistics in Sociology', Macmillan, London.

HINDESS, B. (1977), Marxist Politics and the State, paper read at the British Sociological Association Conference, Sheffield University, April.

HIRSCH, W.Z. and SORENBLUM, S. (1973), 'Governing Urban America in the 1970s', Praeger, New York.

HIRST, D. (1976), 'The Representative of the People?', Cambridge University Press.

HIRST, P. (1977), Economic Classes and Politics, pp. 125-54 in Hunt (ed.) (1977).

HOBSBAWM, E. (1977), Some reflections on 'the Break-up of Britain', 'New Left Review', vol.105, pp.3-23.

HOLLIS, M. (1978), Action and Context: Say it with Flowers, 'Aristotelian Society Supplementary Volume LII', pp.43-56.

HOLLOWAY, J. and PICCIOTTI, S. (eds) (1978), 'State and Capital', Edward Arnold, London.

HUGHES, E.C. (1971), 'The Sociological Eye: vol.2, Selected Papers on Work, Self and the Study of Society', Aldine-Atherton, Chicago.

HUGHES, H.Stuart (1974), 'Consciousness and Society', Paladin, London.

HUNT, A. (ed.) (1977), 'Class and Class Structure',
Lawrence and Wishart, London.

HUSBANDS, C. (1977), 'The Political Economy of Contempo-
rary Cities and the Genesis of Right-Wing Movements: An
Argument for New Approaches to the Study of Support for
Right-Wing Movements, With Special Reference to the
National Front/National Party', paper read at the British
Sociological Association Conference, Sheffield University,
April.

HYMAN, R. (1975), 'Industrial Relations: A Marxist
Introduction', Macmillan, London.

INGLIS, F. (1977), Nation and Community: A Landscape and
a Morality, 'Sociological Review', vol.25(3), Aug., pp.
489-514.

JACKSON, B. (1964), 'Streaming: An Education System in
Miniature', Routledge & Kegan Paul, London.

JACOBS, J. (1965), 'The Death and Life of Great American
Cities', Penguin, Harmondsworth.

JOHNSON, J.H., SALT, J. and WOOD, P.A. (1975), Housing and
the Geographical Mobility of Labour in England and Wales,
pp.91-101 in Kosinski and Prothero (eds) (1975).

JONES, K. and MAYO, M. (eds) (1975), 'Community Work Two',
Routledge & Kegan Paul, London.

JORDAN, A.G., KINKER, J.J. and RICHARDSON, R.H. (1975),
Participation and Conservation: The Chester Conservation
Area Advisory Committee, 'Local Government Studies', vol.
1(4), pp.1-12.

KAPLAN, D. and MANNERS, R.A. (1972), 'Culture Theory',
Prentice Hall, Englewood Cliffs, N.J.

KARIEL, H.S. (ed.) (1970), 'Frontiers of Democratic
Theory', Random House, New York.

KAVANAGH, D. and ROSE, R. (eds) (1977), 'New Trends in
British Politics', Sage, London.

KIDRON, M. (1970), 'Western Capitalism Since the War',
Penguin, Harmondsworth.

KILGANNON, P. (1976), Public Participation - Or the
Abdication of Responsibility, 'London Review of Public
Administration', No.9, pp.7-23.

KOSINSKI, L.A. and PROTHERO, R.M. (eds) (1975), 'People on
the Move', Methuen, London.

KUMAR, K. (1976), Industrialism and Post-Industrialism:
Reflections on a Putative Transition, 'Sociological
Review', vol.3, pp.439-78.

KUMAR, K. (1977), Continuities and Discontinuities in the
Development of Industrial Societies, pp.29-43 in Scase
(ed.) (1977).

LAMARCHE, F. (1976), Property Development and the Economic
Foundations of the Urban Question, pp.85-118 in Pickvance
(ed.) (1976).

LAMBERT, J., BLACKABY, B. and PARIS, C. (1975),
Neighbourhood Politics and Housing Opportunities, pp.
167-99 in Harloe (ed.) (1975).

LASLETT, P. (1977), In an Ageing World, 'New Society',
vol.42(786), 27 Oct., pp.171-3.

LAW, S. (1977), Planning and the Future, 'Town Planning
Review', vol.48(4), pp.365-73.

LEONARD, P. (ed.) (1975), The Sociology of Community
Action, 'Sociological Review Monograph No.21', University
of Keele.

LEVIN, P. (1976), 'Government and the Planning Process',
George Allen & Unwin, London.

LEVIN, P. and DONNISON, D. (1969), People and Planning,
'Public Administration', (Winter), pp.473-9.

LIJPHART, A. (1975), 'The Politics of Accommodation:
Pluralism and Democracy in the Netherlands', University
of California Press.

LINDBERG, L.N., ALFORD, R.R., CROUCH, C. and OFFE, C.
(eds) (1975), 'Stress and Contradiction in Modern
Capitalism', Lexington, London.

LIPSET, S.M. (1950), Bureaucracy and Social Change, pp.
221-32 in Merton et al. (eds) (1952).

LIPSET, S.M. (1969), 'Political Man', Heinemann
Educational Books, London.

LIPSKY, M. (1968), Protest as a Political Resource,
'American Political Science Review', vol.XII, pp.1144-58.

LIPSKY, M. (1970), 'Protest in City Politics', Rand
McNally, Chicago.

LOJKINE, J. (1975), Big Firms' Strategies, Urban Policy
and Urban Social Movements, mimeo.

LUCAS, J.R. (1976), 'Democracy and Participation',
Penguin, Harmondsworth.

LUKES, S. (1975), Political Ritual and Social Integration,
'Sociology', vol.9(2), pp.289-309.

LUKES, S. (1977), 'Essays in Social Theory', Macmillan,
London.

McAUSLAN, J.P.W.B. and BEVAN, R.G. (1977), The Influence
of Officers and Councillors on Procedures in Planning - A
Case Study, 'Local Government Studies', vol.3(3), pp.7-23.

MacEWEN, M. (1963), Planning or Prediction?, 'New Left
Review', No.22, pp.66-74.

McKEOWN, T. (1976), 'The Modern Rise of Population',
Edward Arnold, London.

McKIE, D. (1973), 'A Sadly Mismanaged Affair', Croom Helm,
London.

MacPHERSON, C.B. (1972), 'The Real World of Democracy',
Oxford University Press.

MALIK, R. (1964), 'What's Wrong With British Industry?',
Penguin, Harmondsworth.

MANN, M. (1973), 'Workers on the Move', Cambridge University Press.

MANN, M. (1975), The Ideology of Intellectuals and Other People in the Development of Capitalism, pp.275-91 in Lindberg et al. (eds) (1975).

MANNERS, G., KEEBLE, D., RODGERS, B. and WARREN, K. (1972), 'Regional Development in Britain', Wiley, Chichester.

MANNHEIM, K. (1971), 'Man and Society in an Age of Reconstruction', Routledge & Kegan Paul, London.

MARWICK, A. (1971), 'The Explosion of British Society 1914-70', Macmillan, London.

MASON, T. (1978), Community Action and the Local Authority: A Study in the Incorporation of Protest, pp. 89-116 in Harloe (ed.) (1978).

MASSEY, D. (1971), The Basic Service Categorization in Planning, Centre for Environmental Studies, Working Paper 63.

MELANSON, P.H. (1972), The Political Science Profession, Political Knowledge and Public Policy, 'Politics and Society', vol.2(4), Sept., pp.489-550.

MELLOR, J.R. (1977), 'Urban Sociology in an Urbanised Society', Routledge & Kegan Paul, London.

MERTON, R.K. et al. (eds) (1952), 'Reader in Bureaucracy', Free Press, New York.

MICHELSON, W. (1976), 'Man and His Urban Environment: A Sociological Approach', Addison-Wesley, London.

MILGRAM, S. (1965), Some Conditions of Obedience and Disobedience to Authority, 'Human Relations', vol.18, pp.57-79.

MILIBAND, R. (1964), 'Parliamentary Socialism', Merlin Press, London.

MILIBAND, R. (1973), 'The State in Capitalist Society', Quartet, London.

MILIBAND, R. and SAVILLE, J. (eds) (1975), 'Socialist Register', Merlin Press, London.

MILLS, C. WRIGHT (1956), 'White Collar', Galaxy, New York.

MILLS, C. WRIGHT (1970), The Social Scientist's Task, pp. 423-31 in Kariel (ed.) (1970).

MINGIONE, E. (1977), Theoretical Elements for a Marxist Analysis of Urban Development, pp.89-111 in Harloe (ed.) (1977).

MITCHISON, R. (1977), 'British Population Change Since 1860', Macmillan, London.

MOLLENKOPF, J. (1975), The Post-War Politics of Urban Development, 'Politics and Society', vol.5(3), pp.247-97.

MOLLENKOPF, J. (1976), 'The Fragile Giant: The Crisis of the Public Sector in America's Cities', paper presented at the Conference on the Sociology of Urban and Regional Development, the ISA, Messina, Italy, April, mimeo.

MOLOTCH, H. (1976), The City as a Growth Machine: Toward
a Political Economy of Place, 'American Journal of
Sociology', vol.82(2), pp.309-32.
MOORE Jr, BARRINGTON (1972), 'Reflections on the Causes of
Human Misery', Allen Lane, London.
MOORE, R. (1977), Becoming a Sociologist in Sparkbrook,
pp.87-107 in Bell and Newby (eds) (1977).
MUCHNIK, D.M. (1970), 'Urban Renewal in Liverpool: A Study
in the Politics of Redevelopment', Occasional Papers in
Social Administration 33, Bell, London.
MURIE, A., NINER, P. and WATSON, C. (1976), 'Housing
Policy and the Housing System', George Allen & Unwin,
London.
MUTCH, W.E.S. (1977), The Expansion of Turnhouse,
Edinburgh Airport, pp.43-58 in Sewell and Coppock (eds)
(1977).
NAIRN, T. (1977), 'The Break-Up of Britain', New Left
Books, London.
NEVE, B. (1977), Bureaucracy and Politics in Local
Government: The Role of Local Authority Education
Officers, 'Public Administration', vol.55 (Autumn),
pp.291-303.
NEWTON, K. (1976), 'Second-City Politics', Oxford
University Press.
NORMAN, P. (1975), Managerialism: Review of Recent Work,
pp.62-98 in Harloe (ed.) (1975).
OFFE, C. (1972), Political Authority and Class Structures
- An Analysis of Late Capitalist Societies, 'International
Journal of Sociology', vol.2(1), pp.73-108.
OLIVES, J. (1976), The Struggle Against Urban Renewal in
the 'Cité d'Aliarte' (Paris), pp.174-97 in Pickvance
(ed.) (1976).
OPEN UNIVERSITY (1976), 'Politics of Work and Occupation',
Block 4, Part 1(12-14), Open University Press, Milton
Keynes.
OZBEKHAM, H. (1968), Can Implies Ought, pp.210-40 in
Anderson (ed.)(1968).
PAHL, R.E. (1964), 'Urbs in Rure: The Metropolitan Fringe
in Hertfordshire', LSE Geographical Papers, No.2.
PAHL, R.E. (ed.) (1968), 'Readings in Urban Sociology',
Pergamon, Oxford.
PAHL, R.E. (1968a), 'Spatial Structure and Social
Structure', Centre for Environmental Studies, Working
Paper 10.
PAHL, R.E. (1970), 'Patterns of Urban Life', Longman,
London.
PAHL, R.E. (1971), Poverty and the Urban System, pp.126-45
in Chisholm and Manners (eds) (1971).
PAHL, R.E. (1974), The Sociology of Urban and Regional

Development as a Problem in Political Economy, paper
presented for the Eighth World Congress in Sociology,
Toronto, August, mimeo.
PAHL, R.E. (1975), 'Whose City?', Penguin, Harmondsworth.
PAHL, R.E. (1975a), 'Urban Managerialism' Reconsidered,
pp.265-87 in Pahl (1975).
PAHL, R.E. (1976a), 'Collective Consumption' and the State
in Capitalist and State Socialist Societies, mimeo.
PAHL, R.E. (1976b), Managers, Technical Experts and the
State: Forms of Mediation, Manipulation and Dominance in
Urban and Regional Development, mimeo.
PAHL, R.E. (1977), Playing the Rationality Game, pp.130-49
in Bell and Newby (eds) (1977).
PAHL, R.E. (1977a), Stratification, the Relation Between
States and Urban and Regional Development, 'International
Journal of Urban and Regional Research', vol.1(1), pp.
6-18.
PAHL, R.E. (1977b), A Rejoinder to Mingione and Hill,
'International Journal of Urban and Regional Research',
vol.1(2), pp.340-3.
PAHL, R.E. (1977c), Managers, Technical Experts and the
State: Forms of Mediation, Manipulation and Dominance in
Urban and Regional Development, pp.49-60 in Harloe (ed.)
(1977).
PAHL, R.E. (1978), Castells and Collective Consumption,
'Sociology', vol.12(2), May, pp.309-15.
PAHL, R.E. (1978a), Discussant on 'Theoretical Approaches
to the Study of State Intervention and Urban Development',
pp.11-32 in Harloe (ed.) (1978).
PAHL, R.E. and WINKLER, J.T. (1975), The Coming
Corporatism, 'Challenge', March/April, pp.28-35.
PALMER, J.A.D. (1972), Introduction, pp.9-50 in Goodman
(1972).
PARIS, C. and BLACKABY, B. (1973), 'Research Directions in
Urban Sociology: Neighbourhood Associations and Housing
Opportunities', Centre for Urban and Regional Studies
Working Paper No.16, Sept., University of Birmingham.
PARKIN, F. (1968), 'Middle Class Radicalism', Manchester
University Press.
PARKIN, F. (1973), 'Class, Inequality and Political
Order', Paladin, London.
PARSONS, G.F. (1973), The Giant Manufacturing Corporations
and Balanced Regional Growth in Britain, pp.220-37 in
Blunden et al. (eds) (1973).
PATEMAN, C. (1970), 'Participation and Democratic Theory',
Cambridge University Press.
PERMAN, D. (1973), 'Cublington: Blueprint for Resistance',
Bodley Head, London.
PICKVANCE, C.G. (1974), On a Materialist Critique of Urban

Sociology, 'Sociological Review', vol.22(2), May, pp. 203-20.

PICKVANCE, C.G. (ed.) (1976), 'Urban Sociology: Critical Essays', Tavistock, London.

PICKVANCE, C.G. (1976a), Introduction: Historical Materialist Approaches to Urban Sociology, pp.1-33 in Pickvance (ed.) (1976).

PICKVANCE, C.G. (1976b), On the Study of Urban Social Movements, pp.198-218 in Pickvance (ed.) (1976).

PICKVANCE, C.G. (1976c), From 'Social Base' to 'Social Force', mimeo.

PICKVANCE, C.G. (1977), Physical Planning and Market Forces in Urban Development, 'National Westminster Bank Quarterly Review', Aug., pp.41-51.

PICKVANCE, C.G. (1977a), From 'Social Base' to 'Social Force', pp.175-86 in Harloe (ed.) (1977).

POULANTZAS, N. (1974), Internationalization of Capitalist Relations and the Nation State, 'Economy and Society', vol.3(2), pp.145-80.

RADICE, H. (1975), 'International Firms and Modern Imperialism', Penguin, Harmondsworth.

RATCLIFFE, J. (1976), 'Land Policy', Hutchinson, London.

RAWSTRON, E.M. and COATES, B.E. (1973), Opportunity and Affluence, pp.13-21 in Blunden et al. (1973).

READE, E.J. (1978), 'Identification of "Planning" as a Mode of Decision-Making', paper presented at the Sociologists in Polytechnics Conference, Newcastle-upon-Tyne Polytechnic, March.

REDDAWAY, W.B. (1977), The Economic Consequences of Zero Population Growth, 'Lloyds Bank Review', No.124, pp.14-31.

REX, J. (1968), The Sociology of a Zone of Transition, pp. 211-31 in Pahl (ed.) (1968).

REX, J. (1971), Review of Pahl 'Whose City' (1970), and 'Patterns of Urban Life' (1970), 'Urban Studies', No.2 (June), pp.51-2.

REX, J. (1971a), The Concept of Housing Class and the Sociology of Race Relations, 'Race', vol.12, pp.293-301.

REX, J. (1978), The City, Castells and Althusser, 'International Journal of Urban and Regional Research', vol.2(3), Oct., pp.566-9.

REX, J. and MOORE, R. (1967), 'Race, Community, and Conflict', Oxford University Press.

RICCI, D.M. (1971), 'Community Power and Democratic Theory', Random House, New York.

RIESMAN, D. (1971), 'The Lonely Crowd', Yale University Press, New Haven, Conn.

ROBERTS, N.A. (1976), 'The Reform of Planning Law', Macmillan, London.

ROSE, H. (1968), 'The Housing Problem', Heinemann Educational Books, London.

ROSE, H. and HANMER, J. (1975), Community Participation and Social Change, pp.25-45 in Jones and Mayo (eds) (1975).

ROSENTHAL, D.B. (1970), The Political and the Environmental in Urban Research, 'Polity', vol.11(4), Summer, pp.540-5.

RUNCIMAN, W.G. (1966), 'Relative Deprivation and Social Justice', Routledge & Kegan Paul, London.

RUNCIMAN, W.G. (ed.) (1978), 'Max Weber: Selections in Translation', Cambridge University Press.

RYAN, M.C. and ISAACSON, P. (1976), Planning and Participation: London's Docklands, 'Local Government Studies', vol.12(1), pp.47-57.

SANDERCOCK, L. (1975), 'Cities For Sale', Melbourne University Press.

SANDFORD, C. (1977), 'Social Economics', Heinemann Educational Books, London.

SAPOLSKY, H.M. (1968), Science, Voters, and the Fluoridation Controversy, 'Science', vol.25, pp.432-40.

SARKISSIAN, W. (1976), The Idea of Social Mix in Town Planning, 'Urban Studies', vol.13, pp.23-46.

SAUNDERS, P. (1975), They Make The Rules: Political Routines and the Generation of Political Bias, 'Policy and Politics', vol.4(1), Sept., pp.31-59.

SAVILLE, J. (1957-8), The Welfare State: an Historical Approach, 'New Reasoner', (3), Winter, pp.1-24.

SCASE, R. (ed.) (1977), 'Industrial Society', George Allen & Unwin, London.

SCHATTSCHNEIDER, E.E. (1960), 'The Semisovereign People', Holt, Rinehart & Winston, New York.

SCORER, R.S. (1973), The Atmosphere and Man, 'Atmospheric Environment', vol.7, pp.1155-62.

SCOTT, A.J. and ROWEIS, S.T. (1977), Urban Planning in Theory and Practice: A Reappraisal, 'Environment and Planning', vol.9, pp.1097-1119.

SELF, P. (1961), 'Cities in Flood', Faber & Faber, London.

SELZNICK, P. (1952), Co-optation: A Mechanism for Organizational Stability, pp.135-40 in Merton et al. (eds) (1952).

SENNETT, R. (1970), 'The Uses of Disorder', Penguin, Harmondsworth.

SEWELL, D.W.R. and COPPOCK, J.T. (eds) (1977), 'Public Participation in Planning', Wiley, Chichester.

SEWELL, D.W.R. and COPPOCK, J.T. (1977a), A Perspective on Public Participation in Planning, pp.1-14 in Sewell and Coppock (eds) (1977).

SHARP E., et al. (1978), The Creation of the DOE: A Review Symposium, 'Town Planning Review', vol.49(3), July, pp. 387-92.

SHARPE, L.J. (1977), Whitehall - Structures and People, pp.53-83 in Kavanagh and Rose (eds) (1977).

SILKIN, L. (1948), Housing Layout in Theory and Practice, 'Journal of the Royal Institute of British Architects', vol.55, pp.431-2.

SIMMIE, J. (1974), 'Citizens in Conflict', Hutchinson, London.

SKLAIR, L. (1974), Progress as Ideology, pp.74-83 in Fletcher (ed.) (1974).

SKLAIR, L. (1975), The Struggle Against the Housing Finance Act, pp.250-92 in Miliband and Saville (eds) (1975).

SKLAIR, L. (1977), Ideology and the Sociological Utopias, 'Sociological Review', vol.25(1), pp.51-72.

SMITH, P.J. (1977), One Hundred Days at Windscale, 'New Society', vol.42(790), 24 Nov., pp.405-8.

SMITH, S.A. de (1973), 'Judicial Review of Administrative Action', Stevens, London.

SMITH, S.A. de (1977), 'Constitutional and Administrative Law', Penguin, Harmondsworth.

SPITZER, S. (1975), Toward a Marxian Theory of Deviance, 'Social Problems', vol.22(5), pp.638-51.

STACEY, M., BATSTONE, E., BELL, C. and MURCOTT, A. (1975), 'Power, Persistence and Change: A Second Study of Banbury', Routledge & Kegan Paul, London.

STONE, P.A. (1970), 'Urban Development in Britain' (vol. 1), Cambridge University Press.

STRETTON, H. (1976), 'Capitalism, Socialism and the Environment', Cambridge University Press.

STRINATI, D. (1977), 'Capitalism and the State', paper read at the British Sociological Association Conference, University of Sheffield, April.

STRINGER, P. and TAYLOR, M. (1974), 'Attitudes and Information in Public Participation: A Case Study', Centre for Environmental Studies Research Paper 3.

SWANN, J. (1975), Housing Associations, pp.116-22 in Conference of Socialist Economists, (1975).

TABB, W.K. and SAWERS, L. (eds) (1978), 'Marxism and the Metropolis', Oxford University Press, New York.

TABB, W.K. and SAWERS, L. (1978a), Introduction, pp.3-21 in Tabb and Sawers (eds) (1978).

TAVISS, I. (1969), Futurology and the Problem of Values, 'International Social Science Journal', vol.XXI(4), pp. 574-87.

TAYLOR, I., WALTON, P. and YOUNG, J. (1973), 'The New Criminology', Routledge & Kegan Paul, London.

THOMPSON, D.F. (1970), 'The Democratic Citizen', Cambridge University Press.

THORNLEY, A. (1977), Theoretical Perspectives on Planning Participation, in Diamond and McLoughlin (eds) (1977).

THOULESS, R. (1930), 'Straight and Crooked Thinking', Hodder & Stoughton, London.

WAHLKE, J., EULAN, H., BUCHANAN, W. and FERGUSON, Le Roy C. (1962), 'The Legislative System: Explorations in Legislative Behaviour', John Wiley, New York.

WALKER, J.L. (1978), Setting the Agenda in the US Senate: A Theory of Problem Selection, 'British Journal of Political Science', vol.7, pp.423-45.

WALTON, J. and MASOTTI, L.H. (eds) (1976), 'The City in Comparative Perspective', Sage, London.

WARREN, B. (1974), Capitalist Planning and the State, 'New Left Review', No.72, pp.3-21.

WEBER, M. (1958), 'Gesammelte Politische Schriften', Tübingen.

WEBER, M. (1978), in Runciman (ed.) (1978), from Weber (1958).

WESTERGAARD, J.H. (1964), Land Use Planning Since 1951: The Legislative and Administrative Framework in England and Wales, 'Town Planning Review', vol.35(3), pp.219-37.

WESTERGAARD, J.H. (1977), Class, Inequality and 'Corporatism', pp.165-86 in Hunt (ed.) (1977).

WESTERGAARD, J.H. and RESLER, H. (1975), 'Class in a Capitalist Society', Heinemann Educational Books, London.

WHITELEGG, J. (1976), Births and Deaths of Firms in the Inner City, 'Urban Studies', vol.13, pp.333-8.

WILDAVSKY, A. (1973), If Planning is Everything, Maybe It's Nothing, 'Journal of Policy Sciences', vol.4, pp. 127-53.

WILENSKY, H.L. (1964), The Professionalization of Everyone, 'American Journal of Sociology', vol.70(2), pp. 137-58.

WILLER, D. and WILLER, J. (1973), 'Systematic Empiricism', Prentice Hall, Englewood Cliffs, N.J.

WILLIS, P. (1977), 'Learning to Labour', Saxon House, Farnborough.

WILSON, G.K. (1977), 'Special Interests and Policymaking: Agricultural Policies and Politics in Britain and the USA 1956-70', John Wiley, Chichester.

WILSON, H. (1974), 'The Labour Government 1964-70', Penguin, Harmondsworth.

WILSON, J.Q. (1969), The Mayors Versus the Cities, 'Public Interest', No.16 (Summer), pp.30-40.

WINKLER, J.T. (1976), Corporatism, 'Archives Européennes de Sociologie', vol.XVII(1), pp.100-36.

WRAITH, R.E. and LAMB, G.B. (1971), 'Public Inquiries as an Instrument of Government', George Allen & Unwin, London.

Index

Routledge Social Science Series

Routledge & Kegan Paul   London, Henley and Boston

39 Store Street, London WC1E 7DD
Broadway House, Newtown Road,
Henley-on-Thames, Oxon RG9 1EN
9 Park Street, Boston, Mass. 02108

Contents

*Authors wishing to submit manuscripts for any series in
this catalogue should send them to the Social Science Editor,
Routledge & Kegan Paul Ltd, 39 Store Street,
London WC1E 7DD*

● *Books so marked are available in paperback*
All books are in Metric Demy 8vo format (216 × 138mm approx.)

International Library of Sociology

General Editor   John Rex

GENERAL SOCIOLOGY

Barnsley, J. H. The Social Reality of Ethics. *464 pp.*

Brown, Robert. Explanation in Social Science. *208 pp.*

● Rules and Laws in Sociology. *192 pp.*

Bruford, W. H. Chekhov and His Russia. *A Sociological Study. 244 pp.*

Burton, F. and **Carlen, P.** Official Discourse. *On Discourse Analysis, Government Publications, Ideology. About 140 pp.*

Cain, Maureen E. Society and the Policeman's Role. *326 pp.*

●**Fletcher, Colin.** Beneath the Surface. *An Account of Three Styles of Sociological Research. 221 pp.*

Gibson, Quentin. The Logic of Social Enquiry. *240 pp.*

Glucksmann, M. Structuralist Analysis in Contemporary Social Thought. *212 pp.*

Gurvitch, Georges. Sociology of Law. *Foreword by Roscoe Pound. 264 pp.*

Hinkle, R. Founding Theory of American Sociology 1883-1915. *About 350 pp.*

Homans, George C. Sentiments and Activities. *336 pp.*

Johnson, Harry M. Sociology: *a Systematic Introduction. Foreword by Robert K. Merton. 710 pp.*

●**Keat, Russell** and **Urry, John.** Social Theory as Science. *278 pp.*

Mannheim, Karl. Essays on Sociology and Social Psychology. *Edited by Paul Kecskemeti. With Editorial Note by Adolph Lowe. 344 pp.*

Martindale, Don. The Nature and Types of Sociological Theory. *292 pp.*

●**Maus, Heinz.** A Short History of Sociology. *234 pp.*

Myrdal, Gunnar. Value in Social Theory: *A Collection of Essays on Methodology. Edited by Paul Streeten. 332 pp.*

Ogburn, William F. and **Nimkoff, Meyer F.** A Handbook of Sociology. *Preface by Karl Mannheim. 656 pp. 46 figures. 35 tables.*

Parsons, Talcott, and **Smelser, Neil J.** Economy and Society: *A Study in the Integration of Economic and Social Theory. 362 pp.*

Podgórecki, Adam. Practical Social Sciences. *About 200 pp.*

Raffel, S. Matters of Fact. *A Sociological Inquiry. 152 pp.*

●**Rex, John.** (Ed.) Approaches to Sociology. *Contributions by Peter Abell, Sociology and the Demystification of the Modern World. 282 pp.*

●**Rex, John** (Ed.) Approaches to Sociology. *Contributions by Peter Abell, Frank Bechhofer, Basil Bernstein, Ronald Fletcher, David Frisby, Miriam Glucksmann, Peter Lassman, Herminio Martins, John Rex, Roland Robertson, John Westergaard and Jock Young. 302 pp.*

Rigby, A. Alternative Realities. *352 pp.*

Roche, M. Phenomenology, Language and the Social Sciences. *374 pp.*

Sahay, A. Sociological Analysis. *220 pp.*

Strasser, Hermann. The Normative Structure of Sociology. *Conservative and Emancipatory Themes in Social Thought. About 340 pp.*

Strong, P. Ceremonial Order of the Clinic. *About 250 pp.*

Urry, John. Reference Groups and the Theory of Revolution. *244 pp.*

Weinberg, E. Development of Sociology in the Soviet Union. *173 pp.*

FOREIGN CLASSICS OF SOCIOLOGY

● **Gerth, H. H.** and **Mills, C. Wright.** From Max Weber: *Essays in Sociology. 502 pp.*

● **Tönnies, Ferdinand.** Community and Association. *(Gemeinschaft and Gesellschaft.) Translated and Supplemented by Charles P. Loomis. Foreword by Pitirim A. Sorokin. 334 pp.*

SOCIAL STRUCTURE

Andreski, Stanislav. Military Organization and Society. *Foreword by Professor A. R. Radcliffe-Brown. 226 pp. 1 folder.*

Carlton, Eric. Ideology and Social Order. *Foreword by Professor Philip Abrahams. About 320 pp.*

Coontz, Sydney H. Population Theories and the Economic Interpretation. *202 pp.*

Coser, Lewis. The Functions of Social Conflict. *204 pp.*

Dickie-Clark, H. F. Marginal Situation: *A Sociological Study of a Coloured Group. 240 pp. 11 tables.*

Giner, S. and **Archer, M. S.** (Eds.). Contemporary Europe. *Social Structures and Cultural Patterns. 336 pp.*

● **Glaser, Barney** and **Strauss, Anselm L.** Status Passage. *A Formal Theory. 212 pp.*

Glass, D. V. (Ed.) Social Mobility in Britain. *Contributions by J. Berent, T. Bottomore, R. C. Chambers, J. Floud, D. V. Glass, J. R. Hall, H. T. Himmelweit, R. K. Kelsall, F. M. Martin, C. A. Moser, R. Mukherjee, and W. Ziegel. 420 pp.*

Kelsall, R. K. Higher Civil Servants in Britain: *From 1870 to the Present Day. 268 pp. 31 tables.*

● **Lawton, Denis.** Social Class, Language and Education. *192 pp.*

McLeish, John. The Theory of Social Change: *Four Views Considered. 128 pp.*

● **Marsh, David C.** The Changing Social Structure of England and Wales, 1871-1961. *Revised edition. 288 pp.*

Menzies, Ken. Talcott Parsons and the Social Image of Man. *About 208 pp.*

● **Mouzelis, Nicos.** Organization and Bureaucracy. *An Analysis of Modern Theories. 240 pp.*

Ossowski, Stanislaw. Class Structure in the Social Consciousness. *210 pp.*

● **Podgórecki, Adam.** Law and Society. *302 pp.*

Renner, Karl. Institutions of Private Law and Their Social Functions. *Edited, with an Introduction and Notes, by O. Kahn-Freud. Translated by Agnes Schwarzschild. 316 pp.*

Rex, J. and Tomlinson, S. Colonial Immigrants in a British City. *A Class Analysis. 368 pp.*

Smooha, S. Israel: Pluralism and Conflict. *472 pp.*

Wesolowski, W. Class, Strata and Power. *Trans. and with Introduction by G. Kolankiewicz. 160 pp.*

Zureik, E. Palestinians in Israel. *A Study in Internal Colonialism. 264 pp.*

SOCIOLOGY AND POLITICS

Acton, T. A. Gypsy Politics and Social Change. *316 pp.*

Burton, F. Politics of Legitimacy. *Struggles in a Belfast Community. 250 pp.*

Etzioni-Halevy, E. Political Manipulation and Administrative Power. *A Comparative Study. About 200 pp.*

● Hechter, Michael. Internal Colonialism. *The Celtic Fringe in British National Development, 1536–1966. 380 pp.*

Kornhauser, William. The Politics of Mass Society. *272 pp. 20 tables.*

Korpi, W. The Working Class in Welfare Capitalism. *Work, Unions and Politics in Sweden. 472 pp.*

Kroes, R. Soldiers and Students. *A Study of Right- and Left-wing Students. 174 pp.*

Martin, Roderick. Sociology of Power. *About 272 pp.*

Myrdal, Gunnar. The Political Element in the Development of Economic Theory. *Translated from the German by Paul Streeten. 282 pp.*

Wong, S.-L. Sociology and Socialism in Contemporary China. *160 pp.*

Wootton, Graham. Workers, Unions and the State. *188 pp.*

CRIMINOLOGY

Ancel, Marc. Social Defence: *A Modern Approach to Criminal Problems. Foreword by Leon Radzinowicz. 240 pp.*

Athens, L. Violent Criminal Acts and Actors. *About 150 pp.*

Cain, Maureen E. Society and the Policeman's Role. *326 pp.*

Cloward, Richard A. and Ohlin, Lloyd E. Delinquency and Opportunity: *A Theory of Delinquent Gangs. 248 pp.*

Downes, David M. The Delinquent Solution. *A Study in Subcultural Theory. 296 pp.*

Friedlander, Kate. The Psycho-Analytical Approach to Juvenile Delinquency: *Theory, Case Studies, Treatment. 320 pp.*

Gleuck, Sheldon and Eleanor. Family Environment and Delinquency. *With the statistical assistance of Rose W. Kneznek. 340 pp.*

Lopez-Rey, Manuel. Crime. *An Analytical Appraisal. 288 pp.*

Mannheim, Hermann. Comparative Criminology: *a Text Book. Two volumes. 442 pp. and 380 pp.*

Morris, Terence. The Criminal Area: *A Study in Social Ecology. Foreword by Hermann Mannheim. 232 pp. 25 tables. 4 maps.*

Podgorecki, A. and Łos, M. *Multidimensional Sociology. About 380 pp.*

Rock, Paul. Making People Pay. *338 pp.*

● **Taylor, Ian, Walton, Paul,** and **Young, Jock.** The New Criminology. *For a Social Theory of Deviance. 325 pp.*

● **Taylor, Ian, Walton, Paul** and **Young, Jock.** (Eds) Critical Criminology. *268 pp.*

SOCIAL PSYCHOLOGY

Bagley, Christopher. The Social Psychology of the Epileptic Child. *320 pp.*

Brittan, Arthur. Meanings and Situations. *224 pp.*

Carroll, J. Break-Out from the Crystal Palace. *200 pp.*

● **Fleming, C. M.** Adolescence: Its Social Psychology. *With an Introduction to recent findings from the fields of Anthropology, Physiology, Medicine, Psychometrics and Sociometry. 288 pp.*

● The Social Psychology of Education: *An Introduction and Guide to Its Study. 136 pp.*

Linton, Ralph. The Cultural Background of Personality. *132 pp.*

● **Mayo, Elton.** The Social Problems of an Industrial Civilization. *With an Appendix on the Political Problem. 180 pp.*

Ottaway, A. K. C. Learning Through Group Experience. *176 pp.*

Plummer, Ken. Sexual Stigma. *An Interactionist Account. 254 pp.*

● **Rose, Arnold M.** (Ed.) Human Behaviour and Social Processes: *an Interactionist Approach. Contributions by Arnold M. Rose, Ralph H. Turner, Anselm Strauss, Everett C. Hughes, E. Franklin Frazier, Howard S. Becker et al. 696 pp.*

Smelser, Neil J. Theory of Collective Behaviour. *448 pp.*

Stephenson, Geoffrey M. The Development of Conscience. *128 pp.*

Young, Kimball. Handbook of Social Psychology. *658 pp. 16 figures. 10 tables.*

SOCIOLOGY OF THE FAMILY

Bell, Colin R. Middle Class Families: *Social and Geographical Mobility. 224 pp.*

Burton, Lindy. Vulnerable Children. *272 pp.*

Gavron, Hannah. The Captive Wife: *Conflicts of Household Mothers. 190 pp.*

George, Victor and **Wilding, Paul.** Motherless Families. *248 pp.*

Klein, Josephine. Samples from English Cultures.
  1. Three Preliminary Studies and Aspects of Adult Life in England. *447 pp.*
  2. Child-Rearing Practices and Index. *247 pp.*

Klein, Viola. The Feminine Character. *History of an Ideology. 244 pp.*

McWhinnie, Alexina M. Adopted Children. *How They Grow Up. 304 pp.*

● **Morgan, D. H. J.** Social Theory and the Family. *About 320 pp.*

● **Myrdal, Alva** and **Klein, Viola.** Women's Two Roles: *Home and Work. 238 pp. 27 tables.*

Parsons, Talcott and **Bales, Robert F.** Family: Socialization and Interaction Process. *In collaboration with James Olds, Morris Zelditch and Philip E. Slater. 456 pp. 50 figures and tables.*

SOCIAL SERVICES

Bastide, Roger. The Sociology of Mental Disorder. *Translated from the French by Jean McNeil. 260 pp.*
Carlebach, Julius. Caring For Children in Trouble. *266 pp.*
George, Victor. Foster Care. *Theory and Practice. 234 pp.*
Social Security: *Beveridge and After. 258 pp.*
George, V. and **Wilding, P.** Motherless Families. *248 pp.*
● **Goetschius, George W.** Working with Community Groups. *256 pp.*
Goetschius, George W. and **Tash, Joan.** Working with Unattached Youth. *416 pp.*
Heywood, Jean S. Children in Care. *The Development of the Service for the Deprived Child. Third revised edition. 284 pp.*
King, Roy D., Ranes, Norma V. and **Tizard, Jack.** Patterns of Residential Care. *356 pp.*
Leigh, John. Young People and Leisure. *256 pp.*
● **Mays, John.** (Ed.) Penelope Hall's Social Services of England and Wales. *About 324 pp.*
Morris, Mary. Voluntary Work and the Welfare State. *300 pp.*
Nokes, P. L. The Professional Task in Welfare Practice. *152 pp.*
Timms, Noel. Psychiatric Social Work in Great Britain (1939-1962). *280 pp.*
● Social Casework: *Principles and Practice. 256 pp.*

SOCIOLOGY OF EDUCATION

Banks, Olive. Parity and Prestige in English Secondary Education: a Study in Educational Sociology. *272 pp.*
● **Blyth, W. A. L.** English Primary Education. *A Sociological Description.* 2. Background. *168 pp.*
Collier, K. G. The Social Purposes of Education: *Personal and Social Values in Education. 268 pp.*
Evans, K. M. Sociometry and Education. *158 pp.*
● **Ford, Julienne.** Social Class and the Comprehensive School. *192 pp.*
Foster, P. J. Education and Social Change in Ghana. *336 pp. 3 maps.*
Fraser, W. R. Education and Society in Modern France. *150 pp.*
Grace, Gerald R. Role Conflict and the Teacher. *150 pp.*
Hans, Nicholas. New Trends in Education in the Eighteenth Century. *278 pp. 19 tables.*
● Comparative Education: *A Study of Educational Factors and Traditions. 360 pp.*
● **Hargreaves, David.** Interpersonal Relations and Education. *432 pp.*
● Social Relations in a Secondary School. *240 pp.*
School Organization and Pupil Involvement. *A Study of Secondary Schools.*

- **Mannheim, Karl** and **Stewart, W.A.C.** An Introduction to the Sociology of Education. *206 pp.*
- **Musgrove, F.** Youth and the Social Order. *176 pp.*
- **Ottaway, A. K. C.** Education and Society: An Introduction to the Sociology of Education. *With an Introduction by W. O. Lester Smith. 212 pp.*
- **Peers, Robert.** Adult Education: *A Comparative Study. Revised edition. 398 pp.*
- **Stratta, Erica.** The Education of Borstal Boys. *A Study of their Educational Experiences prior to, and during, Borstal Training. 256 pp.*
- **Taylor, P. H., Reid, W. A.** and **Holley, B. J.** The English Sixth Form. *A Case Study in Curriculum Research. 198 pp.*

SOCIOLOGY OF CULTURE

- **Eppel, E. M.** and **M.** Adolescents and Morality: *A Study of some Moral Values and Dilemmas of Working Adolescents in the Context of a changing Climate of Opinion. Foreword by W. J. H. Sprott. 268 pp. 39 tables.*
- **Fromm, Erich.** The Fear of Freedom. *286 pp.*
- The Sane Society. *400 pp.*
- **Johnson, L.** The Cultural Critics. *From Matthew Arnold to Raymond Williams. 233 pp.*
- **Mannheim, Karl.** Essays on the Sociology of Culture. *Edited by Ernst Mannheim in co-operation with Paul Kecskemeti. Editorial Note by Adolph Lowe. 280 pp.*
- **Zijderfeld, A. C.** On .Clichés. *The Supersedure of Meaning by Function in Modernity. About 132 pp.*

SOCIOLOGY OF RELIGION

- **Argyle, Michael** and **Beit-Hallahmi, Benjamin.** The Social Psychology of Religion. *About 256 pp.*
- **Glasner, Peter E.** The Sociology of Secularisation. *A Critique of a Concept. About 180 pp.*
- **Hall, J. R.** The Ways Out. *Utopian Communal Groups in an Age of Babylon. 280 pp.*
- **Ranson, S., Hinings, B.** and **Bryman, A.** Clergy, Ministers and Priests. *216 pp.*
- **Stark, Werner.** The Sociology of Religion. *A Study of Christendom.*
  Volume II. *Sectarian Religion. 368 pp.*
  Volume III. *The Universal Church. 464 pp.*
  Volume IV. *Types of Religious Man. 352 pp.*
  Volume V. *Types of Religious Culture. 464 pp.*
- **Turner, B. S.** Weber and Islam. *216 pp.*
- **Watt, W. Montgomery.** Islam and the Integration of Society. *320 pp.*

SOCIOLOGY OF ART AND LITERATURE

Jarvie, Ian C. Towards a Sociology of the Cinema. *A Comparative Essay on the Structure and Functioning of a Major Entertainment Industry. 405 pp.*

Rust, Frances S. Dance in Society. *An Analysis of the Relationships between the Social Dance and Society in England from the Middle Ages to the Present Day. 256 pp. 8 pp. of plates.*

Schücking, L. L. The Sociology of Literary Taste. *112 pp.*

Wolff, Janet. Hermeneutic Philosophy and the Sociology of Art. *150 pp.*

SOCIOLOGY OF KNOWLEDGE

Diesing, P. Patterns of Discovery in the Social Sciences. *262 pp.*

● **Douglas, J. D.** (Ed.) Understanding Everyday Life. *370 pp.*

Glasner, B. Essential Interactionism. *About 220 pp.*

● **Hamilton, P.** Knowledge and Social Structure. *174 pp.*

Jarvie, I. C. Concepts and Society. *232 pp.*

Mannheim, Karl. Essays on the Sociology of Knowledge. *Edited by Paul Kecskemeti. Editorial Note by Adolph Lowe. 353 pp.*

Remmling, Gunter W. The Sociology of Karl Mannheim. *With a Bibliographical Guide to the Sociology of Knowledge, Ideological Analysis, and Social Planning. 255 pp.*

Remmling, Gunter W. (Ed.) Towards the Sociology of Knowledge. *Origin and Development of a Sociological Thought Style. 463 pp.*

URBAN SOCIOLOGY

Aldridge, M. The British New Towns. *A Programme Without a Policy. About 250 pp.*

Ashworth, William. The Genesis of Modern British Town Planning: *A Study in Economic and Social History of the Nineteenth and Twentieth Centuries. 288 pp.*

Brittan, A. The Privatised World. *196 pp.*

Cullingworth, J. B. Housing Needs and Planning Policy: *A Restatement of the Problems of Housing Need and 'Overspill' in England and Wales. 232 pp. 44 tables. 8 maps.*

Dickinson, Robert E. City and Region: *A Geographical Interpretation. 608 pp. 125 figures.*

The West European City: *A Geographical Interpretation. 600 pp. 129 maps. 29 plates.*

Humphreys, Alexander J. New Dubliners: *Urbanization and the Irish Family. Foreword by George C. Homans. 304 pp.*

Jackson, Brian. Working Class Community: *Some General Notions raised by a Series of Studies in Northern England. 192 pp.*

● **Mann, P. H.** An Approach to Urban Sociology. *240 pp.*

Mellor, J. R. Urban Sociology in an Urbanized Society. *326 pp.*

Morris, R. N. and **Mogey, J.** The Sociology of Housing. *Studies at Berinsfield. 232 pp. 4 pp. plates.*

Rosser, C. and **Harris, C.** The Family and Social Change. *A Study of Family and Kinship in a South Wales Town. 352 pp. 8 maps.*

● **Stacey, Margaret, Batsone, Eric, Bell, Colin** and **Thurcott, Anne.** Power, Persistence and Change. *A Second Study of Banbury. 196 pp.*

RURAL SOCIOLOGY

Mayer, Adrian C. Peasants in the Pacific. *A Study of Fiji Indian Rural Society. 248 pp. 20 plates.*

Williams, W. M. The Sociology of an English Village: *Gosforth. 272 pp. 12 figures. 13 tables.*

SOCIOLOGY OF INDUSTRY AND DISTRIBUTION

Dunkerley, David. The Foreman. *Aspects of Task and Structure. 192 pp.*

Eldridge, J. E. T. Industrial Disputes. *Essays in the Sociology of Industrial Relations. 288 pp.*

Hollowell, Peter G. The Lorry Driver. *272 pp.*

● **Oxaal, I., Barnett, T.** and **Booth, D.** (Eds) Beyond the Sociology of Development. *Economy and Society in Latin America and Africa. 295 pp.*

Smelser, Neil J. Social Change in the Industrial Revolution: *An Application of Theory to the Lancashire Cotton Industry, 1770–1840. 468 pp. 12 figures. 14 tables.*

Watson, T. J. The Personnel Managers. *A Study in the Sociology of Work and Employment. 262 pp.*

ANTHROPOLOGY

Brandel-Syrier, Mia. Reeftown Elite. *A Study of Social Mobility in a Modern African Community on the Reef. 376 pp.*

Dickie-Clark, H. F. The Marginal Situation. *A Sociological Study of a Coloured Group. 236 pp.*

Dube, S. C. Indian Village. *Foreword by Morris Edward Opler. 276 pp. 4 plates.*

India's Changing Villages: *Human Factors in Community Development. 260 pp. 8 plates. 1 map.*

Firth, Raymond. Malay Fishermen. *Their Peasant Economy. 420 pp. 17 pp. plates.*

Gulliver, P. H. Social Control in an African Society: a Study of the Arusha, Agricultural Masai of Northern Tanganyika. *320 pp. 8 plates. 10 figures.*

Family Herds. *288 pp.*

Jarvie, Ian C. The Revolution in Anthropology. *268 pp.*

Little, Kenneth L. Mende of Sierra Leone. *308 pp. and folder.*

Negroes in Britain. *With a New Introduction and Contemporary Study by Leonard Bloom. 320 pp.*

Madan, G. R. Western Sociologists on Indian Society. *Marx, Spencer, Weber, Durkheim, Pareto. 384 pp.*

Mayer, A. C. Peasants in the Pacific. *A Study of Fiji Indian Rural Society. 248 pp.*

Meer, Fatima. Race and Suicide in South Africa. *325 pp.*

Smith, Raymond T. The Negro Family in British Guiana: *Family Structure and Social Status in the Villages. With a Foreword by Meyer Fortes. 314 pp. 8 plates. 1 figure. 4 maps.*

SOCIOLOGY AND PHILOSOPHY

Barnsley, John H. The Social Reality of Ethics. *A Comparative Analysis of Moral Codes. 448 pp.*

Diesing, Paul. Patterns of Discovery in the Social Sciences. *362 pp.*

● **Douglas, Jack D.** (Ed.) Understanding Everyday Life. *Toward the Reconstruction of Sociological Knowledge. Contributions by Alan F. Blum, Aaron W. Cicourel, Norman K. Denzin, Jack D. Douglas, John Heeren, Peter McHugh, Peter K. Manning, Melvin Power, Matthew Speier, Roy Turner, D. Lawrence Wieder, Thomas P. Wilson and Don H. Zimmerman. 370 pp.*

Gorman, Robert A. The Dual Vision. *Alfred Schutz and the Myth of Phenomenological Social Science. About 300 pp.*

Jarvie, Ian C. Concepts and Society. *216 pp.*

Kilminster, R. Praxis and Method. *A Sociological Dialogue with Lukács, Gramsci and the early Frankfurt School. About 304 pp.*

● **Pelz, Werner.** The Scope of Understanding in Sociology. *Towards a More Radical Reorientation in the Social Humanistic Sciences. 283 pp.*

Roche, Maurice. Phenomenology, Language and the Social Sciences. *371 pp.*

Sahay, Arun. Sociological Analysis. *212 pp.*

Slater, P. Origin and Significance of the Frankfurt School. *A Marxist Perspective. About 192 pp.*

Spurling, L. Phenomenology and the Social World. *The Philosophy of Merleau-Ponty and its Relation to the Social Sciences. 222 pp.*

Wilson, H. T. The American Ideology. *Science, Technology and Organization as Modes of Rationality. 368 pp.*

International Library of Anthropology

General Editor   Adam Kuper

Ahmed, A. S. Millenium and Charisma Among Pathans. *A Critical Essay in Social Anthropology. 192 pp.*
   Pukhtun Economy and Society. *About 360 pp.*

Brown, Paula. The Chimbu. *A Study of Change in the New Guinea Highlands. 151 pp.*

Foner, N. Jamaica Farewell. *200 pp.*

Gudeman, Stephen. Relationships, Residence and the Individual. *A Rural Panamanian Community. 288 pp. 11 plates, 5 figures, 2 maps, 10 tables.*

The Demise of a Rural Economy. *From Subsistence to Capitalism in a Latin American Village. 160 pp.*

Hamnett, Ian. Chieftainship and Legitimacy. *An Anthropological Study of Executive Law in Lesotho. 163 pp.*

Hanson, F. Allan. Meaning in Culture. *127 pp.*

Humphreys, S. C. Anthropology and the Greeks. *288 pp.*

Karp, I. Fields of Change Among the Iteso of Kenya. *140 pp.*

Lloyd, P. C. Power and Independence. *Urban Africans' Perception of Social Inequality. 264 pp.*

Parry, J. P. Caste and Kinship in Kangra. *352 pp. Illustrated.*

Pettigrew, Joyce. Robber Noblemen. *A Study of the Political System of the Sikh Jats. 284 pp.*

Street, Brian V. The Savage in Literature. *Representations of 'Primitive' Society in English Fiction, 1858–1920. 207 pp.*

Van Den Berghe, Pierre L. Power and Privilege at an African University. *278 pp.*

International Library of Social Policy

General Editor Kathleen Jones

Bayley, M. Mental Handicap and Community Care. *426 pp.*

Bottoms, A. E. and **McClean, J. D.** Defendants in the Criminal Process. *284 pp.*

Butler, J. R. Family Doctors and Public Policy. *208 pp.*

Davies, Martin. Prisoners of Society. *Attitudes and Aftercare. 204 pp.*

Gittus, Elizabeth. Flats, Families and the Under-Fives. *285 pp.*

Holman, Robert. Trading in Children. *A Study of Private Fostering. 355 pp.*

Jeffs, A. Young People and the Youth Service. *About 180 pp.*

Jones, Howard, and **Cornes, Paul.** Open Prisons. *288 pp.*

Jones, Kathleen. History of the Mental Health Service. *428 pp.*

Jones, Kathleen, with **Brown, John, Cunningham, W. J., Roberts, Julian** and **Williams, Peter.** Opening the Door. *A Study of New Policies for the Mentally Handicapped. 278 pp.*

Karn, Valerie. Retiring to the Seaside. *About 280 pp. 2 maps. Numerous tables.*

King, R. D. and **Elliot, K. W.** Albany: Birth of a Prison—End of an Era. *394 pp.*

Thomas, J. E. The English Prison Officer since 1850: *A Study in Conflict.*
258 pp.
Walton, R. G. Women in Social Work. *303 pp.*
● **Woodward, J.** To Do the Sick No Harm. *A Study of the British Voluntary Hospital System to 1875. 234 pp.*

International Library of Welfare and Philosophy

General Editors Noel Timms and David Watson

● **McDermott, F. E.** (Ed.) Self-Determination in Social Work. *A Collection of Essays on Self-determination and Related Concepts by Philosophers and Social Work Theorists. Contributors: F. B. Biestek, S. Bernstein, A. Keith-Lucas, D. Sayer, H. H. Perelman, C. Whittington, R. F. Stalley, F. E. McDermott, I. Berlin, H. J. McCloskey, H. L. A. Hart, J. Wilson, A. I. Melden, S. I. Benn. 254 pp.*
● **Plant, Raymond.** Community and Ideology. *104 pp.*
Ragg, Nicholas M. People Not Cases. *A Philosophical Approach to Social Work. About 250 pp.*
● **Timms, Noel** and **Watson, David.** (Eds) Talking About Welfare. *Readings in Philosophy and Social Policy. Contributors: T. H. Marshall, R. B. Brandt, G. H. von Wright, K. Nielsen, M. Cranston, R. M. Titmuss, R. S. Downie, E. Telfer, D. Donnison, J. Benson, P. Leonard, A. Keith-Lucas, D. Walsh, I. T. Ramsey. 320 pp.*
● (Eds). Philosophy in Social Work. *250 pp.*
● **Weale, A.** Equality and Social Policy. *164 pp.*

Primary Socialization, Language and Education

General Editor Basil Bernstein

Adlam, Diana S., *with the assistance of Geoffrey Turner and Lesley Lineker.* Code in Context. *About 272 pp.*
Bernstein, Basil. Class, Codes and Control. *3 volumes.*
● 1. *Theoretical Studies Towards a Sociology of Language. 254 pp.*
2. *Applied Studies Towards a Sociology of Language. 377 pp.*
● 3. *Towards a Theory of Educational Transmission. 167 pp.*
Brandis, W. and **Bernstein, B.** Selection and Control. *176 pp.*

Brandis, Walter and **Henderson, Dorothy.** Social Class, Language and Communication. *288 pp.*

Cook-Gumperz, Jenny. Social Control and Socialization. *A Study of Class Differences in the Language of Maternal Control. 290 pp.*

● **Gahagan, D. M** and **G. A.** Talk Reform. *Exploration in Language for Infant School Children. 160 pp.*

Hawkins, P. R. Social Class, the Nominal Group and Verbal Strategies. *About 220 pp.*

Robinson, W. P. and **Rackstraw, Susan D. A.** A Question of Answers. *2 volumes. 192 pp. and 180 pp.*

Turner, Geoffrey J. and **Mohan, Bernard A.** A Linguistic Description and Computer Programme for Children's Speech. *208 pp.*

Reports of the Institute of Community Studies

Baker, J. The Neighbourhood Advice Centre. A Community Project in Camden. *320 pp.*

● **Cartwright, Ann.** Patients and their Doctors. *A Study of General Practice. 304 pp.*

Dench, Geoff. Maltese in London. *A Case-study in the Erosion of Ethnic Consciousness. 302 pp.*

Jackson, Brian and **Marsden, Dennis.** Education and the Working Class: *Some General Themes raised by a Study of 88 Working-class Children in a Northern Industrial City. 268 pp. 2 folders.*

Marris, Peter. The Experience of Higher Education. *232 pp. 27 tables.*

● Loss and Change. *192 pp.*

Marris, Peter and **Rein, Martin.** Dilemmas of Social Reform. *Poverty and Community Action in the United States. 256 pp.*

Marris, Peter and **Somerset, Anthony.** African Businessmen. *A Study of Entrepreneurship and Development in Keyna. 256 pp.*

Mills, Richard. Young Outsiders: *a Study in Alternative Communities. 216 pp.*

Runciman, W. G. Relative Deprivation and Social Justice. *A Study of Attitudes to Social Inequality in Twentieth-Century England. 352 pp.*

Willmott, Peter. Adolescent Boys in East London. *230 pp.*

Willmott, Peter and **Young, Michael.** Family and Class in a London Suburb. *202 pp. 47 tables.*

Young, Michael and **McGeeney, Patrick.** Learning Begins at Home. *A Study of a Junior School and its Parents. 128 pp.*

Young, Michael and **Willmott, Peter.** Family and Kinship in East London. *Foreword by Richard M. Titmuss. 252 pp. 39 tables.* The Symmetrical Family. *410 pp.*

Reports of the Institute for Social Studies in Medical Care

Cartwright, Ann, Hockey, Lisbeth and **Anderson, John J.** Life Before Death. *310 pp.*

Dunnell, Karen and **Cartwright, Ann.** Medicine Takers, Prescribers and Hoarders. *190 pp.*

Farrell, C. My Mother Said. . . . *A Study of the Way Young People Learned About Sex and Birth Control. 200 pp.*

Medicine, Illness and Society

General Editor W. M. Williams

Hall, David J. Social Relations & Innovation. *Changing the State of Play in Hospitals. 232 pp.*

Hall, David J., and **Stacey, M.** (Eds) Beyond Separation. *234 pp.*

Robinson, David. The Process of Becoming Ill. *142 pp.*

Stacey, Margaret *et al.* Hospitals, Children and Their Families. *The Report of a Pilot Study. 202 pp.*

Stimson G. V. and **Webb, B.** Going to See the Doctor. *The Consultation Process in General Practice. 155 pp.*

Monographs in Social Theory

General Editor Arthur Brittan

● **Barnes, B.** Scientific Knowledge and Sociological Theory. *192 pp.*

Bauman, Zygmunt. Culture as Praxis. *204 pp.*

● **Dixon, Keith.** Sociological Theory. *Pretence and Possibility. 142 pp.*

Meltzer, B. N., Petras, J. W. and **Reynolds, L. T.** Symbolic Interactionism. *Genesis, Varieties and Criticisms. 144 pp.*

● **Smith, Anthony D.** The Concept of Social Change. *A Critique of the Functionalist Theory of Social Change. 208 pp.*

Routledge Social Science Journals

The British Journal of Sociology. *Editor – Angus Stewart; Associate Editor – Leslie Sklair. Vol. 1, No. 1 – March 1950 and Quarterly. Roy. 8vo. All back issues available. An international journal publishing original papers in the field of sociology and related areas.*

Community Work. *Edited by David Jones and Marjorie Mayo. 1973. Published annually.*

Economy and Society. *Vol. 1, No. 1. February 1972 and Quarterly. Metric Roy. 8vo. A journal for all social scientists covering sociology, philosophy, anthropology, economics and history. All back numbers available.*

Ethnic and Racial Studies. *Editor – John Stone. Vol. 1 – 1978. Published quarterly.*

Religion. Journal of Religion and Religions. *Chairman of Editorial Board, Ninian Smart. Vol. 1, No. 1, Spring 1971. A journal with an inter-disciplinary approach to the study of the phenomena of religion. All back numbers available.*

Sociology of Health and Illness. *A Journal of Medical Sociology. Editor – Alan Davies; Associate Editor – Ray Jobling. Vol. 1, Spring 1979. Published 3 times per annum.*

Year Book of Social Policy in Britain, The. *Edited by Kathleen Jones. 1971. Published annually.*

Social and Psychological Aspects of Medical Practice

Editor Trevor Silverstone

Lader, Malcolm. Psychophysiology of Mental Illness. *280 pp.*

● **Silverstone, Trevor** and **Turner, Paul.** Drug Treatment in Psychiatry. *Revised edition. 256 pp.*

Whiteley, J. S. and **Gordon, J.** Group Approaches in Psychiatry. *256 pp.*

Printed in Great Britain by
Lowe & Brydone Printers Limited, Thetford, Norfolk